T0206537

NFLDRAFT
2015 PREVIEW
By
NOLAN NAWROCKI

This book is available in quantity at special discounts for your group or organization. For further information, contact:

Triumph Books LLC
814 North Franklin Street
Chicago, Illinois 60610

Phone: (312) 337-0747
www.triumphbooks.com

Printed in U.S.A.
ISBN: 978-1-62937-076-7

Scouting research: Matt Feminis
Book designed by Bob Peters

PHOTOS COURTESY

Alabama Athletics	University of Florida
Florida State University	University of Iowa
Michigan State Athletics	University of Louisville
Oregon Athletics	University of Minnesota
Rutgers University	University of Nebraska
Stanford University	USC Athletics
UCLA Athletics	West Virginia University

CONTENTS

Jameis Winston

Almost every player in this book was an exceptional college football player or athlete and stands among the best in the country. NFL standards are the most stringent in the world, and it requires immense grit to rigorously compete against the world's most nuanced pros. All players graded were measured against these most demanding measures.

Included with many player profiles is a "Scout's Take," actual feedback reflecting unique and consensus opinions from NFL evaluators, stemming anywhere from veteran area scouts blanketing a region of the country to the savvy GMs going over the top of it when they can fit it into their ever-busy schedules. Much of the information was gathered through the course of the fall, up until the day of publishing this book, and reflects hundreds of conversations aimed at pinpointing the measurables, critical traits, football instincts, work ethic, toughness, competitiveness, leadership, intelligence, temperament, character, scheme fit and league value of the nation's top talent.

Some information and grades might have changed by the time the book is being read, as more workouts, interviews and private workouts take place following the March 17th press date and verified measurements and character research is ascertained.

Much gratitude is owed to everyone who helped contribute to the production of the book in some way, from college coaches and sports information directors to all the NFL executives, scouts and coaches with whom I have had the pleasure to talk football. It takes a community to raise a scout, and I'm very appreciative for all you continue to teach me.

A special thank-you belongs to Noah Amstadter and the Triumph Books team for seeing the project through, Ron Pollack for his insight and guidance, and to Matt Feminis for his brilliance and diligence. Not to be forgotten is the late Joel Buchsbaum and the PFW family that helped found independent draft analysis. I am most grateful for the patience and strength of my inspiration, Christie and the A-team.

— Nolan Nawrocki

DRAFT OUTLOOK

Brandon Scherff   **Leonard Williams**   **Andrus Peat**

The NFL Draft heads to Chicago in a revamped format designed to add flair to the most anticipated football event of the offseason. Perhaps fittingly for a city of broad shoulders, big men dominate the top of this year's draft, with foundational pieces such as USC DL Leonard Williams, Iowa OL Brandon Scherff and Stanford OT Andrus Peat all expected to emerge from this class as key cornerstones.

Williams is the most versatile defensive lineman in the draft and its highest graded player, with rare movement skill for a 6-5, 300-pounder. Florida pass-rusher Dante Fowler and West Virginia WR Kevin White, two ultra-competitive impact players, grade out slightly below Williams at the top of this year's class. Scherff may be the safest selection in this year's draft, with Day One plug-in Pro Bowl potential. Peat is a physical marvel and the draft's most naturally talented blocker. Two very different quarterbacks – Oregon's Marcus Mariota and Florida

State's Jameis Winston – have the potential to become premier passers in a QB class devoid of depth reminiscent of 1998, when Peyton Manning and Ryan Leaf were the first two picks in a class where only eight quarterbacks were selected. Mariota could be immediately impactful in an offense built to his strengths, and Winston has the arm talent and pocket-passing skill to blossom with the right structure around him. Baylor's Bryce Petty and UCLA's Brett Hundley have moldable talent and eventual starter potential. Colorado State's Garrett Grayson offers the accuracy to appeal to a precision passing game.

After being shut out of the first round the last two years, the RB crop features a pair of first-round talents in Georgia's Todd Gurley and Wisconsin's Melvin Gordon, and the class collectively features very good overall depth, with a glut of talent to be found in the middle rounds. Gurley's draft status will suffer from a season-ending knee injury, yet he is the most talented back to emerge from the college ranks since Adrian Peterson. Gordon is an exciting playmaker offering a complete package that figures to make him the first back selected. The class features a good blend of power and speed, with Indiana's do-it-all Tevin Coleman, Boise State's versatile Jay Ajayi, Miami's instinctive Duke Johnson and Nebraska's sleek Ameer Abdullah all capable of becoming instant contributors.

Much like a year ago, the receiving class emerged following a very healthy boost from the underclassmen ranks to become the strongest position in this year's draft. It could feature as many as five first-round picks, beginning with White, Alabama's polished playmaker Amari Cooper and Louisville's sure-handed Devante Parker. Though less polished, Oklahoma's Dorial Green-Beckham is the most imposing mismatch piece, especially as a red-area weapon, and Arizona State's Jaelen Strong the most strong-handed. The crop of catchers is both strong and deep, with starters to be found in the middle rounds.

Following last year's modest crop, talent at the TE position is sparse once again, void of an elite playmaker or any depth. Minnesota's Maxx Williams is distinguished as the top receiving tight end or "F". Rutgers Tyler Kroft is the most well-rounded of the group. The top blocking tight end, or true Y, is Delaware's Nick Boyle. The class is without the distinction of a true first-round talent, and features a vast number of developmental prospects, but little quality depth.

Scherff is the prize of a solid interior offensive line group. The center class is without distinction, though the mid-season conversion of Florida State OLT Cameron Erving to center gives the class a bonafide talent. Oregon's Hroniss Grasu is a prototype zone blocker. Quality guards are more abundant, featuring South Carolina's steady A.J. Cann, Florida State's mauling Tre Jackson, Duke's road-grading Laken Tomlinson and Penn State's athletic Donovan Smith – all of whom possess starter traits.

Peat has rare talent if he could learn to harness it and sits atop a quality OT class that could easily include a handful of first-

rounders, as there has been the last two years. Florida's light-footed D.J. Humphries, Miami's powerful Ereck Flowers, LSU's nasty La'el Collins and Texas A&M's injured Cedric Ogbuehi all have the talent to command first-round attention, though Ogbuehi's season-ending knee injury figures to alter his status. Pittsburgh's T.J. Clemmings also possesses unique upside to develop, though he is far from ready.

It's the best year for edge rushers since a special 2011 crop that produced Von Miller, Aldon Smith, J.J. Watt and Robert Quinn. Florida's powerful Dante Fowler, Nebraska's dynamic Randy Gregory and Clemson's explosive Vic Beasley top the list, capable of fitting as 4-3 defensive ends or 3-4 outside linebackers. Also offering elite speed and versatility are Kentucky's powerful Bud Dupree, Missouri's ultra-competitive Shane Ray and Virginia's strong Eli Harold.

Teams looking to become more stout up front will be enticed by Oregon's fencepost DE Arik Armstead and Washington's massive NT Danny Shelton. Oklahoma's athletic Jordan Phillips and Florida State's stout Eddie Goldman are both capable of disrupting from the NT position. Two one-gap penetrators – Texas' Malcolm Brown and Florida State's Mario Edwards can also factor readily on the inside.

The inside linebacking group lacks an elite playmaker and is headlined by the draft's most instinctive performer, UCLA's Eric Kendricks. Miami's Denzel Perryman compensates for his lack of height with explosive hip snap and violent tackling ability. Michigan's versatile Jake Ryan also has plug-and-play potential.

At a time when long corners have never been more in vogue given rule changes designed to proliferate scoring, this year's CB crop features numerous with ideal length, including Michigan State's speedy Trae Waynes, Washington's physical Marcus Peters, Wake Forest's ball-hawking Kevin Johnson, LSU's angular Jalen Collins and Connecticut's explosive Byron Jones. The safety class is much thinner, with Alabama's Landon Collins standing in a class of his own at the top of the group. Other potential starters include Samford's Jaquiski Tartt and Louisville's James Sample.

QUARTERBACKS

QUARTERBACKS

Nawrocki's TOP 10

1. **JAMEIS WINSTON**
2. Marcus Mariota
3. Bryce Petty
4. Brett Hundley
5. Sean Mannion
6. Garrett Grayson
7. Bryan Bennett
8. Jerry Lovelocke
9. Shane Carden
10. Cody Fajardo

EDITOR'S NOTE:

E — Height, weight and speed are estimated.

e — Only the 40-yard-dash time is estimated.

#00 — Player's jersey number.

PFW GRADE — Player's grade reflects PFW's opinion and occasionally differs from where the player is expected to be drafted based on feedback from the league.

On all positions, 40-yard-dash times are curved to take conditions into account. For instance, a 4.4 40 on a very fast rubber track would be recorded as a 4.52, while a 4.6 on slow grass would be logged as a 4.5.

QB BRYAN BENNETT, #3 (Sr-5)

SOUTHEASTERN LOUISIANA ▶ GRADE: 5.24

Ht: 6-2 ¼ | Wt: 211 | 40: 4.81 | Arm: 31 | Hand: 9 ½

History: Prepped in California, where he also ran track. Began his college career at Oregon, where he was recruited by Chip Kelly and redshirted in 2010. Backed up Darron Thomas in '11 when he appeared in eight games (started in place of injured Thomas against Colorado) and completed 25-of-46 pass attempts (54.3 percent) for 369 yards with six touchdowns and zero interceptions. Rushed 23 times for 200 yards (8.7-yard average) and zero touchdowns. Backed up Marcus Mariota in '12, tossing 20-37-211-3-3 (54.1) with 39-165-6 (4.2) on the ground. Rather than back up Mariota or change positions, transferred to FCS Southeastern Louisiana, where he made an immediate impact. Was the Southland Conference Player of the Year in '13 — started all 14 games and piled up 215-354-3,165-21-11 (60.7) despite playing through a sprained knee ligament. Also coped with a torn ligament in his right (throwing) thumb the last half of the season. Was the Southland Conference Offensive Player of the Year in '14 — started 12-of-13 games played and managed 143-289-2,357-18-8 (49.5). Dealt with a right (shoulder) injury that accounted for his non-start against Stephen F. Austin, and injured his foot against Houston Baptist (was in a walking boot leading up to subsequent McNeese State contest). Was the Lions' leading rusher both seasons, totaling

320-1,701-31 (5.3-yard average). Guided the Lions to two conference championships (14-0 conference mark), as well as the program's first two playoff appearances. Also claimed the school's career records for touchdowns (70). Became the third Lion to participate in the Senior Bowl, and would be the first offensive player drafted out of SELU since 1982.

Strengths: Outstanding athlete with very good speed and nifty open-field running skill to sidestep tacklers. Good escapability and improvisional skill. Has a fluid release with good arm strength and is accurate delivering the ball on the move. Threw with more velocity than any other quarterback at the Scouting Combine, as the only passer to clock 60 miles per hour. Very competitive — has a passion for the game and it shows. Recorded a 37-inch vertical jump and 10-foot, 5-inch broad jump, tops among quarterbacks at the Combine.

Weaknesses: Has not operated a conventional style, NFL offense with pro-style, progression reads and must be able to adapt to working under center. Could improve touch and learn to put more air underneath the ball — throws tend to be very flat. Could improve anticipation and do a better job leading his receivers (who too often must break stride to catch or are forced to adjust). Often sets and throws to primary read and will require some patience adapting to a more sophisticated NFL passing game. Must adjust to calling plays in the huddle in the NFL. Is not comfortable with the bright lights of a big city.

Future: Good-sized, loose-armed, athletic, dual-threat, zone-option read quarterback with a flair for the big play. Despite being unseated by Oregon's Marcus Mariota, Bennett has proven he has NFL-caliber tools and has clear upside to develop. Shows similar developmental potential as 2008 Buccaneers fifth-rounder Josh Johnson, a vagabond No. 3 NFL quarterback.

Draft projection: Fifth- to sixth-round pick.

QB ANTHONY BOONE, #7 (Sr-5)

DUKE ▶ GRADE: 4.80

Ht: 6-0 ¼ | Wt: 231 | 40: 5.06 | Arm: 31 ⅝ | Hand: 9 ⅝

History: Was a four-time all-conference player as a prep in North Carolina, where he also starred in baseball. Redshirted in 2010. Backed up Falcons '13 seventh-rounder Sean

Renfree for two years. Completed 30-of-53 attempts (56.6 percent) for 298 yards with one touchdown and one interception in '11 (10 appearances). Played 12 games in '12, tossing 49-95-531-5-2 (51.6) in 12 games (one start). Did not play against Georgia Tech. Took over in '13 when he started all 11 games played and produced 206-322-2,260-13-13 (64.0), though he missed three games after breaking his collarbone in Week Two. Was team MVP in '14 when started all 13 games and passed 255-453-2,700-19-8 (56.3). For his career, rushed 232 times for 800 yards (3.4-yard average) and 16 scores. Two-time elected team captain. Graduated. Has a 19-6 career starting record.

Strengths: Solid decision-maker — understands where to go with the ball. Fine poise in the pocket. Is surprisingly nimble and light on his feet (despite his girth). Smart and articulate. Respected team leader — organizes offseason workouts and can galvanize a locker room.

Weaknesses: Lacks ideal height. Production is heavily padded from a short, lateral passing game. Operates heavily out of the shotgun. Overall accuracy is very spotty — consistently is off the mark. Tends to drive the ball down and over the top, generating dirtballs and overshoots the deep ball. Weight has fluctuated. Recorded the lowest vertical jump (26 ½ inches), broad jump (8-feet, 2-inches), short shuttle (4.64 seconds) and 3-cone drill time (7.47 seconds) of any quarterback at the Combine.

Future: Compactly built, ball distributor functioned in David Cutcliffe's offense, yet lacks the accuracy and ball placement needed to earn a place in the NFL.

Draft projection: Priority free agent.

Scout's take: "He is erratic. He was that way in the season, and he was that way at the East-West Shrine game. I don't know what you do with him. He's a free agent for us."

QB-WR BRANDON BRIDGE, #7 (Sr-5)

SOUTH ALABAMA ▶ GRADE: 5.10

Ht: 6-4 ⅜ | Wt: 229 | 40: 4.68 | Arm: 34 ¼ | Hand: 9 ¼

History: Grew up in suburban Toronto. Won two championships as a prep. Began his college career at Alcorn State, where he started all 11 games and completed 150-of-291 pass attempts (51.5 percent)

QUARTERBACKS

for 2,086 yards with 19 touchdowns and 13 interceptions. Also carried 120 times for 601 yards (5.0-yard average) and eight touchdowns. Fell out of favor with a new coaching staff in '11 — played the first five games (started the first two) and managed 49-98-632-5-4 (50.0) passing with 39-121-2 (3.1) rushing before a hip flexor injury sidelined him. Transferred to South Alabama and sat out the '12 season. As a backup in '13, appeared in nine games and tossed 29-66-398-1-2 (43.9) with 37-170-1 (4.6) rushing. Damaged ligaments in his right ankle against Louisiana-Lafayette, and did not start the next three games. In '14, started 9-of-11 games played and passed 160-307-1,927-15-8 (52.1) with 101-297-4 (2.9) rushing. Suffered an ankle injury against Louisiana-Lafayette — sat out against Arkansas State and Texas State and did not start against South Carolina. Graduated with a communications degree.

Strengths: Has a cannon arm to zip the ball into tight spots and threaten the field vertically. Very good upper body strength and can brush off tacklers and turn the corner with speed. Good leaping ability — nearly hurdled tackler vs. Mississippi State.

Weaknesses: Very erratic accuracy and ball placement. Struggles to take pace off the ball and throw with touch and precision. Birddogs primary targets and eyes could use more refinement. Limited experience — only a one-year starter at South Alabama. Must improve timing, anticipation and decision-making. Is still learning what it means to lead. Has relatively small hands, wears a glove on his throwing hand to help grip the ball and could stand to improve ball security.

Future: Very raw, developmental thrower with intriguing physical traits to mold in a read-option, vertical passing game. Must refine his delivery and learn to set his feet before he throws. Ability to acclimate to an NFL playbook will determine his success. Has enough athletic talent, speed and toughness to project to receiver, similar to Vikings 2010 sixth-round pick Joe Webb.

Draft projection: Late draftable pick.

Scout's take: "(Bridge) can run and throw. He's not an NFL quarterback. He's a slash (QB/WR). You can get guys like that as free agents. He might go in the seventh (round). …He's a project. He's got a hose, but he sprays it everywhere."

QB TERRANCE BROADWAY, #8 (Sr-5)

LOUISIANA-LAFAYETTE ▶ GRADE: 5.04

Ht: 6-0 ⅝ | Wt: 223 | 40: 4.70e | Arm: 32 ½ | Hand: 9 ⅛

History: Married to a world-class sprinter and has a son. Baton Rouge, La. native. Began his college career at Houston, where he was recruited by Kevin Sumlin. Was slated to redshirt in 2010, but injuries to the Cougars' first two quarterbacks thrust Broadway into action — appeared in four games (one start) and completed 30-of-42 pass attempts for 424 yards with three touchdowns and one interception. Added 19 rushes for 72 yards (3.8-yard average) and zero touchdowns. Would have been third on the depth chart entering '11, so transferred to Louisiana-Lafayette, sitting out the season per NCAA rules. Began '12 as a backup, but took over when Blaine Gautier was injured — Broadway played all 13 games, starting the final nine, and completed 206-315-2,842-17-9 (65.4) with 119-769-9 (6.5) on the ground. Set school single-season records for total offense (3,611 yards) and completion percentage. Started all 12 games played in '13, tossing 166-266-2,419-19-12 (62.4) and running 131-442-8 (3.4). Suffered a broken right (throwing) arm against Louisiana-Monroe, underwent surgery, and missed the regular season finale against South Alabama, though he returned to start in the bowl game. In '14, passed 216-342-2,295-13-9 (63.2) and ran 146-653-3 (4.5) in 13 starts. Guided the Cajuns to three New Orleans Bowl wins, earning game MVP honors twice ('12, '14). Team captain. Was forced out of the Medal of Honor Bowl (all-star game) with an injured index finger.

Strengths: Good athlete with a solid build. Is tough and can take a hit and pop back up. Has shown he will play through injury. Throws with accuracy on the move. Very competitive. Mature, highly respected team leader. Studies the game and works at his craft. Strong personal and football character.

Weaknesses: Lacks ideal height. Average arm strength. Tends to overstride and does not throw on balance when he has time in the pocket. Could be more decisive as a triggerman. Has not faced top competition.

Future: Athletic zone-read quarterback

who found ways to win with an average supporting cast and has enough athletic ability and arm talent to be invited to a camp.

Draft projection: Priority free agent.

QB SHANE CARDEN, #5 (Sr-5)

EAST CAROLINA ▶ GRADE: 5.18

Ht: 6-1 ⅞	Wt: 218	40: 4.94	Arm: 33 ¼	Hand: 9 ¾

History: Father, Jay, played Minor League Baseball for eight years, and mother, Scoti, was a two-sport athlete at Cal Poly. Shane was a three-year starter and two-time all-stater as a Texas prep, earning recognition as Houston's 4A Offensive Player of the Year. Played with a fractured left wrist in 2006. Redshirted in 2010. Earned scout team MVP in '11. Played all 13 games in '12 — took over the starting job in Week Three and completed 273-of-413 pass attempts (66.1 percent) for 3,116 yards with 23 touchdowns and 10 interceptions. Was Conference USA's MVP in '13 when he started all 13 games and piled up 387-549-4,139-33-10 (70.5). Sprained his right ankle against Hawaii and broke his left hand in the season finale vs. Marshall. Was American Athletic Conference Offensive Player of the Year in '14 when he started all 13 games and totaled 392-617-4,736-30-10 (63.5). Rushed 271 times in his career for 253 yards (0.9-yard average) and 24 scores. Two-time captain walks away with 18 ECU single-game, single-season, and career records. Graduated with a degree in sports studies.

Strengths: Confident and competitive. Keeps his eyes downfield in face of the rush and proved tough enough to withstand punishment looking down the barrel of a gun. Mobile enough to avoid the initial rush and extend plays outside the pocket. Throws a catchable ball. Good touch with above-average short-to-intermediate accuracy. Effective fade thrower.

Weaknesses: Marginal scrambling ability. Has a low release point that makes it difficult to find throwing lanes through the trees. Average arm strength lessened by tendency to throw off his back foot. Does not transfer his weight or torque his hips, negating accuracy. Struggles to hasten his delivery when under duress. Hangs the deep out and struggles to drive the ball into tight windows. Statistics are inflated from a lateral passing game. Makes his receivers work for the ball too much. Must acclimate to taking snaps

from under center after working exclusively from the shotgun in college.

Future: Scrappy, undersized, West Coast touch thrower with enough arm to compete for a backup job in a West Coast passing game. Must refine his footwork and improve his ball placement to take the next step.

Draft projection: Late draftable pick.

Scout's take: "For all the yards that he puts up, I expected to like him more. He plays in a dink-and-dunk offense where the receivers create all the yardage. (East Carolina) had a couple receivers that were really productive. They made the offense go."

QB CODY FAJARDO, #17 (Sr-5)

NEVADA ▶ GRADE. 5.12

Ht: 6-1 ½	Wt: 223	40: 4.59	Arm: 31 ⅜	Hand: 9 ½

History: Won a state title at Servite High and was named L.A. Times California Player of the Year. Redshirted in 2010. Appeared in 10 games in '11, starting the final eight he played, and was named Western Athletic Conference Freshman of the Year after completing 150-of-218 pass attempts (68.8 percent) for 1,707 yards with six touchdowns and six interceptions. Sprained his left (non-throwing) shoulder against Texas Tech and did not play against Boise State. Also missed the Idaho contest (left ankle). Started all 12 games played in '12, passing 246-367-2,786-20-9 (67.0) and running 190-1,121-12 (5.9). Did not play against UNLV (back). Completed 243-358-2,668-13-3 (67.9) and rushed 141-621-8 (4.4) in '13 (10 games), though suffered an MCL injury against UC-Davis and did not play against Florida State or Hawaii. Also sprained his foot against Colorado State. Started all 13 games in '14 and totaled 239-405-2,498-18-11 (59.0) through the air, while leading the Wolfpack in rushing with 177-1,046-13 (5.9). Earned team MVP. Two-year captain is Nevada's all-time completions leader (878). Played under Brian Polian his last two years. Graduated with a degree in business management.

Strengths: Experienced four-year starter. Exceptional speed and scrambling ability to create with his feet and escape the rush. Outstanding short-area burst to pop out of the pocket and dash for the sticks. Good arm talent to drive the ball downfield.

Weaknesses: Has a long delivery. Unsophisticated eyes — tends to tuck and run at the flash of coverage and is not patient progressing through reads. Feet are seldom set when he throws, diminishing his accuracy at every layer. Marginal rhythm and anticipation — average passing instincts. Does not consistently convert in critical situations. Regularly faced average Mountain West competition and really struggled vs. Boise State. Not a commanding, vocal leader. Has been nagged by injuries throughout his career.

Summary: An inconsistent, move-the-pocket, athletic pistol passer with exciting speed and enough playmaking ability to buy time and create some plays. Operated behind an average offensive line with a weak supporting cast in college. Shows semblances to Tampa Bay 2006 sixth-rounder and Steelers backup QB Bruce Gradkowski.

Draft projection: Late draftable pick.

Scout's take: "He's a backup or No. 3 type, wildcat QB with good athletic ability. He's too inconsistent as a passer to help us."

QB GARRETT GRAYSON, #3 (Sr-5)

COLORADO STATE ▶ GRADE: 5.26

Ht: 6-2 ½ | Wt: 213 | 40: 4.95e | Arm: 30 | Hand: 10

History: Uncle, Danny, was an All-American linebacker at Washington State before he was drafted in the seventh round of the 1990 NFL Draft by the Steelers. Garrett was a three-year starter and two-year captain as a prep in Washington, where he broke most of the state's 4A passing records, led the nation in completion percentage as a senior (73.2 percent), and piled up more than 10,000 yards of total offense. Also ran track and captained the basketball team. Grayshirted in 2010. Started 3-of-4 games played as an injury replacement in '11, completing 43-of-77 pass attempts (55.8 percent) for 542 yards with two touchdowns and six interceptions. Playing under new head coach Jim McElwain in '12, Grayson passed 78-138-946-7-3 (56.5) in six games — started the first five before suffering a broken left collarbone against Air Force. Missed three games, returned against Wyoming, aggravated the injury, and missed the last three games. Started all 14 games in '13, tossing 297-478-3,696-23-11 (62.1). In April '14, Grayson re-broke his left clavicle moving a couch, requiring surgery. Earned Mountain West Offensive Player of the Year in the fall, managing 270-420-4,006-32-7

(64.3) despite bruising his right (throwing) shoulder against Boston College on Sept. 27 (was on "pitch count" in practices). Also was hampered by a groin injury in November. Rushed 212 times in his career for 279 yards (1.3-yard average) and four touchdowns. Team captain who holds virtually every CSU career passing record. Will be a 24-year-old rookie.

Strengths: Solid passing mechanics and set up. Has a good feel in the pocket — slides to find open throwing lanes and will step up to avoid pressure. Has a clean, efficient, over-the-top delivery and a quick stroke (with the shortest arms of any quarterback at the Combine). Good anticipation and accuracy — consistently hits receivers in stride. Good decision-maker — knows when and where to throw the ball. Is football smart, understands rhythm and tempo and plays with fine poise. Strong work ethic. Vulnerable leader with a likeable personality. Unselfish, team player. Takes pride in his craft. Football is important to him.

Weaknesses: Modest build and stature in the pocket. Average arm strength and ball velocity. Struggles to elude the rush (see Las Vegas Bowl vs. Utah) and takes some needless sacks when unable to get rid of the ball under duress (struggles hastening delivery). Can be a tick late to sort out disguised coverages and trigger. Limited improvisational skill — a bit robotic and overly programmed. Tends to underthrow the deep ball. Not a strong, take-charge, vocal leader. Durability is a concern.

Future: Efficient, game-managing rhythm passer capable of getting a team through a game, yet lacks ideal arm talent to carry an offense. Is similar to Redskins 2012 fourth-round pick Kirk Cousins and is most ideally suited for a backup role in a precision passing game. Requires a clean pocket to function at a high level.

Draft projection: Fourth- to fifth-round pick.

Scout's take: "He's an NFL backup, a quality NFL backup — that's what he is. I've heard some other teams like him in the third (round). He's a (fifth-rounder) for me. For how bad this (QB) class is, I wouldn't be surprised if he pushed up a round. In terms of accuracy, he might be the most proficient in this year's draft. He could go higher than you think (he should)."

QUARTERBACKS

QB **CONNOR HALLIDAY**, #12 (Sr-5)

WASHINGTON STATE ▶ GRADE: 4.75

| Ht: 6-3 | Wt: 196 | 40: 5.0e | Arm: 31 ¼ | Hand: 8 ⅜ |

History: Spokane native who passed for 4,198 yards and 43 touchdowns as a senior. Also played basketball. Redshirted in 2010. Appeared in four games in '11 (one start), completing 59-of-103 pass attempts (57.3 percent) for 960 yards with nine touchdowns and four interceptions. Did not play against Washington after suffering a lacerated liver against Utah. Started 5-of-9 games in '12, tossing 152-291-1,878-15-13 (52.2). Replaced Jeff Tuel (Buffalo Bills) in '13, amassing 449-714-4,597-34-22 (62.9). In '14, started all nine games played before suffering a season-ending broken ankle against USC — totaled 354-526-3,873-32-11 (67.3), including an NCAA single-game record 734 yards (and six touchdowns) against Cal. Set WSU career records with 11,304 passing yards, 90 touchdown passes, 1,013 completions, 1,633 pass attempts, 21 300-yard games and a 62.0 completion percentage. Graduated.

Strengths: Good height and field vision. Functional short accuracy and anticipation.

Weaknesses: Has a slender build and very small hands, the smallest of any quarterback at the Combine. Also the lightest quarterback at the event. Limited arm strength with a push delivery that will not be able to cut through the wind or handle winter conditions. Seldom sets his feet to throw and cannot generate RPMs on the deep out. Hangs the ball in the air and sprays it too often. Can be overly emotional and lose focus too easily. Questionable mental toughness. Average pocket awareness — takes unnecessary sacks and is not built to withstand contact. Marginal durability.

Summary: A shotgun system pocket passer lacking requisite arm talent to survive the rigors of the NFL game. Functioned in a pass-happy, spread offense featuring many pre-determined throws. Could provide an arm in an NFL training camp.

Draft projection: Free agent.

Scout's take: "He has no arm. He might be a good coach."

QB **TAYLOR HEINICKE**, #14 (Sr-4)

OLD DOMINION ▶ GRADE: 5.02

| Ht: 6-1 | Wt: 211 | 40: 4.78 | Arm: 28 ¾ | Hand: 9¼ |

History: Has a sleeve tattoo on his left arm in memory of his father who passed away in December 2011. Prepped at suburban Atlanta Collins Hill, one of the top athletic programs in America. Was Georgia's Old Spice Player of the Year after throwing for 4,218 yards (second in Georgia state history) and 44 touchdowns (third in state history. Was not offered a Division I scholarship. As a true freshman in 2011, saw his first action in Week Five before starting the final eight games and taking ownership of the position. Was runner-up for the Jerry Rice Award (national freshman of the year) after completing 211-of-307 pass attempts (68.7 percent) for 2,385 yards with 25 touchdowns and one interception, a "Hail Mary" pass against Towson. Added 68 rushes for 363 yards (5.3-yard average) and four touchdowns. Was the Walter Payton Award winner (best player in the FCS) in '12 when he broke Steve McNair's 18-year-old passing yardage record, as well as the FCS mark for single-season completions. Led the country in passing yards, passing yards per game, completions, passing touchdowns, total touchdowns, points responsible for, and total offense — racked up 398-579-5,076-44-14 (68.7) passing and 126-470-11 (3.7) rushing in 13 starts, including a record-breaking performance against New Hampshire in which he accounted for 791 yards of offense and six scores. Started all 12 games in '13, totaling 340-486-4,022-33-8 (70.0) through the air and 93-348-5 (3.7) on the ground. Started 11-of-12 games in '14 (offense opened the game in "Wildcat" formation in non-start) — ODU's first season as part of the FBS and Conference USA — tossing 289-457-3,476-30-16 (63.2) and running 80-139-2 (1.7). Played through a right (throwing) shoulder bruise sustained in Week Three. Three-time captain is ODU's all-time leader in passing yards (14,959), attempts (1,829), completions (1,238), completion percentage (67.7) and touchdown passes (132).

Strengths: Nice over-the-top release. Has a knack for finding clear sightlines. Good timing and anticipation and very good accuracy when he has a clean lane and is in rhythm. Extremely competitive,

QUARTERBACKS

11

hardworking and focused. Very good football intelligence. Highly respected leader and self-starter.

Weaknesses: Lacks ideal height and is small-framed. Operates exclusively out of the gun and will need to acclimate to working underneath center. Modest arm strength – does not consistently drive the deep out and tends to hang it. Feet tend to get happy in the pocket. Underwhelming East-West Shrine game showing.

Summary: Smallish, dink-and-dunk, quick-footed, rhythm passer most effective in an offense with moving pockets that allow him to find open throwing lanes. Diminutive stature could hinder his initial opportunities in the NFL, yet possesses the mental fortitude, perseverance and football-playing instincts to eventually overcome his physical limitations with continued focus and dedication.

Draft projection: Priority free agent.

Scout's take: "I wouldn't draft him, but I see some qualities that remind me of Drew Brees. I think he needs to spend some time in Canada and you might have something in a few years."

QB BRETT HUNDLEY, #17 (Jr-4)

UCLA ▶ GRADE: 5.42

Ht: 6-3 ¼ | Wt: 226 | 40: 4.63 | Arm: 32 ⅛ | Hand: 10 ½

History: Highly recruited out of Arizona, where he was named the state's Gatorade Player of the Year. Redshirted in 2011. Took the reins in '12 by starting all 14 games and completing 318-of-478 pass attempts (66.5 percent) for 3,740 yards with 29 touchdowns and 11 interceptions. Started all 26 games the next two seasons — passed 248-371-3,071-24-9 (66.8) in '13; and 271-392-3,155-22-5 (69.1) in '14. Owns UCLA's career touchdown passes record (75), and is the first Bruin quarterback to win at least nine games in three straight seasons. Two-year captain who opted to forgo his final season of eligibility, but not before graduating with a degree in sociology.

Strengths: Excellent size, stature and arm strength. Very good ball velocity when he steps into his throws and fires. Can make all the throws and excels fitting in the back-shoulder throw. Outstanding athlete capable of hurdling defenders as a runner (see Arizona State) and creating chunk yardage with his feet when the pocket breaks down.

Nifty runner with good vision, subtle open-field moves and enough run strength to fall forward. Experienced three-year starter. Recorded a 36-inch vertical jump and the only sub-4-flat-second (3.98) short shuttle among quarterbacks at the Combine.

Weaknesses: Average pocket awareness, passing instincts and overall accuracy. Has a long delivery and mechanics are too varied. Often locks onto receivers, throws to spots and timing and anticipation are off when asked to throw in rhythm (frequently throws behind receivers, forces them to adjust and leads them into traffic). Relies too much on his arm talent and delivers the ball off his back foot even when the pocket is clean. Holds onto the ball too long and takes unnecessary sacks (see 10 taken vs. Utah). Seldom is under center and footwork will need refinement dropping back. Production is camouflaged by a simple, horizontal passing game. Could stand to become more of a student of the game.

Future: A strong, talented pocket passer with physical tools that shout first-round but passing skills that scream developmental project. Has the toughness, arm talent and mobility that fits best in a vertical passing game for teams such as the Cardinals, Panthers or Steelers. Has a similar skill set to Arizona 2014 fourth-round pick Logan Thomas and Redskins 2005 first-round pick Jason Campbell, a league consensus fourth-round talent who was even stacked there for Washington prior to Joe Gibbs' eleventh hour push to fill a pressing quarterback need.

Draft projection: Third- to fourth-round pick.

Scout's take: "Someone probably will take a chance on him in the second (round) in this draft. We wouldn't. He's not even in the conversation with (Winston and Mariota). He's a product of the system. His percentages are inflated. His footwork is bad. It's going to take some time for him to be ready, and even after you coach him up, I'm not sure you'll have a guy you're not trying to replace."

QB JERRY LOVELOCKE, #8 (Sr-5)

PRAIRIE VIEW A&M ▶ GRADE: 5.04

Ht: 6-4 ½ | Wt: 248 | 40: 4.96 | Arm: 10 ½ | Hand: 34 ¼

History: Maryland prep chose FCS Prairie View A&M over offers from FBS schools, including Central Michigan and Temple.

As a true freshman in 2011, started 7-of-10 games played and completed 91-of-177 pass attempts (51.4 percent) for 1,020 yards with 10 touchdowns and four interceptions. Added 57 rushes for 318 yards (5.6-yard average) and three touchdowns. Sprained his right ankle against Grambling and did not play against Southern. Played nine games in '12, starting two, and tossed 98-150-1,033-5-4 (65.3) with 42-71-2 (1.7) rushing. Started 10-of-11 games played in '13, passing 285-429-2,833-23-9 (66.4) and running 75-279-9 (3.7). Did not play against Jackson State after spraining his left AC joint against Mississippi Valley State. In '14, started all 10 games and completed 202-351-2,473-16-9 (57.6) with 60-217-10 (3.6) on the ground.

Strengths: Outstanding size. Very good arm strength — can make every throw and drill it with velocity. Has a high release point and delivers the ball with ease. Is tough and will battle through injuries. Good personal and football character.

Weaknesses: Has a funky, inconsistent release that can be too elongated. Operated an unsophisticated offense and could require additional time to acclimate to NFL terminology. Could stand to accelerate processing time in the pocket. Overly relies on his arm talent and will take unnecessary chances fitting the ball into tight windows. Sporadic deep ball thrower. Seldom works under center. Limited mobility.

Future: A long-term, developmental pocket passer with enough physical talent for a patient positional coach to consider grooming on a practice squad in a vertical, downfield attack such as offenses in Arizona, Pittsburgh or Baltimore.

Draft projection: Priority free agent.

Scout's take: "(Lovelocke) is a developmental player – that's all he is."

QB SEAN MANNION, #4 (Sr-5)

OREGON STATE ▶ GRADE: 5.32

Ht: 6-5⅞ | Wt: 229 | 40: 4.90e | Arm: 33 ½ | Hand: 9

History: Father is a high school football coach. Also played baseball and basketball as a California prep. Redshirted in 2010. Appeared in all 12 games in '11, starting the final 10, and completed 305-of-473 pass attempts (64.5 percent) for 3,328 yards with 16 touchdowns and 18 interceptions. Started 8-of-10 games played in '12, passing 200-309-2,446-15-13 (64.7). Injured his left knee (torn meniscus) against Washington State, had arthroscopic surgery, and missed two games. Upon returning against Washington, threw four interceptions and was benched for two regular season contests and the Beavers' bowl game. Won the job back in '13 when he started all 13 games and totaled 400-603-4,662-37-15 (62.3) — set a Pac-12 record for passing yards and OSU single-season records for touchdown passes, completions, and pass attempts. Started all 12 games in '14, tossing 282-453-3,164-15-8 (62.3). Only three-year captain in school history. Owns 18 school passing records, and his 13,600 passing yards is eighth all-time. Graduated with a liberal studies degree and began working on master's degree.

Strengths: Experienced four-year starter possessing prototype size in a pro-style offense where he consistently operated from underneath center. Clean footwork. Stands tall in the pocket in the face of the rush and delivers. Very good arm strength and fine accuracy (when feet are set). Respected team leader with a calm, cool, even-keeled football-playing temperament. Excellent work habits and football character. Gym rat and film junkie. Takes the game very seriously. Very intelligent and football smart.

Weaknesses: Has small hands (check grip) and does not throw a consistently tight spiral. Underdeveloped frame. Takes too many chances forcing the ball into double coverage (see USC) and has a tendency to lock onto his primary target and telegraph passes. Takes too long to scan the field and needs to hasten internal clock. Average delivery quickness. Could do a better job changing ball speeds. Average athlete. Limited mobility to avoid the rush and move around the pocket under duress. Not a scrambling threat. Rigid mover with tight hips. Does not consistently snap his hips and transfer his weight into his throws. Could be more vocal and demanding as a leader.

Future: A lean, experienced pocket passer groomed in Mike Riley's pro-style offense, Mannion regressed as a senior with fewer weapons, such as Saints 2014 first-round pick Brandin Cooks, and has not proven he can handle pressure. Yet possesses enough arm, experience and desire to emerge as a serviceable NFL starter. Elicited some overly strong comparisons from evaluators

QUARTERBACKS

to Falcons QB Matt Ryan as a junior. Shows more favorably to Buccaneers 2013 third-round pick Mike Glennon.

Draft projection: Fourth- to fifth-round pick.

Scout's take: "You're reaching for him if you take him in the second or third (round). Derek Anderson went in the sixth and was a better quarterback coming out. The kid in Tampa Bay (Glennon) that they don't really like is the same guy, and he has struggled. They reached for him. We had him in the sixth (round)."

QB MARCUS MARIOTA, #8 (Jr-4)

OREGON ▶ GRADE: 6.70

Ht: 6-3 ¾ | Wt: 222 | 40: 4.46 | Arm: 32 | Hand: 9 ⅞

History: Hawaiian native who won a state title as a senior. Also played soccer as a prep. Only drew two FBS scholarship offers. Redshirted in 2011 before starting all 41 games of his college career. Burst onto the scene in '12 when he was named the Pac-12 Offensive Freshman of the Year, becoming the first freshman quarterback to earn first-team all-league honors in 23 years. Set the conference freshman record for most touchdown passes in a season — completed 230-of-336 pass attempts (68.5 percent) for 2,677 yards with 32 touchdowns and six interceptions. Also rushed 106 times for 752 yards (7.1-yard average) and five touchdowns. In '13, became the first player in Oregon history to surpass 4,000 yards of total offense (one of three Pac-12 players to break the previous single-season record). Also broke the conference mark for consecutive pass attempts without an interception (353), and established school records for most points responsible for, completions, and total touchdowns. On the season, passed 245-386-3,665-31-4 (63.5) and rushed 96-715-9 (7.4). Sprained his left MCL against Stanford. Took home major hardware in '14, winning the Heisman Trophy, AP Player of the Year, Walter Camp, Maxwell, Davey O'Brien, Johnny Unitas Golden Arm, and Pac-12 Offensive Player of the Year. Guided the Ducks to the national championship game, totaling 304-445-4,454-42-4 (68.3) through the air with 135-770-15 (5.7) on the ground. The most decorated player in school history, Mariota has a 36-5 career starting record. Also graduated in less than four years with a degree in general science.

Strengths: Poised in the pocket. Can scan the field, read defenses and find the open receiver. Very good arm angles and velocity – can snap it quickly when needed. Good balance in his feet. Decisive triggerman with very good spatial awareness – makes measured throws. Can manipulate his arm and throwing platform and create magic on the move. Extremely athletic with the foot speed to take the corner and avoid the rush. Displays some dazzling run skills and vision to shake defenders out of their shoes. Continues scanning and reading the field while extending plays. Throws with accuracy in the pocket and on the move and is capable of throwing receivers open. Speed and athletic ability are rare for a quarterback. Recorded a 6.87-second three-cone drill time, a 1.56-second 10-yard split and as low as a 4.43-second 40-yard dash, best among quarterbacks at the Scouting Combine. Exceptional work ethic – is known to arrive early at the football office and stay late and possesses exceptional personal and football character. Has special intangibles. Very respectful of authority and humble, yet is described by teammates as able to take command on the field, on the sideline or in the locker room when needed. Is an authentic leader who players respond to and will lead by example and also pull teammates aside and address them when called for. Very durable. Smart, tough, mature and accountable.

Weaknesses: Has a narrow bone structure. Is still developing a feel in the pocket. Operated a spread offense and footwork will require some refinement adjusting to working under center. Is not asked to make a lot of NFL-style, progression reads and often turns and throws in an offense that creates open receivers with wide throwing lanes. Could stand to improve deep accuracy – tends to oversling it. Has not shown the killer instinct and on-field leadership presence to close out games in the clutch with his back against the wall, struggling vs. Stanford throughout his career. Could stand to show more poise in the pocket against pressure and could benefit from becoming a more demanding leader on the field and in the huddle, and understanding the importance of vocal leadership. Not a

Marcus Mariota

true alpha leader.

Future: An athletic, playmaking passer who excelled in an up-tempo, spread, read-option offense, Mariota displayed the poise and vision in the pocket of a seasoned surgeon and has proven he can sit in the pocket, scan and deliver the ball with a high degree of precision. Would be dynamite in Chip Kelly's up-tempo offense in Philadelphia, yet could excel in any offense with a creative coordinator willing to tailor a scheme to Mariota's unique strengths.

Draft projection: Top-10 pick.

Scout's take: "I have seen him too much since he was a freshman. You have to watch his full body of work to appreciate him. It's not his fault that he plays at Oregon and that's the offense they run. He has all the intangibles. The skill set is better than (49ers QB Colin) Kaepernick. He is a smarter, better person and a better passer. They ask (Mariota) to do a lot. He can audible. He knows all the protections. ...People have to start changing the way they view what to do with quarterbacks in the NFL. The game is changing. The Eagles have shown their offense works. They didn't have the 15th or 20th offense this year – they had the third with two bums at quarterback. Why wouldn't you just maximize what (Mariota) does."

QB **BRYCE PETTY**, #14 (Sr-6)

BAYLOR ▶ GRADE: 5.52

Ht: 6-2 ⅞ | Wt: 230 | 40: 4.84 | Arm: 31 ⅞ | Hand: 10

History: Originally committed to Tennessee and then-head coach Phil Fulmer, but following Fulmer's exit, was not wanted by incoming head coach Lane Kiffin. Signed with Baylor, but grayshirted and took classes at Navarro College in 2009. Redshirted in 2010. Backed up Redskins '12 first-rounder Robert Griffin III in '11 when he appeared in five games and completed 3-of-4 pass attempts (75.0 percent) for 43 yards with zero touchdowns and zero interceptions. Backed up Nick Florence in '12, tossing 7-10-97-1-0 (70.0). Was the Big 12 Offensive Player of the Year and finished seventh in the Heisman voting in '13 when he produced 250-403-4,200-32-3 (62.0). Started all 12 games played in '14, managing 270-428-3,855-29-7 (63.1), including a record-setting 550-yard performance in the Cotton Bowl versus Michigan State. Played hurt most of the season after suffering two cracked transverse processes (vertebrae) in the season opener against SMU. Also sustained a concussion against Texas Tech. Rushed 192 times in his career for 338 yards (1.8-yard average) and 21 touchdowns. Petty's career interception percentage (1.18%) established a new NCAA record, passing Billy Volek, while Petty's 9.6 career yards per attempt bested Sam Bradford's previous record. Honored with the Bobby Bowden Award recognizing the epitome of a student-athlete whose conduct is exemplary in the classroom, on the field, and in the community. Graduated in May 2013 with degree in health science studies. Will be a 24-year-old rookie.

Strengths: Looks the part. Outstanding size and pocket stature. Very good arm strength. Is tough and ultra-competitive. Physically tough and has shown he will play through injuries (see SMU when battled through transverse process in back). Good agility to sidestep the first wave of pass rushers. Showed poise rallying team to victory down 21 vs. Baylor. Very good work ethic – works at his craft. Gym rat. Has a very strong support system.

Weaknesses: Operated in a simplified, grip-and-rip offense where he was not asked to work through NFL progressions or handle the complexities of an NFL system. Production was highly inflated by scheme. Tends to stare down his primary target – eyes are not advanced and will require training to look off receivers and manipulate secondaries. Must show he can fit the ball into tighter windows. Often throws off his back foot and arms the ball. Pocket awareness could improve. Deep ball is often too flat, leading to frequent overthrows. Is a bit stiff and rigid in his movement and will need to learn how to protect his body better and slide feet first. Only a two-year starter despite being six years removed from high school. Did not handle adversity well early in career when unseated for the starting job by Nick Florence.

Future: A very well-built, strong-armed thrower who successfully operated a gimmicky vertical passing game with a minimized playbook in college and has the size, arm talent and intelligence to be groomed into an eventual starter with continued refinement. Will require several years before he is ready to assume a job on the front lines and must practice patience and diligence to ascend. Clearly has a lot of physical talent, and showed it at the Senior Bowl, but still has a great deal to learn from

a mental and technical standpoint before he is ready. Similar to Lions 2007 second-round pick Drew Stanton and could wind up having a similar type of career.

Draft projection: Third- to fourth-round pick.

Scout's take: "There are a lot of factions with Petty (in the scouting community). You have all the naysayers that believe Art Briles' quarterbacks can't make it in the league because they haven't yet, from RG3 to Kevin Kolb to Case Keenum, from Baylor to Houston. You have the other group that sees a strong enough arm and a good athlete but see the accuracy being off. And then there are (evaluators) that like him – or see the glass being half-full and believe his accuracy issues are more the fault of his receivers and timing. There are second-round grades and there are free-agent grades. Opinions are all over the board. (Petty) is one of the more polarizing players in this year's draft. He's a love-him-or-hate-him guy."

QB-RB BLAKE SIMS, #6 (Sr-5)

ALABAMA ▶ GRADE: 5.05

Ht: 5-11 ½ | Wt: 218 | 40: 4.48 | Arm: 31 ½ | Hand: 9

History: Two-time all-stater out of Georgia. Redshirted in 2010. Was a running back in '11 — carried 22 times for 107 yards (4.9-yard average) and zero touchdowns. Backed up Bengals '14 fifth-rounder A.J. McCarron the next two seasons — completed 5-of-10 pass attempts (50.0 percent) for 77 yards with zero touchdowns and zero interceptions in '12 (10 games); and 18-29-167-2-0 (62.1) in '13 (eight games). Playing under offensive coordinator Lane Kiffin in '14, won a camp battle over Jacob Coker and broke Alabama's single-season passing yardage record — started all 14 games, passing 252-391-3,487-28-10 (64.5). Bruised his AC joint against Florida. Career rushing totals as a quarterback were 128-598-9 (4.7). Team captain. Graduated with a degree in human environmental sciences.

Strengths: Can handle pre-snap reads and audibles at the line and grew more comfortable in a pro-style offense as the season progressed. Distributes the ball well in the short passing game (slants, digs, screens, outs). Agile and creative runner with enough size, toughness and speed to be tried as a running back.

Weaknesses: Lacks ideal height, measuring

QUARTERBACKS

the shortest of any quarterback at the Combine, and displays limited field vision. Is only a one-year starter. Marginal intermediate-to-deep accuracy — lacks touch and anticipation and frequently overshoots the deep ball. Average awareness and escapability vs. the blitz. Mechanics and accuracy diminish greatly on the move — tends to use a sidearm delivery under duress.

Future: A short, unrefined, dink-and-dunk passer capable of competing for a No. 3 job in a camp but lacks ideal size, accuracy and savvy to earn a spot. Has enough athletic ability to consider position-switching and could warrant the most interest as a developmental runner.

Draft projection: Priority free agent.

Scout's take: "He's too erratic as a passer. He was worked out as a running back at his pro day. He might have a better chance to stick there."

QB JAMEILL SHOWERS, #1 (Sr-5)
UTEP ▶ GRADE: 4.85
Ht: 6-1 | Wt: 231 | 40: 4.75e | Arm: 31 ½ | Hand: 9 ⅝

History: Texas native. Began his college career at Texas A&M, where he redshirted in 2010. Backed up Dolphins '12 first-rounder Ryan Tannehill in '11 — saw limited action in four games and completed 4-of-5 pass attempts (80.0 percent) for 40 yards with zero touchdowns and zero interceptions. Also rushed nine times for 33 yards (3.7-yard average) and a touchdown. Backed up Browns '14 first-rounder Johnny Manziel in '12 — appeared in seven games and recorded 27-44-319-2-1 (61.4) passing and 17-70-0 (4.1) rushing. Graduated in June '13, enabling him to transfer to UTEP and play right away. On the season, started the first seven games and totaled 107-188-1,263-11-4 (56.9) through the air with 62-195-4 (3.1) on the ground before suffering a season-ending dislocated right (throwing) shoulder against Temple. Started all 12 games in '14, tossing 146-262-1,732-12-5 (55.7) and running 83-288-4 (3.5).

Strengths: Good arm talent – throws with velocity and can make all the throws. Has a clean, compact release. Good improvisational skill when the pocket folds. Solid personal and football character.

Weaknesses: Marginal accuracy and touch – too often throws behind receivers. Makes suspect decisions forcing the ball

into coverage. Marginal pocket awareness and poise – presses too much. Holds the ball too long and is late to deliver it, tipping off defensive backs. Late to see and recognize open receivers. Is not a take-charge, vocal leader.

Future: A developmental quarterback who was slow to adapt to a new system at UTEP. Footwork must be refined to avoid spraying the ball so much, yet has enough arm talent to warrant an opportunity.

Draft projection: Priority free agent.

QB JAMEIS WINSTON, #5 (Soph-3)
FLORIDA STATE ▶ GRADE: 6.75
Ht: 6-3 ¾ | Wt: 231 | 40: 4.96 | Arm: 32 | Hand: 9 ⅜

History: Elite recruit out of Alabama, where was the state's Gatorade Player of the Year and a consensus All-American. Two-sport star who was drafted by the Texas Rangers in the 2012 MLB draft and accepted admission into Stanford with a 4.0 GPA prior to accepting a scholarship from FSU. Redshirted in '12 while Buffalo Bills '13 first-rounder E.J. Manuel quarterbacked the Seminoles. In November, Winston and three teammates had a pellet-gun fight at their apartment, causing $4,200 in damage. In the fall, Winston guided FSU to an undefeated national championship and became the youngest player to win the Heisman Trophy. Started all 14 games and completed 257-of-384 pass attempts (66.9 percent) for 4,057 yards with 40 touchdowns and 10 interceptions, including a 20-35-237-2-0 MVP performance against Auburn in the BCS National Championship in which he engineered a game-winning seven-play, 80-yard drive with 1:11 remaining and FSU down 31-27. In April '14, Winston was accused of stealing $32.72 worth of crab legs from a Tallahassee supermarket. He claimed he "forgot" to pay. Ultimately was issued a civil citation and completed community service while suspended from the baseball team. Started all 13 games played in the fall, passing 305-467-3,907-25-18 (65.3). Sprained his right ankle against Louisville. Was suspended for the Clemson contest because he jumped on a table in an FSU dining hall and shouted a profane internet meme. The suspension was originally for just the first half, but the school later announced he would miss the entire game because he was not honest with school officials. Over his two seasons, carried 145 times for 284 yards (2.0-yard average) and seven touchdowns. Finished his two-year run ranked third in school history in passing yards (7,964), second in touchdown passes (65) and sixth in completions (562). Additionally, Winston's 14 300-yard passing games are also tied with Chris Weinke for most in school history. Compiled a 26-1 career starting record. Winston also played two seasons (2013-14) for the FSU baseball team, compiling a 1.94 ERA over 41 appearances (60.1 innings) and a .209 batting average in 158 at-bats.

Strengths: Strong in the pocket and can sidestep the rush, brush off defenders and make difficult, off-balance throws. Very tough, can withstand continual pressure, stand tall and deliver the ball in the face of the blitz. Is quick to see overloaded fronts and find hot routes. Worked from underneath center and out of the gun and was asked to make progression reads. Studies the game, is very football smart and can make checks and handle audibles at the line of scrimmage. Has outstanding arm strength and can make every throw. Anticipates receivers coming open and understands ball placement. Extremely competitive. Has responded very well in critical situations and has shown he can consistently convert on third down. Rallied the team to victory following an 18-point deficit vs. Auburn in the 2013 BCS National Championship game; a 17-point deficit vs. North Carolina State in 2014; and a 21-point deficit vs. Louisville on the road in prime-time while battling thru an ankle injury. Has shown he can handle the pressure of playing on big stages and thrives off it. Has a lot of upside – will only be a 21-year-old rookie. Has the bravado and confidence to question authority and the moxie and on-field temperament needed to command a huddle and ignite comeback victories. In addition to being football smart, is very academically intelligent as evidenced by 4.0 high school GPA and admission into Stanford. Impressed coaches and executives with his ability to talk football concepts and diagram plays on the whiteboard at the Combine.

Weaknesses: Average overall pocket mobility – looked heavier and less fleet-footed in 2014 than he did in 2013. Has a long release that has led to a very high percentage of balls being batted down at the line of scrimmage. Stares down receivers, birddogging his primary target (see Notre Dame) and makes too many risky decisions triggering with a riverboat gambler mentality. Does not manipulate safeties with his eyes. Tends to start games very slowly, and production notably slipped in 2014. Had an exceptional supporting cast with an NFL-caliber offensive line, top-tier receiving talent and an even more talented defense that consistently shut down opponents in the second halves of games. Is still figuring out what it means to lead by example and has invited many questions about his personal character and integrity following multiple off-the-field discretions that resulted in team discipline. Frequently challenged the coaching staff openly on the sidelines and was kicked out of practice prior to the national championship game after Jimbo Fisher reportedly took issue with the way he was performing a two-minute drill. Questions about his shoulder that arose at the Combine require medical clearance.

Future: Regressed following Heisman-winning freshman season after losing his top receiving target to the NFL and battling through an ankle injury the second half of the season. Is still learning how to handle the immense success he attained as a freshman. Yet possesses a pro skill set and has the intelligence and all the physical talent to thrive if paired with a demanding coach willing to challenge him and hold him accountable. The mental toughness and self-confidence he displayed bouncing back from numerous poor first halves only to lead dramatic second-half comebacks last season should serve him well during the difficult rookie QB learning curve that all young, highly touted signal-callers must endure.

Draft projection: Top-10 pick.

Scout's take: "My only problem with (Winston) is he is afraid to or doesn't have any feel to step up in the pocket. He gets a lot of really clean pockets, but he will throw off his back foot, move laterally and get himself in trouble. In three games, I saw him step up in the pocket once. It's surprising because the pocket is that good. The only weakness in the line is at center and it's not like he is awful. When (Winston) gets sacked, it's because he is stationary and doesn't step up."

QUARTERBACKS

RUNNING BACKS

SEAN TAYLOR/UGA ATHLETIC ASSOCIATION

Nawrocki's TOP 10

1. **TODD GURLEY**
2. **Melvin Gordon**
3. **Tevin Coleman**
4. **Jay Ajayi**
5. **Duke Johnson**
6. **Ameer Abdullah**
7. **T.J. Yeldon**
8. **Buck Allen**
9. **Jeremy Langford**
10. **David Johnson**

RUNNING BACKS

RB-RS AMEER ABDULLAH, #8 (Sr-4)

NEBRASKA ▶ GRADE: 5.52

Ht: 5-8 ¾ | Wt: 205 | 40: 4.53 | Arm: 30 | Hand: 8 ⅝

History: Prepped in Alabama. As a true freshman in 2011, appeared in all 13 games and carried 42 times for 150 yards (3.6-yard average) and three touchdowns. Also caught one pass for 11 yards (11.0) and zero touchdowns, while serving as the Huskers' primary return man — returned 15 punts for 107 yards (7.1) and zero touchdowns, and returned 26 kickoffs for 763 yards and a score (29.3). In '12, started 7-of-14 games at the I back spot as an injury replacement for Bengals '13 sixth-rounder Rex Burkhead, rushing 226-1,137-8 (5.0) and catching 24-178-2 (7.4), while returning punts 16-209-1 (13.1) and kickoffs 17-360-0 (21.2). Sprained his right MCL during '13 spring practice. Started all 13 games in each of the next two seasons — toted 281-1,690-9 (6.0), caught 26-232-2 (8.9), and returned kickoffs 4-77 (19.2) in '13; and ran 264-1,611-19 (6.1), snagged 22-269-3 (12.2), and returned kickoffs 14-392-0 (28.0) in '14. Sprained his left MCL against Purdue. Two-time captain, two-time team MVP, and two-time Nebraska Lifter of the Year. Abdullah's 7,186 career all-purpose yards ranks second in Big Ten history behind Ron Dayne, and his 4,588 career rushing yards rank second in school history behind Mike Rozier. Abdullah is the ninth of his siblings to earn a college degree (history). MVP of Senior Bowl. Has 24 career fumbles in 978 career touches with a 5.6-yard rushing average.

Strengths: Very good musculature, especially in the upper body. Sudden mover with very

19

good stop-start acceleration and quickness in the hole to make the first tackler miss. Patient vision — sets up blocks and drives his legs on contact. Efficient open-field runner with a low center of gravity that allows him to bounce off and spin out of tackles. Subtle and nifty to create in the open field. Can line up in the slot and field kicks. Extremely productive. Recorded a 42 1/2-inch vertical jump, 10-foot 10-inch broad jump, 3.95-second 20-yard shuttle and 6.79-second 3-cone drill, all best among running backs at the Combine. Also produced 24 bench-press reps, equivalent to nearly twice his weight.

Weaknesses: Thin-boned (ankles and wrists) and lacks ideal height. Minimal inside-running power — too often tiptoes between the tackles with modest finishing strength. Does not run square to the line or consistently accelerate to and through contact. Lacks top-end gear to kick into overdrive and pull away from defenders — gets tracked from behind. Limited blocking strength — thin-waisted and lacks lead in his pants to anchor. Has small hands and ball security has been an issue — lost 17 of his 24 career fumbles.

Future: A shifty, change-of-pace slasher most ideally suited for a role as a returner and complimentary back, Abdullah lacks the elite speed that makes small backs special and must learn how to protect the football more securely. Is capable of producing a joystick highlight film given his vision, burst and acceleration. Greatest immediate value will be in the return game and as a weapon in the passing game.

Draft projection: Second- to third-round pick.

Scout's take: "He's a tough little player, but he is little and all is weight is up top. He's only had one major injury so far. What scares me is not that he's going to get hurt. I like his run style and production. He has very good acceleration and burst. I just don't see him popping 80-yard runs. He has a lot of 10- and 8- and 20- and 15-yard runs, but you don't see him taking it to the house a lot. I don't see the finishing speed. I couldn't draft a utility back like him before the fourth (round)."

RB JAY AJAYI, #27 (Jr-4)

BOISE STATE ▶ GRADE: 5.81

Ht: 5-11 ¾ | Wt: 221 | 40: 4.56 | Arm: 32 | Hand: 10

History: Last name is pronounced "uh-JYE-ee." Born in England to Nigerian parents. Prepped in Texas, where he averaged nearly 10 yards per carry and scored 35 touchdowns as a senior. Also ran track. Redshirted in 2011, but was arrested in October for trying to steal sweatpants from Walmart (ultimately plead guilty to misdemeanor theft). Soon after, tore his right ACL in practice. Was suspended the first two games of the '12 season, but played the next 11 and carried 82 times for 548 yards (6.7-yard average) and four touchdowns with one catch for 14 yards (14.0) and zero touchdowns. Started 12-of-13 games in '13 (gave way to five receivers against Nevada), producing 249-1,425-18 (5.7) rushing and 22-222-1 (10.1) receiving. Posted the best season by a running back in Boise State history in '14 — set school single-season records for carries, rushing yards, rushing touchdowns by totaling 347-1,823-28 (5.3) on the ground with 50-535-4 (10.7) through the air (14 starts). Also set the BSU record for all-purpose yards (2,358), led the country in scoring (13.7 points per game), and became the only player in FBS history to accumulate 1,800 rushing yards and 500 receiving yards in a single season. Was the only player in the Mountain West Conference to be voted first-team the last two seasons. Has 12 career fumbles in 752 touches with a 5.6-yard average per carry.

Strengths: Well built. Tough, instinctive and very competitive. Runs hard with good body lean, a strong base and fine peripheral vision to navigate through holes and create yardage where there is none. Understands how to get open in the receiving game and catches the ball naturally. Good awareness in pass protection. Willing blocker. Strong goalline/short-yardage runner. Has a 39-inch vertical jump.

Weaknesses: Duck-footed, tight-hipped and will struggle to avoid some direct hits. Average creativity and elusiveness. Lacks the foot speed to turn the corner (see Mississippi) and is not a home-run threat. Could do a better job sinking his hips and uncoiling in pass pro. Regularly faced Mountain West competition.

Future: Big, strong downhill runner who carried a full workload and has the north-south running style to crease defenses and grind out tough yardage. Offers a well-balanced skill set to compete on every down and will bring a power element to a backfield.

Draft projection: Second- to third-round pick.

Scout's take: "He's a poor man's Eddie George. He runs upright like Eddie did, has a similar stride and is put together with big guns. He's rushed for 3,200-some yards the last two years behind a line that is not very good. He ran over Mississippi pretty good and ran all over Arizona in the Fiesta Bowl.

RB JAVORIUS "BUCK" ALLEN, #37 (Jr-4)

USC ▶ GRADE: 5.48

| Ht: 6-0 ½ | Wt: 221 | 40: 4.53 | Arm: 31 ¾ | Hand: 9 ⅜ |

History: Also long-jumped as a Florida prep. Missed his 2009 junior season after breaking his left femur in the season opener. Returned to win a state title in '10. Redshirted in '11. Appeared in three games in '12, recording six carries for 32 yards (5.3-yard average) and zero touchdowns. Came on strong down the stretch in '13, when he was voted team MVP — played all 14 games, starting the final four, and totaled 135-785-14 (5.8) rushing with 22 receptions for 252 yards (11.5) and one touchdown. In '14, started all 13 games and amassed 276-1,489-11 (5.4) on the ground with 41-458-1 (11.2) through the air, while playing through much of the season with a shoulder injury. Has six career fumbles in 480 touches with a 5.5-yard average per carry.

Strengths: Looks the part. Good size, balance, body control and coordination. Light on his feet for his size and carries his weight well. Very good eyes, instincts and run vision — follows his blocks, is quick to find creases and clear through holes. Produces a lot of yardage after contact with consistent leg churn/foot turnover. Outstanding hands — natural catcher. Understands how to settle into soft spots in the passing game and turns upfield quickly after the catch. Has a strong core. Agile and nifty enough to sidestep tacklers in the open field (see Arizona). Above-average run strength to power thru arm tackles and push a pile with defenders draped on his back.

Weaknesses: Runs a bit upright (and consequently leaves his body susceptible to additional punishment). Has room for improvement as a blocker in the way of desire, effort and toughness. Takes some time to get rolling downhill. Average open-field elusiveness to string moves together and create magic vs. clogged lanes. Does not show dynamic speed to consistently take the corner. Was slowed by shoulder injuries as a junior and tied for the fewest bench-press reps (11) of any back at the Combine.

Future: An athletic, finesse big back slowed early in his junior season by a shoulder injury, Allen ran with more urgency and physicality late in the season. Has the receiving skills desired in a West Coast offense and shows semblances to a talented pair of backs known for their receiving skills selected in the second round — 49ers great Roger Craig (pick 49, 1983) and Bears Pro Bowler Matt Forte (pick 44, 2008).

Draft projection: Second- to third-round pick.

Scout's take: "On turf, he lit up Arizona. He looks fast in that game and does everything you want to see. The biggest question I have is how well he is going to adapt to NFL pass protection schemes. I wish I saw more out of him as a blocker."

RB CAMERON ARTIS-PAYNE, #44 (Sr-5)

AUBURN ▶ GRADE: 5.24

| Ht: 5-9 ¾ | Wt: 212 | 40: 4.47 | Arm: 29 ⅝ | Hand: 8 ⅞ |

History: Also played basketball as a Pennsylvania prep. Ran for nearly 2,000 yards with 31 touchdowns as a senior, but poor grades landed him at Milford Prep Academy (N.Y.) in 2008. Spent two years at home before attending Allan Hancock Community College (Calif.). Rushed for 1,364 yards and 18 touchdowns in '11, then carried 261 times for 2,048 yards (7.8-yard average) and 25 touchdowns with seven receptions for 52 yards (7.4) and zero touchdowns in '12. Joined the Tigers in '13 and backed up Rams '14 second-rounder Tre Mason, totaling 91-610-6 (6.7) in 14 games (one start). The Tigers' feature back in '14, started 11-of-13 games and amassed 303-1,608-13 (5.3) rushing and 13-147-0 (11.3) receiving. His 1,755 all-purpose yards doubled the team's next best gainer. Did not lift at the Combine because of a left shoulder (A/C joint) injury and opted not to perform shuttles.

Strengths: Strong, compact and urgent. Is patient and runs with purpose. Slams it hard inside and usually falls forward. Good run skills — has a knack for sifting through traffic and gliding through lanes. Confident and competitive — has a bounce in his step and a resourcefulness as a runner never to go down easy. Drives through contact and plays bigger than his size. Solid Senior Bowl game performance.

Weaknesses: Overaged — will be a 25-year-old rookie (though did not play football from 2009-10). Has small hands. Does not play to timed speed. Rigid route runner. Limited receiving production. Could stand to show more awareness in pass pro. Limited special teams experience.

Future: More quick than fast chunk runner emerged behind the shadow of Tre Mason as a senior and proved capable of carrying a full workload in the SEC. Could require time to acclimate to an NFL playbook, yet is willing to do what it takes to make it and could

RUNNING BACKS

contribute in a rotation.

Draft projection: Late draftable pick.

Scout's take: "He reminds me of (Seahawks 2008 seventh round pick and Ravens RB) Justin Forsett. He's a good football player. He's just not very fast."

RB **DOMINIQUE BROWN**, #10 (Sr-5)

LOUISVILLE ▶ GRADE: 5.12

Ht: 6-1⅞ | Wt: 234 | 40: 4.60e | Arm: 32⅜ | Hand: 9½

History: Was a running quarterback as an Ohio prep — won a state title as a senior, and was named Ohio Division II Co-Offensive Player of the Year. Was recruited to Louisville by then-head coach Charlie Strong. As a true freshman in 2010, appeared in 10 games and carried 20 times for 59 yards (3.0-yard average) and zero touchdowns while operating the "Wildcard" package. Added three catches for 32 yards (10.7) and zero touchdowns. In '11, totaled 140-533-4 (3.8) rushing and 16-98-1 (6.1) receiving in 12 games (three starts). After not playing in Week Two against Florida International, was converted to running back full-time, as the Cardinals' coaching staff said Brown was too talented to keep off the field. Was sidelined by a right MCL tear in '12. Split carries with Senorise Perry in '13 — played all 13 games, starting the final seven, and logged 163-825-8 (5.1) rushing and 24-228-1 (9.5) receiving. Played all 13 games in '14, starting the first three before he took a back seat to Brandon Radcliffe and Michael Dyer — managed 96-378-4 (3.9) on the ground with 7-85-0 (12.1) through the air. Dealt with a nagging ankle injury the second half of the season. Has three career fumbles in 373 touches with 4.4-yard average per carry. Did not perform at the Combine because of a bruised sternum injury. Graduated with a degree in communication.

Strengths: Outstanding size, muscularity and upper-body strength. Runs hard with a bulldozer mentality, lowers his shoulder and almost always falls forward. Brandishes a powerful stiff arm. Reliable receiver who catches the ball cleanly outside his body. Serviceable pass protector with the anchor to stop the blitz. Good football intelligence.

Weaknesses: Runs narrow-based and upright with tight hips. Marginal agility and long speed. Is not elusive and often goes down on first contact. See-and-go reactor — does not anticipate cutback lanes. Limited route runner. Split time in a rotation and wore down at the end of the season. Durability could be an issue given straight-line, track style. Limited special teams experience.

Future: A hard-slamming, straight-ahead, downhill runner best suited to handle a rotational, inside-running role. Can add physicality to a power backfield, though his upright running style could invite injury in the pros.

Draft projection: Late draftable pick.

Scout's take: "(Brown) is not bad. He can't block, but he has good hands. He is a straight-line, one-cut guy who fits a zone scheme."

RB **MALCOLM BROWN**, #28 (Sr-4)

TEXAS ▶ GRADE: 5.24

Ht: 5-11⅜ | Wt: 224 | 40: 4.59 | Arm: 32¾ | Hand: 10¼

History: Highly recruited USA Today and Parade All-American who rushed for 6,663 yards (averaged nearly 10 yards per carry) and scored 86 rushing touchdowns as a Texas prep. As a senior, won a state title and was named 5A Offensive Player of the Year (AP, writers). Suffered season-ending ankle injury seven games into his sophomore season. Also lettered four times in track and field. As a true freshman in 2011, started 7-of-10 games played and was the first true freshman to lead the Longhorns in rushing since Cedric Benson in '01 — carried 172 times for 742 yards (4.3-yard average) and five touchdowns, while grabbing three receptions for 17 yards (5.7-yard average) and zero touchdowns. Did not play against Texas Tech or Missouri (turf toe), then hurt his right knee against Texas A&M and sat out against Baylor. Played eight games in '12 (one start), managing 61-324-4 (5.3) rushing and 15-112-1 (7.5) receiving. Missed five games after spraining his ankle against Oklahoma State. Took home the team's Tenacity Award for Offense in '13 when he played all 13 games, starting the final four in place of injured starter Johnathan Gray, and produced 214-904-9 (4.2) rushing and 17-195-2 (11.5) receiving. In '14, started all 13 games and totaled 183-708-6 (3.9) on the ground and 16-58-0 (3.6) through the air. Graduated with a degree in physical culture and sports (with a minor in social work).

Strengths: Very good size. Keeps his shoulders squared to the line and can step out of tackles. Patient to find cutback lanes. Willing, face-up blocker in pass pro. Can close out games and be effective in 4-minute offensive situations. Strong work habits.

Weaknesses: Limited creativity, elusiveness, agility and burst to make defenders miss. Gathers to cut. Not a big-play threat. Raw route runner. Shut down by BYU, Kansas and Oklahoma State and does not play big

RUNNING BACKS

or run with enough physicality. Split carries as a senior and has yet to prove he could be a featured back.

Future: Patient, downhill, north-south, crease runner with the eyes, anticipation and run strength desired in a zone running scheme.

Draft projection: Fifth- to sixth-round pick.

Scout's take: "He's a powerful inside runner. He was averaging more than four yards per carry until this year. His offensive line is awful. He always falls forward for positive yardage."

FB MIKE BURTON, #46 (Sr-5)
RUTGERS ▶ GRADE: 5.09

Ht: 5-11¼ | Wt: 242 | 40: 4.72 | Arm: 29¼ | Hand: 9½

History: Piled up 4,498 career all-purpose yards as a running back in New Jersey, where he won a state title. Redshirted in 2010. Converted to fullback in '11 when he played 12 games (three starts) and carried 10 times for 44 yards (4.4-yard average) and zero touchdowns. In '12, started the first four games and managed 2-9-0 (4.5) before suffering a season-ending broken ankle injury. Started 10-of-13 games in '13, running 9-61-0 (6.8). Started 10-of-13 games in '14 when his lone carry was a two-yard rush on a fake punt. Also credited with nine tackles. Had 47 career receptions for 401 yards (8.5-yard average) and three touchdowns. Was honored with team awards for performance, leadership and dedication on and off the field, as well as exemplary effort and intensity. Also nominated for the Burlsworth Trophy (top walk-on in college football). Team captain graduated with a communications degree.

Strengths: Good football playing temperament, energy and effort. Smart, versatile blocker — aligns in multiple positions (fullback, H-Back) with varied responsibilities in a pro-style offense. Soft hands. Urgent getting upfield after the catch. Valuable special teams contributor.

Weaknesses: Marginal athlete. Tight-hipped with limited agility and change of direction. Very limited production. Generates little movement on contact and struggles clearing out holes as an isolation-lead blocker. Arms (29 1/4 inches) measured the shortest of any player at the Combine.

Future: A crafty, positional blocker with a special teams temperament to earn a roster spot and contribute as a blocker in limited packages.

Draft projection: Priority free agent.

Scout's take: "He looks like Tarzan, plays like Jane. He doesn't have speed and he is not dynamic or explosive. He's your typical Jersey meathead. When I see that meathead Rob Lowe commercial where he is in the tanning bed, that's who he reminds me of. He's a build-up, finesse blocker. That's what he is. He's not knocking the snot out of anyone."

RB-KR BJ CATALON, #23 (Jr-3)
TCU ▶ GRADE: 5.00X

Ht: 5-7⅝ | Wt: 186 | 40: 4.54 | Arm: 30 | Hand: 9

History: Houston native chose TCU over offers from Baylor and Missouri, among others. As a true freshman in 2012, played all 13 games (one start) and carried 123 times for 582 yards (4.7-yard average) and zero touchdowns with 23 receptions for 152 yards (6.6) and one touchdown. Played 11 games in '13, starting four, and recorded 107-569-6 (5.3) rushing and 11-78-0 (7.1) receiving. Also returned 28 kickoffs for 743 yards (26.5) and a score. Was hurt against West Virginia and sat out against Iowa State. Started the first eight games in '14 — managed 98-493-10 (5.0) on the ground, 14-163-1 (11.6) through the air, and 8-254-1 (31.8) on kickoff returns before a concussion sidelined him for the rest of the year. Has eight career fumbles in 412 touches with a 5.0-yard average per carry. Did not lift at the Combine because of concussion suffered during the season.

Strengths: Shifty returner with enough long speed to go the distance. Can shimmy in the hole and wiggle through creases. Tied for the best 20-yard split (2.50 seconds) of all running backs at the Combine.

Weaknesses: Not built to run between the tackles. Limited power and tackle-breaking ability. Could stand to be more alert, willing in pass protection. Has never been a full-season starter and durability is a concern after a concussion-shortened season. Was the shortest player at the Combine.

Future: Quick, compactly built scatback with the most utility as a returner in the pros. Could offer a change of pace to a backfield.

Draft projection: Priority free agent.

Scout's take: "Geez, he is small. He might not get drafted. He got dinged and was not getting any playing time late in the year with the way they use those multiple backs."

RB DAVID COBB, #27 (Sr-4)
MINNESOTA ▶ GRADE: 5.39

Ht: 5-10⅝ | Wt: 229 | 40: 4.76* | Arm: 31⅝ | Hand: 9⅝

*Strained quad running 40 at Combine.

History: Prepped in Texas. Saw limited action his first two seasons — carried 10

RUNNING BACKS

times for 57 yards (5.7-yard average) and zero touchdowns in 2011 (four games), then carried 1-8-0 (8.0) with one catch for three yards (3.0) and zero touchdowns in '12 (five games). Sprained his right knee during '12 spring practice. Played all 13 games in '13, starting the last seven after Rodrick Williams was injured, and rushed 237-1,202-7 (5.1) with 17-174-0 (10.2) receiving. Was the Gophers' team MVP in '14 when he set school single-season records for rushes and rushing yards — toted 314-1,675-13 (5.2) and caught 16-162-0 (10.1). Strained his left hamstring against Nebraska. Has eight career fumbles in 596 touches with a 5.1-yard average per carry.

Strengths: Excellent size with a thick musculature and well-distributed mass. Can make NFL runs in tight quarters – squares his shoulders, goes downhill and finishes runs. Has a fluid stride and easy running style — shifts his weight seamlessly for a big back. Good vision to pick and slide. Can make subtle moves and shows a strong second surge and natural run instinct at the second level. Fine contact balance. Good durability. Caught the ball and blocked well at the Senior Bowl. Has a strong support system and has learned what it means to take more accountability. Emotional leader.

Weaknesses: Lacks suddenness and burst — only shows one gear. Not explosive on contact. Takes time to get rolling and is easily tracked behind the line of scrimmage. Is not a punishing runner and uses a lot of finesse for a big back. Average speed to the perimeter. Could improve awareness in pass protection and do a better job selling routes. Only a one-and-a-half-year starter. Was shut down vs. TCU.

Future: A finesse, smooth-striding big back who blossomed as a senior despite running behind a meager offensive line. Is at his best when he has some space to operate and has drawn comparisons from evaluators to Steelers 2013 second-round pick Leveon Bell and Bengals 2014 second-round pick Jeremy Hill. Is motivated by a major payday and could be incentivized to produce.

Draft projection: Third- to fourth-round pick.

Scout's take: "Cobb is just a banger — that's all he is. You can't take him too high. If you get him at the right price in the fourth round, you'll love him. He is a good football player. He's not a front-line guy though."

RB-KR TEVIN COLEMAN, #6 (Jr-3)

INDIANA   ▶ GRADE: 5.89

Ht: 5-11 ⅜ | Wt: 206 | 40: 4.45e | Arm: 32 | Hand: 8 ⅞

History: Nicknamed "Rock" for his strength. Parents were born in Liberia, where Tevin's great-great grandfather William David Coleman served as president from 1896-1900. Prepped in suburban Chicago, where he starred as a running back, receiver, cornerback, and kick returner. Also was a track standout. As a true freshman in '12, played all 12 games (two starts) and carried 51 times for 225 yards (4.4-yard average) and one touchdown. Added 10 receptions for 49 yards (4.9) and zero touchdowns, and returned 24 kickoffs for 566 yards (23.6) and a touchdown. Started the first nine games in '13, and recorded 131-958-12 (7.3) rushing, 19-193-0 (10.2) receiving, and 6-124 (20.7) on kickoff returns. Missed the final three games because of an ankle injury. Had a remarkable season in '14 — set IU's single-season rushing record and finished seventh in the Heisman voting by amassing 270-2,036-15 (7.5) on the ground and 25-141-0 (5.6) receiving (12 starts). Missed the second quarter of the Missouri contest because of dehydration. Had toe/foot surgery in December. Since the start of the '13 season (21 games), Coleman ranked second nationally in rushing yards per game (142.6). Team captain. Did not work out at the Combine because of a right turf toe injury.

Strengths: Very strong pound for pound. Has explosive big-play ability. Well built with enough run strength to slam it inside and outstanding acceleration to reach top-end speed in a blink and pull away from a pack. Is quick to and through the hole. Very good balance. Good second-level vision and anticipation. Makes subtle cuts at full speed without breaking stride and shows an exceptional traffic burst. Very good finishing speed. Good short-yardage/goalline surge. Adjusts well to the ball and catches it with ease. Willing blocker able to match up with defensive linemen.

Weaknesses: Average bulk. Tight-hipped and overly muscled, negating lateral agility. Rigid in his routes and has an upright running style that could leave more susceptible to collisions. Could stand to be more aggressive in pass protection and do a better job rolling his hips (tends to block straight-legged). Not patient or creative – runs with blinders on and will pick his spots. Much of his production came untouched. Gets gassed easily and needs to

RUNNING BACKS

Tevin Coleman

exit the game after long runs.

Future: A dynamic, big-play slasher with the speed, strength and explosion to spark an offense. Carried the offense in college and can add a flair to an NFL running game if he can stay healthy given his rigidity.

Draft projection: Top-50 pick.

Scout's take: "(Coleman) has big thighs. He has power and speed. He can go inside and go outside and take it the distance. Playing at Indiana University, he has flown under the radar most of his career, but I'll tell you this – he's one of the top backs in the country. Name one other back who had to carry the offense like he did. You have to look at the resources around them, and he didn't have much. ...He might go in the first (round). The value is in the second."

RB JOHN CROCKETT, #23 (Sr-5)

NORTH DAKOTA STATE ▶ GRADE: 4.85

Ht: 5-11 ¾ | Wt: 217 | 40: 4.57 | Arm: 31 | Hand: 9 ¾

History: Nicknamed "Taz." Won two state titles as a Minnesota prep. Was a finalist for the state's "Mr. Football" as a senior when he averaged 10 yards per carry and scored 34 touchdowns. Also earned seven letters in basketball and track (qualified for state meet in high jump). Spent 2010-11 getting eligible academically. Played all 15 games in 2012 (one start), carrying 194 times for 1,038 yards (5.4-yard average) and nine touchdowns and snagging seven receptions for 54 yards (7.7-yard average) and zero touchdowns. In '13, rushed 190-1,277-11 (6.7) and caught 6-34-0 (5.7) in 15 games. Started all 16 games in '14 — set single-season school records for all-purpose yards (2,419), rushing yards, and rushing attempts by totaling 368-1,994-21 (5.4) on the ground with 30-397-1 (13.2) through the air. Also tossed a 16-yard touchdown pass. Returned 16 career kickoffs for 357 yards (22.3). Won FCS national championship every year at NDSU.

Strengths: Good vision. Presses the line and finds creases. Runs hard and is extremely competitive with the ball in his hand. Can spin out of some tackles and shows good lateral agility. Good effort, energy and desire and lives up to his Tasmanian Devil nickname fighting for yardage. Seeks to finish. Has a 40-inch vertical jump.

Weaknesses: Has a slight build with very limited strength and power to run inside. Runs too upright and gets turned on contact. Spins in place and is not a strong tackle-breaker. Production is inflated from facing modest competition in the Missouri Valley Football Conference and being surrounded by a strong supporting cast. Limited receiving production. Lacks awareness in pass pro. Only a one-year starter. Could do a better job securing the ball.

Future: Productive back emerged as a senior to carry the Bison to their fourth consecutive FCS championship. However, overall skill set is too ordinary for the NFL game, and his greatest trait is his competitiveness, which might be able to carry him to an opportunity.

Draft projection: Priority free agent.

RB **MIKE DAVIS**, #28 (Jr-3)
SOUTH CAROLINA ► GRADE: 5.37
Ht: 5-9 ⅛ | Wt: 217 | 40: 4.58 | Arm: 30 ¼ | Hand: 9 ⅜

History: Brother, James, starred as a running back at Clemson before he was drafted by the Browns (sixth round, 2009). Grew up in crime-infested area of Atlanta, and prepped at Stephenson High, which produced 12 Division I recruits the year he graduated. As a true freshman in 2012, carried 52 times for 275 yards (5.3-yard average) and two touchdowns with four catches for 35 yards (8.8) and zero touchdowns. Did not play against LSU. Started 11-of-12 games played in '13, rushing 203-1,183-11 (5.8) and catching 34-352-0 (10.4). Non-start was against Central Florida when he gave way to a five-receiver formation. Sat out against Coastal Carolina (ankle). Also dealt with shoulder and rib soreness at various times during the season. Missed the first three days of '14 fall camp (hamstring), and was dogged by nagging injuries during the season Started 10-of-13 games — produced 199-982-9 (4.9) on the ground and 32-368-2 (11.5) through the air. Did not start the first two games (bruised ribs), then hurt his right shoulder against Florida and did not start against South Alabama. Has seven career fumbles in 524 touches with a 5.4-yard average per carry.

Strengths: Runs hard with good leg drive and can plow for tough yardage inside. Has quick feet to make the first tackler miss. Good patience and vision to follow his blocks. Very good upper body strength to stiff-arm tacklers.

Weaknesses: Has a heaviness in his body that translates to ordinary burst and acceleration and allows him to be tracked down to the sideline. Measured 19.3 percent body fat at the Combine, higher than any other runner at the event, and has room to trim down and improve conditioning. Runs tilted instead of square,

which has led to a lot of injuries and could create continued durability concerns. Struggles to take the corner. Limited route runner.

Future: Stocky, compact, bowling ball runner who looked more sleek and agile in 2013 than he did in 2014, when he was nagged by injuries and appeared overweight.

Draft projection: Third- to fourth-round pick.

Scout's take: "(Davis) runs hard inside, but he doesn't have a lot of power. For a shorter back, he runs tall and gets shocked. I don't see a lot of acceleration or juice. He's solid, not special. I have him in the fourth (round). I know he is going to go higher."

RB **MICHAEL DYER**, #5 (Sr-4)
LOUISVILLE ► GRADE: 4.92
Ht: 5-8 ½ | Wt: 218 | 40: 4.57 | Arm: 30 ⅝ | Hand: 9 ½

History: Father was killed in a car accident when Michael was five. Highly recruited Parade All-American who was Arkansas' 2009 Gatorade Player of the Year. Finished his high school career with 8,097 yards and 84 touchdowns. Began his college career at Auburn, where he broke Bo Jackson's freshman rushing record — started 8-of-14 games for the national champions, carrying 182 times for 1,093 yards (6.0-yard average) and five touchdowns. Was MVP of the BCS Championship. Started 6-of-12 games played in '11, rushing 242-1,242-10 (5.1). Was suspended for the Tigers' bowl game against Virginia, and left the program soon after. Reportedly failed drug tests, had his grades altered to maintain eligibility, and was late to meetings while at Auburn. In '12, transferred to Arkansas State to play for Gus Malzahn, who was Dyer's offensive coordinator at Auburn, but was dismissed in late July after testifying that a gun he owned was used in a robbery carried out by some of his Auburn teammates (Dyer refused to participate). Also admitted to synthetic marijuana use. Earned his associate's degree from Arkansas Baptist before transferring to Louisville, where Dyer agreed to a behavior contract and zero-tolerance policy. In '13, played the first seven games (one) and managed 44-223-2 (5.1) before a sports hernia sidelined him and required surgery in December. Started 4-of-9 games played in '14, totaling 110-481-5 (4.4), though he missed the first three games with a quad contusion, and was academically ineligible for the Belk Bowl against Georgia. For his career, caught eight passes for 64 yards (8.0) and zero touchdowns. Will turn 25 during his rookie season. Strained his right hamstring during drills at the Combine and did not perform shuttles. Has seven career fumbles in 159 touches with a 4.6-yard average per carry.

Strengths: Strong between the tackles. Nice spin move. Slithers through traffic. Good upper-body strength. Steps hard downhill and sidesteps tacklers.

Weaknesses: Short-stepper with tight hips. Not elusive and makes few tacklers miss. Gets tracked to the perimeter. Lacks burst and acceleration – only shows one gear. Seldom used as a receiver. Overaged – will be a 25-year-old rookie. Character and durability must be taken into consideration.

Future: Short, stocky fireplug with enough strength and vision to work between the tackles. Could provide depth as a complimentary power back in the same mold as Rams RB Zac Stacy.

Draft projection: Priority free agent.

RB JAHWAN EDWARDS, #32 (Sr-4)

BALL STATE ▶ GRADE: 5.07

Ht: 5-9 ½ | Wt: 220 | 40: 4.73 | Arm: 31 ⅝ | Hand: 8 ⅞

History: Prepped at nationally ranked Butler High in North Carolina, where he won two state championships (MVP of both games). Was 235 pounds when he was recruited to BSU. As a true freshman in 2011, played all 12 games, starting the final seven, and carried 178 times for 786 yards (4.4-yard average) and 11 touchdowns with 11 receptions for 43 yards (3.9-yard average) and zero touchdowns. Started 12-of-13 games in '12, producing 232-1,410-14 (6.1) rushing and 10-51-0 (5.1) receiving. Sprained his ankle against Western Michigan and did practice leading up to the Central Michigan, yielding the start to Barrington Scott. In '13, rushed 212-1,110-14 (5.2) and caught 7-31-0 (4.4) in 11 starts. Did not play against Army and North Texas (concussion). Was voted team MVP in '14 — started all 12 games and totaled 262-1,252-12 (4.8) on the ground with 29-236-0 (8.1) through the air. Returned 16 career kickoffs for 258 yards (16.1) and zero scores. Team captain owns BSU records for rushing yards (4,558), touchdowns (51), points (306), and rushing attempts (884). Has seven career fumbles in 957 touches with a 5.2-yard average per carry.

Strengths: Good leg churn and balance through traffic. Does not stop his feet on contact and powers through tacklers. Very strong lower body. Runs decisively. Attacks the line and can create a surge in goalline / short-yardage situations – has 51 career TDs. Good spin move. Functional outlet valve. Three-and-a-half-year starter who made an immediate impact upon his arrival.

Weaknesses: Tight hips. Stiff route runner. Recorded the slowest 20-yard split (2.94 seconds) of all running backs at the Combine. Needs to learn to bring his feet with him in pass protection and not overextend. Was not challenged vs. lesser MAC competition.

Future: Thickly built, compact grinder who will take everything a defense gives him and create his own holes. A tough, productive college bellcow with enough competitive fire, inside run skill, power and leg drive to fend for a role in the pros.

Draft projection: Priority free agent.

FB JALSTON FOWLER, #45 (Sr-4)

ALABAMA ▶ GRADE: 5.24

Ht: 5-11 | Wt: 254 | 40: 4.87 | Arm: 32 ¾ | Hand: 10 ½

History: Has a son, Jalston Jr. All-state running back-linebacker as a prep in Alabama, where he won a state title. As a true freshman backup in 2011, appeared in all 13 games and carried 56 times for 385 yards (6.9-yard average) and four touchdowns. Was working at running back, fullback and h-back/tight end in '12 — rushed 11-85-0 (7.7) and caught one pass for six yards (6.0) and zero touchdowns before a torn left ACL ended his season. Returned to play all 13 games in '13, rushing 20-88-0 (4.4) and catching 7-15-5 (2.1). Played all 14 games in '14, starting five, and recorded 12-69-0 (5.8) on the ground with 11-129-2 (11.7) receiving. Team captain has a master's degree in sports management. Was the heaviest (254) running back weighed at the Combine.

Strengths: Very thickly built. Powerful isolation-lead blocker. Can locate defenders and latch on. Catches the ball very well out of the backfield. Squares his shoulders to the line, runs hard through contact and almost always falls forward. Has soft hands. Football smart and understands protections. Exceptional football character. Terrific weight-room work habits. Unselfish, committed team player willing to do the dirty work.

Weaknesses: Limited career production. Average elusiveness and body control. Lacks foot speed to avoid direct contact. Limited run skills after the catch.

Future: A tough, physical hammer with the special teams makeup to become a core special teams player. Saw limited duty in a talented backfield, yet possesses the tools to earn a starting job in the pros for a traditional, run-first offense that still values the position.

Draft projection: Fourth- to fifth-round pick.

Scout's take: "I don't put a lot of value on

RUNNING BACKS

fullbacks. For me, Fowler will be in the fifth round. I just can't put a fullback any higher. If one fits and you're looking for one, he has enough talent to go in (the fourth round). Fowler has a chance to be a starter, but because he won't be a full-time player on the field and has limitations, I don't like taking one in the fourth. He has to be special."

RB MELVIN GORDON, #25 (Jr-4)

WISCONSIN ▶ GRADE: 6.27
Ht: 6-0 ⅝ | Wt: 215 | 40: 4.46 | Arm: 32 ⅜ | Hand: 9 ¾

History: Kenosha native who was Wisconsin's Gatorade Player of the Year and Offensive Player of the Year. As a true freshman in 2011 (wore jersey No. 3), carried 20 times for 98 yards (4.9-yard average) and a touchdown in three games before having season-ending hernia surgery. In '12, backed up Doak Walker winner and Broncos '13 second-rounder Montee Ball — rushed 62-621-3 (10.0) and caught two balls for 65 yards (32.5) and a touchdown in 14 games (four starts). Backed up Patriots '14 fourth-rounder James White in '13, when Gordon toted 206-1,609-12 (7.8), setting a UW sophomore rushing record. In '14, won the Doak Walker Award, was the Heisman runner-up, and was named Big Ten Offensive Player of the Year — piled up 343-2,587-29 (7.5) rushing and 19-153-3 (8.1) receiving in 14 starts, including an epic 25-408-4 performance (in three quarters) against Nebraska, which broke the FBS single-game record (later broken by Oklahoma's Samaje Perine). Also took home Outback Bowl MVP honors after rushing for a record 34-251-3 (7.4) in an overtime win over Auburn. Sat out second half of LSU game (hip), and twisted his right ankle against Minnesota. Gordon's single-season rushing total established a conference record and is second-most all-time behind Barry Sanders' 2,628-yard 1988 season. Gordon's 32 touchdowns tied for the NCAA lead in 2014. Exceptional work ethic. Has 12 career fumbles in 661 touches with a 7.8-yard average per carry.

Strengths: Good size with long arms and big hands and a very sculpted, strong upper body. Extremely productive despite regularly facing stacked boxes. Terrific competitor. Exceptional perimeter speed – field fast and plays faster than timed speed. Decisive runner – outstanding short-area burst to and through the hole. Churns his legs through contact as an inside runner and will fight for yardage. Has superb feet with an uncanny knack for slipping and avoiding contact (his most defining trait).

Exceptional balance and body control – knows how to set up tacklers and makes dynamic speed cuts. Quick to see cutback lanes and explode through lanes. Very good open-field elusiveness – spins out of tackles. Quick, explosive stiff-arm. Ran thru and around a stingy Nebraska defense. Has operated out of the slot and has kickoff-return experience.

Weaknesses: Not a true, home-run hitter – lacks elite top-end speed and can be tracked from behind. Minimal receiving production in a run-first offense. Did not become a full-time starter until junior season. Ran behind a very well-coached, efficient offensive line that often left him untouched through the second and even third level. Will miss some open backside lanes pressing the line, tending to bounce outside. Average upper-body strength. Could show more awareness in pass protection and lacks ideal core strength to anchor in pass pro against big bodies. Not a powerful inside runner to push the pile and cannot be his own blocker – gets smothered inside. Needs to do a better job protecting the football.

Future: Beefed up his body and ran with more determination and leg churn inside in 2014 in his first year as a truly featured back, proving he could shoulder a full workload. However, like Reggie Bush and Barry Sanders, to maximize Gordon's skill set, he will be best deployed to operate in space, where he could spin out of tackles, sidestep and create. Is not as dynamic or explosive as Jamaal Charles, but has a very similar slashing style and like Charles exiting Texas, still needs to learn to protect the football better. Has the run skills and creativity to emerge as a game-changing back in the pros, but is not a complete bell cow.

Draft projection: First-round pick.
Scout's take: "He's not an inside runner. Someone is going to take him in mid to late 1, maybe sooner, but he is not a real dynamic inside runner. You got to be able to lower your pads. He will make a living running off-tackle or bouncing outside …I thought he was really good. I just didn't think he was great."

RB-KR TODD GURLEY, #3 (Jr-3)

GEORGIA ▶ GRADE: 6.60
Ht: 6-0 ⅝ | Wt: 222 | 40: 4.45e | Arm: 31 ½ | Hand: 10

History: Won three North Carolina state titles at Tarboro High. Was the state's AP Player of the Year as a senior when he rushed for 2,600 yards and 38 touchdowns, including 242 yards and four scores in the championship game. Also ran track. As a true freshman in 2012, started 12-of-14 games and carried 222

Todd Gurley

JOHN KELLEY / UGA ATHLETIC ASSOCIATION

yards for 1,385 yards (6.2-yard average) and 17 touchdowns. Added 16 receptions for 117 yards (7.3) and zero scores, and returned seven kickoffs for 243 yards (34.7) and a score. Did not start the season opener or bowl game. Started all 10 games played in '13, producing 165-989-10 (6.0) and 37-441-5 (11.9) receiving. Missed three games after spraining his left ankle against LSU. Played six games in '14, starting five, and managed 123-911-9 (7.4) on the ground, 12-57-0 (4.8) through the air, and 4-179-1 (44.8) on kickoffs. Also tossed a 50-yard completion. Served a four-game, mid-season suspension for accepting more than $3,000 for autographed memorabilia and other items over a two-year period. Returned against Auburn (non-start), but suffered a torn ACL. Will be a 21-year-old rookie. Has three career fumbles in 586 touches with a 6.4-yard average per carry.

Strengths: Big, strong, physical and explosive – can run around tacklers almost as seamlessly as he can run through them and continually produces NFL-caliber runs. Runs behind his pads and gains speed whipping around corners with terrific bend for a big back. Very confident and competitive. Exceptional body control, contact balance, leg drive and functional, football-playing body power – does not go down easy. Can slice through the line and take the corner with surprising acceleration and burst. Runs through arm tackles and almost always falls forward. Wears down defenses and gets better with a lather. Regularly converts losses into big gains and bounces off tacklers, brandishing a violent stiff arm. Possesses home-run, finishing speed and has explosive, big-play ability as a kickoff returner. Catches the ball cleanly and is dangerous on screens, with very good lateral agility to make sharp cuts in the open field. Alert in pass protection. Very good ball security. Quick healer who is ahead of schedule in his rehabilitation.

Weaknesses: Short-term durability will require closer evaluation – may not be at full health for his rookie season. Will need to become more nuanced in pass protection, improving hand placement and positioning.

Future: A special talent with the sheer size, run strength, body power, vision, balance and tackle-breaking ability to dominate. A true workhorse back capable of carrying an offense. Has perennial all-Pro potential if he can return to full form, and could be drafted lower than he is graded because of uncertainty surrounding knee injury.

Draft projection: First-round pick.

Scout's take: "He reminds me a little bit of Steven Jackson. (Gurley) might fall because of the ACL, the same way Willis McGahee did, but if you are picking in the bottom of the first, you'd never expect to get an opportunity to draft a player as talented as he is. (The knee injury) didn't affect Jamal Lewis coming out of (Tennessee). He still went fifth (overall). To me, Gurley is one of the top five players in this draft talent-wise. He's my third-highest graded player."

RB DEE HART, #10 (Sr-4)

COLORADO STATE ▶ GRADE: 5.03

Ht: 5-7 ½ | Wt: 199 | 40: 4.78 | Arm: 29 ¾ | Hand: 9

History: Highly recruited out of Dr. Phillips in Orlando — rushed for 2,224 yards and 41 touchdowns as a senior, earning 6A Florida Player of the Year. Was MVP of U.S. Army All-American Bowl. Originally committed to Michigan, but re-opened his recruiting after Rich Rodriguez was fired. Began his college career at Alabama — redshirted in 2011 after tearing his ACL during a summer 7-on-7. Appeared in five games in '12 (wore jersey No. 1) before suffering another ACL injury — carried 21 times for 88 yards (4.2-yard average) and zero touchdowns, while returning four punts for 50 yards (12.5). Also forced a fumble on special teams. Played 12 games in '13 and recorded 22-78-1 (3.5) rushing with 4-58 (14.) on punt returns. Was dismissed from Alabama in February '14 after he was arrested and charged with possession of marijuana and giving a false name to law enforcement — Hart reportedly gave a gas station cashier counterfeit money, and a subsequent search of his vehicle found eight grams of marijuana. Transferred to Colorado State to play for Jim McElwain, who was Alabama's offensive coordinator when Hart signed with the Crimson Tide. By virtue of earning his degree — in three years — in criminal justice from Alabama, Hart was eligible to play in '14, when he started 10-of-13 games for the Rams, totaling 194-1,275-16 (6.6) with 18-189-2 (10.5). Fumbled five times in 2014. Did not lift at the Combine because of a left hand sprain.

Strengths: Has natural run skill and vision to sort through congestion and find open running lanes. Extra-effort type who gets what is blocked and fights for a little extra. Runs hard and carries a swagger. Is tough and extremely competitive.

Weaknesses: Has a small frame with small hands and a thin bone structure, especially in the lower body. Has had multiple knee injuries, and long-term durability is a concern given hard running style. Struggles to generate power through his hips. Marginal long speed. Struggled to earn carries at Alabama competing with better competition. Character requires close scrutiny. Needs to do a better job securing the ball.

Future: Quicker than fast, hard-nosed runner lacking the frame to support his running style. Is too short and too slow on paper, but he is also too instinctive and productive as a senior to overlook when you factor his heart into the equation.

Draft projection: Priority free agent.

RB BRAYLON HEARD, #5 (Jr-4)

KENTUCKY ▶ GRADE: 4.95

Ht: 5-9 ⅝ | Wt: 198 | 40: 4.54 | Arm: 30 ¼ | Hand: 9

History: Prepped at Cardinal Mooney in Ohio, where he won state championships in football and the 4X100 meter relay. Began his career at Nebraska — as a true freshman in 2011, rushed 25 times for 114 yards (4.6-yard average) and a touchdown in seven games. Played 12 games in '12, carrying 52-348-3 (6.7) with three receptions for 18 yards (6.0-yard average) and zero touchdowns. Did not play against Michigan or Michigan State (groin). Transferred to Kentucky, and sat out the '13 season per NCAA rules. In '14, started 10-of-11 games played and totaled 73-379-4 (5.0) rushing with 21-108-0 (5.1) receiving. Also returned two kickoffs for 33 yards (16.5). Sat out against Ohio after spraining his right ankle in the season opener versus Tennessee-Martin. Yielded the start against Missouri to freshman Stanley "Boom" Williams. Fumbled once in 2014. Did not run the 60-yard shuttle because of a right hamstring strain.

Strengths: Good balance. Clocked a 1.56-second, 10-yard split and is quicker than fast. Dependable hands. Willing blocker. Caught the ball very naturally at the Combine and displayed clean footwork going through bag drills.

Weaknesses: Marginal career production. Runs too upright and lacks run strength and power – is easily turned on contact. Does not keep his shoulders squared to the line and has a soft running style. Average athletic ability and finishing speed. Has a 30 1/2-inch vertical jump. Is not a creative playmaker. Lacks substance in pass pro.

Future: A third-down back with no distinguishing quality to separate himself from the pack. Best trait are his hands. Could fend for a spot in camp.

Draft projection: Priority free agent.

RB-FB KENNY HILLIARD, #27 (Sr-4)

LSU ► GRADE: 4.82

Ht: 5-11⅝ | Wt: 226 | 40: 4.82 | Arm: 31¼ | Hand: 9¼

History: Father of twin daughters with high school sweeheart. Uncle, Dalton, starred as a running back at LSU before playing for the Saints (1986-93), and cousin, Ike, played for the Giants and Buccaneers (1997-2008). As a Louisiana prep, Kenny set the state's career record with 8,603 rushing yards. As a true freshman in 2011, appeared in 13 games and carried 62 times for 336 yards (5.4-yard average) and eight touchdowns. In '12, played 12 games (one start) and totaled 82-464-6 (5.7). In '13, played 13 games and logged 68-310-7 (4.6). Started 6-of-11 games played in '14, recording 90-447-6 (5.0). Missed two games after hurting his left shoulder against Alabama. For his career, caught 11 passes for 69 yards (6.3-yard average) and a score. Did not lift at the Combine because of a left shoulder injury. Graduated.

Strengths: Good size and lower-body strength. The game is important to him. Outstanding personal and football character. Fairly versatile and has also seen some time at fullback. Has NFL pedigree.

Weaknesses: Marginal athletic ability and foot speed. Produced the lowest vertical jump (27 inches) of all running backs at the Combine. Gathers to cut. Tentative blocker and seldom is asked to pass protect. Runs with blinders on. Not creative. Loud hands. Was never a full-time starter and has minimal special teams experience. Limited career production.

Future: A nondescript, try-hard, grunter with enough size to warrant an opportunity in a camp as an inside runner. Did not distinguish himself in a very talented backfield and lacks the physical tools to distinguish himself in the pros.

Draft projection: Priority free agent.

FB-RB JOEY IOSEFA, #27 (Sr-5)

HAWAII ► GRADE: 4.97

Ht: 5-11¾ | Wt: 247 | 40: 5.01 | Arm: 31¾ | Hand: 10¼

History: Given name is Marvin. Born in American Samoa, where he played quarterback, linebacker, and safety and won two championships. Also played rugby, soccer and volleyball as a prep. Grayshirted in 2009 after arriving as a 190-pound quarterback, then redshirted in '10. Was the team's leading rusher in '11 when he played all 13 games (wore jersey No. 30), starting 11, and carried 110 times for 548 yards (5.0-yard average) and seven touchdowns with 20 receptions for 122 yards (6.1-yard average) and a touchdown. Started 7-of-8 games played in '12, recording 125-463-1 (3.7) rushing and 19-153-1 (8.1) receiving. Missed four games because of a stress fracture in his right foot. Broke his left foot in July '13, missed the first two games of the season, returned against Nevada and aggravated the injury, which required surgery. On the season, started all five games played and managed 126-590-5 (4.7) on the ground with 10-87-1 (8.7) through the air. In '14, logged 151-617-8 (4.1) rushing with 11-76-0 (6.9) receiving in six starts. Broke his right ankle against Oregon State, then was arrested for DUI — missed seven games (three while suspended) and was stripped of his co-captaincy. Completed 4-of-7 career pass attempts (57.1 percent) for 71 yards with two touchdowns and zero interceptions. Two-time team captain.

Strengths: Very thickly built with natural strength and tree-trunk legs. Has a powerful stride with good inside, plowing strength. Runs hard downhill. Produced the most bench-press reps (30) of any running back at the Combine. Surprisingly agile and light on his feet for a big back. Set the school record in the hang clean (366 pounds).

Weaknesses: Ran the slowest 40-yard dash (5.04 seconds) of any running back at the Combine. Poor long speed. Has been slowed by a chronic foot injury that requires medical scrutiny. Not elusive. Lacks foot speed to reach the corner. Was not asked to block a lot and is not nuanced in pass pro.

Future: A battering ram who outgrew the tailback position and could have a chance to make it as a fullback conversion or power back in the pros. Could find a niche as a short-yardage / goalline runner if he proves valuable on special teams.

Draft projection: Priority free agent.

RB-KR DAVID JOHNSON, #7 (Sr-5)

NORTHERN IOWA ► GRADE: 5.39

Ht: 6-0⅝ | Wt: 224 | 40: 4.46 | Arm: 31¼ | Hand: 9⅝

History: Triplet along with two sisters. Iowa all-stater who scored 42 touchdowns as a senior. Also ran track and played basketball. Chose UNI over Illinois State, who wanted

RUNNING BACKS

him as a linebacker, and a grayshirt offer from Iowa. Redshirted in 2010. Played all 13 games in '11, starting five, and carried 179 times 822 yards (4.6-yard average) and nine touchdowns. Added 33 receptions for 422 yards (12.8) and three touchdowns. Started 7-of-11 games in '12 (shared starts with Carlos Anderson), rushing 178-1,021-13 (5.7) and catching 32-383-5 (12.0). Started 10-of-11 games played in '13, totaling 222-1,291-10 (5.8) on the ground with 38-393-4 (10.3) through the air. Sprained his left ankle against ISU, did not play against Youngstown State, and did not start against Missouri State. In '14, amassed 287-1,553-17 (5.4) rushing and 38-536-2 (14.1) receiving in 14 games (12 starts). Two non-starts came when he needed a breather after returning the opening kickoff. Also returned 12 kickoffs for 438 yards and a score (36.5). Led the Panthers in all-purpose yards in three of his four years. Also had two career completions to his credit, including a 36-yard touchdown. Three-year captain who owns 15 UNI records, and is poised to become the first UNI running back drafted since 1966. Has 13 career fumbles in 1,019 touches with a 5.4 average per carry.

Strengths: Outstanding size-speed combination. Tied for the fastest 40-yard dash (4.40 seconds) of all running backs at the Combine – and it translates to the field with breakaway speed. Very solid showing at the Senior Bowl, including scoring a 19-yard TD where he weaved through a number of tacklers. Snags the ball with ease and catches outside his frame. Good ball skills. Showed very well against better competition (see Iowa). Self-driven, competitive team leader. Has a 41 1/2-inch vertical jump.

Weaknesses: Shows some tightness in his hips and tends to run tall with long strides, negating his power. Runs small – is not a strong finisher and does not break a lot of tackles. Average elusiveness and agility – does not string moves together or make many tacklers miss. Could play with more urgency. Average anchor in pass protection. Lets the ball into his body as a receiver and does not run crisp routes. Did not regularly face top competition. Could do a better job of securing the football – tends to flag it in the open field, creating too many career fumbles (13).

Future: A finesse, one-cut, downhill slasher in the mold of Chicago Bears 2008 second-round pick Matt Forte, Johnson combines natural receiving skills with explosive big-play ability and could readily contribute as a zone runner if he improves in pass protection.

Draft projection: Third- to fourth-round pick.

Scout's take: "He has big lanes to run through due to the wide splits their line uses. He has adequate feet. He does not play to his size. I left the school expecting to see more from him."

RB DUKE JOHNSON, #8 (Jr-3)

MIAMI (FLA.) ▶ GRADE: 5.57

Ht: 5-9 ⅞ | Wt: 207 | 40: 4.53 | Arm: 30 ⅜ | Hand: 9 ¼

History: Highly recruited out of Miami Norland, where he won a state championship. As a true freshman in 2012, was voted ACC Rookie of the Year (coaches and media) after piling up 2,060 all-purpose yards — played all 12 games, starting five, and carried 139 times for 947 yards (6.8-yard average) and 10 touchdowns with 27 receptions for 221 yards (8.2-yard average) and a touchdown. Also set a UM single-season kickoff return yardage record by returning 27 for 892 yards (33.0-yard average) and two scores. Started 7-of-8 games played in '13 before suffering a season-ending broken right ankle injury against Florida State — finished totaling 145-920-6 (6.3) rushing, 4-77-0 (19.2) receiving, and 14-396-0 (28.3) on kickoff returns. Lone non-start was against Savannah State when he needed a breather after returning the opening kickoff 95 yards. Left the North Carolina game after being diagnosed with a concussion. Started all 13 games in '14 and produced 242-1,652-10 (6.8) rushing and 38-421-3 (11.1) receiving. Broke or tied 11 school records, including the Hurricanes' all-time rushing lead (3,519 yards). Suffered an ankle injury in the final five minutes of the Independence Bowl, on the same play that he fumbled and gave South Carolina the ball that set up a 24-21 win. Opted not to lift at the Combine and did not run shuttles because of a strained right hamstring. Has seven career fumbles in 637 touches with a 6.7-yard rushing average. Wore a single pink bandage below his left eye at the Combine to honor the mother of one of his friends who twice has survived breast cancer.

Strengths: Outstanding eyes, anticipation and run patience to set up and follow his blocks. Makes subtle, shifty moves to avoid the first wave and spring free. Very decisive zone runner – sticks his foot in the dirt and goes. Outstanding short-area burst, as confirmed at the Combined where he tied for the best 10-yard split (1.50 seconds) of all running backs. Is not easy to hit squarely and does not go down easy. Can pull a rabbit out of his hat, reverse field and turn a four-yard loss into an

RUNNING BACKS

eight-yard gain. Has shown he can carry a full workload despite his lack of overall bulk and mass and has battled through injuries. Savvy route runner effective on screens and wheel routes. Catches the ball without breaking stride and runs with great urgency and vision after the catch. Willing, unselfish blocker who will sacrifice his body. Extremely competitive and determined.

Weaknesses: Average size. Can be overwhelmed in pass protection. Tends to cut block and has taken some knees to the helmet (see 2013 Florida Atlantic) that led to concussion testing. Lacks top-end finishing speed and finishing strength to push the pile inside.

Future: A smooth, patient, stretch-zone runner with the short-area burst, natural run instincts and anticipation to pick up yardage in chunks. Plays bigger than his size and has the desire and heart of an NFL rushing champion, if he could stay healthy. Could be very productive in a zone-based, running scheme.

Draft projection: Second- to third-round pick.

Scout's take: "Duke is a really good runner. He has the ability to do anything – run inside or outside, he catches everything and can return. I thought he did a decent job blocking the couple times you see him as a lead blocker. I think he can be a three-down back."

RB GUS JOHNSON, #6 (Sr-4)

STEPHEN F. AUSTIN ▶ GRADE: 5.09

Ht: 5-9 ⅞ | Wt: 215 | 40: 4.66 | Arm: 29 ⅝ | Hand: 9 ⅛

History: Texas native. As a true freshman in 2011, played 10 games and carried 45 times for 194 yards (4.3-yard average) and three touchdowns, while snagging five catches for 60 yards (12.0-yard average) and zero touchdowns. Did not play against Sam Houston State. Started 8-of-10 games played in '12, rushing 154-969-14 (6.3) and catching 14-86-1 (6.1). Did not play against Lamar (hip pointer). In '13 started 9-of-11 games played and ran for 176-1,061-11 (6.0) with 21-108-0 (5.1) receiving. Did not play against Central Arkansas (right ankle). Was the Southland Conference Player of the Year in '14 when he set the SFA and SLC single-season rushing record — amassed 256-1,683-23 (6.6) on the ground and 17-165-0 (9.7) through the air. Tops SFA's career rushing (3,907 yards) and touchdowns (52) lists. *Strengths:* Thickly built and layered with muscle. Outstanding weight-room strength and work ethic. Can squat a small house and has a very sturdy

lower body to carry tacklers draped on his back and pick up additional yardage. Good contact balance – bounces off tacklers and produces a lot of yardage after contact. Slams the ball hard inside and drives through contact. Picks up yardage in chunks. Tied for the best 10-yard split (1.50 seconds) of all running backs at the Combine. Outstanding small-school production. Functional outlet receiver. Competitive runner. Loves the game.

Weaknesses: Not explosive with average burst and top-end speed. Is tight in the hips, straight-linish and only shows one gear. Could do a better job pressing the line of scrimmage and anticipating. Average elusiveness. Is late to reach the corner. Tends to carry the ball loosely away from his body. Regularly faced Southland competition. Underdeveloped blocker.

Future: A strong, tough inside runner with enough power and desire to fend for a job in a camp. Will require time to acclimate to better competition and pass protection in the pros.

Draft projection: Priority free agent.

RB MATT JONES, #24 (Jr-3)

FLORIDA ▶ GRADE: 5.22

Ht: 6-2 ⅜ | Wt: 231 | 40: 4.57 | Arm: 32 | Hand: 8 ⅝

History: Native Floridian who won a state championship at Armwood, which finished ranked in the top five nationally. In the summer of 2011, tore his left MCL and missed four games of his senior season. As a true freshman in '12, played 12 games (one start) and carried 52 times for 275 yards (5.3-yard average) and three touchdowns, while catching three balls for 10 yards (3.3-yard average) and zero touchdowns. Did not play against Georgia. Missed part of '13 fall camp while recovering from a viral infection. On the season, started 4-of-5 games played before tearing his left meniscus against LSU (required two surgeries) — managed 79-339-2 (4.3) rushing and 5-25-0 (5.0) receiving. Started 10-of-11 games played in '14, totaling 166-817-6 (4.9) on the ground and 11-65-1 (5.9) through the air. Sprained his ankle against Tennessee, dealt with left knee swelling, and did not start against LSU. Sat out the Gators' bowl game against East Carolina (shoulder). Did not complete shuttles at the Combine after straining his right hamstring. Has five career fumbles in 316 touches with a 4.8-yard average per carry. Did not play in the bowl game after the interim head coach suggested he avoid getting hurt following Jones' announcement that he would be turning pro.

Strengths: Outstanding size. Functional

RUNNING BACKS

inside run strength to pick up tough yardage in confined quarters. Runs with good body lean and usually falls forward. Lowers his shoulder and can step out of some arm tackles in space. Efficient cut blocker.

Weaknesses: Has very small hands. Has a 31 1/2-inch vertical jump. Adequate vision, foot speed and make-you-miss in the hole. Lacks lower-body power to bore through contact. Struggles to clear his feet through traffic and is easily tripped. Impatient – runs up the back of blockers and does not allow lanes to develop or show wide-eyed, peripheral vision to make the cutback. Questionable competitiveness. Durability could be an issue given direct hits he repeatedly sustains to his lower body.

Future: A big-bodied, between-the-tackles runner capable of providing some depth in the pros. Does not have the vision, power or agility desired on the front lines and ability to factor on special teams could determine his value.

Draft projection: A fifth- to sixth-round pick.

Scout's take: "He is a little heavy-footed. He runs hard. Someone could draft him late as a good backup. I thought his value was late in the fifth round. He's not a real hammer."

RB JEREMY LANGFORD, #33 (Sr-5)

MICHIGAN STATE ▶ GRADE: 5.42

Ht: 5-11 ⅞ | Wt: 208 | 40: 4.41 | Arm: 31 ½ | Hand: 8 ¾

History: Running back-safety who earned All-Michigan recognition as a senior when he rushed for 1,932 yards and 24 touchdowns. Redshirted in 2010. Was switched to cornerback during '11 fall camp before playing all 14 games, primarily on special teams, and tallying five tackles, zero pass breakups, and zero interceptions with a sack. Spent '12 spring practice at receiver before switching back to running back in the fall — played in nine games and recorded nine rushes for 23 yards (2.6-yard average) and zero touchdowns. Added six tackles and a forced fumble on special teams. In '13, inherited the tailback position from Steelers '13 second-rounder Le'Veon Bell — started all 13 games and toted 292-1,422-18 (4.9) with 28-157-1 (5.6) receiving. Started all 13 games in '14, carrying 276-1,522-22 (5.5) and catching 11-62-0 (5.6). Sprained his left ankle in the season opener versus Jacksonville State. Rushed for 100-plus yards his final 16 games against Big Ten foes. Graduated with a degree in sociology. Medically excluded from lifting at the Combine because of a right shoulder injury. Had five career fumbles in 616 touches with a 5.1-yard average per carry.

Strengths: Patient and follows his blocks

on traps and powers, letting the running game develop. Good short-area burst when lanes develop. Good eyes and anticipation to cut back against the grain. Can slip and avoid tacklers. Effective in the screen game and has good hands. Gets better with a lather and smells blood near the goalline – wills his way to pay dirt driving and carrying defenders and creating a second surge. Tied for the best 10-yard split (1.50 seconds), 20-yard split (2.50 seconds) and 40-yard dash (4.40 seconds) of all running backs at the Combine. Football is very important to him.

Weaknesses: Has small hands and carries the ball too loosely in the open field. Lacks bulk. Tends to run a bit tall for his size and does not generate maximum power through his lower half or produce a lot of yardage after contact. Limited knee churn. Does not consistently play to his timed speed or show top finishing speed.

Future: An ideal change-of-pace back in the pros with enough strength, toughness and vision to carry an offense if pressed into duty and could turn out to be a solid starter in a zone running scheme.

Draft projection: Second- to third-round pick.

Scout's take: "I was a little disappointed in terms of his size. I expected him to be a little bigger in person. … The good news is they rotate and he has not taken a lot of hits. He has no wear and tear on his body. He is a space player. He is truly a third-down back. You have to remember, third-down backs are really first-down backs in the NFL with the way the game has changed. He will be a better pro than college player. They tried him at receiver and even corner at one time trying to get him on the field. It only enhances his resume when they tell me that."

RB TERRANCE MAGEE, #18 (Sr-4)

LSU ▶ GRADE: 5.17

Ht: 5-8 ½ | Wt: 213 | 40: 4.55e | Arm: 30 | Hand: 9

History: High school quarterback who won a 4A Louisiana state championship (was named outstanding player of the game) and was honored as the 4A Most Outstanding Offensive Player of the Year — accounted for 4,000 yards of offense and 54 touchdowns. Also an honorable mention all-state baseball player (pitcher and center fielder). As a true freshman in 2011, appeared in five games and carried 27 times for 133 yards (4.9-yard average) and a touchdown. Was sidelined the final three games with a strained left PCL. Was a receiver in '12 when he saw limited action in nine games. Back at running back in '13, rushed 86-626-8 (7.3) and caught 6-49-0 (8.2) in 13 games. Played all 13 games in '14 (one start), toting 112-571-3 (5.1) with 17-171-0 (10.1) receiving. Had three career kickoff returns for 94 yards (31.3). Team captain who wore jersey No. 14 prior to his senior season, when he was honored with jersey No. 18, bestowed upon the player who best exemplifies what it means to be a Tiger on and off the field. Did not run the 40 at the Combine because of a strained right hamstring. Has two career fumbles in 250 touches with a 5.9-yard average per carry.

Strengths: Quick to and through the hole – good short-area acceleration and burst. Catches the ball with ease. Has a 37-inch vertical jump. Outstanding work habits. Loves the game. Smart and accountable. Pays attention to detail and will work to be great.

Weaknesses: Has small hands. Below-average run strength and power. Not an elusive runner in the open field and does not break a lot of tackles. Average eyes, anticipation and vision. Lacks breakaway speed and gets tracked down to the perimeter. Developing blocker.

Future: Short, compact, zone runner was overshadowed by sensational freshman Leonard Fournette in a talented backfield-by-committee, yet possesses the intelligence and desire to make a living and could prove to be valuable in a zone-based ground game such as that of the Falcons, 49ers or Broncos. Might be a better pro than college player given his professional approach and that he played in a rotation with two of the best backs in the country during his career.

Draft projection: Late draftable pick.

RB-RS MARCUS MURPHY, #6 (Sr-5)

MISSOURI   ▶ GRADE: 5.20

| Ht: 5-8 ⅞ | Wt: 193 | 40: 4.54 | Arm: 31 | Hand: 8 ⅝ |

History: Prepped at Texas football factory DeSoto. As a true freshman in 2010, rushed 22 times for 181 yards (8.2-yard average) and two touchdowns, caught two balls for five yards (2.5) and zero touchdowns, and returned 24 kickoffs for 475 yards (19.8) and zero touchdowns. Redshirted in '11 while recovering from surgery to repair a torn right labrum suffered in a July 7-on-7. Played all 26 games the next two seasons — recorded 46-251-1 (5.5) rushing, 9-22-0 (2.4) receiving, 27-374-3 (13.9) on punt returns, and 19-458-1 (24.1) on kickoff returns in '12 (12 games); and 92-601-9 (6.5) rushing, 11-79-1 (7.2) receiving, 21-146-0 (7.0) on punt returns, and

27-599-0 (22.2) on kickoff returns in '13 (14 games led the Tigers with 1,425 all-purpose yards). Suffered a broken finger against Vanderbilt in '12. Was the SEC Special Teams Player of the Year in '14 when he started 10-of-14 games at tailback (non-starts went to co-starter Russell Hansbrough), totaling 177-924-4 (5.2) on the ground, 28-212-1 (7.6) through the air, 27-281-1 (10.4) on punt returns, and 17-504-2 (29.6) on kickoff returns. Murphy's 4,905 career all-purpose yards rank second in school history behind Jeremy Maclin. Did not run all shuttles at the Combine because of a left hamstring injury. Graduated with a degree in Parks, Recreation, and Tourism.

Strengths: Good stop-and-start acceleration and urgency climbing to the second level. Very confident and competitive. Outstanding body control and balance. Plays faster than his timed speed and shows electricity with the ball in his hands, making sharp speed cuts and weaving to avoid tacklers. Superb vision, toughness and traffic burst in the return game with the finishing speed to hit home runs – has seven career TD returns in the Southeastern Conference.

Weaknesses: Has very small hands. Tied for the fewest bench-press reps (11) of any running back at the Combine. Marginal lower-body explosion. Has a pedestrian 29-inch vertical jump. Is not a nuanced route runner. Lacks bulk to be effective in pass protection.

Future: A diminutive, quicker-than-fast back with the run instincts, vision and short-area burst to make an immediate impact in the return game in the pros and contribute as a change-of-pace back.

Draft projection: Late draftable pick.

FB CONNOR NEIGHBORS, #43 (Sr-5)

LSU   ▶ GRADE: 5.09

| Ht: 5-10 | Wt: 232 | 40: 4.65e | Arm: 29 ⅜ | Hand: 8 ⅞ |

History: Comes from a football family — grandfather, Billy, played for Bear Bryant, and father, Wes, also played at Alabama. Connor played middle linebacker (and hockey) as an Alabama prep. Walked on and appeared in one game in 2010. Saw action in four games in '11 without recording any stats. Played all 13 games each of the next two seasons — carried once for five yards (5.0-yard average) and zero touchdowns in '12; and tallied 2-0-0 (0.0) with seven catches for 92 yards (13.1) and zero touchdowns in '13 (started final seven). Was recognized as the Tigers' Co-Outstanding Offensive Player in '14 when he started 10-

of-12 games played and snagged 4-27-0 (6.8). Sprained his right wrist in practice leading up to UL-Monroe contest. Sprained his ankle against Auburn, sidelining him against Florida. Graduated with a degree in business. Nicknamed "Bone Saw."

Strengths: Extremely tough and competitive. Outstanding football intelligence. Will sacrifice his body as an isolation-lead blocker and seal running lanes. Very good second effort and blocking urgency climbing up to the next level. Aggressive and alert in pass protection. Has NFL pedigree and a passion for the game. Exceptional football character.

Weaknesses: Does not look the part with an underdeveloped body, short arms and small hands. Not strong on contact and will fall off some blocks – gets rocked at the point of contact vs. big linebackers. Does not run with power and is not elusive in space. Poor career production.

Future: A determined, self-made overachiever with enough grit, football smarts and determination to warrant an opportunity as a part-time lead blocker and full-time special teams performer.

Draft projection: Priority free agent.

RB THOMAS RAWLS, #34 (Sr-4)

CENTRAL MICHIGAN ▶ GRADE: 5.17

Ht: 5-9 | Wt: 215 | 40: 4.54 | Arm: 30 ¾ | Hand: 9 ½

History: Flint, Mich. native. Played his first three years at Michigan, where he wore jersey No. 38. As a true freshman in 2011, carried 13 times for 79 yards (6.1-yard average) and zero touchdowns in 10 games. Played eight games in '12 (one start), totaling 57-242-4 (4.2) with one catch for six yards (6.0-yard average) and zero touchdowns. Could not climb the depth chart in '13 when he scratched together 3-12-1 (4.0) in nine games. Did not play the last two games because of an MCL injury. Earned bachelor's degree in communications from Michigan, making him eligible to play right away at CMU. With the Chippewas in '14, toted 210-1,103-10 (5.3) with 10-93-0 (9.3) receiving in nine games (six starts). Was suspended for September contests against Syracuse and Kansas after he was arrested on felony charges of larceny and stealing credit cards (warrants had been issued in May). The crime took place in April in a casino, where Rawls and two other men were caught on tape stealing an unattended purse. He later used a stolen credit card from the purse to buy food and gas. Ultimately pleaded guilty to a high-

court misdemeanor count of attempted larceny from a building in exchange for the other two charges being dropped. Was sentenced to one year probation and 104 hours of community service. Did not play against Eastern Michigan (knee), and was academically ineligible for the Bahamas Bowl against Western Kentucky. Did not run shuttles at the Combine because of bilateral hamstring tightness.

Strengths: Ultra-competitive. Good inside running power with strong, active leg churn, good lower-body power and a lot of energy (knees fire like pistons). Runs angry with a terrific sense of urgency and falls forward. Presses the line and powers his way through contact. Can stick his foot in the dirt and go. Improves with a lather and can wear down defenses with his hard running style and grit. Showed well vs. better competition. An offensive tempo-setter.

Weaknesses: Not overly elusive. Can do a better job of securing the football through traffic. Very limited receiving production – shows rigidity in his routes as a receiving outlet and has hard hands. Long-term durability could be a concern given his physical running style and penchant for delivering punishment. Overall character and integrity issues will invite closer scrutiny and have knocked him off some draft boards.

Future: Tough, hard-nosed, downhill runner with the competitive run style and innate toughness to earn a job and become a productive pro if he can learn how to stay out of trouble. Would rather run over than around tacklers and enjoys making his presence felt on opposing defense.

Draft projection: Late draftable pick.

Scout's take: "He is just an inside bulldozer, tough guy. …He's difficult to tackle. He runs violently, with high knees – it's like a drummer in the marching band. He's a one-year wonder with off-the-field issues though. I'm not sure he will be drafted. We'd consider signing him after the draft."

RB JOSH ROBINSON, #34 (Jr-4)

MISSISSIPPI STATE ▶ GRADE: 5.28

Ht: 5-7 ⅞ | Wt: 217 | 40: 4.66 | Arm: 29 ¾ | Hand: 10 ⅛

History: Prepped in Louisiana, where he won a 4A state championship (through he broke his right arm in the final game). Also ran track. Was born to a teenage mother who was not a constant presence in his life. Josh was raised by his grandmother before she died of a heart attack when he was 12, then received care and support from a "village" of family friends and had to live out of car at points. Redshirted in 2011. Played all 12 games in '12, carrying 55 times for 335 yards (6.1-yard average) and one touchdown. Added three catches for eight yards (2.7-yard average) and zero touchdowns. Did not play against Ole Miss. Played all 13 games in '13 (two starts), totaling 78-480-3 (5.9) rushing and 12-115-0 (9.6) receiving. Started 11-of-13 games in '14 — was the Bulldogs' leading rusher with 190-1,203-11 (6.3) on the ground and 28-370-1 (13.2) through the air. Did not start against South Alabama and Vanderbilt. Wore jersey No. 13 prior to junior season. Has four career fumbles in 366 touches with a 6.2-yard average per carry. Opted not to run shuttles at the Combine.

Strengths: Runs with a low center of gravity and superb lower-body power to sink his hips and surge through traffic. Good run vision – can pick and slide and weave through congestion. Makes NFL quality runs – see Kentucky when he broke free from the grasps of nearly every defender on a single run. Battles and scraps for extra yardage and does not go down easy. Effective short-yardage/goalline runner. Good hand-eye coordination to make one-handed snags over his shoulder (see Arkansas). Willing blocker. Has a lot of tread left on his tires. Has an energetic, playful personality and can add a spark to a locker room.

Weaknesses: Lacks ideal foot speed to pull away from a pack. Can become more nuanced in pass protection. Weight has fluctuated throughout career (weighed 230 pounds in 2012) and may need to be monitored.

Future: A thickly built, smooth-striding, strong-based, instinctive runner who moves like a rolling ball of butcher knives and grinds up tacklers in his way. The type of player you root for, Robinson has overcome great adversity in his life to get where he is and has a make-it mentality.

Draft projection: Fourth- to fifth-round pick.

RB-WR [F]-KR ROSS SCHEUERMAN, #29 (Sr-4)

LAFAYETTE ▶ GRADE: 5.10

Ht: 5-11⅞ | Wt: 204 | 40: 4.53 | Arm: 30 | Hand: 8¾

History: Running back-safety who also wrestled as a New Jersey prep. Was the Patriot League Rookie of the Year in 2011 when he started 9-of-11 games, and carried 104 times for 499 yards (4.8-yard average) and zero

touchdowns with 20 receptions for 188 yards (9.4-yard average) and one touchdown. Added 31 kickoff returns for 715 yards (23.1-yard average) and one score. Started 7-of-11 games in '12, totaling 146-701-5 (4.8) rushing, 21-151-0 (7.2) receiving, and 18-304-0 (16.9) on kickoff returns. In '13, ran for 218-1,113-14 (5.1), caught 31-337-4 (10.9), and returned kickoffs 19-470-0 (24.7) in 12 games (11 starts). Started all 11 games in '14, toting 236-1,191-31 (5.0), catching 57-521-3 (9.1), and returning kickoffs 4-156-1 (39.0). Concluded his career with a memorable performance at Yankee Stadium in the 150th meeting between Lafayette and Lehigh — set a Patriot League single-game record with 45-304-3 (6.8). Was forced out of the Sacred Heart contest with a hip pointer. Team captain.

Strengths: Good cutback ability with enough elusiveness to sidestep the first tackler. Lines up in the slot and catches the ball outside his frame with ease. Protects the football in traffic and seldom puts it on the ground. Very smart, competitive, unselfish team player. Experienced four-year starter. Flashed the ability to dominate (see final game vs. Lehigh). Has a special teams personality and kickoff return experience. Caught the ball very naturally at the Combine and appeared smooth in his transition.

Weaknesses: Runs upright and leaves his body susceptible to some big hits. Not a strong inside runner or overly creative in space. Has room to improve technique as a stalk blocker. Faced inferior competition in the Patriot League.

Future: A jack-of-all-trades with intriguing versatility to contribute in multiple phases and earn a roster spot for a creative coach who understands his value as a utility runner, slot receiver and return man.

Draft projection: Late draftable pick.

RB-FB TYLER VARGA, #30 (Sr-4)

YALE ▶ GRADE: 5.22

Ht: 5-10⅝ | Wt: 222 | 40: 4.65e | Arm: 30⅜ | Hand: 10⅛

History: Born in Sweden (speaks three languages). Parents are body builders. Kitchener, Ont. native who was recognized as the most valuable high school player in Canada. Multi-sport athlete who also competed in baseball, basketball, alpine skiing, swimming, judo, and track and field growing up. Suffered a torn peroneal tendon in his final game, incurred compartment syndrome, and lost 20 pounds. Received offers from U.S. colleges, including Baylor and Dartmouth, but began his college career at University of Western Ontario. In 2011, ran for 799 yards and a national-best 15 touchdowns, garnering Canadian Interuniversity Sport National Freshman of the Year honors. Sat out two games because of eye and neck injuries. Transferred to Yale, and sat out two games while the NCAA confirmed his eligibility, but made an immediate impact when he hit the field — led the country in all-purpose yardage per game (194.2), carrying 171 times for 935 yards (5.5-yard average) and eight touchdowns, catching 16 balls for 100 yards (6.2) and a touchdown, and returning 22 kickoffs for 519 yards (23.6) in eight games. Even was called upon to play quarterback in an emergency role against Columbia when he ran for 220 yards and three scores. Played six games in '13 (started first five), managing 125-627-1 (5.0) rushing and 10-33-0 (1.7) receiving. Missed four games (foot). Healthy in '14, earned Ivy League Offensive Player of the Year by logging 233-1,423-22 (6.1) on the ground and 12-107-4 (8.9) through the air. His 26 touchdowns led the FBS and set a Yale single-season record. Finalist for the William Campbell Trophy, awarded for the nation's top football playing scholar-athlete. Selected for the Senior Bowl. Did not work out at the Combine because of a bone spur in his right ankle.

Strengths: Is chiseled like he was made out of granite and looks the part. Runs hard and plays with power. Good run instincts and anticipation. Functional core strength to drive thru defenders on contact. Hands (10 5/8) measured the biggest of any running back at the Combine – and he catches the ball naturally. Very solid showing during Senior Bowl week.

Weaknesses: Too much of a tweener, lacking ideal foot speed for a tailback and the girth and blocking power desired as a fullback. Has short arms and limitations show up in pass pro. Production is inflated from facing modest Ivy League competition. Not elusive.

Future: A compactly built, hard-charging power back whose best chance could come as a West Coast fullback in the pros, with the versatility to factor in multiple phases most effectively as a short-area receiver out of the backfield, complimentary inside runner and special teams kamikaze.

Draft projection: Fifth- to sixth-round pick.

RB-KR KARLOS WILLIAMS, #9 (Sr-4)

FLORIDA STATE ▶ GRADE: 5.23

Ht: 6-0 ¾ | Wt: 230 | 40: 4.47 | Arm: 33 | Hand: 9 ¾

History: Brother, Vince, also played at FSU and is a linebacker for the Steelers. Karlos was a highly recruited safety as a Florida prep. Contributed mostly on special teams as a true freshman in 2011 — recorded eight tackles, zero pass breakups and zero interceptions, while returning 13 kickoffs for 397 yards (30.5-yard average) in 12 games. Missed the Champs Sports Bowl against Notre Dame after breaking his right wrist against Florida. Played all 14 games in '12, recording 32-2-1 with one tackle for loss, including 11 tackles and a game-clinching interception against Georgia Tech in his lone (and first career) start. Added 13-340 (26.2) on kickoff returns. After struggling in coverage, was moved to running back in Week Two of the '13 season. Backed up Falcons '14 fourth-rounder Devonta Freeman, carrying 91 times for 730 yards (8.0-yard average) and 11 touchdowns with eight receptions for 63 yards (7.9-yard average) and zero touchdowns in 14 games. Also returned kickoffs 5-88 (17.6) and tallied seven tackles. Started 10-of-12 games played in '14, producing 150-689-11 (4.6) rushing, 29-265-1 (9.1) receiving, and 3-41 (13.7) on kickoff returns. Sprained his ankle against Wake Forest, did not play against Syracuse, and did not start against Notre Dame. Was investigated for domestic battery, but charges were never filed and the investigation was dropped. Was also questioned in a drug robbery in June 2014. Will be a 22-year-old rookie. Has three career fumbles in 307 career touches with a 5.9-yard average per carry.

Strengths: Looks the part. Exceptional size and straight-line speed for a big back. Good athlete. Has the longest arms (33 inches) and wingspan (80 3/8 inches) of any running back at the Combine. Enough size and run strength to run between the tackles. Has special teams experience.

Weaknesses: Only a one-year starter. Plays too small and narrow-based. Is hesitant in the hole and does not trust his eyes. Runs with a choppy stride, stopping and going, and does not hit spots like he is capable if he just cut it loose. Only bench-pressed 16 reps at the Combine and needs to get stronger. Not a strong finisher. Too straight-linish – marginal lateral agility and elusiveness. Clocked a 4.5-second short shuttle at the Combine, indicative of tight hips.

Future: A slow-processing, undisciplined,

non-instinctive, out-of-control safety whose issues on defense have not dissipated since being converted to the offensive backfield. Looks pretty on paper with intriguing measurables, but remains very much a developmental project and may never figure it out. Will need to prove his way on special teams to stick on an NFL roster.

Draft projection: Fifth- to sixth-round pick.

Scout's take: "We all know he is a good athlete from what he did as a safety in the bowl game. He is raw. He tries to stick his foot in the ground and go. Once he gains a little more playing time and feel for vision, he will show more patience and learn to set up his runs. Right now, he lacks patience and just thinks he is going to run through everyone."

RB-KR TREY WILLIAMS, #3 (Jr-3)

TEXAS A&M ▶ GRADE: 5.20

Ht: 5-7 ½ | Wt: 195 | 40: 4.43 | Arm: 29 ⅞ | Hand: 8 ¼

History: Parade All-American who played for Danny Amendola's father as a prep in Texas, where he carried 935 times for 8,110 yards (8.7-yard average) and 86 touchdowns over three seasons and was the 5A Offensive Player of the Year as a senior. Played all 13 games as a true freshman in 2012, carrying 65-376-5 (5.8) with 12 receptions for 171 yards (14.2-yard average) and zero touchdowns. Added 25 kickoff returns for 557 yards (22.3). Strained his hamstring against Mississippi State. Backed up Ben Malena in '13 when Williams rushed 58-407-6 (7.0), caught 10-54-0 (5.4), and returned kickoffs 28-706 (25.2). Sprained his ankle against Rice and did not play against Sam Houston State or Alabama. Played 12 games in '14, starting two, and ran for 81-560-7 (6.9), caught 16-105-1 (6.6), and returned kickoffs 17-421 (24.8). Was suspended for the Louisiana-Monroe contest — head coach Kevin Sumlin explained by saying, "Trey Williams didn't handle his business the week before the way that we wanted him to, so consequently he didn't see any action Saturday."

Strengths: Good muscularity and definition with big thighs and an athletic overall build. Very good feet, lateral quickness and agility – can shake defenders out of their shoes in the open field with dynamic jump cuts and by stringing together subtle moves. Shifty and explosive and can squirt through small lanes and create. Strong pound-for-pound. Very good vision, body control and balance. Turns over his feet rapidly. Has big-play kickoff-return ability.

Weaknesses: Marginal height. Hands (8

1/4) measured the smallest of any player at the Combine. Not strong or powerful tackle-breaker and looks to bounce outside a lot. Played behind a very talented offensive line with wide splits and often saw big running lanes. Limited mass to stop a charge in pass pro. Did not handle punts.

Future: A gadget back and dynamic return specialist who can carve a role as a creative, make-you-miss specialty runner. Will make his mark in the return game and must prove dependable as a punt returner to maximize value.

Draft projection: Fifth- to sixth-round pick.

RB T.J. YELDON, #4 (Jr-3)

ALABAMA ▶ GRADE: 5.52

Ht: 6-1 ¼ | Wt: 226 | 40: 4.56 | Arm: 31 ⅝ | Hand: 9

History: Alabama native who was highly recruited out of Daphne High, where he won a state championship and was named Mr. Football. As a true freshman in 2012, complimented Packers '13 first-rounder Eddie Lacy by carrying 175 times for 1,108 yards (6.3-yard average) and catching 11 balls for 131 yards (11.9-yard average) and one touchdown. Set the Alabama freshman rushing record, and tied Mark Ingram's freshman rushing touchdown record, as he and Lacy became the first pair of Tide running backs to rush for 1,000 yards in the same season. Started 11-of-12 games played in '13, producing 207-1,235-14 (6.0) rushing and 20-183-0 (9.2) receiving. Was suspended the first quarter of the Colorado State contest as punishment for an unsportsmanlike conduct penalty against Texas A&M — mocked Johnny Manziel's "money" celebration and made a throat slash gesture. Sat out against Chattanooga while nursing an ankle injury. Started 10-of-13 games in '14 when he totaled 194-979-11 (5.0) on the ground with 15-180-1 (12.0) through the air. Yielded the start to Kenyan Drake against Florida. Coped with nagging ankle and hamstring injuries during the season — did not start against Mississippi State, sat out against Western Carolina, and did not start in the Sugar Bowl against Ohio State. Has 10 career fumbles in 622 touches with a 5.8-yard career rushing average.

Strengths: Outstanding size. Tough competitor and will play through noticeable injuries. Runs hard. Can pick and slide, wiggle through traffic and grind out tough yardage inside. Good vision, feet and cutback ability – instinctively sorts out traffic, anticipates angles and has a knack for finding narrow running

RUNNING BACKS

lanes. Runs with urgency and steps downhill with authority. Has good lateral agility for his size and an effective spin move. Good anchor strength in pass pro to absorb a charge. Played in a pro-style system. Has a 36-inch vertical jump. Works hard. Football is important to him and it shows.

Weaknesses: Has small hands, is not a natural catcher and could do a better job holding onto the ball. Duck-footed, short-stepper with a stiff lower body that lends to an upright running style. Labors to open up his stride and make defenders miss. Lacks suddenness and takes time to get started. Limited long speed — gets caught in traffic and from behind. Ran behind a powerful line and often only produced what was blocked for him. Looked heavy-hipped and plodding with limited knee extension in Combine drills.

Future: A big, strong, early-down back, Yeldon bulked up and battled through nagging injuries as a junior that negated a half-step and led to diminished playing time alongside more powerful sophomore Derrick Henry. Is capable of earning a role as a complementary power back, though has room to continue making strides in the passing game and must learn to secure the ball better. Could prove more valuable if he shed 10 pounds and returned to the form he showed earlier in his college career when healthy.

Draft projection: Second- to third-round pick.

Scout's take: "I'm not a Yeldon fan. I think he is a third-round guy. He is a short-stepper who is so stiff in his hips, and he doesn't have long speed. I worry about his football smarts too. He looks lost in pass pro and doesn't know how to run a route. His awareness in space is not good. He is a little one-dimensional."

RB ZACH ZENNER, #31 (Sr-5)

SOUTH DAKOTA STATE ▶ GRADE: 5.16

Ht: 5-11 ½ | Wt: 223 | 40: 4.54 | Arm: 32 | Hand: 9 ⅝

History: Did not get a single FBS offer out of high school despite being a finalist for Minnesota's Mr. Football (also played baseball). Played in all 51 games of his SDSU career. As a true freshman in 2011, carried 107 times for 470 yards (4.4-yard average) and three touchdowns with 18 receptions for 130 yards (7.2-yard average) and two touchdowns in 11 games (two starts). Added 31 kickoff return yards for 754 yards (24.3-yard average), while tallying seven tackles on special teams. Started every game the next three seasons — was the FCS' leading rusher with 300-

2,044-13 (6.8) on the ground and 28-197-0 (7.0) receiving in '12 (13 games); toted 351-2,015-23 (5.7) and caught 21-251-2 (12.0) in '13 (14 games); and piled up 337-2,061-22 (6.0) rushing and 28-331-4 (11.8) receiving in '14 (14 games). Two-time captain. Three-time Payton Award finalist owns the Missouri Valley Football Conference career records for rushing yards (6,548), all-purpose yards (8,211), rushing touchdowns (61), and total touchdowns (69). Only player in FCS history to rush for 2,000-plus yards in three straight seasons. Graduated with a biology degree. Campbell Trophy ("academic Heisman") finalist and inaugural winner of the Mickey Charles Award to the top student-athlete in the FCS. Had nine career fumbles in 1,222 touches with a 6.0-yard rush average.

Strengths: Mentally tough and very competitive. Dominated lesser competition. Produced well vs. better competition (see Nebraska and Missouri). Good vision. Enough run strength to push his way through a pile. Adequate speed to reach the perimeter. Has soft hands and catches the ball with ease without breaking stride. Carried a full workload. Has a 41-inch vertical jump. Has special teams experience, covering and returning kicks, and an unselfish, special teams mentality. Willing blocker. Extremely intelligent and football smart – excellent retention. Outstanding durability – has not missed any time during his career and is very workman-like and dependable.

Weaknesses: Average foot quickness and lateral agility to elude tacklers. Runs upright and gathers to cut and is very choppy in his movement with a laboring run style – not fluid or graceful and won't win any style points. Runs up the backs of blockers. Had more than a 1,000 carries in college.

Future: Productive, downhill Division II standout with the vision and cutback ability desired in a zone-based, ground game, such as Denver's or Seattle's. An ideal backup capable of making an impact on special teams.

Draft projection: Late draftable pick.

Scout's take: "He lit up Nebraska for 200 (yards) and racked up 150 vs. Missouri and you go see him in person and he looks like a high school player. They said he has four percent body fat, but there's no way he looks 220 pounds. ... Before you put together a full evaluation, he is a player you need to see in person. ... I have raised and lowered grades based on how they look physically when I see their body types. This is a case where you can't go strictly off tape."

RUNNING BACKS

WIDE RECEIVERS

DALE SPARKS / WVU

Nawrocki's TOP 10

1. **KEVIN WHITE**
2. **Amari Cooper**
3. **Devante Parker**
4. **Jaelen Strong**
5. **Nelson Agholor**
6. **Dorial Green-Beckham**
7. **Devin Funchess**
8. **Devin Smith**
9. **Breshad Perriman**
10. **Sammie Coates**

WR [F,X] - RS **NELSON AGHOLOR**, #15 (Jr-3)

USC ▶ GRADE: 5.92

Ht: 6-0 ⅛ | Wt: 198 | 40: 4.42 | Arm: 32 ¼ | Hand: 9 ¼

History: Born in Nigeria, where his father played soccer. Nelson moved to the U.S. when he was five. Prepped in Florida, where he was a highly recruited USA Today All-American. Also played basketball. Lined up at flanker for the Trojans. As a true freshman in 2012, played all 13 games (three starts) and recorded 19 receptions for 340 yards (17.9-yard average) and two touchdowns. Added five kickoff returns for 121 yards (24.2-yard average). Started all 14 games in '13, producing 56-918-6 (16.4) receiving and 10-175 (17.5) on kickoff returns. Added 18 punt returns for 343 yards (19.1) and two scores. Started all 13 games in '14 — caught 104-1,313-12 (12.6), returned kickoffs 9-147 (16.3), and returned punts 19-197-2 (10.4). Had seven career rushes for 18 yards (2.6-yard average) and zero touchdowns. Team captain. Dislocated his left middle finger during Combine drills and did not perform jumps or shuttles.

Strengths: Outstanding athlete with long arms and a wide catching radius. Very good ball skills and body control – contorts his body in the air and makes difficult grabs. Can sky for the ball and pluck it out of the air. Makes dynamic speed cuts and can create separation out of his breaks with quickness. Runs a full route tree. Can pierce zones from the slot and stretch the field from the inside or outside. Continues working to uncover. Elusive and creative after the catch. Explosive punt returner with good vision, traffic burst and breakaway speed.

Weaknesses: Thin-framed with small hands. Makes some concentration drops. Lacks physicality and can be knocked off routes

WIDE RECEIVERS

and struggle releasing vs. press coverage. Not strong or tough after the catch and can be affected by bodies in the middle of the field. Not a consistent blocker.

Future: A big-play weapon with excellent speed and athletic ability, Agholor emerged as a big-play weapon in the slot and adds value as an explosive return man. Has the resume of a playmaker.

Draft projection: Top-40 pick.

Scout's take: "That's my guy. I love him. I hope he doesn't go in the first (round). He had some drops (in 2013) but he straightened that out. He catches everything. I thought he was more explosive and a better receiver than Marquise Lee (in 2013) and he stepped up his game this year when he had to be the guy."

WR [X,F] - KR **MARIO ALFORD**, #5 (Sr-4)
WEST VIRGINIA ▶ GRADE: 5.42
Ht: 5-8 ½ | Wt: 180 | 40: 4.39 | Arm: 31 ¼ | Hand: 9 ⅜

History: One of 14 children. Prepped in Georgia, where he played quarterback and won the 100-meter state championship (10.77 seconds). Spent two years at Georgia Military College. In 2011, tallied 10 receptions for 122 yards (12.2-yard average) and a touchdown with 33 carries for 226 yards (6.8-yard average) and four touchdowns (nine games). In '12, recorded 8-199-2 (24.9) receiving and 52-541-6 (10.4) rushing in eight games. Added eight kickoff returns for 188 yards (23.5-yard average) and a score. With the mountaineers in '13, started 5-of-12 games — one at the "Y" (inside) receiver and the final four at the "X" (outside) receiver — and produced 27-552-2 (20.4) receiving and 11-229-0 (20.8) on kickoff returns. Started all 13 games at "X" in '14 when he led the Atlantic Coast Conference in receiving touchdowns — caught 65-945-11 (14.5) and returned kickoffs 26-743-2 (28.6). Had seven career rushes for 61 yards (8.2-yard average) and zero touchdowns.

Strengths: Outstanding all-purpose production. Plays bigger than his size. Explosive driving off the line of scrimmage. Unique gear change with ability to accelerate to top gear rapidly. Ran a 6.64-second short shuttle, tied for the second quickest time at the Combine. Very good ball skills – tracks it extremely well downfield. Catches the ball well in a crowd. Can pull a rabbit out of his hat and make multiple tacklers miss in the open field. Dynamic kickoff returner with home-run, finishing speed. Is tough and will play through pain.

Weaknesses: Very undersized. Ran a limited route tree and is a not a refined route runner. Lacks strength releasing off the line. Will need to learn how to read coverages and acclimate to a more sophisticated offense. Average leaping ability – has a 34-inch vertical jump. Offers a small target and does not have a wide catching radius or adjust easily to off-target throws. Limited blocking strength.

Future: Diminutive, explosive playmaker capable of taking the top of a defense, operating inside or outside. Could factor readily in the return game.

Draft projection: Third- to fourth-round pick.

Scout's take: "He is a poor man's Steve Smith. He is a little returner. I am putting him in the third round."

WR [X,F] - KR **DRES ANDERSON**, #6 (Sr-5)
UTAH ▶ GRADE: 5.35
Ht: 6-1 ⅛ | Wt: 187 | 40: 4.50e | Arm: 31 ⅝ | Hand: 9 ⅜

History: Son of 10-year NFL receiver Willie "Flipper" Anderson. Dres was recruited out of California. Redshirted in 2010. Played all 13 games in '11 (four starts), recording 23 receptions for 355 yards (15.4-yard average). Started 11-of-12 games in '12 (gave way to two-tight end starting formation against Washington State), catching 36-365-3 (10.1). In '13, was the Utes' leading receiver for the second year in a row — started 11-of-12 games (gave way to two-tight end starting formation against Oregon) and snagged 53-1,002-7 (18.9). In '14, managed 22-355-4 (16.1) receiving before suffering a left knee injury against USC and undergoing season-ending surgery. For his career, rushed 44 times for 143 yards (5.7-yard average) and one touchdown, and returned 12 kickoffs for 251 yards (20.9-yard average). Team captain graduated with a degree in communications. Medically excluded at the Combine because of left knee injury.

Strengths: Uses his hands well to brush off press coverage and gets into routes quickly. Very fluid movement skill. Efficient route runner with little wasted motion in his routes. Good spatial awareness and feel for soft spots in coverage. Fine body control. Makes difficult catches look easy. Produces in the clutch. Very good speed and field vision to turn upfield and weave through traffic after the catch. Has NFL pedigree. Quick study. Functional positional blocker – gets in the way.

Weaknesses: Has small hands and a wiry frame. Long-strider – not explosive in and out of cuts. Does not do a lot of dirty work in the middle of the field – hears footsteps and could be more susceptible to injury in the pros tiptoeing through traffic. Makes as many easy drops as difficult snags and must become more consistent catching the ball. Lacks physicality as a blocker.

Future: A skinny, sleek, athletic, big-play receiver who consistently gets on top of defensive backs and has natural receiving skills that could translate well outside the numbers in the pros. Had received some second-round grades from evaluators prior to his injury and could prove to be a value pick later in the draft.

Draft projection: Fourth- to fifth-round pick.

Scout's take: "If he is healthy, we're talking about him in the second round. He has that type of talent to be discussed with some of the other top receivers. Where he goes is going to depend largely on how he runs and works out coming off the injury. I like him."

WR [X] - KR KENNY BELL, #80 (Sr-5)

NEBRASKA ▶ GRADE: 5.27

Ht: 6-1⅛ | Wt: 197 | 40: 4.39 | Arm: 31⅝ | Hand: 9¼

History: Father, Ken, was a kick returner for the Denver Broncos (1986-89). Kenny prepped in Colorado, where he also ran track. Missed six games of his senior season in 2009 (broken collarbone). Redshirted in 2010. Took ownership of the "X" position in '11 when he played all 13 games, starting the final 11, and recorded 32 receptions for 461 yards (14.4-yard average) and three touchdowns. Started all 14 games in '12, producing 50-863-8 (17.3). In '13, caught 52-577-4 (11.1) in 13 games (12 starts). Did not start against Minnesota. Started 12-of-13 games in '14, managing 47-788-6 (16.8). In his non-start (McNeese State), suffered a groin injury that nagged him the first half of the season and also knocking him out of the Michigan State contest. Sustained a concussion against Iowa. For his career, rushed six times for 109 yards (18.2-yard average) and one touchdown, while returning 51 kickoffs for 1,277 yards (25.0-yard average) and one score. Walks away as Nebraska's all-time leader in receptions (181) and receiving yards (2,689). Team captain graduated with a degree in ethnic studies.

Strengths: Very good straight-line speed. Has a 41 1/2-inch vertical jump and posted a 6.66-second three-cone drill, demonstrating exceptional agility. Climbs the ladder to get the ball and can take it out of the air and makes acrobatic in-air adjustments. Makes difficult one-handed snags and is effective on reverses in the run game. Outstanding career production. Experienced four-year starter.

Has big-play kickoff return ability. Has NFL pedigree. Experienced, four-year starter.

Weaknesses: Very slight, underdeveloped frame. Tied for the fewest bench-press reps (7) of any player at the Combine. Lacks functional strength to beat the jam and factor as a blocker. Has tight hips, takes long strides and is not fluid transitioning out of speed cuts. Outmuscled on jump balls. Not strong after the catch. Only adequate athletic ability – stumbles in his routes and is not fluid. Does not play to timed speed. Limited blocker easily discarded.

Future: An outside, vertical receiver capable of competing for a job as a No. 4 or 5 receiver with added value as a kickoff returner. Must refine his route-running and get stronger to match up with NFL defensive backs.

Draft projection: Fourth- to fifth-round pick.

Scout's take: "He's overrated. I don't think he is very tough or that good of an athlete. He's tight and you see it when he has to make sharp cuts – he has to take an extra step with choice routes or slants. I don't know how much he likes to go inside. He is the all-time leading receiver in Nebraska history, but they have always been a running team – what receivers have they produced? ... He does not have a quarterback who can get him the ball – that was part of their problem."

WR [Z] DA'RON BROWN #4 (Sr-5)

NORTHERN ILLINOIS ▶ GRADE: 5.09

Ht: 6-0⅛ | Wt: 205 | 40: 4.53 | Arm: 32 | Hand: 10¼

History: Chicago Public League product who played quarterback in high school, rushing for 3,700 yards his final two seasons. Redshirted in 2010 when he earned Work Team Player of the Year. Played all 14 games in '11, starting five, and recorded 24 receptions for 322 yards (13.4-yard average) and two touchdowns. Started 6-of-14 games in '12, tallying 17-156-2 (9.2). In '13, started 11-of-13 games played and produced 46-752-9 (16.3). Was bothered by a hamstring injury late in the season — did not start against Western Michigan, did not play against Bowling Green, and did not start against Utah State. Led the Huskies in receiving for the second straight year in '14 when he started all 14 games and produced 68-1,065-6 (15.7). Rushed 21 times in his career for 160 yards (7.6-yard average) and two touchdowns. Will be a 24-year-old rookie.

Strengths: Has big, strong hands. Very good hand-eye coordination and hand placement. Adjusts well to the low ball and tracks it well over his shoulder. Gets upfield quickly after the catch and has good strength to power through some arm tackles. Good effort blocking on the perimeter.

Weaknesses: Runs a limited route tree. Not dynamic or elusive after the catch. Lacks the speed to separate vertically. Shows only one gear and struggles to pop out of breaks or separate with quickness.

Future: Well-built, possession receiver effective on digs, slants and bubble screens and working inside where he could flex his muscle.

Draft projection: Late draftable pick

WR [F] - RS **KAELIN CLAY**, #8 (Sr-5)
UTAH   ▶ GRADE: 5.10
Ht: 5-9 ⅝ | Wt: 195 | 40: 4.49 | Arm: 30 ⅞ | Hand: 9

History: Long Beach Poly product who also ran track as a prep, recording a 10.46 100 meters. Began his career at Cal, where he redshirted in 2010. Did not play in '11 after having surgery to repair a torn meniscus. Left Cal and spent two years at Mt. San Antonio College (Calif.). Played all 12 games in '12, catching 38 balls for 659 yards (17.3-yard average) and eight touchdowns, while returning 17 kickoffs for 679 yards (39.9-yard average) and three touchdowns. Played all 11 games in '13, racking up 52-995-16 (19.1) receiving with 25-772-2 (30.9) on kickoff returns, and 17-245-1 (14.4) on punt returns. In those two years, rushed seven times for 77 yards (11.0-yard average) and two touchdowns. With the Utes in '14, snagged 43-523-4 (12.2), and returned kickoffs 22-548-1 (24.9) and punts 23-346-3 (15.0) in 13 games (10 starts). Won the College Football Performance Awards Punt Returner trophy, as his three scores tied for first in the nation.

Strengths: Field fast and determined returner with good vision and anticipation – quick to go north and south and push the ball upfield. Runs with good body lean and awareness and has a knack for dodging live bullets and slipping tacklers. Is effective in the short-passing game, capable of weaving through traffic and converting short, lateral tosses into big gains. Has 10 career return touchdowns.

Weaknesses: Will struggle releasing vs. press coverage in the pros. Did not run a full route tree and needs to learn how to use stems and nods to set up his routes. Takes choppy strides and is not fluid transitioning out of breaks. Is tight in the hips and not a savvy or crisp route runner.

Future: A strong, shifty slot receiver, Clay stepped up in the absence of the injured Dres Anderson in 2014, yet brought the most value to the Utes flipping the field in the return game.

Similar to former Chiefs RS Dante Hall, Clay's calling card will be returning punts, where he could make a living.

Draft projection: Late draftable pick.

WR [Z,X] **SAMMIE COATES**, #18 (Jr-4)
AUBURN   ▶ GRADE: 5.56
Ht: 6-1 ⅜ | Wt: 212 | 40: 4.42 | Arm: 33 ⅜ | Hand: 9 ⅜

History: Lost his father in an industrial accident when Sammie was in fifth grade. Won an Alabama state championship as a prep. Also starred in basketball and baseball. Broke his ankle in the summer of 2009. His first season at Auburn was '11, though he didn't play that year after having right foot surgery that required two pins be inserted. In '12, played 12 games (one start) and tallied six receptions for 114 yards (19.0-yard average) and two touchdowns. Did not play against Mississippi State. Started 12-of-14 games at split end in '13, totaling 42-902-7 (21.5). Did not start against Western Carolina or Texas A&M. Appeared in 12 games in '14, starting seven at split end, and managed 34-741-4 (21.8). Suffered a deep bone bruise in his left knee in the season opener against Arkansas — hampered him throughout the season, as he sat out against San Jose State and did not start five other contests, including the Outback Bowl against Wisconsin. By virtue of graduating with a degree in public administration, was eligible to participate in the Senior Bowl. Honored with the Uplifting Athletes Rare Disease Champion Award, presented to a leader in the world of college football who has realized his or her potential to make a positive and lasting impact on the rare disease community.

Strengths: Looks every bit the part with a unique size-strength-speed combination. Has a 41-inch vertical jump and can jump through the roof. Tied for the most bench-press reps (23) among all receivers at the Combine. Has a powerful stride and runs with physicality after the catch. Has explosive big-play ability. Beat Mississippi talented Senquez Golson deep for a TD and creates big matchups problems for undersized corners.

Weaknesses: Lacks route discipline, rhythm and focus. Very inconsistent hands. Breaks stride to catch. Tends to fight the ball and double-catch it – is not a natural, clean catcher. Too many concentration lapses.

Future: A big-time playmaker that will tease evaluators with his rare talent and break their hearts with his case of the drops. Has some likeness to Vikings 2012 first-round pick (29th overall pick) Cordarrelle Patterson, and his rare physical talent will likely attract a WR coach who believes his hands can be corrected. Could have as much value as a downfield decoy.

Draft projection: Second- to third-round pick.

Scout's take: "He has a ton of ability, but it's difficult to get past his inconsistent hands. He does not have a lot of polish. He runs fast and has all the tools. There are just inconsistencies to him. He is really raw as a route runner. Talent-wise, he reminds me of (Steelers 2014 fourth-round pick) Martavis Bryant (out of Clemson), who had the blazing speed and inconsistent hands. He could have gone in the second if not for some of his off-field issues."

WR [Z] CHRIS CONLEY, #31 (Sr-4)

GEORGIA   ▶ GRADE: 5.33

Ht: 6-1 ⅞	Wt: 213	40: 4.36	Arm: 33 ¾	Hand: 9 ⅞

History: Georgia native who was raised by a teacher mother and Air Force father. As a true freshman in 2011, was slated to redshirt before injury forced him into action in Week Four — appeared in 11 games and recorded 16 receptions for 288 yards (18.0-yard average) and two touchdowns. Sustained a concussion in September. Missed '12 spring practice because of a broken right foot and right wrist surgery. Played all 14 games in '12, starting three at flanker, and tallied 20-342-6 (17.1). Started 9-of-11 games played in '13 — seven at flanker, two at split end — and snagged 45-651-4 (14.5). Did not play against Florida and Appalachian State and did not start against Auburn and Kentucky because of a high right ankle sprain. Started 11-of-13 games at flanker in '14 and caught 36-657-8 (18.2) playing through a partially dislocated shoulder injury. Gave way to an extra tight end and fullback against Tennessee and Vanderbilt, respectively. Earned team award for dedication to strength and conditioning. Graduated with a degree in Journalism.

Strengths: Outstanding size. Registered the most explosive vertical jump (45 inches) for any position at the Combine in the last decade and paced all receivers with a 11-foot, 7-inch broad jump. Had the longest arms (33 3/4 inches) of any receiver at the Combine. Accelerates at the top of his routes to create some separation. Catches on contact and is effective working through traffic. Efficient stalk blocker. Extremely coachable. Strong leadership presence. Relentless work ethic. Strives for greatness. Very tough and will battle through injuries. Showed well at the NFLPA Collegiate Bowl, separating himself

from the competition. Very smart, tough and accountable. Impressed teams in Combine interviews.

Weaknesses: Long strider with tightness in his body. Does not play to his timed speed or regularly display the rare leaping ability and explosiveness put on display at the Combine. Gets hung up at the line vs. the jam. Does not consistently create separation. Is not a natural hands catcher. Shows little creativity or elusiveness after the catch. Has been slowed by a lot of injuries and overall body stiffness could continue to create issues in the pros.

Future: More of a possession receiver than a true downfield vertical threat, Conley will win over a coaching staff with his sterling intangibles, relentless drive, toughness and leadership ability. As physically talented as he is, he has never emerged as a go-to receiver in a run-first offense, yet could prove to be a better pro than college player with continued refinement and if he can stay healthy. Greatest value could be the strong presence he will add to a locker room.

Draft projection: Fourth- to fifth-round pick.

Scout's take: "I gave him a fourth-round grade when I went through the school. He made some plays. I think he was better as a junior when he had a better quarterback and wasn't playing hurt. I think that affected him this year. ... He ran well at the Combine, but he was very average in the ball drills. He had some clunkers that hit off his hands. That is some of the inconsistency in his game. He was one of the most difficult evaluations I had this fall. I kept wrestling with where to put him. It was hard to get a good feel for what he could become. ... At his best, I think he will be a no. 3 receiver. I didn't grade him as a starter."

WR [X,Z,F] AMARI COOPER, #9 (Jr-3)

ALABAMA   ▶ GRADE: 6.65

Ht: 6-0 ⅞	Wt: 211	40: 4.34	Arm: 31 ½	Hand: 10

History: Prepped at Miami Northwestern, where he played with Vikings 2014 first-rounder Teddy Bridgewater. Played the "X" receiver for the Tide, leading the team in receiving all three years. In '12, broke Julio Jones' freshman records for receptions and receiving yards — played all 14 games, starting the final nine, and produced 59 receptions for 1,000 yards (16.9-yard average) and 11 touchdowns. Was bothered by heel, turf toe, and knee injuries in '13 when he started 7-of-12 games played and managed 45-736-4 (16.4). Sat out against Colorado State, and did not start any games between Weeks One and Eight.

ALABAMA ATHLETICS

WIDE RECEIVERS

Amari Cooper

Healthy in '14, was the Biletnikoff winner, Southeastern Conference Offensive Player of the Year (coaches, AP) and a Heisman finalist — racked up 124-1,727-16 (13.9) in 14 starts, setting the Alabama and SEC single-season record for catches. His junior season yards and touchdowns rank second in conference history. Will be a 21-year-old rookie. Did not lift at the Combine because of a left shoulder injury and opted not to run the 60-yard shuttle.

Strengths: Very good hands. Terrific stop-and-start acceleration, as confirmed by recording the fastest short shuttle (3.98 seconds) of any receiver at the Combine. Is deceptively fast and closes cushion in a blink. Makes tough catches in traffic. Will climb the ladder and sky for the ball in a crowd, consistently highpointing it. Is smart and versatile, having played all three spots in a pro-style offense and having a very good understanding of how to read coverages. Exceptionally crafty route runner – runs a full route tree and understands how to set up defenders with subtle nods and stems and sell his routes. Superb athlete with outstanding balance and body control to snap out of breaks and make plays in the air. Cat-quick to create separation out of his breaks. Makes difficult catches look routine. Effective creating after the catch on bubble screens and can convert lateral tosses into chunk yardage. Tough, physical blocker. Has playmaking ability and comes through in the clutch. Had instant impact potential in a sophisticated, NFL-style offense.

Weaknesses: Lacks elite size. Can improve escaping press coverage and release more cleanly vs. physical corners. Will make some concentration drops Was slowed by injuries on an inconsistent offense as a sophomore.

Future: A legitimate play-making No. 1 receiver with the confidence, route savvy, athletic talent and receiving skill to become an impact pass-catcher in the pros. So smooth he makes the extraordinary look routine. High-floor prospect from a proven program with instant impact potential.

Draft projection: Top-10 pick.

Scout's take: "When you try to think of weaknesses, you're really only nitpicking. It's difficult to find many. He does it all."

WR [F] - PR JAMISON CROWDER, #3 (Sr-4)

DUKE ▶ GRADE: 5.38

| Ht: 5-8 ⅜ | Wt: 185 | 40: 4.48 | Arm: 30 ⅜ | Hand: 8 ¾ |

History: Starred on the field and hardwood as a South Carolina prep — earned conference player of the year in both sports, and was part of a basketball state championship. Missed two games as a senior because of a strained hamstring. As a true freshman in 2011, had 14 receptions for 163 yards (11.6-yard average) and one touchdown. Also returned 38 kickoffs for 814 yards (21.4-yard average) and zero touchdowns and 13 punts for 122 yards (9.4) and zero touchdowns. Started all 40 games the next three seasons. In '12, set the Atlantic Coast Conference single-season record for receiving yards by a sophomore by producing 76-1,074-8 (14.1) with 5-90-0 (18.0) on kickoff returns and 5-66-0 (13.2) on punt returns. Teamed with Connor Vernon to establish an ACC single-season record for most receptions (161) by two teammates. Was voted team MVP in '13 when he set the ACC single-season record for catches and set school single-season records for receiving yards and most 100-yard games (seven) — caught 108-1,360-8 (12.6) and returned punts 25-401-2 (16.0). Was the Blue Devils' leading receiver

for the second straight year in '14 when he snagged 85-1,044-6 (12.3), adding 22-280-2 (12.7) on punt returns. Also tossed a 12-yard touchdown pass. Was All-ACC as a receiver and return specialist his last two seasons. Led the team in all-purpose yardage all four years, including 21 career rushes for 135 yards (6.4-yard average) and a touchdown. Tied for the ACC career receptions record (283), and is Duke's all-time leader in punt return scores (four). Team captain. Graduated. Will be a 22-year-old rookie.

Strengths: Dependable hands. Plays smart. Nuanced route runner – stems and sets up defensive backs to separate underneath. Good sideline and field awareness. Has a 37-inch vertical jump. Very good vision and awareness as a punt returner. Has a passion for the game. Experienced, three-year starter in an NFL-style offense. Selfless, team player. Strong showing at the Senior Bowl.

Weaknesses: Small-framed with small hands and offers a small throwing target. Average long speed. Not explosive. Has some tightness in his hips that negates lateral agility. Cannot consistently fend off the jam. Not a strong tackle-breaker. Marginal blocking strength to sustain.

Future: A quicker than fast, shifty, competitive, undersized receiver and punt returner with a desirable makeup to earn a role as a slot machine in the pros. Has the work ethic, football smarts and toughness to find a way to produce.

Draft projection: Fourth- to fifth-round pick.

Scout's take: "He's a little return specialist and slot guy. He probably made himself a little bit of money at the Senior Bowl. He's a good little football player. He makes plays. He is going to play in the league."

WR [Z] DAVARIS DANIELS, (Jr-4)

EX-NOTRE DAME ▶ GRADE: 5.10

| Ht: 6-1 ½ | Wt: 201 | 40: 4.64 | Arm: 31 ¼ | Hand: 9 |

History: Father, Phillip, was a 15-year NFL defensive end with the Seahawks, Bears, and Redskins. Davaris was highly recruited out of Chicago's northern suburbs. Did not play as a freshman in 2011. Played 11 games in '12, starting three, and recorded 31 receptions for 490 yards (15.8-yard average) and zero touchdowns. Missed the last two games of the regular season because of a broken collarbone. Started 8-of-13 games in '13, producing 49-745-7 (15.2). Was not admitted for the '14 spring semester (academics) then was suspended in August while the university

WIDE RECEIVERS

investigated academic fraud. Opted to forgo remaining eligibility in order to declare for the draft. Did not run shuttles at the Combine because of cramps.

Strengths: Good functional strength to beat the jam. Will work across the middle and catches on contact. Secures the ball well through traffic and churns for extra yardage. Adjusts well to the thrown ball and tracks it well over his shoulder. Good hand strength. Has sneaky speed and knows how to stem and open the hips of defensive backs before breaking off his route. Can 'dot the i' along the sideline, showing very good field awareness and concentration. Good competitive playing speed and leaping ability. Has a 37-inch vertical jump. Has NFL pedigree.

Weaknesses: Has small hands and is an inconsistent hands-catcher. Lacks top-end speed and short-area burst to separate. Slow out of the blocks. Cannot run by cornerbacks vertically. Must show that he is willing to put in the hard work and be accountable to his team. Could stand to show more tenacity as a blocker.

Future: A good-sized, possession receiver who was ascending prior to academic suspension and must prove that he is willing to work to create his own legacy and do what it takes to be great. Could be very humbled on Draft Day and need to prove his way in training camp to make it.

Draft projection: Late draftable pick.

Scout's take: "He has too much entitlement and was never where he was supposed to be. They could not count on him in the program."

WR [Z] **DEVANTE DAVIS**, #81 (Sr-4)

UNLV ▶ GRADE: 5.09

Ht: 6-2 ⅞ | Wt: 220 | 40: 4.61 | Arm: 32 ⅜ | Hand: 9 ½

History: High school tight end who also played basketball and was an all-state triple jumper as a Texas prep. Had his right knee scoped as a ninth grader. Played 11 games as a true freshman in 2011, starting three, and tallied four catches for 42 yards (10.5-yard average) and zero touchdowns. Was suspended against Boise State (violation team rules). Started all 13 games in '12, totaling 61-854-4 (14.0). Sat out '13 spring practice after having surgery to repair torn right meniscus. In the fall, started all 13 games and reeled in 87-1,290-14 (14.8). Started the first eight games of the '14 season — managed 34-599-4 (17.6) before suffering a season-ending right wrist injury. Team captain graduated in less than four years with a degree in public administration. Was the first UNLV

player invited to the Senior Bowl since Ickey Woods in 1987, but missed the game because of a hamstring injury.

Strengths: Functionally strong beating the jam and pushing off cornerbacks. Good field awareness, ball reactions, hand quickness and body control. Uses his body well to position and post up defensive backs. Good concentration in traffic. Has a knack for finding openings in zone coverage and works to uncover. Good football intelligence and character. Studies the game and has a passion for it.

Weaknesses: Lacks speed, burst and acceleration. Only shows one gear and gathers to cut. Struggles to separate and most of his catches are contested. Does not play fast. Not creative or elusive after the catch. Lets the ball get on top of him. Could be more imposing as a blocker given his size.

Future: A very big, physical possession receiver who will fit most ideally as a flanker in a rhythm passing game. Could have to prove that he could contribute on special teams to hold a No. 4 or No. 5 receiver job. Somewhat similar to Dolphins 2012 seventh-round pick Rishard Matthews.

Draft projection: Late draftable pick.

Scout's take: "He can't run. The one thing he had was hands, and he dropped a bunch at the Combine. He could possibly be drafted late. I graded him as a priority free agent."

WR [Z,F] **GEREMY DAVIS**, #85 (Sr-5)

CONNECTICUT ▶ GRADE: 5.01

Ht: 6-2 ⅝ | Wt: 216 | 40: 4.60e | Arm: 9 ½ | Hand: 32 ¼

History: Prepped in Georgia. Redshirted in 2010 (knee). Appeared in 12 games in '11, catching seven balls for 73 yards (12.2-yard average) and zero touchdowns. Started 11-of-12 games in '12 and produced 44-613-1 (13.9). In '13, was the Huskies' leading receiver for the second year in a row — pulled in 71-1,0853 (15.3). Totaled 44-521-3 (11.8) in '14 (10 starts), but suffered a foot injury against East Carolina and sat out against Army and Central Florida. Team captain. Did not run at the Combine because of tightness in his right hamstring.

Strengths: Very dependable hands-catcher who extends outside his frame and can make difficult grabs. Is not fazed entering traffic. Tied for the most bench-press reps (23) among all receivers at the Combine. Very well-conditioned athlete with only 4 percent body fat. Works hard in the weight room and is diligent with game-day preparation. Very good football intelligence. Competitive stalk blocker.

Weaknesses: Stiff, segmented route runner who signals routes and gives up break points. Below-average functional playing speed – is not quick or explosive off the line and does not turn his feet over quickly. Lacks discipline in his routes. Could stand to do a better job working back to the ball. Limited creativity and gear change after the catch.

Future: Lanky, long-armed possession receiver with make-it intangibles and effort that could allow a team to take a chance on his subpar talent. Best chance to earn a spot will come on special teams.

Draft projection: Priority free agent.

WR [X] - RS **TITUS DAVIS**, #84 (Sr-4)
CENTRAL MICHIGAN ▶ GRADE: 5.25

| Ht: 6-0 ¾ | Wt: 196 | 40: 4.54 | Arm: 29 ⅝ | Hand: 8 ¼ |

History: Prepped in suburban Chicago, where he won a state championship at Wheaton-Warrenville South. Also was a state qualifier in the long jump, 4X100 and 4X200. Manned the "Z" receiver for the Chippewas. As a true freshman in 2011, started 7-of-11 games and set the CMU record for single-season touchdown receptions for a freshman — caught 40 balls for 751 yards (18.8-yard average) and eight touchdowns. Led the Mid-American Conference and ranked No. 1 in the nation in yards per catch in '12 when he started all 12 games and totaled 43-860-8 (20.0). Was suspended for the team's bowl game against Western Kentucky. In '13, pulled in 61-1,109-8 (18.2) in 11 starts despite missing the Ohio contest and playing the final five games with a torn left labrum. Was CMU's team MVP for the second straight year in '14 when he posted 60-980-13 (16.3) in nine starts. Missed September contests against Purdue, Syracuse and Kansas because of a knee strain. For his career, rushed 15 times for 113 yards (7.5-yard average) and zero touchdowns, returned 21 punts for 195 yards (9.3-yard average) and returned 18 kickoffs for 387 yards (21.5-yard average). Team captain is CMU's career leader in touchdown receptions (37), receiving yardage (3,705) and is the only receiver in FBS history to make at least eight TD receptions in each of his four seasons. Medically excluded from lifting at the Combine because of a right shoulder injury.

Strengths: Acrobatic catcher with very good ball skills and body control. Versatile and plays inside and outside with a good understanding of offensive concepts. Is quick off the line and shows nifty feet to slip and avoid the jam and get into his routes. Field fast. Advanced route runner. Understands how to work through zones. Attacks the ball in the air and climbs to get it, doing a very good job tracking it in the air. Quick to turn upfield after the catch. Outstanding career production. Has return experience.

Weaknesses: Has a very lean frame with short arms and was tied for the smallest hands (8 1/4 inches) of any receiver at the Combine. Struggles escaping press coverage. Lacks top-end speed to consistently separate. Not a strong tackle-breaker. The Combine event appeared too big for him as he pressed too much and showed a lack of awareness. Has a 32 1/2-inch vertical jump. Underwhelming blocker with limited mass. Has not faced top competition.

Future: A good functional football player with the athletic talent, body control and receiving skill to produce outside the numbers in the red zone where he exceled most in college. Could provide added value in the return game.

Draft projection: Late draftable pick.

WR [F,X] - KR **STEFON DIGGS**, #1 (Jr-3)
MARYLAND ▶ GRADE: 5.37

| Ht: 6 0 | Wt: 195 | 40: 4.44 | Arm: 31 ¼ | Hand: 10 |

History: Maryland native who was a blue chip recruit coming out of high school. Was voted team MVP as a true freshman in 2012 when he started 7-of-11 games played and recorded 54 receptions for 848 yards (15.7-yard average) and six touchdowns. Also returned 25 kickoffs for 713 yards (28.5-yard average) and two scores, and returned 22 punts for 221 yards (10.0). Sat out against Clemson (ankle). In '13, totaled 34-587-3 (17.3) receiving and 12-281-0 (23.4) on kickoff returns in seven starts before suffering a season-ending broken right fibula injury against Wake Forest. Started nine games in '14, pulling in 62-792-5 (12.8) and returning kickoffs KR 20-478-0 (23.9). Was suspended against Michigan State for his role in a pre-game confrontation with Penn State players in which he made contact with an official's face. During the PSU game, suffered a season-ending lacerated kidney injury. In his career, rushed 32 times for 187 yards (5.9-yard average) and zero touchdowns. Opted not to lift at the Combine.

Strengths: Has very big hands and excellent hand-eye coordination. Outstanding speed to separate down the field. Catches the ball in stride. Very competitive with the ball in his hands and is nifty and creative running after

WIDE RECEIVERS

the catch. Attacks the ball in the air and will compete in a crowd. Makes some spectacular concentration catches (see Connecticut). Plays with a sense of urgency and will attack defenders as a blocker. Very confident and plays with an edge.

Weaknesses: Has a very thin build and is tight in the hips. Lacks weight-room strength and functional strength. Could struggle to beat tight press coverage in the pros. Not strong after the catch. Could stand to refine his route running.

Future: A sleek, speedy slot receiver who plays with surprising physicality for his frame, Diggs could always be vulnerable to injury in the pros. However, he is a very good football player, offers return ability and versatility to play inside or outside.

Draft projection: Third- to fourth-round pick.

Scout's take: "I don't think he likes the noise across the middle. He will block, but all his routes are outside the numbers. He doesn't do the dirty work inside – they leave that to Deon Long."

WR [X] - RS **PHILLIP DORSETT**, #4 (Sr-4)
MIAMI (FLA.) ▶ GRADE: 5.47

| Ht: 5-9 ¾ | Wt: 185 | 40: 4.31 | Arm: 30 ¼ | Hand: 9 ⅜ |

History: Won a Florida state championship at St. Thomas Aquinas. As a true freshman in 2011, recorded 14 receptions for 147 yards (10.5-yard average) and one touchdowns in 12 games (one start). Started 10-of-12 games in '12, pulling in 58-842-4 (14.5). Started 6-of-8 games played in '13 and managed 13-272-2 (20.9) — suffered a partially torn left MCL against North Carolina, missed five games and was limited in the final two. Healthy in '14, started all 13 games and posted 36-871-10 (24.2). Also returned 25 career kickoffs for 477 yards (19.1-yard average) and 25 punt returns for 136 yards (5.4).Named the Hurricanes' Strength Training Athlete of the Year.

Strengths: Rare acceleration and explosion to run by defenders and stretch the field vertically -- looks like a blur zooming across the field. Tied for the fastest 10-yard split (1.49 seconds) of any player at the Combine and has unique short-area burst. Can turn short gains into big plays. Is elusive with the ball in his hands.

Weaknesses: Runs a very limited route tree. Hands are inconsistent. Is not a crafty route runner and could do a better job escaping the jam. Lacks physicality and shies from contact in a crowd. Does not give consistent effort on the perimeter as a blocker.

Future: One of the fastest players in the draft, Dorsett possesses rare speed to challenge deep and keep defenses honest. Is still relatively unpolished and must learn the nuances of route running to maximize his potential.

Draft projection: Second- to third-round pick.

Scout's take: "He's a pure speed guy. I put him in the third round. He has a chance to go in the second. The only problem I have with him is his overall size and whether he has good enough hands. He is a vertical guy that lacks polish."

WR [F,Z] - TE **DEVIN FUNCHESS**, #1 (Jr-3)
MICHIGAN ▶ GRADE: 5.67

| Ht: 6-4 ¼ | Wt: 232 | 40: 4.63 | Arm: 33 ½ | Hand: 9 ¾ |

History: Michigan native won a state championship at Harrison High. Was considered a tight end his first two seasons in Ann Arbor. Started 5-of-13 games in '12 (wore jersey No. 19), tallying 15 receptions for 234 yards (15.6-yard average) and five touchdowns. Started 9-of-13 games in '13 (wore jersey No. 87), grabbing 49-748-6 (15.3). In '14, moved to wide receiver — started all 11 games played and produced 62-733-4 (11.8). Did not play against Miami (OH) because of a toe injury on his right foot that he suffered in the fourth quarter vs. Notre Dame. Will be a 21-year-old rookie. Opted not to run shuttles at the Combine.

Strengths: Big and strong to press off defensive backs and power through the jam. Exceptional athlete with a 38-inch vertical jump and superb leaping ability to sky for the ball. Looks like a small forward playing basketball on grass making acrobatic, in-air adjustments. Eats ground with long strides. Creates mismatches with unique length and body control – can crack peanuts off the helmets of defensive backs and pluck it out of the air.

Weaknesses: Shaky hands – double-catches and misjudges the ball too often and makes too many concentration drops. Does not compete as a blocker and gives little effort on the backside – takes plays off and does not keep working to uncover. Not a disciplined or focused route runner. Gathers to cut. Hears footsteps and gets alligator-armed at times in the middle of the field – easily distracted. Lacks run strength and creativity after the catch. Inconsistent effort. Clocked a 4.7-second 40-yard-dash electronically at the Combine and does not show top-end speed, burst or acceleration to stretch the field vertically. Disinterested blocker.

Future: A talented athlete who lacks the focus, route savvy, attention to detail and desire to become a consistent receiver. Does not show the toughness or physicality to be a factor in-line as a tight end. Can create some mismatches with his length inside the red area and will likely fit best working the slot in the pros. Will require an attitude adjustment and needs to figure out what it means to really work to maximize his immense physical talent. Has bust potential.

Draft projection: Second-round pick.

Scout's take: "He plays small for a tight end. He does not play big through contact. He goes down pretty easy. He has a different personality. He didn't connect with our coaches (in the interview process). He had a boatload of drops. He has some talent, but I really struggle with what to do with him. He is a tweener."

WR [Z,F] ANTWAN GOODLEY, #5 (Sr-5)

BAYLOR   ▶ GRADE: 5.31

| Ht: 5-10 ¼ | Wt: 209 | 40: 4.46 | Arm: 30 ¾ | Hand: 9 ¼ |

History: Has a son, Antwan III. Also played basketball and ran track as a Texas prep. Redshirted in 2010. Appeared in 11 games in '11 (one start), tallying two receptions for 26 yards (13.0-yard average) and zero touchdowns. Added 19 kickoff returns for 451 yards (23.7-yard average). Started 5-of-13 games in '12, snagging 17-171-2 (10.1) and returning kickoffs 24-542 (22.6). In '13, started all 13 games at outside receiver and produced 71-1,339-13 (18.9). Started all 11 games played at outside receiver in '14, hauling in 60-830-6 (13.8). Hurt his quad during fall camp, then aggravated the injury in the season opener against SMU, costing him two games. Also had 18 career rushes for 130 yards (7.2-yard average) and zero touchdowns. Medically excluded from lifting at the Combine because of a left AC sprain and did not jump or run shuttles because of a right hamstring cramp.

Strengths: Fights through the jam. Good run strength to barrel through arm tackles. Extremely sturdy lower-body – can squat three times his weight. Tracks the ball very effortlessly downfield and catches in stride. Deceptively fast and strong on contact. Very effective short-area receiver – can turn short catches into long gains and can be very effective in the screen game. Durable.

Weaknesses: Has small hands and made too many concentration drops. Played in a simplified, spread offense with a limited playbook where he ran a limited route tree. Production is inflated from spread offense. Takes plays off on the backside and is a lackadaisical blocker.

Future: A receiver trapped in a running back's body, Goodley has intriguing run-after-the-catch ability and long speed, yet could require some time to acclimate to a more complex NFL offense.

Draft projection: Third- to fourth-round pick.

Scout's take: "He's built like (Lions WR) Golden Tate but thicker. He looks more like a running back than a receiver. He can run and track it. He only runs four routes – a stop, hitch, in-cut and nine route – that's it."

WR [X,F] DORIAL GREEN-BECKHAM (Jr-3)

OKLAHOMA   ▶ GRADE: 5.85

| Ht: 6-5 ⅛ | Wt: 237 | 40: 4.47 | Arm: 32 ½ | Hand: 9 |

History: Did not know his biological father. Was adopted by his high school football coach's family in 2009. Was the most highly sought after receiver recruit in the nation as a prep in Missouri — broke the state's single-season receiving yard mark as a sophomore; finished his career as high school football's all-time leading receiver with 6,353 yards and 75 touchdowns; won state titles in the 100-meter dash and triple jump; and won a basketball state title. Two-time All-American and the consensus national player of the year in 2011. As a true freshman in 2012, recorded 28 receptions for 395 yards (14.1-yard average) and five touchdowns in 11 games. Was suspended against Vanderbilt after he was arrested for possession of marijuana (ultimately pleaded guilty to a lesser charge and paid a fine). Started all 14 games at the "X" receiver in '13, producing 59-883-12 (15.0). Sprained his right ankle against Kentucky then sprained his left shoulder against Auburn in the SEC Championship. In January '14, was arrested for alleged possession of a controlled substance with intent to distribute — was riding in a car when a traffic-stop search when one pound of marijuana was found. Ultimately another person took responsibility for the drugs, and Green-Beckham did not face charges. Was dismissed from Missouri in April '14 following a domestic incident — reportedly broke into his girlfriend's home by kicking down the door then pushed a friend of his girlfriend down stairs. Transferred to

WIDE RECEIVERS

Oklahoma, but was denied a waiver to make him eligible to play immediately. Did not play for the Sooners before declaring early for the draft.

Strengths: Has a rare size-speed combination with natural hands and will create mismatches inside or outside, showing the ability to dominate beyond 20 yards and inside the 20-yard-line. Outstanding balance and body control – and can sky for the ball and make grabs well above the rim. Catches the ball very cleanly with terrific hand placement – natural catcher. Can serve as a downfield decoy and open up the short passing game. Caught every ball through the gauntlet with ease at the Combine. Has legitimate play-making ability. Despite off-the-field transgressions, receives high praise from Oklahoma coaches and support staff for his improved maturity and the way that he has conducted himself since arriving on campus.

Weaknesses: Has small hands for as big as he is. Can do a better job using his hands to ward off defensive backs at the line of scrimmage. Does not play strong. Recorded an ordinary short shuttle time (4.46 seconds) at the Combine, and can become more efficient getting in and out of his breaks – rounds out of his breaks. Could clean up his arm action transitioning – telegraphs where he is going and has not yet learned the nuances of route running. Makes some concentration drops. Is immature and can be too much of a follower, having been raised with little structure in his life. Has a history of off-the-field concerns that require closer scrutiny. Should be a more physical blocker for his size.

Future: A high-risk / high-reward prospect with as much receiving talent as any player in the draft, Green-Beckham will require additional seasoning if he ever wants to become great, yet possesses the physical tools to contribute readily and eventually emerge as a No. 1 receiver. Has been removed from a number of draft boards for off-field concerns that could have a negative impact on his draft status, yet has too much upside not to intrigue a patient team with a strong locker room.

Draft projection: Top-50 pick.

Scout's take: "The guy is tough, competitive and catches everything. The NFL wants big receivers. He is a weapon in the red zone. The guy he might be is (Steelers 2000 eighth overall pick) Plaxico Burress. There are a lot of similar traits. DGB is bigger and faster and

a better player. He is a matchup nightmare."

WR [X] - PR RASHAD GREENE, #80 (Sr-4)

FLORIDA STATE ▶ GRADE: 5.46

| Ht: 5-11 ⅝ | Wt: 182 | 40: 4.49 | Arm: 31 ⅝ | Hand: 9 |

History: Won a state championship at Florida's St. Thomas Aquinas, where he teamed with Phillip Dorsett. Also starred in track and field (sprints and jumps). As a true freshman in 2011, caught 38 balls for 596 yards (15.7-yard average) and seven touchdowns, while returning three kickoffs for 65 yards (21.7-yard average) in nine games (three starts). Missed four games because of an injury to his left Achilles. Manned the "X" receiver the next three seasons. Started 13-of-14 games in '12, totaling 57-741-6 (13.0). Started 13-of-14 games for the national champs in '13 when he hauled in 76-1,128-9 (14.8). Was the Seminoles' leading receiver for the fourth straight year in '14 — set FSU single-season catches record by racking up 99-1,365-7 (13.8). For his career, rushed nine times for 81 yards (9.0-yard average) and one touchdown. Team captain owns FSU records for career catches (270) and receiving yards (3,830). Medically excluded from lifting at the Combine because of a left wrist injury.

Strengths: Outstanding hands. Polished route runner with fluid hips to transition quickly out of his breaks and make sharp speed cuts without breaking stride. Extremely productive. Has a feel for coverage and where to fit. Competitive after the catch and shows fine elusiveness to create. Smart, hardworking and accountable. Plays with confidence and carries a swagger.

Weaknesses: Very lean with limited functional strength to beat the jam. Does not have elite foot speed to outrun defenders after the catch. Does not play big inside or run strong after the catch. Limited punt return experience earlier in career and muffed several punts early – one vs. Miami and another against North Carolina State. Limited blocker – gets overwhelmed.

Future: A smart, savvy, clutch, go-to receiver who could continue getting stronger, yet possesses the hands and route savvy to wear out defenses and consistently move the sticks. Could enhance his value by proving he could contribute in the punt return game.

Draft projection: Second- to third-round pick.

Scout's take: "I don't think the quarterback has any confidence in any of the other receivers if Greene is not in the game – that's when you see (Jameis Winston) holding, holding and taking a sack. He is always looking for number 80. I like (Greene's) makeup. ... He would have been great for Rams when they were the greatest show on turf. He reminds me of an Isaac Bruce-type."

WR [X] - KR RANNELL HALL, #6 (Sr-4)
CENTRAL FLORIDA ▶ GRADE: 5.12
Ht: 6-0 ⅜ | Wt: 198 | 40: 4.58 | Arm: 30 ½ | Hand: 8 ⅝

History: Also ran track as a Miami, Fla. prep. As a true freshman in 2011, played all 12 games and scratched together four receptions for 34 yards (8.5-yard average) and zero touchdowns. Played all 14 games in '12 (one start), recording 35-631-4 (18.0). Was the Knights' leading receiver in '13 when he started all 13 games and produced 57-886-5 (15.5). Started 9-of-10 games played in '14, managing 49-500-0 (10.2). Missed the season opener against Penn State (elbow) then hurt his left hamstring and did not play against UCONN or Tulsa. Non-start was against Houston when he served a one-game suspension for a targeting penalty against Bethune-Cookman. For his career, rushed 43 times for 264 yards (6.1-yard average) and two touchdowns, while returning 82 kickoffs for 2,083 yards (25.4).

Strengths: Good separation quickness in his routes coming out of breaks. Flashes some creativity with the ball in his hands to weave in and out of traffic after the catch. Very good weight-room strength and explosion with a strong lower body. Has a 41-inch vertical jump. Good football character. Has a passion for the game and it shows.

Weaknesses: Very small hands. Inconsistent catcher – lets the ball into his body a lot. Lacks physicality releasing off the line and could be hemmed by physical press cornerbacks. Does not play to his weight-room numbers. Average ball skills. Lacks the long speed to separate or pull away in the open-field and gets tracked down from behind. Could stand to be more physical as a blocker. Lacks the finishing speed desired in the return game. Did not handle punts.

Future: More quick than fast, Hall shows enough creativity and elusiveness with the ball in his hands to earn a job in the return game, though must prove he can handle punts. May need to play in the slot where he could see more open releases.

Draft projection: Late draftable pick.

Scout's take: "I am not a big fan. He is not polished. He is a jack of multiple trades, but he doesn't jump out in any special way. I gave a draftable grade, but I don't think I would want him."

WR [Z] JUSTIN HARDY, #2 (Sr-4)
EAST CAROLINA ▶ GRADE: 5.36
Ht: 5-10 ¼ | Wt: 192 | 40: 4.58 | Arm: 32 ⅛ | Hand: 10

History: North Carolina native who played receiver and quarterback as a prep. Also earned two letters as a basketball player and one as a high jumper. Originally signed with Fayetteville State, but was released from his commitment in order to walk on at ECU. Made an immediate impact as a true freshman in 2011 when he started 7-of-10 games played at inside receiver caught 64 balls for 658 yards (10.3-yard average) and six touchdowns. Missed two games because of a hairline fracture in his right knee. Started all 12 games in '12 — eight at inside receiver, four at outside receiver — and hauled in 88-1,105-11 (12.6). Sustained a concussion against Houston. Lost his father to a heart attack in the spring of '13, but started all 13 games in the fall, totaling 114-1,284-8 (11.3). Started all 13 games at IR in '14 and piled up 121-1,494-10 (12.3). For his career, returned 64 punts for 495 yards (7.7-yard average). Set the FBS career receptions record (387) while leading the Pirates in receiving all four years, three of which rank amongst ECU's top five receiving seasons. Team captain earned his degree in sport studies, and was named the Burlsworth Trophy winner as the best FBS player who began his career as a walk-on.

Strengths: Efficient and balanced route runner with good body control. Very strong hands. Has very long arms for his size and a wide catching radius. Produced the fastest 3-cone drill time (6.63 seconds) of any receiver at the Combine. Highly competitive former walk-on and plays with a chip on his shoulder. Scrappy blocker who plays bigger than his size. Unselfish, team leader. Film junkie.

Weaknesses: Lacks strength to escape physical press coverage. Average speed – lacks an explosive top gear and does not create off the stop and challenge down the field. Does not string moves together with the ball in his hands and goes down easy. Durability is a concern – has a history of knee injuries dating back to high school.

Future: A very natural-catching, possession receiver who can carve a niche in the slot on

WIDE RECEIVERS

third downs in the pros. Has the toughness, desire and secure hands to play a long time in the league.

Draft projection: Fourth- to fifth-round pick.

Scout's take: "I think he has the best hands in the draft. In all the games I saw, I only saw one drop and it was behind him. He makes a lot of catches that he shouldn't. He is just speed deficient. I don't know if he could be a No. 2 (receiver), but he could be a great No. 3."

WR [Z] JOSH HARPER, #3 (Sr-5)

FRESNO STATE   ▶ GRADE: 5.27

Ht: 6-0 ⅞ | Wt: 191 | 40: 4.61 | Arm: 30 ⅞ | Hand: 8 ¾

History: Father, Willie, was a linebacker for the 49ers (1973-83), and brother, Matt, is the assistant defensive backs coach for the Eagles. The youngest of nine children, Josh also played basketball as a California prep. Redshirted in 2010. In '11, recorded 35 receptions for 497 yards (14.2-yard average) and five touchdowns in 11 games (three starts). Missed two games because of a sprained ankle. Started 4-of-5 games played in '12 — managed 24-333-4 (13.9) despite missing the season opener (hamstring) and the final seven games (hernia). Started all 11 games played in '13, producing 79-1,011-13 (12.8) before tearing his left groin against San Jose State and undergoing season-ending surgery. Started 13-of-14 games in '14, racking up 90-1,097-7 (12.2). Team captain.

Strengths: Agile and quick with very good body control to make in-air adjustments and stretch for the ball. Can make difficult one-handed snags (see San Jose State) and will lay out and sacrifice his body to make spectacular grabs. Competes for the ball like it belongs to him and wins jumpballs.

Weaknesses: Very thinly built with small hands. Marginal play strength. Tied for the lowest broad jump (8 feet, 9 inches) of any receiver at the Combine and registered a pedestrian 32-inch vertical jump. Production is padded from playing in a spread-heavy passing game. Limited blocking strength and efficiency. Has had some durability issues.

Future: A lithe, graceful outside receiver in a similar mold as San Francisco 49ers 2003 fourth-round pick Brandon Lloyd, Harper has a bionic way of catching the ball and pedigree that could allow him to hold a job a long time as a complimentary, possession receiver.

Draft projection: Fourth- to fifth-round pick.

Scout's take: "He didn't have a great year (in 2014). He was hot (in 2013) with (David) Carr throwing and (Davante) Adams carrying most of the load as the primary receiver but struggled this year when he had to be the guy."

WR [F] - RS CHRIS JONES, #22 (Sr-4)

ALABAMA   ▶ GRADE: 5.05

Ht: 5-10 ⅛ | Wt: 182 | 40: 4.64 | Arm: 30 | Hand: 9

History: Alabama native. As a true freshman in 2011, played 12 games — caught three balls for 49 yards (16.3-yard average) and zero touchdowns, returned three punts for 33 yards (11.0-yard average) and returned one kickoff for 32 yards (32.0-yard average). Did not play against Auburn. In '12, started 10-of-14 games at the "H" position, producing 27-368-4 (13.6) receiving, 21-213 (10.1) on punt returns and 8-213 (26.6), including a 99-yard score against Ole Miss. Was the Southeastern Conference Special Teams Player of the Year (coaches) in '13 — started 7-of-13 at slot receiver, catching 36-349-2 (9.7), returning punts 23-321-2 (14.0) and returning kickoffs 22-631 (28.7), including a 94-yard score against Virginia Tech. Started 8-of-14 games at the "H" in '14 when he totaled 19-264-1 (13.9) receiving, 19-152-0 (8.0) on punt returns and 37-851-0 (23.0) on kickoff returns. Suffered a bruised ankle against Florida Atlantic. Also notched 20 career tackles on special teams. Graduated.

Strengths: Good short-area quickness, agility, balance and burst. Shifty and competitive with the ball in his hands. Good vision to find open lanes and contact balance to keep his feet through traffic. Makes good decisions fielding the ball.

Weaknesses: Has small hands. Tied for the slowest 10-yard split (1.75 seconds) and ran the registered the slowest 40-yard dash (4.76 seconds) of any receiver at the Combine. Only bench-pressed 8 reps. Marginal route runner – struggles to separate. Limited blocker. Average career receiving production.

Future: Quicker-than-fast, competitive return specialist with enough vision, burst and balance to compete for a job. Offers limited value as a slot receiver and is not special in the return game.

Draft projection: Priority free agent.

WR [Z] DEZ LEWIS, #5 (Sr-4)

CENTRAL ARKANSAS   ▶ GRADE: 5.23

Ht: 6-3 ¾ | Wt: 214 | 40: 4.57 | Arm: 32 ½ | Hand: 9 ⅞

History: Also played basketball as a Texas prep. Did not receive a Division I scholarship offer. As a true freshman in 2011, played 13 games (two starts) and caught 27 balls for 386 yards (14.3-yard average) and two touchdowns. Started all 12 games in '12, grabbing 61-797-7 (13.1). In '13, started 10-of-11 games played and snagged 50-721-7 (14.4). Did not play against Nebraska Kearney after spraining his left ankle against McNeese State. Wore jersey No. 89 in the season finale against Sam Houston State in honor of a teammate who was lost to injury. Started all 12 games at the "X" receiver in '14, totaling 64-945-9 (14.8). Wore jersey No. 85 prior to his junior season.

Strengths: Outstanding body length. Good strength to fend off press coverage. Will go up for the ball and create mismatches with his size. Shows some run skill on slip screens. Leader by example. Solid Senior Bowl showing.

Weaknesses: Long strider who builds to speed. Is not quick off the line. Only shows one gear. Has some lower-body tightness. Struggles sinking his hips, getting in and out of breaks and creating separation. Ran a limited route tree and rounds out of breaks. Average run strength after the catch. Does not play to his size on the perimeter as a blocker. Did not face top competition.

Future: Long-limbed, small-school, go-to receiver who climbs the glass like a basketball player in the red zone and must prove that he is more than a big fish in a small pond.

Draft projection: Late draftable pick.

WR [X] - RCB TONY LIPPETT, #14 (Sr-6)

MICHIGAN STATE   ▶ GRADE: 5.34

| Ht: 6-2 ½ | Wt: 192 | 40: 4.61 | Arm: 32 ¾ | Hand: 9 ⅞ |

History: Quarterback-defensive back also ran track as a Detroit prep. Redshirted in 2010. Played cornerback in '11 — recorded 18 tackles, five pass breakups and zero interceptions with one-half tackle for loss in 14 games, though he also saw limited time as a receiver and scratched together four receptions for 44 yards (11.0-yard average) and zero touchdowns. Back at receiver in '13, caught 36-392-2 (10.9) in 13 games (five starts at split end). Started 10-of-14 games at split end in '13, grabbing 44-613-2 (13.9). Also tossed a five-yard touchdown pass. Missed time during '14 spring practice because of a right ankle injury. In the fall, was the Big Ten Receiver of the Year and team MVP after starting all 13 games at split end and hauling in 65-1,198-11

(18.4). In his career, rushed six times for 51 yards (8.5-yard average) and one touchdown. Started at WR and CB against Penn State and Baylor, becoming the first Spartan two-way starter since 1968.

Strengths: Very good length. Runs a precise route with the savvy to separate out of his breaks. Has long arms and good body control to pluck the ball outside his frame. Functional stalk blocker – walls off and gets in the way. Effective on reverses and is elusive in the open field. Offers position versatility – played receiver and cornerback. Energetic personality. Responds well to coaching.

Weaknesses: Very lean, especially in the lower body with thin calves. Leggy, long strider. Not explosive off the line or sudden out of his breaks. Runs a limited route tree. Lacks physical strength and toughness. Not a strong tackle-breaker.

Future: Very lean, long-limbed, finesse outside receiver with enough route savvy and separation quickness to be effective outside the numbers as a No. 3 or No. 4 receiver. Offers intriguing developmental potential as a press cover man.

Draft projection: Third- to fourth-round pick.

Scout's take: "He reminds me of Harry Douglas a little bit. (Lippett) needs to get stronger. He is a good athlete. He plays faster than he ran at the Combine. He is a good value guy in the mid-round area. … He might have a chance as a cornerback. The last three games he played it. He is a man cover guy."

WR [F] - RS TYLER LOCKETT, #16 (Sr-4)

KANSAS STATE   ▶ GRADE: 5.52

| Ht: 5-9 ⅞ | Wt: 182 | 40: 4.34 | Arm: 30 | Hand: 8 3/8 |

History: Father, Kevin, is KSU's all-time leading receiver, and uncle, Aaron, is fifth all-time. Tyler won a state title as an Oklahoma prep. Was the Big 12 Offensive Freshman of the Year in 2011 when he started 6-of-9 games played and snagged 18 receptions for 246 yards (13.7-yard average) and three touchdowns. Missed four games because of a lacerated kidney. Started 11-of-13 games played in '12, catching 44-687-4 (15.6). Led the Big 12 in receiving yards per game (105.2) and all-purpose yards (1,859) in '13 — started all 12 games played and amassed 81-1,262-11 (15.6). Set a KSU single-game record with 440 all-purpose yards against Texas, and was named Offensive MVP of the Buffalo Wild Wing's

Bowl against Michigan. Sat out against Baylor while nursing a left hamstring strain. Was the Big 12 Special Teams Player of the Year for the second straight year in '14 when he led the nation in punt-return average (19.0), and paced the Big 12 in receiving yards per game (112.6) and all-purpose yards (2,047) again, racking up 106-1,515-11 (14.3) in 13 starts. Was recognized as the Big 12 Scholar Athlete of the Year. In his career, rushed 22 times for 192 yards (8.7-yard average) and zero touchdowns. Was also one of the nation's best return men, finishing his career with 77-2,196-4 (28.5) on kickoffs and 32-488-2 (15.2) on punts. Two-time team captain set 17 KSU records, including career receptions (249), receiving yards (3,710), receiving touchdowns (29) and 100-yard receiving games (17). Graduated with a business management degree. Did not lift at the Combine because of a left shoulder strain suffered at the Senior Bowl.

Strengths: Extremely productive. Tied for the fastest 20-yard split (2.45 seconds) and produced the event's fastest 60-yard shuttle (11.14 seconds) of any receiver at the Combine. Has rare burst and acceleration. Dominated the second half of the Alamo Bowl vs. UCLA, when he grabbed 10-116-2 and nearly sparked a come-from behind victory. Terrific game-day competitor. Exceptional return specialist with home-run, finishing speed. Excels as a gunner on special teams. Leads by example and became a respected, vocal team leader. Willing, scrappy blocker for his size. Experienced, three-and-a-half-year starter. Battles through injuries. Coaches described him as being "wired right" at the Senior Bowl.

Weaknesses: Had the shortest wingspan (70 3/4 inches) of any receiver at the Combine and offers a small catching radius. Played at 175 pounds in college and does not have a frame to withstand the rigors of the NFL. Runs a very limited route tree and struggles some shaking man off coverage out of the slot given his lack of stature. Can be re-routed easily by bigger cornerbacks.

Future: A dynamic, diminutive slot receiver with true blazing speed. Is explosive long and short and as capable of creating plays in short areas as he is taking the top off a defense. Lack of size will create greater difficulties at the pro level and could challenge him to stay healthy. Has created a buzz in the scouting community, yet similar to Rams eighth overall pick Tavon

Austin, could struggle living up to lofty draft expectations if drafted too early.

Draft projection: Third- to fourth-round pick.

Scout's take: "The receiver who is climbing is Lockett. The area (scouts) are all saying second (round) and it's trickling up. I just talked to (a GM) who loves him. He's so small – it's more risk than I would like to take. I do like the player a lot at the right price. We couldn't think about him before the (middle of the) third (round). You'd like to get him in the fourth."

WR [F] DEON LONG, #6 (Sr-6)

MARYLAND   ▶ GRADE: 5.09

| Ht: 5-11 ⅝ | Wt: 192 | 40: 4.48 | Arm: 31 | Hand: 9 ½ |

History: Has a son, Deon Jr. Prepped at Dunbar High in Washington D.C. Graduated in 2009, but failed to qualify academically and spent a semester at Hargrave Military Academy (Va.). Moved on to West Virginia, but left in April '10 because he wasn't happy with the school or his role in the offense. Transferred to New Mexico, where his high school coach was hired to coach the receivers by then-head coach Mike Locksley, a D.C. native. Sat out the '10 season per NCAA transfer rules. Was the Lobos' leading receiver in '11 — wore jersey No. 20 and caught 47 balls for 809 yards (17.2-yard average) and four touchdowns. Added 18 kickoff returns for 425 yards (23.6-yard average) and a score. Missed two games because of turf toe. Did not want to play for a new coaching staff the following year, so transferred to Iowa Western Community College — won the '12 NJCAA National Championship and earned All-American honors after posting 100-1,625-25 (16.3) in 12 games. Chose Maryland (where Locksley is now offensive coordinator) over offers from Florida and Nebraska. Was suspended for two weeks in the spring of '13 for a violation of university policy. In the fall, managed 32-489-1 (15.3) in seven games (six starts) before suffering a season-ending broken right tibia and fibula. Recovered to start all 13 games in '14 when he totaled 51-575-2 (11.3). Will be a 24-year-old rookie. Did not run the 60-yard shuttle because of a left hamstring strain.

Strengths: Good enough speed to create some separation down the field. Is athletic with good body control. Catches on contact. Aggressive attacking upfield after the catch.

Tracks the ball well downfield. Solid showing during the East-West Shrine week.

Weaknesses: Average size. Tight in the hips. Lacks weight-room strength. Struggles some beating press coverage. Is not a precise or disciplined route runner and needs to learn to appreciate more of the finer points of the game. Has been troubled by character and work ethic issues throughout his career and has played for five schools in six seasons. Could stand to improve as a blocker.

Future: A well-travelled, competitive receiver who began to show more maturity in his final year of college. Must prove that he can adopt a professional work ethic and approach to the game for a team willing to take a chance on developing him. Could have to prove capable of contributing on special teams to make it. Proving he could contribute in the return game would enhance his draft value.

Draft projection: Priority free agent.

Scout's take: "I know a lot of (scouts) are turned off by his instability. He showed enough at the East-West Shrine game that someone could take a chance on him late."

WR [Z]/RB/KR DONATELLA "TELLO" LUCKETT, #6 (Sr-5)
HARDING ► GRADE: 5.07

| Ht: 5-11 ¾ | Wt: 211 | 40: 4.57 | Arm: 31 | Hand: 9 ¼ |

History: Has eight siblings. Prepped in Mississippi, where he carried 204 times for 1,888 yards (9.3-yard average) and 30 touchdowns as a senior. Redshirted in 2010. Playing fullback in a triple-option offense, played all 11 games in '11 (one start) and carried 51-333-1 (6.5). Also returned eight kickoffs for 305 yards (38.1-yard average) and two scores. Moved to receiver in '12 when he caught 28 balls for 453 yards (16.2-yard average) and seven touchdowns in 11 games (10 starts). Added 9-122-2 (13.6) rushing and 10-155-0 (15.5) on kickoff returns. Started all 11 games in '13 — grabbed 28-570-3 (20.4), rushed 11-99-0 (9.0) and returned kickoffs 17-437 (25.7). Started all 10 games played in '14, totaling 23-602-5 (26.2) receiving, 7-25-2 (3.6) rushing and 3-35 (11.7) on kickoff returns. Did not play against East Central (ankle). His 22 career touchdowns averaged nearly 50 yards each. Team captain. Garnered a Senior Bowl invite. Also ran track at Harding. Will be a 24-year-old rookie.

Strengths: Well-muscled and physically strong. Looks every bit the part. Competes hard. Good open-field run skill – vision, wiggle and run strength to finish. Extremely physical

blocker and stands out like a man among boys delivering some violent crackback blocks. Very durable. Had a solid showing in one-on-one drills at the Combine vs. better defensive backs.

Weaknesses: Registered the slowest 3-cone drill time (7.53 seconds) of any receiver at the Combine and the second slowest short shuttle time (4.54 seconds) among receivers at the Combine. Body stiffness shows up in his routes. Lacks field awareness and is still learning how to use his hands to avoid press coverage. Football IQ will require a learning curve.

Future: Physical Division II standout who played in a run-first, triple-option offense in college and stood out most for his dominant blocking style and functional strength. A converted running back with natural run skill, Luckett could warrant some interest in the return game and has a chance to be groomed as a No. 4 or No. 5 receiver. Will fit most naturally as a "Z" or jumbo slot receiver in a West Coast offense and will add the most immediate value to a roster as a core special teams contributor.

Draft projection: Priority free agent.

WR [Z] VINCE MAYLE, #1 (Sr-6)
WASHINGTON STATE ► GRADE: 5.29

| Ht: 6-2 | Wt: 224 | 40: 4.66 | Arm: 31 ¾ | Hand: 9 |

History: Played running back (in a Wing-T offense) and linebacker as a California prep. Began his college athletic career playing basketball at Shasta Community College (Calif.) in 2009-10. Took the following year off to care for his ailing mother. Moved on to Sierra College (Calif.) in '11, but did not have enough credits to play immediately. Returned to football in '12 and earned All-American honors after recording 61 receptions for 984 yards (16.1-yard average) and 16 touchdowns. Transferred to Washington State in '13 — appeared in all 13 games, producing 42-539-7 (12.8). In '14, tied for the Pac-12 lead and set a WSU single-season record for catches, while pacing the conference and setting a school single-season receiving yards record — started all 12 games at "X" receiver and racked up 106-1,483-9 (14.0). Also returned nine kickoffs for 177 yards (19.7-yard average). Medically excluded from lifting with a right thumb injury and did not run the 60-yard shuttle because of a right hamstring cramp.

Strengths: Outstanding size. Powers off the line to beat the jam. Uses his body to shield defensive backs and is tough in a crowd. Good functional strength to make plays on the ball and run through contact after the catch. Willing blocker. Has a passion for the game and a lot of upside to develop.

Weaknesses: Has small hands. Average long speed. Tied for the slowest 10-yard split (1.75 seconds) of any receiver at the Combine. Only played on the left side in college. Marginal field awareness. Is still learning how to run routes – drifts and gives away too many indicators. Does not run a full route tree. Not sudden or quick off the line of scrimmage. Gauntlet performance at the Combine is characteristic of his play – looked very unpolished, running through at a slow, measured pace, dropping two and double-catching another, and then showed improvement the second time through.

Future: A big, athletic, developmental "Z" receiver who still has a long way to go before he is ready for prime time. Yet possesses the size, length, muscularity and upside to intrigue teams. Marginal Combine performance detracted from draft value, yet similar to Broncos 2006 fourth-round pick Brandon Marshall, could turn out to be a very productive pro in a West Coast offense that allows him to maximize his strengths. Has a high ceiling if the light comes on.

Draft projection: Fourth- to fifth-round pick.

Scout's take: "He's a former basketball player and second-year starter. Based on what I saw in the fall, I would like to take him and develop him. He is a very interesting player. He is big and physical and athletic. He is still learning, but the arrow is pointing up. He is a talented dude. You might have something special in a few years."

WR [X] - RS DOUGLAS "TRE" McBRIDE, #3 (Sr-4)

WILLIAM & MARY ▶ GRADE: 5.47

Ht: 6-0 ¼ | Wt: 210 | 40: 4.41 | Arm: 32 ⅛ | Hand: 9

History: Also lettered in basketball and track as a Georgia prep. In 2011, was the first W&M true freshman receiver to play since 2005 — appeared in all 11 games and recorded 14 receptions for 146 yards (10.4-yard average) and zero touchdowns. Started all 11 games in '12, producing 55-897-10 (16.3) receiving, while returning nine kickoffs for 171 yards (19.0-yard average). Was the Colonial Athletic Association Special Teams Player of the Year in '13 when he started 11-of-12 games and totaled 63-801-5 (12.7) receiving with 22-605 (27.5) on kickoff returns and

3-59 (19.7) on punt returns. Was the Tribe's leading receiver and all-purpose gainer for the third straight year in '14 when he started all 11 games played and piled up 64-809-4 (12.6) receiving, 25-518 (20.7) returning kickoffs and 8-63 (7.9) returning punts. Set single-season school record with 359 all-purpose yards against Villanova. Did not play against Hampton (ankle). In his career, rushed 28 times for 212 yards (7.6-yard average) and zero touchdowns.

Strengths: Looks the part with long arms and a trim frame. Outstanding body control to make deft in-air adjustments and pluck the ball out of the air over his head. Gets into and out of breaks very quickly, making sharp cuts. Tied for the fastest 10-yard split (1.49 seconds) of any player at the Combine. Has the burst to separate. Has a smooth, fluid stride and appears to be gliding downfield. Effective on screens and reverses and can create with the ball in his hands. Stood out at the East-West Shrine practices for ability to separate and make plays on the ball. Has a 38-inch vertical jump. Sets high standards for himself and will work at his craft. The game is important to him. Has the top-end speed to play big in the return game.

Weaknesses: Has small hands. Tight in the hips. Still very raw and lacks ideal functional football-playing speed. Has not yet learned the nuances of route running. Was talking to himself through Combine testing and will require positive reinforcement at times to avoid falling in the tank. Average blocker.

Future: A very well-built, well-proportioned, athletic small-school receiver in a similar mold as Texas 2006 third-round pick Jacoby Jones. Stock ascended with strong post-season performances vs. better competition and has the speed and receiving talent to emerge as a legitimate vertical threat.

Draft projection: Third- to fourth-round pick.

Scout's take: "If you want him, you probably have to get him in the third (round). He is raw but very talented."

WR [Z] - RB - RS TY MONTGOMERY, #7 (Sr-4)

STANFORD ▶ GRADE: 5.38

Ht: 5-11 ⅞ | Wt: 221 | 40: 4.53 | Arm: 31 | Hand: 10 ⅛

History: Full name is Ty Anthony Montgomery II. Also played baseball and lacrosse as a Texas prep. As a true freshman in 2011 (wore jersey No. 88), played all 13 games (started final four) and recorded 24 receptions for 350 yards (14.6-yard average) and two touchdowns. Added 27 kickoff returns for 680 yards (25.2-yard average), including a 96-yard score against Washington State. Played 11 games in '12, starting four, and managed 26-213-0 (8.2) receiving with 10-258 (25.8) on kickoff returns. Was bothered most of the season by a partially torn PCL which sidelined him for three games. Started 12-of-14 games in '13 (gave way to extra tight ends in non-starts), catching 61-958-10 (15.7). Ranked second nationally in kickoff returns with 36-1,091-2 (30.3). Hurt his left knee in the Rose Bowl. Had right shoulder surgery in the spring of '14. In the fall, started 6-of-11 games played and logged 61-604-3 (9.9) receiving with 17-429-0 (25.2) on kickoff returns and 13-238-2 (18.3) on punt returns. Hurt his right shoulder against Cal and missed the final two games. In his career, rushed 39 times for 334 yards (8.6-yard average) and four touchdowns. Did not lift at the Combine because of a left A/C (shoulder) sprain.

Strengths: Well built with a very strong lower body and good overall musculature. Has big strong hands. Powers through press coverage and is swift out of his breaks. Outstanding gear change – accelerates and separates out of double moves. Very versatile and lined up all over the field – at all three WR positions (X, Z, F), as a kick returner, running back and wildcat QB. Good run strength and toughness. Has a 40 1/2-inch vertical jump. Explosive returner – can power thru arm tackles, open up his stride and finish. Very good all-purpose production. Hard-working, coachable and football is important to him.

Weaknesses: Very inconsistent hands. Does not have a good feel for zone coverage. Stiff, segmented route runner – too rigid and mechanical in his movement. Often has to be schemed open. Could stand to improve blocking effort – does not play to his size. Lets the ball get on top of him, as it did running through the gauntlet drill at the Combine, and lacks confidence in his hands. Has been very injury-prone, and durability is a concern.

Future: A jack-of-all-trades, master of none. Is most consistently impactful in the return game and creating plays out of the backfield and might be ripe for a RB conversion given his run strength and toughness with the ball in his hands and inconsistent hands.

Draft projection: Third- to four-round pick.

Scout's take: "He is a slash player – part running back and part receiver. He is not a no. 1, 2 or 3 receiver. He is just one of those gadget guys. He handles kickoff and punt returns and has size. He is always struggling to catch it – that's his greatest knock. He has a lot of drops. … The no. 1 trait you need to have as a receiver is the ability to catch the ball, and he doesn't do it consistently. I think that's why they put him in the backfield and hand it to him. He has thick legs – he looks like a running back."

WR [Z] KEITH MUMPHERY, #25 (Sr-5)
MICHIGAN STATE   ▶ GRADE: 4.88
Ht: 5-11 ⅝ | Wt: 215 | 40: 4.54 | Arm: 31 ⅛ | Hand: 9 ⅛

History: Also ran track as Georgia prep — was a member of the 4x100 meter relay team that broke the state record (41.9). Redshirted in 2010 and was named Scout Team Player of the Year. Appeared in all 14 games in '11, grabbing two catches for 39 yards (19.5-yard average) and zero touchdowns. Was the Spartans' leading receiver in '12 when he started 12-of-13 games at flanker, producing 42-515-1 (12.3). Played all 14 games in '13, starting three of the first four at the "Z" receiver, and totaled 18-299-3 (16.6). Started 11-of-13 games at "Z" in '14, snagging 26-495-3 (19.0). Gave way to extra tight end in non-starts. Had 14 career rushes for 125 yards (8.9-yard average) and one touchdown. Graduated with a communications degree.

Strengths: Has a thick build with very good strength. Good field and sideline awareness. Will keep working to uncover and come back to the ball. Good run strength after the catch. Functional blocker in the run game. Sterling intangibles. Charismatic, vocal leader with the mental toughness and work ethic to command the respect of teammates in the locker room.

Weaknesses: Is slow off the line and builds to speed. Average separation quickness and route savvy. Rounds cuts and drifts in his routes. Creates little after the catch. Cradle catcher. Not a blazer. Very nondescript career production given his number of starts. No return experience.

Future: A strong, short-area, possession receiver who brings the most value as a tempo-setting competitor in the WR room. Has a special team's personality to fend for a roster spot.

Draft projection: Priority free agent.

WR [X,F] - RS JAMARCUS "J.J." NELSON, #1 (Sr-5)
ALABAMA-BIRMINGHAM   ▶ GRADE: 5.10
Ht: 5-10 ¼ | Wt: 156 | 40: 4.24 | Arm: 31 ⅛ | Hand: 8 ¼

History: Prepped in Alabama, where also starred in basketball and track — 4A state champ in the 100 meters (twice, 10.49) and

200 meters (21.76). Redshirted in 2010. At "X" receiver in '11, played all 12 games and notched 17 catches for 358 yards (21.1-yard average) and four touchdowns. Added 24 kickoff returns for 422 yards (17.6-yard average) and zero touchdowns. In '12, grabbed 22-414-4 (18.8) and returned kickoffs 3-53-0 (17.7) in 10 games (four starts at the "Z" receiver). Hurt his right groin against East Carolina and missed two games. Started 7-of-10 games at "Z" in '13 — caught 42-846-8 (20.1), returned kickoffs 27-614-1 (22.7) and returned punts 8-88-1 (11.0). Sat out against Florida Atlantic and Florida International while nursing a high left ankle sprain sustained against Vanderbilt. Started 11-of-12 games at "X" and hauled in 39-399-3 (10.2) in '14 when he was Conference USA's Special Teams Player of the year — returned kickoffs 22-843 (38.3), including four scores (Western Kentucky, Arkansas, Louisiana Tech and Southern Miss), and returned punts 26-277 (10.7). Became the first Blazer to receive All-American honors since Roddy White in 2004, though as a returner. Had 18 career rushes for 90 yards (5.0-yard average) and one touchdown. Has played in three different offenses since his arrival. Graduated. Opted not to lift at the Combine.

Strengths: Explosively fast with rare acceleration and burst to threaten the seam. Tied for the fastest 10-yard split (1.49 seconds) of any player at the Combine and posted the event's best 40-yard dash (4.21 seconds). Very nifty with the ball in his hands and can stick his foot in the ground and fly when a lane develops. Surprisingly willing blocker (given his slight frame).

Weaknesses: Lacks strength. Gets knocked off routes easily. Was the lightest player weighed at the Combine and tied for the smallest hands (8 1/4 inches) of any receiver. Limited run strength and tackle-breaking ability. Durability could always be an issue given his narrow build and lack of bulk.

Future: A pure, outside-the-numbers, vertical receiver with rare burst and breakaway speed to factor in the return game if he could add some bulk and get stronger. Lacks the stature to withstand the physicality of the NFL game.

Draft projection: Priority free agent.

Scout's take: "I had (graded) him in the sixth round for his speed and return ability. After watching him struggle to field punt returns at his pro day, I think he'll be a priority free agent.

I thought the only way he would make it is as a punt returner and he was not natural catching the ball. A few bounced off his chest and it was just how he was setting up and catching. He could be the latest in a line of the fastest guys at the Combine who did not make it."

WR [X,Z] DEVANTE PARKER, #9 (Sr-4)

LOUISVILLE ▶ GRADE: 6.27

Ht: 6-2 ⅝ | Wt: 209 | 40: 4.42 | Arm: 33 ¼ | Hand: 9 ¼

History: Father, Anthony Shelman, played running back at Louisville. Devante also played basketball and ran track as a Kentucky prep. Piled up 68 catches for 1,793 yards (26.4-yard average) and 19 touchdowns as a senior. As a true freshman in 2011, played 11 games (four starts) and tallied 18-291-6 (16.2). Did not play against North Carolina and Cincinnati. Played all 13 games in '12, starting three, and caught 40-744-10 (18.6). Was the Cardinals' leading receiver in '13 when he started all 12 games played and posted 55-885-12 (16.1). Did not play against Rutgers (right shoulder), and sustained a high right ankle sprain against Miami in the Russell Athletic Bowl. Suffered a broken fifth metatarsal in his left foot (required surgery) late in '14 fall camp — missed the first seven games before starting 4-of-6 games played and managing 43-855-5 (19.9). Graduated with a communications degree. Did not perform shuttles at the Combine because of left foot injury.

Strengths: Exceptional hands. Outstanding body control to adjust to the ball and make in-air adjustments and acrobatic, over-the-shoulder catches. Smooth strider with supple hips and fluid movement skill. Is able to create last-second separation and make contested catches look easy. Deceptively fast to gain a step on defensive backs. Sets up cornerbacks and is quick out of his breaks. Superb hand-eye coordination. Wins jump-ball situations. Very good leaping ability. Confident and carries a swagger – wants the ball in the clutch. Has big-play potential.

Weaknesses: Has a modest build with little muscle definition. Could struggle avoiding press coverage in the pros and needs to develop more moves at the line. Does not run crisp routes with multiple, quick cuts. Average run strength after the catch – powers through few tackles and lacks physicality in his game. Takes plays off on the backside and appears disinterested and content to coast as a blocker. Scouts have questioned his maturity. Has never had more than 55 catches in a season or

Devante Parker

the type of superstar production typically seen in early draft picks.

Future: A lithe, silky smooth, speedy playmaker. Emerged as the go-to receiver for Teddy Bridgewater in 2013 and when healthy, assumed the role again as a senior, though he did not appear fully recovered. Has the combination of length, balance, body control, elevation and top-end speed to become a No. 1 receiver in the pros, though durability could remain an issue given his thin frame. Best trait is his ability to pluck the ball downfield and create big plays. Durability concerns require closer scrutiny.

Draft projection: First-round pick.

Scout's take: "He is kind of a prima donna. Maturity could be an issue. We interviewed him, and I tracked him last year when there was word he was going to come out. He doesn't understand coverages very well or understand offensive concepts. He doesn't play that fast. You watch him against man coverage and he is really not separating the way you would think an explosive receiver would separate."

WR [Z] BRESHAD PERRIMAN, #11 (Jr-3)

CENTRAL FLORIDA ▶ GRADE: 5.57

Ht: 6-2 | Wt: 212 | 40: 4.55e | Arm: 32 | Hand: 9 ¼

History: Father, Brett, was a 10-year NFL receiver (1988-97), most notably with the Lions and Saints. Breshad also ran track as a prep in the Atlanta area, where attended three different high schools. Suffered a broken femur during his junior season of high school. As a true freshman in 2012, played all 14 games (four starts) and caught 26 balls for 388 yards (14.9-yard average) and three touchdowns. Started 10-of-12 games played in '13, snagging 39-

811-4 (20.8). Sustained a concussion against Houston and did not play against Temple. In '14, started 10-of-13 games and totaled 50-1,044-9 (20.9). Medically excluded from working out at the Combine because of a right hamstring injury and opted not to lift.

Strengths: Very good size and body length. Extends outside his frame and can make some very acrobatic, highlight-reel catches. Eats up ground with long strides and can create several steps of separation on vertical routes. Tracks the ball well over his shoulder and climbs the ladder to pluck it outside his frame. Outstanding hand-eye coordination. Good run-after-the-catch strength. Can be a red-zone weapon. Functional perimeter blocker. Has NFL pedigree and the game is not too big for him.

Weaknesses: Is too easily hemmed by press coverage and needs to work on his release vs. the jam. Is not a polished or sophisticated route runner and does not run a full route tree. Lacks suddenness changing direction. Makes too many concentration drops. Lets the ball get on top of him.

Future: A big-play weapon capable of making an inaccurate quarterback look good. Offers a catching radius that needs its own zip code and makes spectacular grabs that could produce a very impressive highlight film. However, his lack of consistency as a catcher is concerning, and he must show improved focus to win the trust of quarterbacks.

Draft projection: Second- to third-round pick.

Scout's take: "(Perriman) has some size and speed, but he doesn't play fast. He is a build-up speed guy. He is not real good coming out of his breaks because he is tight in the hammies and a thicker built guy. He will makes some wow catches and also drops the ball sometimes. It's a mixed body of work. … If someone is talking about drafting him in the first (round), they are shopping hungry. When you watch him live, you wonder if he can run."

WR [Z,F] EZELL RUFFIN, #3 (Sr-5)

SAN DIEGO STATE ▶ GRADE: 4.82

Ht: 5-11 ⅝ | Wt: 218 | 40: 4.68 | Arm: 31 ⅛ | Hand: 8 ¾

History: First name is pronounced "ee-ZELL." Also competed in track as a California prep. Redshirted in 2010 after sustaining a concussion during fall camp. Was academically ineligible in '11. Played 12 games in '12, starting four, and caught 17 balls for 319 yards (18.8-yard average) and zero touchdowns. Played with a broken left hand in September then sprained his left AC

joint against Hawaii and did not play against Colorado State. Started 12-of-13 games at the "Z" receiver in '13, producing 68-1,136-3 (16.7). In '14, started 6-of-7 games played at the "Z," managing 26-422-2 (16.2). Suffered a broken collarbone against North Carolina and missed five games. Team captain.

Strengths: Very good size and thickness – built like a running back. Flashes some power after the catch. Sacrifices his body to make difficult grabs. Offers some physicality in the run game blocking on the perimeter.

Weaknesses: Stiff and unsudden. Is heavy out of the blocks and slow getting into his routes. Shows little polish or refinement as route runner. Body-catcher. Poor production after the catch – most catches are contested and is often tackled on contact. Recorded the lowest vertical jump (27 1/2 inches), tied for the lowest broad jump (8 feet, 9 inches) and produced the slowest short shuttle (4.59 seconds) and 60-yard shuttle (12.65 seconds) of any receiver at the Combine. Measured 16.6 percent body fat at the Combine, very high for a receiver. Injury-prone.

Future: A compact, thickly built possession receiver lacking the requisite speed and explosion for the pro game. Limitations showed heavily at the Combine.

Draft projection: Priority free agent.

WR [Z] DEANDRE SMELTER, #15 (Sr-5)

GEORGIA TECH ▶ GRADE: 5.39

Ht: 6-2 ⅛ | Wt: 226 | 40: 4.55e | Arm: 32 ⅝ | Hand: 11

History: Multi-sport standout as a Georgia prep — in addition to playing quarterback, running back, receiver and safety, also played basketball and was drafted by the Minnesota Twins in the 14th round of the 2010 MLB draft. Was a key member of the Georgia Tech baseball team (pitcher-outfielder) from 2011-13, but labrum damage forced him off the diamond and back to the gridiron. Started 8-of-13 in '13 and recorded 21 receptions for 345 yards (16.4-yard average) and four touchdowns. Added 11 punt returns for 124 yards (11.3-yard average) and five kickoff returns for 65 yards (13.0). Started all 12 games played in '14 — totaled 35-715-7 (20.4) before suffering a torn left ACL against Georgia. Also had four career rushes for 115 yards (28.8-yard average) and one touchdown. Medically excluded from the Combine because of knee injury.

Strengths: Exceptional size and body length with very good muscle definition and strong legs. Tied for the biggest hands (11 inches) of any player at the Combine and shows very strong hands to take the ball out of the air. Very good hand-eye coordination to track the ball in the air and haul it in over his shoulder. Powers his way off the line of scrimmage. Runs with urgency with the ball in his hands. Fights for yardage after the catch and will barrel through defensive backs. Works hard and does extras – spends time on the jugs machine. Prideful, physical blocker and uses his frame well to wall off defenders. Very focused with solid personal and football character. Could have more upside than most players given hw little football he has played as a result of his baseball background.

Weaknesses: Is still learning how to beat the jam and will need to be trained how to read coverages and make sight adjustments. Ran a limited route tree. Gathers to cut. Lets the ball get into his body. Lacks elite top-end speed. Only played two years of college football, and baseball remains as a potential distraction. Durability must be evaluated closely.

Future: A strong, physical, possession receiver hailing from a program that has produced a number of No. 1 receivers in recent years. Smelter has the toughness and physicality ideally sought in a West Coast flanker and could prove to be a great value pick for a team with the luxury to wait on his return.

Draft projection: Fourth- to fifth-round pick.

Scout's take: "He is hurt. He may never work out (before the draft). No one will know how well he can run. He plays in a (triple-option) offense, not a natural route-running pass offense, and because of it, he didn't catch 70 balls. And they weren't wow catches. He is a talented player, but I think he will slip some because of the unkowns."

WR [X] - RS **DEVIN SMITH** #9 (Sr-4)

OHIO STATE ▶ GRADE: 5.64

Ht: 6-0 ⅜	Wt: 196	40: 4.38	Arm: 31	Hand: 9

History: Ohio native who won the state long jump championship and qualified in the high jump and 4x200 relay. As a true freshman in 2011, played all 13 games and caught 14 balls for 294 yards (21.0-yard average) and four touchdowns. Started 10-of-12 games at flanker in '12, snagging 30-618-6 (20.6). Started 12-of-14 games in '13, catching 44-660-8 (15.0). Sustained a concussion during a one-car accident in late June '14. In the fall, snagged 33-931-12 (28.2) in 15 games (11 starts) to lead the country in yards per catch for the national champs. Returned 13 career kickoffs for 233 yards (17.9-yard average) and five punts for 18 yards (3.6). Also competed

in track and field for the Buckeyes. Did not complete shuttles at the Combine because of a right hamstring strain.

Strengths: Has an uncanny ability to track and adjust to the deep ball and was the most consistently explosive, big-play receiving threat in college football in 2014. Runs to the spot like a centerfielder. Has a 39-inch vertical jump and can climb the ladder to secure the ball. Shows some elusiveness after the catch. Has return and gunner experience. Very durable. Experienced, three-year starter in the Big Ten Conference on a national championship team.

Weaknesses: Has a very lean, narrow build with small hands. Does not like to do the dirty work in the middle of the field and will shy away from contact and alter his routes too much to avoid it. Struggles against physical, press coverage. Route-running could use more refinement. Has a big ego and is sensitive to criticism. Blocking could stand to improve, especially away from the ball. Has never caught a high volume of passes in a season, and his explosive big plays as a receiver did not translate to the return game.

Future: A finesse, big-play, deep-ball, vertical receiver with exceptional downfield tracking skills to run underneath the ball and create big plays. Would be best paired with a patient WR coach and will need to adopt a professional work ethic to maximize his potential. Could bring additional value on special teams.

Draft projection: Second- to third-round pick.

Scout's take: "He is similar to (Ravens 2011 second-round pick) Torrey Smith. Smith was far more productive, but they are going to bring the same qualities to an offense."

WR [F] **EVAN SPENCER**, #6

OHIO STATE ▶ GRADE: 5.24

Ht: 6-1 ¼	Wt: 212	40: 4.50e	Arm: 32 ⅝	Hand: 10 ¼

History: Father, Tim, was one of the most productive backs in OSU history, played 78 games for the Chargers (1985-90) and currently works as the running backs coach for the Buccaneers. As a true freshman in 2011, Evan appeared in 10 games and recorded three receptions for 78 yards (26.0-yard average) and one touchdown. Played all 12 games in '12, starting four, and recorded 12-136-0 (11.3). Started 12-of-14 games at the "Z" in '13, catching 22-216-3 (9.8). Broke his right fibula in the Orange Bowl against Clemson and missed '14 spring practice. In the fall, started all 15 games and snagged 15-149-3 (9.9) for the national champions. Graduated with a degree in economics.

Strengths: Born tough and has a special teams personality. Tone-setter. Knocked Landon Collins out of the Sugar Bowl with a shoulder injury following a tenacious block. Plays big. Good football intelligence. Very efficient, powerful blocker. Extremely durable. Has NFL pedigree.

Weaknesses: Poor career production. Not elusive in the open field. Tightly wound and creates little separation in his routes. Limited catching radius. Not a blazer.

Future: A physical, determined possession receiver with enough toughness to make a living in the slot or as a flanker. Could bring the most value as a blocker and on special teams. Is likely to be overlooked in the draft process but will spend the rest of his career proving why he belongs and make a mark as a core special teams performer.

Draft projection: Late draftable pick.

Scout's take: "He could get drafted late. We'd sign him after the draft. Special teams will be his ticket."

WR [X] JAELEN STRONG #21 (Jr-4)

ARIZONA STATE   ▶ GRADE: 5.97

| Ht: 6-2 ⅜ | Wt: 217 | 40: 4.43 | Arm: 32 ½ | Hand: 9 |

History: Lost his father to Leukemia in 2003. Prepped in Philadelphia, but was a non-qualifier coming out of high school. Went to Pierce College (Calif.), where he redshirted in '11 and posted 67 catches for 1,263 yards (18.9-yard average) and 15 touchdowns in '12. Made an immediate impact in '13 when he started all 14 games at the "X" receiver and hauled in 75-1,122-7 (16.1). Led the Sun Devils in receiving for the second straight season in '14 — started all 12 games when he played at the "X" and totaled 82-1,165-10 (14.2). Sustained a concussion against Oregon State and sat out against Washington State. Did not lift at the Combine because of a right A/C (shoulder) sprain and did not perform shuttles because of a right hamstring strain.

Strengths: Extremely strong hands, defined perhaps best in his game-winning, Hail Mary TD reception against USC. Has a powerful stride and the strength to slip off the jam. Good hand-eye coordination. Deceptively fast and can gain a step on defenders downfield and separate with length and leaping ability at the last second. Good ball skills and body control to make in-air adjustments and effectively work along the sidelines. Has a 42-inch vertical jump and very good leaping ability to sky for the ball and take it away from defenders in a

crowd. Makes one-handed snags extended outside his frame. Good run strength after the catch. Exceptional two-year production.

Weaknesses: Has small hands. Did not run a full route tree. Is not a nifty or polished route runner. Does not consistently separate and many of catches are contested. Does not play to his timed speed. Came across as "very guarded" during the interview process and questions about his focus and work ethic must be answered.

Future: Big, athletic, strong-handed, physical receiver with enough speed, length and leaping ability to be effective down the field and the size, hand strength and run-after-the-catch ability to work underneath. His commitment to the finer points of game will determine how good he will become.

Draft projection: Top-40 pick.

Scout's take: "I like him as much as any receiver in the West. The only downfall is the system. I would like to see a more traditional passing tree. From a physical standpoint, he has everything you want in a receiver. He could be a no. 1 (receiver). I see him as more of a 2."

WR [X] - TE DARREN WALLER, #88 (Sr-4)

GEORGIA TECH   ▶ GRADE: 5.26

| Ht: 6-6 ⅛ | Wt: 238 | 40: 4.46 | Arm: 33 ¼ | Hand: 9 |

History: Also played basketball as a Georgia prep. Missed his sophomore season after tearing elbow ligaments, and sustained a concussion early in his senior season. As a true freshman in 2011, appeared in 12 games as a special-teams player. Sat out against Middle Tennessee State (bruised left quad). Started 10-of-14 games in '12, catching eight balls for 162 yards (20.2-yard average) and zero touchdowns. Was suspended for the '13 season opener against Elon (violation team rules). On the season, snagged 17-367-3 (21.6) in 12 games (four starts). Was suspended the first two games of the '14 season (failed drug test), but started 8-of-12 contests and collected 26-442-6 (17.0). Graduated with a management degree.

Strengths: Rare size – measured the tallest and heaviest receiver at the Combine. Very good arm length. Has a 37-inch vertical jump. Has the long speed and length to create separation downfield. Intelligent, experienced three-year starter. Willing blocker. Has lined up at multiple positions (Z and X).

Weaknesses: Has small hands. Smooth-muscled with little definition in his body and lacks weight-room strength. Does not play big. Needs to do a better job consistently catching the ball in contested situations that he often draws given his lack of separation quickness. Is not strong-handed and does not take the ball away in a crowd or dominate in the red area the way his size would seem to suggest. Long strider. Ran a limited route tree and does not show polish in his routes – cannot make quick cuts and pop out of breaks. Disinterested blocker. Marginal football character. Lacks focus and plays bored.

Future: Looks like a Top 10 pick on paper and plays like an undrafted free agent, lacking the passion and football temperament desired in a productive pro. Career underachiever who must learn to better harness his natural talent and apply himself more to his craft if he is going to develop into a successful pro. Was not featured as a jumbo receiver in a run-first, triple-option offense and could warrant interest as a 'flex' tight end operating out of the slot in the pros. Will be best paired with a motivating WR coach who understands how to push the buttons of underachievers. Future depends on whether the light ever goes on.

Draft projection: Fourth- to fifth-round pick.

Scout's take: "I am not a big fan. I just don't care for him. He's not really productive as a receiver. He's been benched a number of times. He has off-field issues. He comes across as a very lackadaisical blocker. He only plays to one side of the field. I like his size. I don't like the makeup."

WR [F] DeANDREW WHITE, #2 (Sr-5)
ALABAMA ▶ GRADE: 5.19

Ht: 5-11 ½ | Wt: 193 | 40: 4.42 | Arm: 31 | Hand: 9 ¼

History: Also ran track as a prep in Texas, where he captured the 5A 200-meter dash state title. Redshirted in 2010. Played 12 games in '11, starting two, and tallied 14 catches for 151 yards (10.8-yard average) and two touchdowns. Added two punt returns for 34 yards (17.0-yard average). Was suspended for the Georgia Southern contest (violation team rules). Sustained a concussion during an altercation on the Tuscaloosa strip at 2 a.m. in April '12 the night before the team was to depart for the White House for winning the 2011 national championship. In the fall, started the first five games at the "X" receiver and logged 8-105-2 (13.1) before suffering a season-ending torn right ACL injury. Backed up Amari Cooper in '13, but was called upon to start 7-of-13 games at the "X" receiver — totaled 32-534-4 (16.7). Had postseason surgery to repair a broken sesamoid bone in his left foot, sidelining him for '14 spring practice. In the fall, started 10-of-12 games played at the

"Z" and hauled in 40-504-4 (12.6). Separated his right shoulder in the season opener against West Virginia and missed two games, then hurt his left toe against Florida in Week Four. Had five career kickoff returns for 81 yards (16.2-yard average). Graduated prior to senior season with a degree in human environmental science. Did not lift at the Combine because of a right shoulder sprain.

Strengths: Good route-running strength and quickness. Catches the ball naturally. Is not fazed entering traffic. Runs through arm tackles after the catch. Very good weight-room strength. Is tough and competitive and it shows on special teams, where he excels as a gunner. Good work ethic.

Weaknesses: Average size with a physical playing temperament that could leave him more susceptible to injury. Shows some stiffness in his body, and it showed up in the gauntlet drill at the Combine when he weaved a lot off the line. Could stand to be more precise with his routes – did not show great field awareness. Has some diva in his receiver personality and wants the ball more than it comes his way and will get pouty with limited opportunities. Minimal production given starting experience. Durability issues are a concern.

Future: A strong, tough, tightly-wound receiver who could make the most immediate impact as a core special teams contributor in the pros. Has the grit and swagger to earn his way into the receiving rotation.

Draft projection: Fifth- to sixth-round pick.

Scout's take: "He's a great kid to talk to. I liked his personality. He catches the ball really well. I don't think he is a very good returner. He does not have a lot of polish when you break down his game tape. I don't think he is as good as (former Alabama WR and Seahawks 2014 fourth-round pick) Kevin Norwood. There's no way White has his route-running ability and hands. I think he is a sixth-round-type of player."

WR [Z,X] KEVIN WHITE, #11 (Sr-5)
WEST VIRGINIA ▶ GRADE: 6.75

Ht: 6-2 ⅝ | Wt: 215 | 40: 4.31 | Arm: 32 ⅝ | Hand: 9 ¼

History: Played receiver and defensive back as a New Jersey prep, but was a non-qualifier coming out of high school. Went to Lackawanna College, but sat out the 2010 season because of a right shoulder injury. Also missed the '11 season because he missed the deadline for financial aid. Back on the field in '12, totaled 36 receptions for 535 yards (14.9-yard average) and six touchdowns in nine games. With the

WIDE RECEIVERS

Mountaineers in '13, missed the season opener against William & Mary (right ankle), but started 9-of-11 games and produced 35-507-5 (14.5). Was a Biletnikoff finalist and WVU's team MVP in '14 when he piled up 109-1,447-10 (13.3) in 13 starts. Graduated with a degree in multidisciplinary studies.

Strengths: Built like Adonis. Exceptional size-speed combination with very long arms and outstanding strength to press off the jam to get into his routes. Tied for the most bench-press reps (23) among all receivers at the Combine. Runs crisp routes and shows very good field awareness against man or zone coverage. Field fast. Runs with urgency after the catch and shows the ability to take a short toss the distance. Is strong and explosive with the ball in his hands and a dangerous open-field threat on bubble screens – attacks the field and does not go down easy. Plucks the ball out of the air and can make difficult catches over the top of defensive backs. Has rare speed to separate down the field and pull away from defensive backs. Plays with physicality. Very good football intelligence. Can make difficult one-handed snags. Plays big on the biggest of stages and consistently comes through in the clutch (see Baylor). Impressed teams with football IQ in the interview process and "lit up the room" with his charisma. Extremely competitive, unselfish, team player with a tremendous work ethic.

Weaknesses: Took a junior-college route and only had one year of top, big-school production. Was only asked to run a handful of routes in a streamlined, simplified offense in college. Is a bit mechanical coming in and out of breaks. Only played one position in college. Did not consistently separate or run away from cornerbacks. Will need to learn how to read coverages – was not asked to make sight adjustments.

Future: A big, strong, physically imposing, playmaking receiver who elevated his game as a senior and showed he could be a difference-maker with a backup quarterback. Followed up an incredibly productive, dominating season with an even better Combine showing in all facets to eliminate any questions about his speed or the offense in which he thrived. A top-10 cinch with instant impact, perennial Pro Bowl potential.

Draft projection: Top-10 pick.

Scout's take: "Kevin White is the top player in the East hands down. I don't know how he can't be. He has consistently done it every week. It's not like he had a drop off one week or disappeared for a few like a lot

of guys do. This guy is winning the game. He is the reason they are in every game. He's like Larry Fitzgerald. The other kid (Mario Alford) makes a lot of plays too. They have a great combination."

WR [X] JOHN "CAM" WORTHY, #9

EAST CAROLINA   ▶ GRADE: 5.09

Ht: 6-2 ¼ | Wt: 211 | 40: 4.60e | Arm: 33 ½ | Hand: 10 ⅛

History: Played quarterback as a South Carolina prep. Began his college career at Catawba, where he redshirted as a quarterback in 2010. Did not keep pace academically and landed at Yuba College (Calif.), where he was shifted to receiver — caught 16 balls for 383 yards (23.9-yard average) and three touchdowns in nine games. Was offered a preferred walk-on spot at ECU. After using 2012 to get up to speed, appeared in all 13 games in '13, recording 19-295-2 (15.5). Also tossed a 13-yard touchdown pass. Earned a more prominent role in '14 when he started all 11 games played at the "X" receiver, producing 55-1,016-4 (18.5). Was suspended by the ECU Office of Rights and Responsibilities for two games (North Carolina and SMU) for an argument with another student in the summer. Medically excluded from working out at the Combine because of injuries to both feet.

Strengths: Looks every bit the part. Outstanding size with very long arms and big hands. Breaks off his routes quickly. Competes for the ball in the air. Lit up Virginia Tech for 6-224-0 and Connecticut for 7-138-0, including three catches where he kept working to come free vs. Byron Jones. Shows some strength after the catch and shows good concentration down the field. Keeps working to uncover and helps his quarterback out of a jam.

Weaknesses: Average positional instincts and processing speed. Lets the ball get on top of him. Not quick off the line and builds to speed. Will struggle with physical bump coverage. Not a refined route runner and struggles to separate with quickness or savvy – most of his catches are contested. Not elusive after the catch. Will require time to acclimate to an NFL playbook.

Future: A raw, long, big-bodied strider with the hands to function as a possession receiver. Made his senior year his best and has developmental potential as an outside-the-numbers, move-the-chains-type receiver. Will be best with simplified assignments and will need to earn a job on special teams to stick on a roster as a No. 4 or No. 5 receiver.

Draft projection: Priority free agent.

WIDE RECEIVERS

TIGHT ENDS

Nawrocki's TOP 10

1. **MAXX WILLIAMS**
2. Tyler Kroft
3. Clive Walford
4. Busta Anderson
5. Jeff Heuerman
6. Nick Boyle
7. AJ Derby
8. Blake Bell
9. Jesse James
10. Nick O'Leary

TE [F] RORY "BUSTA" ANDERSON, #81 (Sr-4)

SOUTH CAROLINA ▶ GRADE: 5.32

Ht: 6-4⅝ | Wt: 244 | 40: 4.70e | Arm: 32¼ | Hand: 8¾

History: Also played basketball as a Georgia prep. As a true freshman in 2011, recorded eight receptions for 188 yards (23.5-yard average) and three touchdowns in 13 games (two starts). In '12, caught 14-271-5 (19.4) in 13 games (two starts). Missed the '13 season opener against North Carolina (hamstring), but started 9-of-12 games and snagged 17-235-0 (13.8). Partially tore his right triceps during '14 spring practice (required surgery). In the fall, started 6-of-10 games played, managing 22-260-1 (11.8) before suffering a left triceps strain against Furman and missing games against Auburn and Tennessee. Medically excluded from Combine workouts because of a left tricep injury.

Strengths: Willing positional blocker – can get in the way, reach and seal. Quick into his routes and is able to create some separation with quickness. Good balance and body control – adjusts well to the ball in the air. Has enough speed to threaten the seam. Efficient working up a level and fitting on linebackers.

Weaknesses: Very small hands (only tight end to measure below 9 inches). Lacks bulk and functional football-playing strength. Struggles to match up vs. ends and sustain in-line as a blocker. Is easily knocked off his routes. Could stand to be more focused. Weight has fluctuated significantly and has struggled to keep it on. Durability has been a concern throughout his career with back, foot, hamstring and recurring triceps injuries that require more careful scrutiny. Likes to chirp too much.

Future: An athletic pass-catcher ideally suited to play in the slot and create some mismatches down the field. Durability concerns could hinder draft status.

Draft projection: Fourth- to fifth-round pick.

Scout's take: "He reminded me of (2013 third-round pick) Jordan Reed for the Redskins, who no one really liked coming out, but he found his niche as a pass catcher. This

TIGHT ENDS

kid could be the same way."

TE [H] **BLAKE BELL**, #10 (Sr-5)

OKLAHOMA ▶ GRADE: 5.22

Ht: 6-6 ¼ | Wt: 252 | 40: 4.79 | Arm: 33 ⅛ | Hand: 10

History: Father, Mark, played defensive end for Seahawks and Colts (1979-84), and uncle, Mike, played defensive end for the Chiefs (1979-91). Blake was a highly recruited quarterback out of Kansas. Redshirted in 2010. Backed up Steelers '13 first-rounder Landry Jones the next two years. Was used as a short-yardage runner from the QB position in '11, when he appeared in seven games and completed 1-of-4 pass attempts (25.0 percent) for eight yards with zero touchdowns and one interception while also carrying 44 times for 171 yards (3.9-yard average) and 13 touchdowns. Broke the OU record for rushing touchdowns by a freshman quarterback, as 26 of his 44 carries went for either a first down or touchdown, and he was named Offensive MVP of the Insight Bowl. Appeared in all 13 games in '12 when he passed 9-16-107-0-0 (8.2) and ran 60-201-11 (3.3). Split time with Trevor Knight in '13 — started 8-of-11 games played, totaling 140-233-1,648-12-5 (60.1) through the air and 75-255-0 (3.4) on the ground. Sustained a concussion and did not play against Kansas State. Also did not play in the Sugar Bowl against Alabama (coach's decision). Was sidelined during '14 spring practice with a knee sprain. With Knight entrenched as the starter, Bell converted to tight end and caught 16 balls for 214 yards (13.4-yard average) and four touchdowns in 12 games (eight starts). Did not play against Kansas (strained knee). Graduated.

Strengths: Very good body length – provides a big catching target. Strong, effortful, short-yardage / goal-line runner – churns his legs through contact and grinds out some tough yardage. Understands how to settle into zones. Recorded the best 3-cone drill time (6.85 seconds) of any tight end at the Combine. Solid character. Pedigreed, works hard and applied himself to learning the craft. Solid football character.

Weaknesses: Raw, developing blocker still adapting to run-game fits. Too slippery as soft-shouldered as a blocker and could do a better job sustaining in-line. Must learn how to roll his hips and drive defenders. Bench-pressed a TE-low 14 reps at the Combine and must continue developing his strength in the weight room. Breaks stride to catch and does not sink his hips and run through tacklers after

the catch with the same gusto he has shown in short-yardage situations. Builds to speed and is not an instant accelerator off spots. Raw positional instincts and blocking technique.

Future: Big-bodied, underpowered converted quarterback still learning to play the TE position. Intriguing developmental prospect with upside to be groomed. Will require patience and could have the career arc and longevity Tim Tebow did not enjoy in the NFL because of his willingness to change positions.

Draft projection: Late draftable pick.

Scout's take: "He is probably a good fifth-round value, but he is not very strong. He is an ex-quarterback, and his body looks like it. He is really a developmental tight end."

TE [H] **E.J. BIBBS**, #11 (Sr-5)

IOWA STATE ▶ GRADE: 5.18

Ht: 6-2 | Wt: 258 | 40: 4.85e | Arm: 31 ⅛ | Hand: 10 ¼

History: Parents are police officers. Chicago native who played receiver and linebacker as a prep. Grayshirted at Iowa in 2010, but did not remain in Iowa City. Spent the next two years at Arizona Western College. Played four games in '11 and caught six balls for 79 yards (19.8-yard average) and one touchdown. Played 12 games in '12, snagging 22-230-6 10.5). With the Cyclones in '13, started 9-of-12 games and produced 39-462-2 (11.8). Had surgery to repair a torn meniscus during '14 fall camp, but started all 10 games played — totaled 45-382-8 (8.5) before an injury to the same knee required arthroscopic surgery, which knocked him out of the final two games and the Senior Bowl. Team captain. Only performed skill drills at the Combine because of a bone bruise on his left knee.

Strengths: Naturally thick-framed and strong bodied and moves well for his size. Versatile with his alignment – plays in line, flexed, as a wing and on special teams. Smooth route runner. Understands how to find soft spots on option routes and works over the middle without fear. Strong at the top of his routes to create some separation. Natural hands catcher. Adjusts to poorly thrown balls outside his frame and can make difficult one-handed snags (see Oklahoma State). Drives his legs on contact and battles for extra yardage after the catch (good leg drive). Solid production. Willing blocker – creates good fits in the run game and on the flanks. Works hard and has a passion for the game.

Weaknesses: Below-average height and arm length. Is not a crafty route runner – tends to

TIGHT ENDS

drift too much, signal routes and give up break points (see Texas). Not elusive after the catch and cannot make many tacklers miss. Lacks suddenness and acceleration. Does not have ideal speed to threaten the seam. Can do a better job sustaining blocks.

Future: Strong, stocky, compact, leverage blocker and possession receiver with enough agility to function in the slot and on the move. Could develop into a solid contributor in a simple scheme and would be best paired with a patient coaching staff.

Draft projection: Late draftable pick.

Scout's take: "It's going to take him some time to figure it out, but he'll work at it. Our coaches wouldn't have the patience to coach him up."

TE [Y] **NICK BOYLE**, #86 (Sr-4)

DELAWARE ▶ GRADE: 5.26

Ht: 6-4 ½ | Wt: 268 | 40: 5.06 | Arm: 33 ⅜ | Hand: 10 ⅝

History: Captained the football and basketball teams as a New Jersey prep and entered the program as a 230-pound freshman. Was expected to redshirt in 2011, but an injury to another player forced him into action — started 5-of-7 games played and caught two balls for 25 yards (12.5-yard average) and one touchdown. Started 7-of-10 games played in '12, catching 20-181-0 (9.1). Missed the Bucknell contest because of a partially torn left ACL. Started all 12 games in each of the next two seasons — totaled 42-474-7 (11.3) in '13 and 37-304-4 (8.2) in '14. Team captain. Participated in the Senior Bowl.

Strengths: Looks the part. Exceptional size with a short trunk and long torso characteristic of a prototype offensive lineman. Natural knee bender with good in-line power and leverage. Takes good angles to the second level and can reach and cut off linebackers. Dependable short-area receiver with secure hands and good hand-eye coordination. Experienced, three-and-a-half-year starter. Very good football intelligence – only needs to be instructed once to retain and can assimilate a complex playbook readily. Vocal leader. Very solid character with strong work habits and perfectionist tendencies. Craves hard coaching. Solid Senior Bowl showing. Versatile and has lined up inline, at fullback and as an H-back. Recorded the best 20-yard shuttle time (4.23 seconds) and 60-yard shuttle (11.65 seconds) of any tight end at the Combine.

Weaknesses: Marginal foot quickness, acceleration and short-area burst. Labors to clear the line and escape the jam. Pedestrian

route runner. Gathers to cut. Cannot challenge the field vertically. Average body control – gets overextended at the second level. Marginal separation quickness and elusiveness with the ball in his hands. Has not consistently faced top competition or dominated. Limited leaping ability, confirmed with a 30 1/2-inch vertical jump (tied for lowest among tight ends at the Combine).

Future: Big, strong, hulking base blocker who fits ideally as a true "Y". Has starter traits as an in-line blocker in a power offense and could add value as a dependable, underneath target. Might have a chance as a developmental, zone-blocking guard conversion project.

Draft projection: Fourth- to fifth-round pick.

Scout's take: "You could justify taking a pure Y starter in the third round. I can't go any higher than the fourth. I haven't seen one better than (Boyle) this year."

TE [F,H] **GERALD CHRISTIAN**, #18 (Sr-5)

LOUISVILLE ▶ GRADE: 5.21

Ht: 6-3 | Wt: 244 | 40: 4.84 | Arm: 32 ½ | Hand: 10 ¾

History: Highly sought after recruit who played receiver and linebacker as a Florida prep. Had a high ankle sprain during the playoffs of his senior year. Began his college career at the University of Florida, where he redshirted in 2010. Appeared in eight games in '11 without recording any receiving stats. Decided to transfer because he was unhappy being used as a blocking tight end. Sat out '12 per NCAA rules. With the Cardinals in '13, started 11-of-13 games and produced 28 receptions for 426 yards (15.2-yard average) and four touchdowns. Tore his left meniscus vs. Temple but did not miss a game. Started 10-of-13 games in '14, catching 32-384-5 (12.0). Played for three different offensive coordinators. Graduated with a degree in justice administration. Medically excluded from jumps at the Combine because of left knee injury.

Strengths: Athletic marvel with a tapered waist, well-muscled hamstrings and evenly cut, striated upper-body – looks every bit the part. Led all tight ends at the Combine with 28 bench-press reps despite being tied for the lightest – extremely strong pound for pound. Is effective catching the ball on the move on drags, crossers and underneath routes. Functional stalk blocker most effective on the move. Football smart and lined up at multiple positions – in line, flexed and on the move.

Weaknesses: Average overall bulk and body mass and can be controlled too easily by

TIGHT ENDS

linebackers and mugged too much at the line. Tends to catch too much in pass-protection and does not attack, drive and sustain on the second level. Does not consistently finish and tends to slip off blocks. Rigid, upright route runner – marginal hip flexibility to sink in and of breaks. Does not play fast or put fear into deep safeties as a seam-stretcher. Double-caught the ball too much at the Combine. Produced the slowest shuttle times of any tight end at the Combine, registering a 4.76-second short shuttle and 7.62-second 3-cone drill time.

Future: A tightly-wound, overly muscled, body beautiful, short-to-intermediate receiver with enough strength and desire to function as a move blocker if he could learn how to unlock his hips.

Draft projection: Fifth- to sixth-round pick.

Scout's take: "He's undersized and not as athletic as you would like for an undersized guy. His routes need a lot of work. He's not much of a blocker either. He is a true tweener. You'd probably take him in the sixth round."

TE [Y] CLEAR CAMERON, #85 (Sr-4)

TEXAS A&M ▶ GRADE: 4.93

Ht: 6-5⅝ | Wt: 277 | 40: 4.94 | Arm: 33⅜ | Hand: 9⅜

History: Played tight end, offensive tackle, and defensive end as a Tennessee prep. Also attracted Division I basketball offers. Began his career at Tennessee, where he played all 12 games (two starts) and caught one pass for four yards (4.0-yard average) and zero touchdowns. Was kicked off the team after he was arrested for stealing the laptop of a Tennessee baseball player. Spent '12 at Arizona Western, where he tallied 5-54-0 (10.8) in seven games. With the Aggies in '13, played all 13 games (one start) and caught 4-42-1 (10.5). Started 5-of-11 games played in '14, snagging 5-34-0 (6.8). Missed two games after spraining his ankle against South Carolina. Medically excluded from the bench press at the Combine because of right elbow injury.

Strengths: Outstanding body mass. Has a big frame with an 82-inch wingspan (tied for longest among tight ends) and offers a big target to post up linebackers as a short-area receiver. Enough in-line blocking strength to match up against power and wash defenders down the line on double teams. Has special teams experience (contributed as a wedge blocker on kickoff return team).

Weaknesses: Very limited receiving production – ordinary route runner with limited burst to uncover vs. man coverage. Not a natural catcher – got beat up by the ball at the Combine, letting it into his body and double-catching (though did gain more confidence as it progressed). Average athlete for the TE position – not quick or sudden to climb or separate. Is late to reach the block point and connect with linebackers on the second level. Average sustain on the move. Not a glass-eating in-line blocker. Limited role player in a spread offense. Weight has fluctuated and weight-room strength could stand to improve. Must prove more focused and disciplined.

Future: A functional, base blocker with the body mass to fend for a job as a situational No. 3 or jumbo tight end. Has a frame to fill out and could be tried as a Jason Peters-type tackle conversion project in a zone-blocking scheme, though he must harden to withstand the rigors of the NFL's trenches.

Draft projection: Late draftable pick.

Scout's take: "He has no twitch in his lower body. He is not a very good blocker. He's just big."

TE [F,H] AJ DERBY, #11 (Sr-5)

ARKANSAS ▶ GRADE: 5.24

Ht: 6-3 3/4 | Wt: 251 | 40: 4.72 | Arm: 30 1/2 | Hand: 9 1/2

History: Father, John, was an All-Big Ten linebacker and team captain at Iowa. AJ also played basketball and baseball as a prep in Iowa, where he won state titles in football and basketball. Coming out of high school, was considered the top prospect in the state. Began his college career at Iowa, where he redshirted as a quarterback in 2010. Backed up James Vandenberg in '11 — completed 3-of-6 pass attempts (50.0 percent) for 30 yards with zero touchdowns and zero interceptions in nine appearances. Was arrested in early October for fourth-degree criminal mischief and public intoxication — drunkenly punched out the window of a bus near an Iowa city bar. Served a two-game suspension then was moved to linebacker, which prompted a transfer to Coffeyville (Kan.) Community College. Played 10 games in '12, passing 149-321-1,936-22-14 (46.4). Transferred to Arkansas in '13 — backed up Brandon Allen, seeing action in seven games (one start as an injury replacement) and tossing 19-36-178-1-1 (52.8). Converted to tight end in '14 — started 7-of-11 games played and caught 22 balls for 303 yards (13.8-yard average) and three touchdowns. Did not play the final two games (knee scope). Medically excluded from running, jumping and skill drills at the Combine because of a left foot injury.

Strengths: Good athlete with loose hips.

TIGHT ENDS

Fluid mover. Good enough positional blocker to get in the way and steer defenders. Explosive angle blocker – see chip block vs. LSU's Danielle Hunter. Very dependable hands-catcher – adjusts well to the ball and is comfortable with it in his hands. Versatile – lines up at fullback, on the wing, in-line, flexed and in motion.

Weaknesses: Very short-armed with small hands. Bench-pressed only 15 reps at the Combine and lacks functional football-playing strength. Is easily walked back and lacks substance in his body to withstand a charge and anchor. Easily knocked off his release and does not come off the line with intent. Tends to drift in his routes and gathers to cut. Only a one-year starter.

Future: An athletic, versatile pass-catcher most effective on delayed releases, crossers and drag routes, Derby displays the fluidity, foot speed, body control and receiving skill to continue developing in the slot or as an H-back. Has intriguing developmental potential.

Draft projection: Fourth- to fifth-round pick.

Scout's take: "Most of this class belongs in the fifth or sixth round. You're creating guys if you draft them any sooner. ...Derby didn't work out because of the injury at the Combine. We have to look at it more closely. He's probably a fifth-round guy. But he's another creation."

TE [Y,H] JEFF HEUERMAN, #5 (Sr-4)

OHIO STATE ▶ GRADE: 5.31

Ht: 6-5⅛ | Wt: 254 | 40: 4.75e | Arm: 33¼ | Hand: 10⅛

History: Wore no. 5 in tribute to the injured Braxton Miller as a senior. Father, Paul, was a Michigan basketball captain, and younger brother, Mike, is a tight end at Notre Dame. Jeff also played hockey growing up. Was recruited to Ohio State by then-head coach Jim Tressel. As a true freshman in 2011, caught one pass for 25 yards (25.0-yard average) and zero touchdowns in 10 games (one start). Started 9-of-12 games in '12, recording 8-94-1 (11.8). Also caught a crucial two-point conversion in the final seconds against Purdue — sent the game to overtime, allowing the Buckeyes to win and preserve an undefeated season. In '13, started 13-of-14 games and produced 26-466-4 (17.9). Sprained his left foot during '14 spring practice (also suffered a broken nose during tug-of-war exercise). Started all 14 games in '14, posting 17-207-2 (12.2). Sprained his right ankle in Sugar Bowl against Alabama — played through it against Oregon in the national title game, but did not participate at the Senior Bowl. Team captain. Only performed skill drills at the Combine because of ankle injury.

Strengths: Very good size and length. Functional in-line strength to turn and seal defenders. Good technician. Battles for positioning and works to sustain. Good body control to reach and hook defenders. Can stretch the field vertically. Catches on contact and breaks arm tackles after the catch. Catches the ball cleanly outside his frame. Outstanding weight-room worker. Bench-pressed 26 reps at the Combine. Smart and assignment-sound. Is tough and plays through injuries, competing with a noticeable limp as a senior.

Weaknesses: Long-strider — builds to speed and is not quick in and out of his cuts. Only shows one gear. Not elusive in the open field and makes few tacklers miss. Not overly strong or physical as a blocker and does not drive defenders off the line. History of foot injuries will require closer scrutiny.

Future: A well-rounded, self-made tight end who can run, catch and block, Heuerman was slowed by nagging injuries and a revolving door at quarterback as a senior, yet possesses enough starter-caliber traits to contribute readily if healthy. Could prove to be a solid value pick if he could return to early form.

Draft projection: Fourth- to fifth-round pick.

Scout's take: "If you talk to (Ohio State strength coach) Mickey (Marotti), he will tell you that you have to go back to (2013) to get a true indication of what (Heuerman) can do. He played with the (ankle) injury all year and couldn't fully train and was not the same player as a senior. A lot of scouts were backpedaling on him during the fall. Mickey personally loves the kid. You would think Heuerman is a first rounder the way Mickey talks about him."

TE [Y] JESSE JAMES, #18 (Jr-3)

PENN STATE ▶ GRADE: 5.22

Ht: 6-7 | Wt: 261 | 40: 4.81 | Arm: 33 | Hand: 9 ⅜

History: Three-time captain as a Pennsylvania prep. As a true freshman in 2012, started 6-of-11 games played (sat out season opener versus Ohio) and had 15 receptions for 276 yards (18.4-yard average) and five touchdowns. Started all 25 games the next two seasons — totaled 25-333-3 (13.3) in '13 (12 starts) and 38-396-3 (10.4) in '14 (13 starts). Will be a 21-year-old rookie.

Strengths: Excellent body length. Adjusts well to balls thrown behind him. Scrappy in-line blocker. Paced all tight ends with a 10-foot, 1-inch broad jump. Bench-pressed 26 reps at the Combine and recorded a 37-inch vertical

TIGHT ENDS

jump. Measured taller than any receiver at the Combine and has the leaping ability and length to create a very large throwing target and win with size. Adequate core strength in pass pro.

Weaknesses: Takes choppy steps and doesn't open his stride. Weaved a lot in the gauntlet drill at the Combine, exposing his tight hips. Lacks ideal top-end speed to stretch the field. Average burst at the top of his routes – plodding mover with too much rigidity to create separation. Gathers to cut, signals his routes and gives up break points. Is too tall to sink his hips and bore defenders off the line in the run game.

Future: A lean, long-limbed, competitive in-line blocker capable of factoring as a short-to-intermediate receiver. Similar to Falcons 2013 fourth-round pick Levine Toilolo and has a chance to develop into a functional No. 2.

Draft projection: Fourth- to fifth-round pick.

Scout's take: "I put (James) in the sixth round. There's no 'wow' factor. He's a backup at best. I don't see much upside."

TE [F] BEN KOYACK, #18 (Sr-4)

NOTRE DAME ▶ GRADE: 4.97

Ht: 6-4⅞ | Wt: 255 | 40: 4.75e | Arm: 32⅞ | Hand: 10¾

History: Was one of the most highly recruited tight ends in the country coming out of Pennsylvania, where he totaled 152 career receptions for 2,591 yards (17.0-yard average) and 28 touchdowns. Missed three games as a junior after tearing his right meniscus. Also won the state javelin championship (192-11). As a true freshman in 2011, played 12 games (did not see action in season opener versus South Florida) and caught 1-5-0 (5.0). In '12, tallied 3-39-0 (13.0) in 12 games (one start). Did not see action against Pittsburgh. Started 5-of-13 games in '13 and caught 10-171-3 (17.1). After waiting his turn behind Bengals '13 first-rounder Tyler Eifert and Cardinals '14 second-rounder Troy Niklas, Koyack started all 13 games in '13, producing 30-317-2 (10.6). Elected not to perform at the Combine.

Strengths: Has very big hands. Improved positioning and leverage as a blocker as a senior. Understands angles and is an effective stalk blocker. Can hook and seal and will run his feet on contact. Deceptively athletic and can lull defenders to sleep with his long strides. Uses his length to uncover. Very intelligent.

Weaknesses: Extremely lean build and lacks power in his body. Straight-linish mover – rounds out of breaks. Is not a precise route runner. Is fazed by traffic and shows shaky concentration in a crowd. Not natural tracking

the ball and tends to body the ball and double-catch. Breaks few tackles. Only a one-year starter with modest career production. Does not seem like he loves football. Average football character.

Future: Career underachiever. Was overshadowed by a talented cast of tight ends and did not produce until his senior season, when he dealt with erratic QB play. The light came on enough as a senior to warrant a developmental opportunity.

Draft projection: Priority free agent.

Scout's take: "(Koyak) catches the ball well. He is a push-and-pester type. He doesn't move particularly well. He can go to a camp and be a college free agent, but I am not drafting him. … I saw him live, and he looked like a good camp body."

TE [Y.H] TYLER KROFT, #86 (Jr-3)

RUTGERS ▶ GRADE: 5.62

Ht: 6-5½ | Wt: 246 | 40: 4.74 | Arm: 33 | Hand: 9⅝

History: Prepped in Pennsylvania. Redshirted in 2011. Appeared in 11 games in '12 (one start) and recorded three receptions for 59 yards (19.7-yard average) and one touchdown. Was Rutgers' leading receiver in '13 when he played all 13 games in '13, starting the final 12, and caught 43-573-4 (13.3). Missed most of '14 spring practice with a shoulder injury. In the fall, started 11-of-13 games and snagged 24-269-0 (11.2). Played for three different offensive coordinators and two different position coaches. Medically excluded from performing drills and running at the Combine because of a left ankle injury.

Strengths: Smooth, efficient route runner. Good sustain as an in-line blocker – moves his feet, slides and sticks on blocks. Scrappy competitor – understands leverage and positioning and consistently blocks his man. Efficient releasing off the line and getting into his routes. Can drop his hips and get in and out of cuts. Plays fast and bigger than his size. Has a frame to grow into.

Weaknesses: Only bench-pressed 17 reps at the Combine and needs to get stronger in the weight room. Is not a blazer. Marginal leaping ability – does not consistently highpoint or attack the ball in the air. Not quick-handed or a confident hands-catcher and can be fazed by traffic and make concentration drops. Struggles clearing zones and finding openings in coverage. Is late to adjust to the ball. Struggles handling spin and counter moves in pass protection and could do a better job anticipating block points. Tends to be a little

TIGHT ENDS

Tyler Kroft

grabby and can improve hand placement.

Future: A solid, all-around tight end still growing into his body, yet has a well-balanced skill set to be molded. Is surprisingly efficient as a blocker despite his lack of mass and possesses enough grit to be effective in-line blocking in the pros with continued physical development.

Draft projection: Second- to third-round pick.

Scout's take: "I see this guy running down the middle of the field, and he looks like (former Giants TE) Mark Bavaro to me. I think he can run the seam. He is not a stone-cold killer, but he blocks well. He is more of a position blocker. He's not going to Canton. ...He only caught 24 balls, but his quarterback can't hit the broad side of a barn. He's got everything you want. He's more than a slow-footed, possession, blocking Y. ...I wish I could see

him leave his feet. I have not seen him jump two inches off the ground yet."

TE [H] / FB **NICK O'LEARY**, #35 (Sr-4)

FLORIDA STATE   ▶ GRADE: 5.22

Ht: 6-3 ¼ | Wt: 252 | 40: 4.94 | Arm: 29 ¾ | Hand: 9 ⅜

History: Comes from an athletic family — Nick's parents were scholarship athletes at Georgia, and he is the grandson of Jack Nicklaus. Prepped in Florida, where he won a state championship as a junior. Was suspended two games as a senior after he was caught by television cameras flipping off players from the other team. As a true freshman in 2011, played all 13 games (two starts) and had 12 receptions for 164 yards (13.7-yard average) and one touchdown. Started 11-of-13 games in '12, catching 21-252-3 (12.0). Did not play against Savannah State while nursing a right thigh bruise. Sustained a concussion during '13 spring practice, then was fortunate to suffer only minor injuries in a motorcycle accident in which he was thrown from his bike. Was a Mackey Award finalist in '13 when he started 13-of-14 games and totaled 33-557-7 (16.9). Twenty-seven of 33 receptions went for a first down or touchdown. Missed the final six spring practices in '14 after he got into another motorcycle accident which left him with a swollen ankle. Won the Mackey Award in '14 after producing 48-618-6 (12.9) in 14 starts. Owns nearly all of FSU's tight end records.

Strengths: Very good hand-eye coordination. Has a natural feel for settling in zones and finding soft spots in coverage. Quick to turn upfield after the catch. Strong and tough battering ram with the ball in his hand. Puts his head down after the catch and will barrel for extra yardage. Competitive run blocker. Versatile and lines up in multiple spots and understands angles to position, fit and sustain on the move.

Weaknesses: Extremely short arms characteristic of a fullback. Measured the shortest wingspan (74 inches) of any tight end at the Combine and tied for the lowest vertical jump (30 1/2 inches). Short-stepper with tight hips. Not explosive on contact. Has a sense of entitlement and is still learning what it means to really work and be a pro.

Future: More strong than explosive, O'Leary's best traits are his reliable hands as a short, dump-off outlet and intermediate receiver on drags and delayed crossers in the play-action passing game. Profiles as an H-back in the pros.

Draft projection: Fifth- to sixth-round pick.

Scout's take: "(O'Leary) is a very productive type, but he does not have a lot of speed. He has a knack for creating leverage in his routes with good hands. He is never going to knock the (expletive) out of anyone, but he can block. He is a tweener – a cross between a true H and a Y. He is not big or strong enough to be a Y."

broken right leg against Missouri State. Was the College Football Performance Awards FCS Tight End of the Year for the second straight season in '14 when he led the Missouri Valley Football Conference in receptions (and set an SIU single-season mark) with 81-861-13 (10.6) in 12 starts. Led all Division I tight ends (FBS and FCS) in receptions, receiving yards and receiving touchdowns. Honored as the best tight end in MVFC history as part of the conference's 30-year anniversary. Wore jersey No. 85 prior to junior season. Team captain. Graduated with a degree in industrial technology.

Strengths: Excellent receiving production. Good speed with a low center of gravity and fine balance. Sets up routes with stems and nods and can create some separation at the top of his routes. Runs hard after the catch. Can stretch the field vertically and will sacrifice his body to make difficult catches. Recorded a 38-inch vertical jump, a 2.60 20-yard split and 4.52-second 40-yard dash, best among tight ends at the Combine. Extremely competitive, hates to lose and will rise to big occasions. Experienced three-and-a-half-year starter.

Weaknesses: Underpowered blocker – appears disinterested at times. Tight in his hips and does not uncoil in-line. Bench-pressed 225 pounds only 17 times and could stand to improve upper-body strength. Braces himself for contact and takes direct hits on the second level given his lack of creativity and desire to run thru rather than around tacklers. Limited body control to extend outside his frame. Tends to body the ball and let it get on top of him too quickly in the gauntlet and drills at the Combine.

Future: A strong, compact, mudder ideally suited for an H-Back role, Pruitt shares similarities with Buffalo Bills 2013 seventh-round pick Chris Gragg and could find a niche role. Special teams could have to be his ticket.

Draft projection: Late draftable pick.

TE [H] MYCOLE PRUITT, #4 (Sr-5)
SOUTHERN ILLINOIS   ▶ GRADE: 5.14
Ht: 6-2 ¼ | Wt: 251 | 40: 4.54 | Arm: 33 ½ | Hand: 10 ¼

History: Tight end-defensive end who also played basketball and volleyball as a Missouri prep. Redshirted in 2010. Played all 11 games in '11, starting seven, and recorded 43 receptions for 562 yards (13.1-yard average) and three touchdowns. Was the Salukis' leading receiver in '12 when he started all 11 games and caught 49-577-4 (11.8). In '13, snagged 48-601-5 (12.5) in 10 starts before suffering a

TE [F,H] WES SAXTON, #13 (Sr-4)
SOUTH ALABAMA   ▶ GRADE: 5.18
Ht: 6-3 ⅜ | Wt: 248 | 40: 4.66 | Arm: 32 | Hand: 9 ⅝

History: Cousin, Tony Nathan, was a running back for the Dolphins (1979-87). Saxton prepped in Alabama. Started at Itawamba (Miss.) Community College, where he caught 10 balls for 137 yards (13.7-yard average) and one touchdown in 2011. Started 6-of-12 games in '12, snagging 26-336-1 (12.9). Started all 12 games in '13 and caught 50-635-0 (12.7). Sprained his right ankle against Navy. In '14,

TIGHT ENDS

started 9-of-12 games and totaled 20-155-0 (7.8). Sustained an ankle injury against Troy and was hampered the second half of the season (did not play against Texas State). Medically excluded from lifting at the Combine because of left sternoclavicular joint injury.

Strengths: Well-built and looks the part. Smooth, fluid movement skills. Very good body control. Recorded the fastest 10-yard split (1.60 seconds) of any tight end at the Combine, and displays outstanding short-area burst to open up his stride and accelerate in and out of breaks. Has a 36-inch vertical jump. Can make quick, dynamic speed cuts. Runs hard through contact after the catch.

Weaknesses: Does not understand leverage and positioning – tends to lunge too much and get overextended as a blocker. Raw hand usage and placement – tends to shoot hands wide of the target. Measured an unusually high 17 percent body fat at the Combine, indicating a lack of nutritional discipline. Undisciplined route runner still learning the finer points of the game. Inconsistent hands catcher. Has some limitations in the weight room because of childhood wrist injury.

Future: A very athletic receiver best on the move, Saxton has the quickness, burst and body control to be developed into a play-making weapon in the slot. Has natural talent that cannot be coached and many flaws that are correctable alongside a nuanced coaching staff. Will command interest as a developmental H-back and will benefit from being paired with a more accurate passer.

Draft projection: Fifth- to sixth-round pick.

Scout's take: "He is not ready for prime time. He does not always play fast or to the speed that he timed. He drops a lot of balls – there are a lot of concentration drops if you really break him down. You can't take him before the fifth round."

TE [F] JEAN SIFRIN, #87 (Jr-4)
MASSACHUSETTS ▶ GRADE: 5.10
Ht: 6-5 ¼ | Wt: 245 | 40: 4.82 | Arm: 33 ⅜ | Hand: 11

History: Moved from the Bahamas to Florida when he was three. Moved constantly as a child and went to seven elementary schools. Dropped out of high school in 2005 and got his GED. Worked at a warehouse, incurring two herniated disks which required epidural steroid injections. Got back into sports at Asa College in '11 when he caught five balls for 52 yards (10.4-yard average) and a touchdown in six games. Also played basketball, but ultimately got kicked out ("for something I didn't even

do," according to Sifrin). Redshirted at El Camino College (Calif.) in '12 because his credits didn't transfer. In '13 (wore jersey No. 1), posted 18-328-5 (18.2) in eight games. Reportedly had offers from Oklahoma and USC, but chose to join UMASS in '14. Was not eligible to join the team until September. After missing the season opener against Boston College, started 9-of-11 games and totaled 42-642-6 (15.3). Was a 27-year-old junior and has a seven-year-old son named Jabari.

Strengths: Has a long, rangy, athletic frame with big mitts. Tied for the biggest hands (11 inches) of any player at the Combine and for the longest wingspan (82 inches) among tight ends, translating to a huge catching radius. Has shown he can win in crowds and make the one-handed snag (see sensational highlight-reel TD grab against Colorado). Flashes playmaking ability and can make difficult catches look easy. Has upside to be groomed.

Weaknesses: Inconsistent hands – makes too many concentration drops. Fought the ball at the Combine – had four drops and a number of double-catches in the gauntlet drill and the stage appeared to be too big for him. Has not regularly faced top competition in the Mid-American Conference. Unrefined route runner. Is still learning how to leverage and fit in the run game. Has a big learning curve and will require time to get acclimated to the NFL. Overaged.

Future: A raw, developmental project and basketball player on grass. Flashes some intriguing traits and has tools that cannot be taught. Has a chance to contribute in the slot with very simplified responsibilities and assignments. However, age and unsophistication could leave him undrafted.

Draft projection: Late draftable pick.

TE [Y] RANDALL TELFER, #82 (Sr-5)
USC ▶ GRADE: 4.92
Ht: 6-3¾ | Wt: 250 | 40: 4.85e | Arm: 33½ | Hand: 9⅝

History: California native. Redshirted in 2010. Played all 12 games in '11, starting five, and caught 26 balls for 273 yards (10.5-yard average) and five touchdowns. Started 9-of-12 games played in '12, snagging 12-100-4 (8.3). Sprained his right ankle against Utah and did not play against Washington. Tore his right meniscus during '13 spring practice. Started 8-of-11 games played in '13, snagging 6-78-1 (13.0). Missed three games after spraining his right MCL against Notre Dame. Missed time during '14 spring practice after having his right knee scoped. In the fall, started 12-of-13

TIGHT ENDS

games and totaled 21-197-2 (9.4). Suffered a hip pointer against Arizona State. Was named USC's Most Inspirational Player. Graduated with a political science degree. Medically excluded from working out at the Combine because of left foot injury.

Strengths: Good size. Fairly athletic. Effort blocker. Battles and competes. Has enough strength to match up with base ends in pass pro. Sits down in soft spots in zones. Has special teams experience.

Weaknesses: Consistently late to reach the block point at the second level. Tends to play too tall. Runs a limited route tree. Slow off the line. Builds to speed and only shows one gear. Cannot separate vs. man coverage or threaten the deep middle. Limited run-after-the-catch skill and creativity – straight-line mover. Marginal career production. Has been nicked a lot and struggles to avoid the training room.

Future: A functional college tight end lacking any distinguishable, redeeming trait to warrant drafting. Could fend for a role as a rotational No. 3 tight end.

Draft projection: Priority free agent.

TE [Y] ERIC TOMLINSON, #87 (Sr-5)

UTEP   ▶ GRADE: 5.10

Ht: 6-5 ⅝ | Wt: 263 | 40: 4.99 | Arm: 32 ⅞ | Hand: 10

History: Also played basketball as a Texas prep. Redshirted in 2010. Played all 12 games in '11, starting five, and caught six balls for 83 yards (13.8-yard average) and two touchdowns. In '12, managed 4-26-0 (6.5) in 10 games (three starts). Missed two games because of a broken right wrist. Started all 13 games in '13 and pulled in 30-304-1 (10.1). In '14, managed 19-134-1 (7.1) in 10 starts, though he missed two games because of a sprained MCL.

Strengths: Has a short trunk and long torso and is well built to create leverage in the run game. Has natural point-of-attack strength and plays with physicality as an in-line blocker. Good base and grip strength to create a surge in the running game. Drives his legs and works to finish. Tough, gritty competitor. Works across the middle and catches on contact. Functional short-area receiver with reliable hands. Good football intelligence. Blue-collar worker with a very serious, workmanlike approach. Played full game with broken wrist and will play through injuries.

Weaknesses: Very heavy in his movement and limited as a route runner and after-the-catch, open-field runner. Marginal elusiveness to avoid tacklers – creates little yardage after the catch. Limited athletic ability, foot speed

and burst – cannot threaten the seam. Straight-linish. Creates no separation out of breaks. Recorded a 30 1/2-inch vertical jump and an 8-foot, 9-inch broad jump, the lowest of any tight end at the Combine. Marginal weight-room strength.

Future: Big, country strong in-line blocker whose calling card will be re-establishing the line of scrimmage in the run game. Will bring his hard hat every day and get the job done. Could compete readily as a no. 2 blocking tight end.

Draft projection: Late draftable pick.

TE [Y,H] CLIVE WALFORD, #46 (Sr-5)

MIAMI (FLA.)   ▶ GRADE: 5.40

Ht: 6-4 | Wt: 251 | 40: 4.76 | Arm: 34 | Hand: 10 ¼

History: Has a son with his fiancée, Aneliz, and spends most of time with his family. Was a basketball player until his senior year of high school at Glades Central, and then-head coach Randy Shannon offered a Miami scholarship before Walford even debuted on the football field. Redshirted in 2010. Started 8-of-12 games in '11 and recorded 18 receptions for 172 yards (9.6-yard average) and one touchdown. Played all 12 games in '12, starting five, and caught 25-451-4 (18.0). Started 12-of-13 games in '13 (gave way to an extra receiver against Savannah State), grabbing 34-454-2 (13.4). Was a Mackey Award finalist in '14 — started 10-of-12 games played and pulled in 44-676-7 (15.4). Did not start against Florida A&M (extra receiver), and missed the Russell Athletic Bowl against Louisville after tearing his right meniscus against Pittsburgh. Team captain graduated with a degree in sports administration.

Strengths: Looks the part with good overall length. Good balance, body control and vision running after the catch. Makes deft moves to set up his routes and create separation vs. man coverage. Understands how to work through zones. Tracks the deep ball well. Effective climbing to the second level and picking off linebackers. Has only 5.7 percent body fat, the lowest of any tight end at the Combine, and is a very well-conditioned athlete. Solid showing during Senior Bowl week. Caught the ball effortlessly running through the gauntlet at the Combine. Versatile and lines up all over the field. Showed gradual improvement every year in the program and works at his craft. Identifies with the game and it's important to him.

Weaknesses: Tight in the hips and dull at the top of his routes, opening up break points to defenders. Average lateral agility. Not an explosive downfield seam-stretcher. Can be tracked from behind. Tends to play too narrow-based as an in-line blocker, negating lower-body power. Could stand to improve weight-room strength, especially in the lower half.

Future: A skilled receiver most ideally suited for a move role where he can work angles with momentum on his side. Warford has enough size to function in-line but is most ideally suited for a H-Back role and working out of the slot in the pros.

Draft projection: Third- to fourth-round pick.

Scout's take: "(Walford) is not explosive. He has some quickness and catches the ball well, but he does not scare you going down the field. He is a 4.8 guy. He might be one of the better tight ends in this year's class, but it's a bad class. They all will get pushed up a little higher than they should by teams in need."

TE [F] MAXX WILLIAMS, #88 (Soph-3)

MINNESOTA   ▶ GRADE: 5.72

Ht: 6-3⅞ | Wt: 249 | 40: 4.86 | Arm: 33½ | Hand: 10⅜

History: Father, Brian, played at Minnesota and was a first-round pick of the Giants (1989-99). Maxx played quarterback, linebacker and kicker as a Minnesota prep. Redshirted in 2012. Started 7-of-13 games in '13 and caught 25 balls for 417 yards (16.7-yard average) and five touchdowns. In '14, became only the third sophomore Mackey Award finalist — totaled 36-569-8 (15.8) in 12 games (10 starts). Did not play against San Jose State (right knee). Twenty-eight of 36 receptions went for a touchdown or first down. Will be a 21-year-old rookie.

Strengths: Has long arms and big hands and is a superb athlete. Plays faster than timed speed and flashes playmaking ability. Releases cleanly into routes. Reliable hands catcher – very natural, soft hands. Caught every ball effortlessly through the gauntlet drill at the Combine and makes it look easy. Very coordinated and balanced feet to 'dot the i.' Times jumps well. Nifty after the catch. Shows very good field awareness and hand-eye coordination – runs to the ball with the precision of a center-fielder and makes quick, in-air adjustments. Plucks the ball out of the air. Has NFL pedigree, is very young and has a lot of upside.

Weaknesses: Choppy short-stepper. Struggles to shake man coverage and needs to be schemed free on arrows, drags, digs and short underneath routes vs. zone coverage. Can do a better job setting up routes. Does

Maxx Williams

not produce many contested catches in crowds and short-arms the ball in traffic. Lacks girth and can be controlled with ease at the line of scrimmage. Bench-pressed only 17 reps at the Combine and needs to get stronger. Limited in-line blocking power, hip snap and on-the-move efficiency – falls off blocks and does not finish.

Future: A finesse, soft-handed, reliable receiver who could have really used another year in college to mature physically, yet could factor as a receiver readily. Is most ideally deployed as an inside, slot receiver. Still has a long way to go as a blocker and may never be great. Will make his mark in the league moving the sticks and producing big plays in the passing game.

Draft projection: Second- to third-round pick.

Scout's take: "He kind of reminds me of (Jets 2014 second-round pick) Jace Amaro. I thought (Williams) could have used another year of school to continue refining his game, but I understand why he decided to (declare early). This TE class is the worst I have seen in a while, and he might be the best of the group. He made that one highlight reel catch in the (Citrus Bowl) where he hurdled the guy and everyone thinks he is a great athlete. I think he's a bit overrated. He's one dimensional for what we do. ... I put him in the third (round)."

TIGHT ENDS

OFFENSIVE LINE

Nawrocki's TOP 10

1. **BRANDON SCHERFF**
2. **Andrus Peat**
3. **Ereck Flowers**
4. **Cameron Erving**
5. **D.J. Humphries**
6. **La'el Collins**
7. **Donovan Smith**
8. **A.J. Cann**
9. **Laken Tomlinson**
10. **Tre' Jackson**

ORT **DARRYL BALDWIN**, #76 (Sr-5)

OHIO STATE ▶ GRADE: 4.92

Ht: 6-5 ¾ | Wt: 305 | 40: 5.40e | Arm: 34 ⅞ | Hand: 9 ⅝

History: Lost his father to lupus in 2002. Played defensive tackle as a prep in Ohio, where he also competed in basketball and track and field. Redshirted in 2010. Appeared in seven games in '11 (wore jersey No. 90), collecting three tackles, one for loss and one sack. Switched to offensive line in '12 before appearing in all 12 games (101 snaps primarily on special teams). Played 12 games in '13, drawing one start at left tackle against Michigan in place of injured starter Jack Mewhort, who was drafted by the Colts in the second round of the '14 draft. Seized his opportunity in '14 when he started all 15 games at right tackle for the national champions. Graduated in May with a degree in business marketing and is working on a master's degree in sports management.

Strengths: Good length and overall body mass. Functional lower-body power. Can seal and turn defenders in the run game. Solid anchor in pass pro to stop a charge.

Weaknesses: Only a one-year starter. Limited foot quickness and lateral agility to handle quickness and speed. Can be slow off spots and reacting to second moves. Heavy climbing to the second level and struggles connecting and cutting off linebackers.

Future: Overshadowed by Colts 2014 second-round pick Jack Mewhort much of career, Baldwin emerged as a functional college starter on a national championship team as a senior and has enough size and length to warrant developing in a power-based scheme.

Draft projection: Priority free agent.

ORG-ORT **AL BOND**, #54 (Sr-5)

MEMPHIS ▶ GRADE: 5.01

Ht: 6-3 ¾ | Wt: 303 | 40: 5.58 | Arm: 33 ⅜ | Hand: 10 ¼

History: Prepped in Tennessee, where he captained the football team for three years and played basketball. Redshirted in 2010. Played

10 games in '11, starting the final seven at right tackle. Started all 12 games at ORT in '12. Played all 12 games in '13, starting 10 at right guard. Suffered a herniated disk in December. Moved back to ORT in '14 and started all 13 games. Graduated with a degree in Correctional Administration.

Strengths: Outstanding size. Good strength and lower-body power to move defenders in the run game. Good base, anchor strength to absorb a charge and control defenders in confined spaces. Experienced four-year starter. Is tough and played with a herniated disk (back) injury in 2013. Competes hard. Fairly versatile in college, lining up at center in the offseason workouts and having played guard and tackle.

Weaknesses: Limited hip flexibility and knee bend. Lacks ideal agility to adjust to movement and is heavily stressed by speed and inside counters. Too grabby in pass protection. Tends to overset, play too upright and extends over his toes too much. Late to see, recognize and adjust to the blitz. Is a bit top heavy. Could stand to improve weight-room strength. Has a 23 ½-inch vertical jump. Average Combine showing.

Future: A square-hipped, thick-bodied, short-area, interior blocker with enough versatility to fend for a job as a backup.

Draft projection: Priority free agent.

ORT BRETT BOYKO, #69 (Sr-5)

UNLV　　　　　　　　　　▶ GRADE: 4.95

Ht: 6-7 | Wt: 301 | 40: 5.59 | Arm: 32 | Hand: 9

History: Played defensive end and quarterback as a prep in Canada, where he also played basketball. Redshirted in 2010 after undergoing shoulder surgery. Stepped in to start all 12 games at left tackle in '11. Started all four games at OLT in '12 — tore cartilage in his left knee in Week Two, causing him to miss three games, then tore his left ACL in Week Four. Returned to start all 13 games at OLT in '13. Considered transferring to Missouri following graduation. Started all 13 games in '14 — the first eight at OLT, the final five at left guard. Suffered a left elbow injury in the season finale against Nevada and was not able to participate in the East-West Shrine Game. Team captain graduated with a psychology degree. Is rated the No. 1 prospect for the CFL Draft. Elected not to lift at the Combine because of a left elbow injury.

Strengths: Good body length. Solid technician in pass pro — efficient kickslide and

hand replacement. Understands how to play angles. Comes off the ball with urgency and creates good fits in the run game. Experienced four-year starter.

Weaknesses: Has small hands and short arms for as tall as he is, creating issues with leverage and balance. Sets too narrow-based and is not a natural knee-bender, translating to a lack of stoutness and point-of-attack strength. Limited athletic ability and foot speed to handle inside counters. Late to reach the second level and cut off linebackers.

Future: Scrappy, angular, underpowered college left tackle lacking the core strength ideally suited inside and the foot speed to handle wide rushers. Right tackle only. Increased value to the CFL could lessen NFL interest.

Draft projection: Priority free agent.

ORG-ORT JAMON BROWN, #79 (Sr-4)

LOUISVILLE　　　　　　　▶ GRADE: 5.26

Ht: 6-3 ⅝ | Wt: 323 | 40: 5.50e | Arm: 34 ⅜ | Hand: 9 ¾

History: Engaged with a child. Two-way lineman who also competed in power lifting as a Kentucky prep. As a true freshman in 2011, switched from defensive tackle in September — played nine games and started two at left guard. Moved to right tackle in '12, starting all 13 games. Started all 26 games at left tackle 2013-14. Graduated. Will be a 22-year-old rookie. Did not lift at the Combine after straining his right pectoral muscle during warmups and also did not run, jump or perform positional drills.

Strengths: Outstanding overall mass with very good arm length. Is strong and can lock up and mash defenders in confined quarters. Good point-of-attack strength in the run game. Is athletic enough to pull and lead up through holes (though often does not reach block point) and able to ride speed rushers wide of the pocket. Good anchor strength in pass pro. Versatile and has played left and right-handed. Extremely durable.

Weaknesses: Too much heaviness in his body and gets fatigued and tends to play tall. Weight has tended to fluctuate and could stand to improve conditioning. Subpar agility, body control and change of direction — struggles handling quickness and inside moves and lets defenders cross his face. Technique deteriorates the further he is asked to travel. Struggles to adjust to linebackers and movement at the second level. Could play with more awareness recognizing the blitz. Could improve overall

OFFENSIVE LINE

sustain and do a better job finishing. Is still learning what it means to really work and be a consummate pro.

Future: Very thick-bodied, strong-side college tackle lacking ideal height and agility to handle speed rushers in the pros and would be best suited playing on the right side or kicking in to right guard.

Draft projection: Fourth- to fifth-round pick.

ORT TRENTON BROWN, #74 (Sr-4)

FLORIDA ▶ GRADE: 5.22

Ht: 6-8 ½ | Wt: 355 | 40: 5.26 | Arm: 36 | Hand: 10 ⅞

History: Georgia native who played basketball prior to his junior season of high school. Spent 2011-12 at Georgia Military College, where he was an NJCAA All-American as a sophomore. With the Gators in '13, appeared in all 12 games and started the final five at right tackle after Tyler Moore was injured. In '14, started 6-of-11 games played at right guard. Did not play against Vanderbilt (knee bruise).

Strengths: Rare body and arm length and a wingspan of an aircraft carrier. Was the tallest and heaviest player measured at the NFL Combine and is a $25 cab ride to get around, also possessing the Combine's longest wingspan (87 ⅜ inches). Can control defenders when he gets his hands on them and generate some movement in the run game. Flashes a mean streak and seeks to finish. Plays heavy-handed and creates good extension. Adequate anchor strength to handle power — is seldom inverted. Good durability. Has upside (only played two years of high school football).

Weaknesses: Raw technician — turns his shoulders too early and falls off blocks. Tips when he is pulling with his stance and could stand to clean up his footwork. High-hipped and will get out-leveraged at the line. Lumbering movement skill. Does not play fast or get into blocks quickly. Could do a better job sustaining. Was only a part-time starter at Florida and did not prove fully committed. Could learn to be more vocal communicating with other offensive lineman pre-snap.

Future: A thickly built, long-levered size prospect with ability to bump-and-steer and control defenders for a big-bodied, mashing offensive line such as the Steelers, Lions or Colts. Will require some patience to be groomed.

Draft projection: Late draftable pick.

Scout's take: "I kept him alive in the sixth round for his size. He is really (an NFL) tackle playing guard (in college). He has balance issues that bothered me."

OLG A.J. CANN, #50 (Sr-5)

SOUTH CAROLINA ▶ GRADE: 5.78

Ht: 6-2 ¾ | Wt: 313 | 40: 5.25e | Arm: 32 ⅝ | Hand: 10 ¼

History: South Carolina native who was a dominant two-way lineman as a prep. Redshirted in 2010. Took ownership of the left guard position in '11 when he started all 13 games. In '12, started 12-of-13 games — lone non-start was against Florida (coach's decision). Started all 26 games from 2013-14. Did not play in the Senior Bowl (knee), and did not work out at the Combine (left calf). Two-time captain graduated with a degree in African American studies in December 2013. Did not run the 40-yard dash at the Combine because of left hamstring injury.

Strengths: Good functional, football-playing strength. Natural knee-bender with good lower-body explosion. Understands leverage and positioning. Agile and athletic enough to climb to the second level and pick off linebackers. Very good anchor strength and agility in pass protection. Shuffles, slides and stays square. Consistently controls the line of scrimmage. Matched up very well vs. Auburn's Gabe Wright. Experienced four-year starter in the Southeastern Conference. Outstanding intangibles. Respected leader of the line. Energetic and upbeat and will boost morale in the locker room. Has a strong support system. Studies the game and works at the craft. Extremely durable.

Weaknesses: Average arm length. Not a glass-eater. Does not explode off the ball and could do a better job finishing blocks. Gets caught up in traffic and can be late to locate targets on the move (see Clemson) and consistently seal linebackers. Limited versatility.

Future: A compact, dependable, NFL-ready left guard with the strength, mass, intelligence and work ethic to be a 10-year starter in the pros. Should be able to contribute immediately and elevate the play of those around him. Compares favorably to Falcons 2007 second-round pick (39th overall) Justin Blalock.

Draft projection: Top-50 pick.

Scout's take: "I have a problem with his balance and body control. I didn't see the power to him. Maybe some of it had to do with how much the team was struggling. ... Of all the guards, I think he probably winds up being the first off (the board). I graded him in the low

OFFENSIVE LINE

second. I think he'll go higher."

ORT T.J. CLEMMINGS, #68 (Sr-5)

PITTSBURGH   ▶ GRADE: 5.56

Ht: 6-4 ¾ | Wt: 309 | 40: 5.14 | Arm: 35 ⅛ | Hand: 10 ⅜

History: Highly recruited New Jersey prep who also received multiple Division I basketball offers. Did not play football until his junior season, but won a pair of Non-Public Group 1 state championships. As a true freshman defensive lineman in 2010 (wore jersey No. 90), appeared in eight games and recorded three tackles, one for loss and zero sacks. Redshirted in '11. Started 6-of-8 games at defensive end in '12, tallying 20-1-0 before moving to offensive line prior to the Compass Bowl against Mississippi (did not play). Dealt with a lower-back injury in September. Became a full-time right tackle and started all 26 games 2013-14. Team captain played for three different coaching staffs.

Strengths: Looks every bit the part with exceptional arm length, good musculature and a very athletic, well-distributed frame. Has a basketball background and terrific feet to shuffle and mirror. Can match up with speed and power. Fires off the ball and runs his feet in the run game to generate movement. Quick to the second level and is effective scaling defenders. Can throw his hips in the hole and reach defenders. Climbs quickly to the second level. Has piston feet in pass pro in his kickslide and gets good depth. Flashes good pop in his punch. Has a 32-½-inch vertical jump and recorded a 4.54-second short shuttle time at the Combine, among the best for offensive linemen. Immense upside. Very durable.

Weaknesses: Marginal blocking instincts and awareness. Slides off blocks too easily and gives up the inside. Not enough coordination between his hands and feet and is too easily short-circuited by stunts and games and late to recognize the blitz.

Future: An unpolished athletic specimen who will enamor evaluators with his physical tools and drive them crazy with his inconsistent technique. Would be best next to a very smart blocker who could help him with assignments. Played right tackle but has athletic traits to play on the left side if he could continue to refine his game. Would be most ideally suited in a zone-blocking scheme, where his quick feet and athletic ability are big pluses. An overhyped, media darling lacking the same love within the scouting community.

Draft projection: Second-round pick.

Scout's take: "The coaches have to hit the reset button every day to coach him. He doesn't see it. He's a developmental project. It's very clear on the school call watching him in practice and was even more evident at the Senior Bowl. I have him in the fifth round. I realize he probably will be taken in the second (round) because he has length and tools to work with. His upside is off the charts. The learning curve and how long it is going to take him is going to be key. If you take him too early, the expectations could create too much pressure to perform right away, and he's not ready."

OLG TAKOBY COFIELD, #73 (Sr-5)

DUKE   ▶ GRADE: 5.12

Ht: 6-4 ¼ | Wt: 310 | 40: 5.17 | Arm: 34 | Hand: 10

History: Also lettered in track and field as a prep in North Carolina, where he won a football state title. Redshirted in 2010. Played 10 games in '11, starting the final two at left tackle. Missed two games with an upper-body injury. Started all 40 games at OLT 2012-14. Missed '14 spring practice while nursing a sprained left MCL.

Strengths: Has a thick trunk with a big bubble, good lower-body strength and good arm length. Has enough size to bump, steer and wall off. Tough competitor. Physically tough and will battle through injuries.

Weaknesses: A bit knock-kneed and does not look the part. Lacks ideal height for a tackle. Could do a better job staying square in pass protection. Below-average hand quickness and technique – catches too much. Needs to improve his hand placement and learn to replace his hands in pass pro. Limited body control and recovery quickness. Is stressed by outside speed too much to handle the edges. Gives up ground vs. power. Struggled at the NFLPA Collegiate Bowl.

Future: Undersized, body-blocking college left tackle most ideally suited to zone block from the inside where he has help on both sides of him.

Draft projection: Late draftable pick.

Scout's take: "I thought he could have a chance to move into guard because of his lack of athleticism at tackle. He has that big wide body. He has to play guard because it helps cover up the deficiencies he has out at tackle."

OLG-ORT LA'EL COLLINS, #70 (Sr-4)

LSU   ▶ GRADE: 5.95

Ht: 6-4 ½ | Wt: 305 | 40: 5.14 | Arm: 33 ¼ | Hand: 10 ⅜

History: Recently reunited with father who was released from jail after 20 years. Elite recruit coming out of Louisiana, where he was

OFFENSIVE LINE

a Parade and USA Today All-American who garnered all-state recognition three times. As a true freshman in 2011, appeared in seven games (46 snaps). Started all 13 games at left guard in '12, notching an impressive, team-leading 64.5 knockdowns. Shifted to left tackle in '13 when he started all 12 games played and logged 65 knockdowns. Sat out against Furman (MCL sprain). Was the Jacobs Blocking Trophy winner (top offensive lineman in the Southeastern Conference) and LSU's most outstanding player in '14 when he piled up 88 knockdowns in 13 starts at OLT. Team captain will be a 22-year-old rookie.

Strengths: Powerfully built with a strong frame, wide shoulders, long arms and massive hands. Very good weight-room strength and functional, football-playing strength and power. Knocks defenders off the line and generates a surge in the run game. Good hip roll and lower-body explosion. Plays with a chip on his shoulder and seeks to finish. Has grappler grip strength to control and ragdoll linebackers. Consistently runs pass-rushers wide of the pocket and shows he can handle speed. Dropped nearly 20 pounds from his junior to senior season and showed more foot agility and quickness. Versatile and has played inside and outside. Very durable.

Weaknesses: Lacks ideal height for the outside. Has some hip tightness that leaves him on the ground more than he should be. Average lateral agility to adjust to movement. Tends to get too overextended and grab a lot on the move. Could do a better job striking in pass protection and playing with more consistent knee bend (will lock his knees and get too upright). Struggled to handle the edge speed of sensational Texas A&M freshman DE Myles Garrett.

Future: A very thickly-built, wide-bodied, college left tackle who plays a power game more ideally suited for the right side or the interior. Is a good enough foot athlete to handle the left side, but could be a road-grading interior presence, with the ability to pull, anchor and plow holes open. Versatility is a plus that could drive up his draft status.

Draft projection: Top-50 pick.

Scout's take: "(Collins) is good-looking in the upper body but thin in the lower. He doesn't have great hip flexibility. He is athletic and has balance and footwork, but he's not a great foot athlete. And I don't think he is overly powerful. He does a good job when he got his hands on guys. I didn't see him creating consistent movement. He tries to create it a lot out of his upper body."

OLT ROB CRISP, #78 (Sr-5)

NORTH CAROLINA STATE   ▶ GRADE: 5.21

Ht: 6-6 ⅝ | Wt: 301 | 40: 5.29 | Arm: 34 ½ | Hand: 10

History: Highly recruited Parade All-American. As a true freshman in 2010, saw limited action in 13 games (started the season opener at left tackle). Played all 13 games in '11 (413 snaps), starting two at right tackle. In '12, started all eight games played at OLT. Suffered a broken tailbone in the season opener against Tennessee and missed four games. Started the first two games of the '13 season before he was sidelined by a concussion. Was granted a medical hardship, and returned to start all 13 games at OLT in '14.

Strengths: Exceptional body length. Looks the part with a rangy, athletic build. Quick-footed and athletic enough to handle edge speed and run speed rushers wide of the pocket — showed well matching up against Clemson's Vic Beasley. Fine balance in pass protection. Recorded a 32 ½-inch vertical jump and a 4.60 short shuttle, among the best measurables of OL participants at the Combine.

Weaknesses: Plays with too much finesse. Can be out-leveraged and overpowered and give up a lot of ground vs. mass. Is late to adjust to inside counters (soft power step and anchor). Below-average functional strength. Inconsistent eyes recognizing the blitz. Late to locate targets on the second level. Could struggle with hard coaching. Durability concerns must be vetted carefully after concussion issues ended his junior season prematurely and took a psychological toll.

Future: Fairly athletic, quick-footed zone blocker with the size, body and arm length to warrant interest as a developmental left tackle prospect. Durability issues could affect his draft status and playing performance, but he could develop into a contributor if he can stay healthy and focused.

Draft projection: Late draftable pick.

Scout's take: "I'm not sure if he is good enough of a player to overcome some of the issues in his past. He is 6-6 with long arms, big hands and athletic tools. Someone will give him a chance late."

C REESE DISMUKES, #50 (Sr-4)

AUBURN   ▶ GRADE: 5.26

Ht: 6-2 ¾ | Wt: 296 | 40: 5.31 | Arm: 32 ¼ | Hand: 8 ⅞

History: Parade All-American who was one of the top center recruits in America coming out of Spanish Fort, Ala., where he won a state title, was voted 5A Lineman of the Year and was runner-up for Mr. Football. Had his right labrum surgically repaired prior to his senior season. Two-year captain. Stepped right into the lineup as a true freshman in 2011 when he started all 13 games. In '12, started all 10 games played — was arrested in August for public intoxication and served a one-game suspension (season opener against Clemson) then missed the Ole Miss contest with a dislocated right elbow. Was a Rimington finalist in '14 when he started all 14 games. Won the Rimington and was an Outland finalist in '14 when he started all 13 games. His 50 career starts is the second most in school history. Two-year captain. Graduated.

Strengths: Plays with solid technique and understands his responsibilities. Good snap-and-step quickness. Alert and aware to inside pressure. Plays with an edge and seeks to finish blocks. Experienced, four-year starter in the Southeastern Conference. Holds teammates accountable.

Weaknesses: Is narrow-shouldered and light-framed with a smooth-muscled body, short arms and very small hands, the smallest of any offensive lineman at the Combine. Is troubled by size and power (see Alabama). Has a tendency to bend at the waist and get overextended. Measured 28 percent body fat at the Combine and could stand to improve conditioning. Personal character requires closer scrutiny – could have some issues fitting in the locker room.

Future: Stiff, overly-muscled, grind-it-out blocker with the toughness and grit to earn a starting job in the pros.

Draft projection: Fourth- to fifth-round pick.

Scout's take: "(Dismukes) is highly touted, but he plays short-armed. He is a good technician, but he is not explosive or powerful. He lacks a lot of pop. I was not wowed by him. (Coaches) tell you how tough and nasty he is, but I just don't see it in games. It's all about turning and positioning and walling off.

To me, he is probably no worse than (Patriots 2014 fourth-round pick) Bryan Stork, who was a hit-and-fit guy with short arms. I want my center to have some size and length and be athletic."

ORT-ORG ANDREW DONNAL, #78 (Sr-5)

IOWA　　　　　　　　　　▶ GRADE: 5.25

Ht: 6-5 ⅞ | Wt: 313 | 40: 5.32 | Arm: 33 ½ | Hand: 10

History: Last name is pronounced "duh-NELL." Prepped in Ohio, where he also played basketball and competed in track and field (throws). Redshirted in 2010. Appeared in four games in '11. Appeared in seven games in '12, starting three at left guard. Missed the last five games of the season after tearing the MCL, PCL and meniscus in his right knee. Was a reserve in '13 when he saw action at right guard and tackle (13 games). Started all 13 games at right tackle in '14.

Strengths: Quick into blocks and can reach and hook. Works up to the second level and can fit on linebackers. Can steer and control. Very active hands. Understands angles. Good recovery speed. Tough competitor. Versatile and has played inside and outside.

Weaknesses: Underpowered with limited lower-body strength and explosion. Tends to play a bit tall and does not drive defenders off the ball in the run game. Only a one-year, full-time starter. Average finishing strength. Bench-pressed only 17 reps at the Combine and needs to spend more time in the weight room and get stronger.

Future: More explosive than strong, Donnal is a light-footed, zone blocker with intriguing versatility to contribute as a four-position swing backup and has upside to continue developing.

Draft projection: Fifth- to sixth-round pick.

OLG JAMIL DOUGLAS, #74 (Sr-5)

ARIZONA STATE　　　　　▶ GRADE: 5.27

Ht: 6-4 | Wt: 304 | 40: 5.22 | Arm: 33 ⅜ | Hand: 10 ¾

History: Prepped in California. Redshirted in 2010. Was arrested in October on suspicion of second-degree burglary — reportedly stole a laptop and video-game equipment from a dorm. Was a reserve/special-teams player in '11 when he appeared in all 13 games. Started all 27 games at left guard 2012-13. Moved to left tackle in '14 when he started all 13 games. Team captain won the Sun Devils' weight room performance award. Graduated with criminal justice degree.

Strengths: Good explosive power. Can pull and kick out defenders. Good pop and power in his hands. Very solid base in pass pro – good hands fighter. Can handle power. Solid football character. Works hard in the weight room and translates his weight-room strength to the field. Tough, chippy and aggressive blocking temperament. Generally blocks his man.

Weaknesses: Lacks ideal length to play outside. Average body control to adjust on the move and often lands on the ground when he redirects. Will fall off blocks on the perimeter and mechanics break down the further he travels. Overall balance could stand

OFFENSIVE LINE

to improve.

Future: Moved to left tackle as a senior as the bell cow of the offensive line, yet is most naturally suited at left guard in the pros. Explosive zone blocker with the movement skill and strength to develop into a solid pro. Looked out of place on an island as a senior and much more comfortable operating from the interior.

Draft projection: Fourth- to fifth-round pick.

C-OLG CORNELIUS EDISON, #77 (Sr-4)

Portland State   Grade: 5.10

Ht: 6-2 ⅞ | Wt: 299 | 40: 5.25e | Arm: 33 ½ | Hand: 9 ½

History: Two-way lineman from the state of Washington. Tore his right meniscus in the winter of 2009. As a true freshman in '11, sustained a concussion during fall camp before appearing in three games on the season. Started all 23 games at left guard 2012-13. Shifted to center in '14 and won the FCS Rimington Award (12 starts). Team captain.

Strengths: Good arm length for the interior. Moves well for his size. Can pull and reach defenders on the second level. Takes good angles and runs his feet on contact. Good awareness in pass protection. Is tough and will play through injuries. Mentally tough and competitive. Good personal and football character.

Weaknesses: Undersized. Plays a bit narrow-based. Could do a better job of running his feet through contact — gets stalled and does not finish. Regularly faced lesser FCS competition.

Future: A swing, interior blocker who moved to center as a senior and made the most of the opportunity. Could take some time adapting to NFL competition, yet possesses enough strength, agility and competitiveness to earn a job.

Draft projection: Late draftable pick.

C-OLT CAMERON ERVING, #75 (Sr-5)

FLORIDA STATE   ▶ GRADE: 6.12

Ht: 6-5 ½ | Wt: 313 | 40: 5.12 | Arm: 34 ⅛ | Hand: 10 ⅜

History: Played defensive tackle as a Georgia prep, recording 98 tackles as a senior. Suffered a bulging disc and redshirted in 2010. Was a backup defensive tackle in '11 (wore jersey No. 98) — tallied 20 tackles, 2 1/2 for loss and one sack. Converted to OLT the following spring and started all 28 games 2012-13. After his junior season, lost his aunt (heart failure) and grandmother (pancreatic cancer) in a three-month span. Started all 14 games in '14 — nine at OLT and the final five at center. Two-time Jacobs Trophy winner as

the ACC's top blocker according to coaches. Has torn his right meniscus twice.

Strengths: Outstanding size – has long arms, big hands and natural girth. Terrific balance and body control — is seldom on the ground. Natural knee bender with outstanding lateral agility. Uses his hands very well to keep defenders off his frame. Quick into his blocks. Takes good angles to the second level and has a very good feel for positioning and run fits. Generates some power through his lower half to and is strong enough at the point of attack to handle massive wide-bodies. Very smart and versatile and can play anywhere along the line. Very good football intelligence. Charismatic leader and people pleaser.

Weaknesses: Can get sloppy and slow with his hands on the edge and get rocked handling speed-to-power moves. Struggles some with elite edge speed on the outside and is susceptible to inside moves. Not consistently powerful driving defenders. Scouts have questioned his toughness.

Future: One of the few players in the draft with the football smarts, agility, length and mass to line up at any position on the offensive line. Has been a very consistent performer in an elite program and possesses unique potential to be a five-position player. Will require some more refinement adjusting to the inside, but his skill set is best suited inside. Can be plugged in Day One

Draft projection: Top-40 pick.

Scout's take: "Athletic tackles get pushed up. He is no worse than (Dolphins 2014 19th overall pick) Ja'Wuan James and some of the others that have gone in the first round. He's stronger and more physical than James. He might not be as agile or as quick to recover. ... If Erving plays center (in the pros), he might be the best in the class. He's intriguing there because he is so big."

ORT TAYO FABULUJE, #59 (Sr-5)

TCU   ▶ GRADE: 5.02

Ht: 6-6 ⅜ | Wt: 353 | 40: 5.56 | Arm: 34 | Hand: 9 ⅞

History: Name is pronounced "TIE-oh fa-BOO-LOU-ZHAY." Born in Nigeria. Won a football state championship and lettered in basketball and track as a Texas prep. Began his college career at BYU, where he redshirted in 2010. Transferred to TCU to be closer to home and sat out the '11 season per NCAA rules. In '12, started 12-of-13 games — the first 10 at left tackle, the final two at right tackle. Did not play football in '13 — with his mother in legal trouble, was forced to take a job in order to support his mother and sister. Transferred back to BYU (as a student only) in order to save money on his tuition and living expenses (family friend offered him a place to stay). At the time was working three jobs. Transferred back to TCU and re-joined the football team in '14 — missed time during spring practice (high ankle sprain), but started all 12 games played at OLT. Sat out against SMU (back). Graduated with a degree in psychology. Did not lift at the Combine because of a right shoulder injury and did not perform the broad jump or three-cone drill because of a left hip flexor injury.

Strengths: Good arm length and grip strength. Possesses raw power and brute strength in his body. Consistently creates a surge in the run game and relishes moving defenders off the line. Physical finisher. Once he gets his hands on defenders, they are done. Sets a wall in pass protection and gives up little ground.

Weaknesses: Does not look the part, with too much smooth muscle. Average foot quickness and agility to handle elite speed. Tends to open his shoulders too quickly and becomes susceptible to inside counters. Could stand to do a better job latching on and controlling pass rushers. Marginal football character. A follower too easily persuaded — has transferred between BYU and TCU three times. Lacks mental toughness desired in the trenches and is still learning what it means to work.

Future: A big-bodied, lumbering mauler who profiles as a right tackle only in the pros. Is very strong and could make it on a power-based offensive line.

Draft projection: Late draftable pick.

ORG JON FELICIANO, #70 (Sr-5)

MIAMI (FLA.)   ▶ GRADE: 5.12

Ht: 6-3 ⅞ | Wt: 323 | 40: 5.36 | Arm: 32 ⅜ | Hand: 9 ¾

History: A Florida native, Feliciano grew up poor and was raised by his mother, who has been diagnosed with cancer twice. At one point, slept in a condemned house. Also played basketball in high school. Broke his right foot in the spring of 2009. Created his own scholarship opportunity by personally seeking out a Miami assistant. Redshirted in '10. Al Golden replaced Randy Shannon in '11, and Feliciano started 7-of-10 games at left guard. Missed two games with a high right ankle sprain. Tore his right meniscus during '12 spring practice. In the fall, started all 12 games at OLG. Sustained a concussion during '13 spring practice. On the season, started all 13 games — 11 at OLG, two at right tackle. Started all 13 games in '14 — nine at OLG, three at ORT and one at left tackle. Team captain became the first in his family to earn a degree. Did not lift at the Combine because of a left shoulder injury and elected not to run the 3-cone drill.

Strengths: Effective cut blocker. Good football-playing temperament. Is strong at the point of attack and can anchor in pass protection. Alert vs. the blitz and quick to recognize stunts and games and switch off blocks. Good inside hand placement. Versatile and has played inside and outside.

Weaknesses: Does not run his feet through contact and falls off blocks. Average athletic ability. Tight-hipped. Is late to reach the second level. Marginal contact balance. Tends to bend at the waist too much and consequently spends too much time on the ground.

Future: A big, strong, short-area blocker who played on the left side most of his career, yet has a skill set that looks best suited for the ORG position in a power scheme.

Draft projection: Late draftable pick.

Scout's take: "Feliciano is a tough mauler. He's heavy-handed with a strong upper (body). He is not a good athlete or a good foot athlete. He is slightly better than a phone-booth guy. He'll get drafted late. I put him in the bottom of (the sixth round). He is just a tough kid with size – nothing special."

C B.J. FINNEY, #66 (Sr-5)

KANSAS STATE   ▶ GRADE: 5.19

Ht: 6-3 ¾ | Wt: 318 | 40: 5.31 | Arm: 32 | Hand: 10

History: Won state championships in football and wrestling as a Kansas prep. Walked on and redshirted in 2010. Started all 13 games in '11 — the season opener at left guard and the final 12 at center. Started all 39 games at center 2012-14. As a senior, was a Rimington finalist and the Big 12's Co-Offensive Lineman of the Year. Saw time at left tackle against West Virginia and UCLA. Three-time captain. Graduated with a degree in history.

Strengths: Stout at the point of attack with solid base, anchor strength to handle mass and power. Did not give much ground against Oklahoma NT Jordan Phillips. Plays strong-handed. Highly respected, vocal team leader. Is accountable and sets a good example. Experienced, durable four-year starter — never missed a game. Good communicator — makes all the line calls.

Weaknesses: Tends to set tall and is not a natural knee-bender. Limited lateral agility and

OFFENSIVE LINE

quickness, confirmed in laboring to change direction at the Combine. Is slow to get out to the second level and cut off linebackers and can be vulnerable and require help vs. quick penetrators. Late to reach blocking point pulling and leading upfield on screens. Slow to switch off blocks and pick up the blitz. Average arm length. Bench-pressed only 20 reps at the Combine and could stand to improve upper-body strength. Tied for the shortest arms (32 inches) of any offensive lineman at the Combine. Recorded 29.4 percent body fat at the Combine, the second highest of any offensive lineman, and could stand to improve conditioning.

Future: A big-bodied, country-strong, base blocker best in a phone booth. Has the size, intelligence and intangibles to compensate for his lack of agility and athletic ability, yet could always leave evaluators wanting more.

Draft projection: Fifth- to sixth-round pick.

OLT JAKE FISHER, #75 (Sr-4)

OREGON ▶ GRADE: 5.54

| Ht: 6-6 ⅛ | Wt: 306 | 40: 5.02 | Arm: 33 ¾ | Hand: 10 ⅜ |

History: Played tight end and defensive line as a Michigan prep. Originally committed to the University of Michigan and then-head coach Rich Rodriguez — de-committed when Rodriguez was fired before signing with Oregon (and then-head coach Chip Kelly). Was a reserve as a true freshman in 2011, appearing in 13 games. Played all 13 games in '12, starting 11 at right tackle. In '13, started 11-of-12 games played at ORT — did not play against Washington State and did not start against Washington State because of a hip flexor injury. Started all 13 games played at left tackle in '14 — sprained his left MCL against Wyoming and was sidelined against Washington State and Arizona. Was moved to left tackle in training camp as a senior to replace the injured Tyler Johnstone.

Strengths: Good overall length. Keeps his hands inside and can lock down defenders once he gets his hands on them. Flashes a rapid punch. Nifty enough to reach and hook defenders. Shows awareness vs. the blitz. Is physically tough and will battle through injuries. Showed very well in movement drills at the Combine, besting all offensive linemen with a 4.33-second short shuttle, 7.25-second three-cone drill, 1.70-second 10-yard split and 5.01 40-yard dash (second-best).

Weaknesses: Average core strength and recovery speed. Does not dominate at the point of attack and can be stressed by speed inside

and outside. Is late to reach the second level and cut off linebackers. Tends to lunge and overextend the further he is asked to travel and slips off blocks on the move. Tends to set tall in pass pro and could do a better job sinking his hips and anchoring. Does not consistently finish in the run game. Too grabby.

Future: A light-framed, positional-blocking, swing tackle with enough toughness to play on the right side and enough foot speed to help in a pinch on the left side. Is best in confined areas and most ideally suited for a No. 3 role in a zone-blocking scheme. Possesses eventual starter potential. Exceptional Combine testing could drive up his value.

Draft projection: Second- to third-round pick.

Scout's take: "He came in to the Combine and really showcased himself after having a solid week at the Senior Bowl. He was decent in the game — not great. It's the practice that matters."

OLT ERECK FLOWERS, #74 (Jr-3)

MIAMI (FLA.) ▶ GRADE: 6.32

| Ht: 6-6 ¼ | Wt: 329 | 40: 5.34 | Arm: 34 ½ | Hand: 9 ⅞ |

History: Miami, Fla. native won a state championship as a senior. As a true freshman in 2012, played all 12 games with four early-season starts at right tackle. Started all 13 games at left tackle in '13. Started 11-of-12 games played at OLT in '14 — missed the North Carolina contest after having surgery to repair a torn meniscus suffered against Virginia Tech. Elected not to perform jumps or shuttles at the Combine. Will be a 21-year-old rookie.

Strengths: Massive bodied with a long torso and short trunk. Plays with terrific leverage, locking out and keeping defenders at bay in pass protection. Understands angles and positioning. Climbs to the second level and is surprisingly light on his feet for his size to reach linebackers. Collapses the line on down blocks and sets a wall sealing off at the second level. Flashes a nasty steak. Good balance in his feet and recovery speed – runs defenders wide of the pocket. Matches up very well against power. Very good weight-room strength. Paced all players at the Combine with 37 bench-press reps. Buried Nebraska's Randy Gregory in the run game in Week Four and matched up very well in pass pro.

Weaknesses: Has some heaviness shuffling and sliding. Labors more in his kick slide than is desired in a blind-side protector. Can be late to cut off the edge. Needs to show more awareness vs. stunts and games and can be knocked off balance from his inside. Struggles some anchoring vs. power-leverage rushers (see Virginia vs. Eli Harold). Plays a bit out of control on the move and will get overextended lunging and fall off blocks.

Future: A powerfully built, college left tackle with good enough length, feet and agility to handle elite NFL speed rushers, though would be most at home playing on the right side where he could use his unique power to mash defenders in the run game and would be more often matched vs. power than speed. Is just a pup and his best football is still ahead of him.

Draft projection: First-round pick.

Scout's take: "I am a Flowers fan. I think he goes anywhere from 25 in the first (round) to 50 in the second. I lean towards higher. He's big, long and has played the position. He's not the niftiest, but he could be a good right tackle. He could play on both sides, but is more of a right (tackle) looking at his overall athleticism if you had to start him off somewhere."

C ANDY GALLIK, #59 (Sr-5)

BOSTON COLLEGE ▶ GRADE: 5.23

Ht: 6-2 ¾ | Wt: 306 | 40: 5.51 | Arm: 32 ¾ | Hand: 10 ¼

History: Chicago Catholic League product. Redshirted in 2010. Played nine games in '11, starting three early-season games at center. Took ownership of the center spot and started all 37 games 2012-14. Was a Rimington finalist as a senior. Suffered an ankle injury in the Pinstripe Bowl against Penn State and did not play in the Senior Bowl. Team captain graduated with a sociology degree.

Strengths: Has very good overall body mass with a sturdy frame and a thick, stout trunk. Good lower-body, base strength to stop a charge in pass pro. Flashes a mean streak. Football smart, makes the line calls and sets the protection. Good lateral agility. Ran a 4.58-second short shuttle time at the Combine, tied for the best of any interior offensive lineman. Hard working, committed, tough and very durable.

Weaknesses: Duck-footed with heavy legs. Limited athletic ability. Lets blockers cross his face and can be overwhelmed by stunts. Gives up the edge too easily in pass pro and is not quick to adjust to movement or switch off blocks. Average lower-body explosion. Limited versatility — center only.

Future: A heavy-legged, short-stepping, zone center with the toughness, football smarts and competitiveness to play a long time in the league. Blue-collar worker who will bring his lunch pail and hard hat every day and find a way to get the job done.

Draft projection: Fourth- to fifth-round pick.

Scout's take: "(Gallik) is kind of like the guy in Green Bay now (Corey Linsley). He has a little shorter arms. He's tough, smart, could pull and has some trouble with size because of those short arms. But he is athletic and tough. He is not a sexy pick. He's just going to be solid."

C-OG MAX GARCIA, #76 (Sr-5)

FLORIDA ▶ GRADE: 5.20

Ht: 6-4 ⅛ | Wt: 309 | 40: 5.35e | Arm: 33 ⅛ | Hand: 10 ¼

History: Also competed in track and field (throws) as a Georgia prep. Began college at Maryland, where he was recruited by Ralph Friedgen and James Franklin. Was slated to redshirt in 2010, but injuries forced him to appear in two games as a reserve left tackle. Started all 12 games at OLT in '11 before requesting a release from his scholarship. Transferred to UF and sat out '12 per NCAA rules. Dealt with a bulging disc in his back in summer '13, but was good to go in the fall when he started all 12 games — seven at left guard, five at OLT. Shifted to center in '14 and started all 12 games, grading out at 97 percent. Following the season, was voted a team captain and co-offensive MVP in addition to receiving separate awards for leadership, tenacity and community service. Was a medical exclusion from working out at the Combine because of a left shoulder injury (pectoralis).

Strengths: Outstanding size with good arm length for the interior. Good anchor strength to match up against size and power. Smart and tough. Extremely versatile — has played all five positions. Makes all the line calls. Good weight-room strength.

Weaknesses: Tends to lock his knees and play too straight-legged, which translates to getting overextended and struggling to sustain. Bends too much at the waist. Could stand to do a better job sinking his hips and firing off the ball low. Not a consistently strong finisher. Is challenged by the speed of quick penetrators. Late to reach linebackers at the second level and gets too grabby attempting to fit.

Future: Tight-hipped, top-heavy, upper-body blocker best in close quarters. Size prospect with enough functional strength and versatility to compete for a job as an interior swing backup.

Draft projection: Late draftable pick.

Scout's take: "What I really like about Garcia – he has started at all five positions on

OFFENSIVE LINE

the offensive line. There is a lot to be said for that when you are looking for a backup player. He has starts at every position. He can put either hand down in the dirt and have some ability. And he has size. (Look at the) center (Jonotthan Harrison) out of Florida last year that went undrafted to Indianapolis. Because of injuries, he wound up starting a lot of games for them."

OLT LAURENCE GIBSON, #63 (Sr-5)

VIRGINIA TECH   ▶ GRADE: 5.26

Ht: 6-5 ¾ | Wt: 305 | 40: 5.08 | Arm: 35 ⅛ | Hand: 10 ⅜

History: Played just two years of football as an Arizona prep. Spent 2009 at Hargrave Military Academy (Va.). Redshirted in '10; appeared in one game in '11; and saw limited action in 12 games in '12. Started 6-of-12 games played at right tackle in '13. Missed time during '14 fall camp with a foot sprain. On the season, started all 13 games at left tackle. Owns two degrees (sociology and psychology). Will be a 24-year-old rookie.

Strengths: Outstanding athlete. Extremely long arms. Locks on in the run game and runs his feet. Very quick working to the second level. Was the most explosive jumper among offensive linemen at the Combine, registering a 33 ½-inch vertical jump and a 9-foot-5-inch broad jump. Has an extremely low 10.80 percent body fat, the lowest of any offensive lineman at the Combine, and is a very well-conditioned athlete who looks like he is moving better in the fourth quarter than he does in the first. Humble and grounded.

Weaknesses: Tends to set tall in pass pro and can be out-leveraged by speed and power. Does not play strong. Needs to improve his functional football-playing core strength and learn to sink his hips to anchor. Took a long time to become a full-time starter in college and lacks confidence in his immense abilities.

Future: Developmental left tackle with very intriguing size, length and movement skill. Made considerable strides as a senior when he bulked up, but must hone his technique and continue to get stronger to handle NFL edge rushers. Would fit best in a zone-based blocking scheme and has a lot of upside to be groomed.

Draft projection: Fourth- to fifth-round pick.

ORG-C MARK GLOWINSKI, #64 (Sr-5)

WEST VIRGINIA   ▶ GRADE: 5.26

Ht: 6-4 ⅜ | Wt: 307 | 40: 5.21 | Arm: 33 ⅛ | Hand: 9 ¾

History: Prepped in Pennsylvania. Was a two-year starter (2010-11) at Lackawanna College (Pa.) before redshirting at WVU in

'12. Started all 25 games at right guard 2013-14. Graduated.

Strengths: Looks the part. Solid in pass protection – can shuffle, slide and mirror and is alert to the blitz. Keeps his head on a swivel. Flashes pop in his punch. Can seal and wall off. Tied for the best broad jump (9-feet, 5-inches) among offensive linemen at the Combine and also recorded the top short shuttle (4.58 seconds) among guards. Handled the quickness of Texas DT Malcom Brown and battles vs. better competition.

Weaknesses: Plays small. Tight in the lower body. Needs to learn how to use his hands better to strike and control defenders. Plays short-armed and is very grabby. Not powerful. Limited body control on the move and unable to come to balance and redirect to cut off linebackers at the second level.

Future: Fairly athletic chest-blocker who does not play to his workout numbers, yet shows enough quickness, agility and balance to function in a zone-blocking scheme. A better tester than football player.

Draft projection: Middle-round pick.

Scout's take: "I was surprised. When you look at the top performers from the Combine, Glowinski was one of the better performers in most categories. He tested really well and then worked out pretty good (in the positional drills)."

C HRONISS GRASU, #55 (Sr-5)

OREGON   ▶ GRADE: 5.58

Ht: 6-3 | Wt: 297 | 40: 5.02 | Arm: 32 ⅛ | Hand: 10 ¼

History: Two-way lineman as a Los Angeles, Calif. prep. Born to Romanian immigrants. Redshirted in 2010 before taking ownership of the center position. Started all 40 games 2011-13. Had arthroscopic surgery on his left wrist after his sophomore season. Started all 12 games in '14, though he did not play against Colorado, Oregon State and Arizona (left ankle) and played through the injury late in the season. Also sat out the Senior Bowl. Two-time Rimington finalist. Team captain. Was a medical exclusion from the Combine because of a left ankle and left shoulder (pectoralis) injury.

Strengths: Has big hands. Quick into his blocks. Can wall off and seal. Natural knee bender. Takes good angles. Good ankle flexion. Works up to the second level and can initiate contact and fit on linebackers. Plays with good leverage and technique. Very good balance and lateral agility to handle quick, gap penetrators.

OFFENSIVE LINE

Quick to recognize the blitz. Experienced four-year starter. Outstanding football character. Respected team leader. Mentally tough and will play through injuries.

Weaknesses: Average hip roll and explosion — lacks the core functional strength to drive defenders off the ball. Can be overpowered by big-bodied pluggers. Lacks sand in his pants to anchor in pass protection. Small-framed and has had some difficulty staying healthy.

Future: A finesse, zone-blocking center with the quickness, balance and blocking range to fit seamlessly into a slide-protection scheme. Was slowed by injury as a senior and graded out more highly playing on a healthy set of wheels in 2013. Could contribute readily and be a very solid pro if he is able to stay healthy.

Draft projection: Fourth- to fifth-round pick.

Scout's take: "I like him. I just wish he were stronger. He runs well and is a good athlete. He is a lot bigger in person than he looks on tape. He is 290 and has a frame to play at 305-310. His hip strength and snap are not great. He is built for speed — Oregon linemen are racehorses, not Clydesdales."

ORT CHAZ GREEN, #75 (Sr-5)
FLORIDA   ▶ GRADE: 5.14

Ht: 6-4 ⅝	Wt: 314	40: 5.18	Arm: 33 ⅝	Hand: 10 ⅞

History: Highly recruited out of Tampa. Redshirted in 2010. Started all nine games played in '11 (eight at right tackle, one at left tackle). Missed four games while nursing a high left ankle sprain. In '12, Started 10-of-11 games played at ORT — did not play against Tennessee and Kentucky and did not start against LSU because of a left ankle injury. Missed the '13 season after tearing his left labrum during fall camp. In '14, started 11-of-12 games (nine at ORT, two at OLT). Did not start the bowl game against East Carolina. Team captain.

Strengths: Very good size. Good athletic ability. Takes good angles to seal and wall off. Plays hard and competes. Strong football character. Experienced, three-year starter in the Southeastern Conference. Versatile and has played on both edges.

Weaknesses: Soft run blocker. Is not stout. Lets defenders come up and underneath him and cross his face and struggles to anchor. Tends to play too upright. Gives up too much ground in pass protection — can be walked back against power. Raw footwork in his kick slide and very inconsistent hand placement and overall technique. Average lateral agility for the left side — gave up too much pressure vs.

Alabama. Durability has been an issue.

Future: A big, finesse swing tackle prospect that has struggled to stay healthy in college and lacks the ideal core strength for the front lines. Could be very well suited for a backup role in a zone-blocking scheme and has enough talent and desire to develop.

Draft projection: Late draftable pick.

C-OT CHAD HAMILTON, # (Sr-5)
COASTAL CAROLINA   ▶ GRADE: 5.09

Ht: 6-2	Wt: 292	40: 5.10e	Arm: 34	Hand: 9 ⅜

History: South Carolina native. Redshirted in 2010. Played all 11 games in '11, starting the final four at left guard. Moved to left tackle in '12 and started all 12 games played. Missed the first-round playoff game against Bethune-Cookman (knee). Started all 29 games 2013-14. Graduated with a degree in education. Elected not to run or lift at the Combine.

Strengths: Has very long arms and good movement skill. Light on his feet. Flashes pop in his punch. Is athletic enough to fan the rush when all his moving parts are coordinated. Energetic playing temperament — competes and blocks to the whistle.

Weaknesses: Was the shortest (6-2) and lightest (292 pounds) offensive lineman at the Combine and lacks the bulk and body length to stay outside. Is underpowered and could be overwhelmed by NFL big bodies. Did not face top competition in college.

Future: A small-school, college left tackle who projects to center in the pros. Will require some time in an NFL strength program and need to learn the nuances of the center position before he is ready. Developmental project.

Draft projection: Priority free agent.

Scout's take: "To me, (Hamilton) is a free agent all the way. The reason: One, he is short. Two, he has never played center before. I projected him to center and have never even seen him take a snap. I hate projections, but I thought he had a chance. I graded him as priority free agent."

OLG-OLT JARVIS HARRISON, #51 (Sr-5)
TEXAS A&M   ▶ GRADE: 5.28

Ht: 6-4 ⅛	Wt: 330	40: 5.22	Arm: 33 ½	Hand: 9 ¾

History: Also competed in basketball and track and field as a Texas prep (played just two years of football). Redshirted in 2010. Backed up right guard Cedric Ogbuehi in '11 — appeared in 11 games, starting four as an injury replacement. In '12, started all 13 games at left guard. Started all 13 games in '13 — 11 at left guard and two (Vanderbilt, UTEP) at left tackle when Falcons '14 first-rounder Jake Matthews shifted to right tackle to replace the injured Ogbuehi. Suffered a calf injury in the Chick-fil-A Bowl against Duke. Missed '14 spring practice and the first two games of the season while recovering from shoulder surgery, but played 10 games and started the final seven (five at OLG, two at OLT).

Strengths: Outstanding athletic ability and movement skill for his size. Is extremely strong and physical (when he wants to be) and can move defenders off the line of scrimmage at will. Natural knee bender. Outstanding grip strength. Versatile and has played guard and filled in at left tackle.

Weaknesses: Weight has fluctuated throughout his career and needs to take better care of his body. Marginal football character and work habits — needs to be motivated and pushed. Plays down to the competition and has a lazy streak in his play. Did not dominate lesser competition at the NFLPA Collegiate Bowl.

Future: A massive wide body in a similar mold as former Cowboys great Nate Newton or Saints 2008 fifth-round pick Carl Nicks. Has underachieved throughout his career, but, when Harrison is motivated, he can be as destructive and dominant in the run game as any offensive lineman in the draft. A high-risk, high-reward pick with legitimate talent for a hard-nosed coach such as Jaguars OL coach Doug Marrone who is capable of molding him. Possesses the athletic talent to be an emergency left tackle.

Draft projection: Fourth- to fifth-round pick.

Scout's take: "(Harrison) is one of those players whose first love is basketball. He is a big powerful guy like Charles Barkley (who) can two-handed dunk. He will surprise people when he runs and jumps. When you see him, he looks like one of those old Dallas Cowboys offensive lineman that were (destroying) people. I like him. There are issues that scare you. If you want to talk about pure talent, he is a second-round talent all day long. I'm not saying he goes there. But he has that type of talent. It's like he came straight out of (the movie) North Dallas Forty."

ORG-ORT **BOBBY HART**, #51 (Sr-4)

FLORIDA STATE   ▶ GRADE: 5.10

Ht: 6-4 ¾ | Wt: 329 | 40: 5.35e | Arm: 33 | Hand: 10 ⅛

History: Played his senior season at St. Thomas Aquinas, where he won a state title and was recruited coast-to-coast. Also played basketball and wrestled. As a 17-year-old true

freshman in 2011, appeared in 11 games and started the final nine (one at left tackle, eight at right tackle). Was a reserve in '12, appearing in eight games. Started all 28 games at ORT 2013-14. Graded out at a mediocre 73 percent as a senior. Will be a 21-year-old rookie. Was a medical exclusion at the Combine because of a left hamstring injury.

Strengths: Good lower-body thickness and base. Good grip strength once he latches on and has enough functional strength to anchor vs. power.

Has been very durable and not missed any time during his career to injury. Football is important to him.

Weaknesses: Plays small. Tends to bend at the waist and overset. Average athletic ability and foot quickness to handle edge speed. Relies too much on his upper body. Not explosive. Is just beginning to learn what it means to really work. Overly analytical, asks a lot of questions and takes time to digest what he is taught. Has to be re-trained a lot and lost starting job as a sophomore as a result.

Future: A big-bodied, heavy-legged waist bender with enough mass and power to kick inside in the pros. Admittedly underachieved in college and is gaining newfound appreciation for what it takes to make it.

Draft projection: Late draftable pick.

Scout's take: "He is a very young. He entered college when he was 16. It reminds me of when Amobi Okoye was entering the league. … Hart is a guard all day. He has that big (butt) and bulk and good size and weight to him. I just think he has to become a little better football player. I do not think he can play tackle."

ORT **ROB HAVENSTEIN**, #78 (Sr-5)

WISCONSIN   ▶ GRADE: 5.26

Ht: 6-7 ⅜ | Wt: 321 | 40: 5.46 | Arm: 33 ¾ | Hand: 9 ⅞

History: Last name is pronounced "HAY-ven-stine." Also lettered in basketball as a Maryland prep. Arrived weighing 380 pounds and redshirted in 2010 — underwent left labrum surgery and left knee surgery (MCL, meniscus) that summer. Had his right labrum repaired prior to the '11 season when he served as the backup right tackle, appearing in 13 games (one start). Took ownership of the position the following season and started all 41 games at ORT 2012-14. Was a game captain 11 times as a senior.

Strengths: Rare body length. Flashes some nastiness and will maul defenders in the run game once he gets his hands on them. Takes good angles and understands leverage. Solid technician — showed a strong power step and great feel for positioning in one-on-one drills at the Senior Bowl. Functional base strength to handle and re-direct power. Seeks to finish blocks.

Weaknesses: Limited athlete with average recovery speed. Tends to play too tall, flat-footed and straight-legged and consequently gets out-leveraged and winds up on the ground a lot. Limited shock in his punch. Had labrum surgery on both shoulders early in college career and has had to modify workouts to alleviate pressure from shoulders, translating to only 16 reps in the bench-press test, the lowest of any offensive linemen at the Combine. Late to arrive at the second level and has limited blocking range, as confirmed with the slowest three-cone drill time (8.30 seconds) of any player at the Combine.

Future: A lumbering positional blocker who wins with intelligence, toughness and angles. Has enough grit to eventually earn a starting job in the pros as a right tackle only. Limited positional value and shoulder concerns could hinder his draft status.

Draft projection: Fourth- to fifth-round pick.

Scout's take: "He looked more athletic on tape than he did in person. He is a foot pounder. I think he is a right tackle only. He is hard to get around. On the edges, he struggles. I graded him in the late fifth (round). He might go higher. Andrew Whitworth went in the second. Big stiff guys have a place in the league."

OLG SEAN HICKEY, #60 (Sr-5)

SYRACUSE ▶ GRADE: 5.11

Ht: 6-5⅜ | Wt: 309 | 40: 5.35e | Arm: 32¾ | Hand: 10½

History: Prepped in Pennsylvania. Tore both labrums as a junior in 2008. Redshirted in 2010. Missed '11 spring practice because of a right PCL tear, then was sidelined for the year after tearing his left ACL. Healthy in '12, started all 13 games, including the first four at left tackle and the final nine at right tackle opposite Giants '13 first-rounder Justin Pugh. Started all 13 games at OLT in '13. Sprained his left ankle against Pittsburgh and was limited against Boston College. Started all 12 games at OLT in '14. Team captain allowed just two sacks his final three seasons. Did not run at the Combine because of a tweaked left hamstring injury.

Strengths: Has enough agility to shuttle and slide and get in the way. Solid anchor strength to match up with power. Can seal running lanes and hold blocks in short areas. Exceptional weight-room strength — bench-pressed 35 reps at the Combine. Has a passion for the game and lives at the football facility.

Weaknesses: Has short arms for a tackle and lets defenders into his frame at the snap. Is not quick to strike with his hands or replace them. Marginal functional speed. Is stressed by edge rushers. Lumbers in space and struggles to adjust to linebackers on the second level. Average blocking instincts and awareness. Not a strong finisher. Durability has been an issue throughout his career, with three surgeries in college.

Future: A strong, gritty college left tackle most ideally suited for the inside in the pros. Lacks the arm length and lateral agility to be effective on the edges, yet could compete for a job as an interior backup.

Draft projection: Late draftable pick.

OLT D.J. HUMPHRIES, #70 (Jr-3)

FLORIDA ▶ GRADE: 6.08

Ht: 6-5 | Wt: 307 | 40: 5.09 | Arm: 33⅝ | Hand: 10

History: Four-year starter as prep in North Carolina, where he was a USA Today All-American and considered the top offensive tackle recruit in America by multiple services. Enrolled in January 2012 and appeared in all 12 games, making three starts (two at left tackle, one as a blocking tight end). In '13, started six of the first seven games at OLT. Left the season opener against Toledo after spraining his left MCL then was benched against Missouri, which preceded a season-ending torn left MCL injury suffered in practice. Started all 10 games played at OLT in '14 — hurt his left ankle against Eastern Michigan and did not play against Kentucky or Alabama.

Strengths: Has a well-distributed frame. Excellent foot quickness and athletic ability. Very light on his feet. Quick to the second level fitting on linebackers. Natural bender. Good recovery speed. Played with surprising strength for a 290-pounder and was able to handle power (see Florida State vs. Mario Edwards). Flashes a mean streak. Understands leverage and positioning. Plays with very good balance and makes it look easy. Natural pulling. Effortless pass protector.

Weaknesses: Narrow-shouldered and narrow-hipped. Does not play with a lot of strike in his hands and must continue to improve his core strength. Tends to overextend too much and will fall off blocks. Can be beat at the snap by elite speed (see Missouri). Could stand to continue developing core strength. Struggled to gain weight in college, never playing greater than 290 pounds, and must

OFFENSIVE LINE

prove that he can hold weight added prior to the Combine and that it's not manufactured.

Future: Surprised many scouts by showing up at the Combine weighing 307 and still showing superb agility, knee bend and movement skill in drills. Has all the athletic skills to handle the left side in the pros and best football is still ahead of him. Should be able to step into an OLT job immediately in the pros.

Draft projection: Late first-round pick.

Scout's take: "If Terron Armstead came out in this draft, would we be talking about him as a first-rounder too. Terron is longer, bigger and a better athlete. My point about Armstead is — shouldn't there be some concern about a guy who finishes the bowl game at 290 and was 280 as a sophomore and then shows up at the Combine weighing 310? I worry about the manufactured part of it. I do like the athlete though."

ORG TRE' JACKSON, #54 (Sr-4)

FLORIDA STATE   ▶ GRADE: 5.66

Ht: 6-3 ¾ | Wt: 330 | 40: 5.51 | Arm: 32 ⅝ | Hand: 10 ⅞

History: Georgia prep missed his junior season after tearing his left ACL. As a true freshman in 2011, appeared in eight games and made his first start at right guard in the Champs Sports Bowl against Notre Dame. In '12, started all 14 games at ORG. Started all 13 games played at ORG in '13, missing just the Nevada contest (right ankle). Started all 14 games at ORG in '14. Was named South Team MVP at the Senior Bowl. Elected not to lift at the Combine.

Strengths: Exceptional size with a thick trunk. Outstanding weight-room strength. Very good base anchor strength to handle mass and power in pass protection. Has a very strong core and is seldom inverted. Can short set and stop a defender in his tracks. Very good grip strength to control defenders once engaged. Outstanding Senior Bowl showing — excelled in one-on-one drills.

Weaknesses: Smooth-muscled with relatively short arms. Average foot speed and athletic ability. Hand placement could be more consistent – hands go wide. Does not always bring his feet with him or play on balance, translating to sustain issues, especially on the second level. Average Combine results and positional workout.

Future: A big, strong wide body, Jackson has the girth and functional strength to be effective in a power-based scheme. Is capable of re-establishing the line of scrimmage in the run game and fortifying the pocket in pass pro. Is at his best in confined quarters when not asked to travel far.

Draft projection: Second-round pick.

Scout's take: "(Jackson) has been a little disappointing. I don't think he has been as solid or as physical as I thought he was last year. I saw more explosive power and lower-body drive last year. This year, he is not grinding as much. His game is more about placement. I think the left tackle (Cameron Erving) may have displaced him as the best blocker on the offensive line."

ORG ARIE KOUANDJIO, #77 (Sr-5)

ALABAMA   ▶ GRADE: 5.28

Ht: 6-4 ¾ | Wt: 301 | 40: 5.48 | Arm: 34 ⅛ | Hand: 10 ⅞

History: Last name is pronounced "KWON-joe." Brother, Cyrus, was an All-Southeastern Conference offensive tackle for the Tide before being selected by the Bills (second round, 2014). DeMatha Catholic (Md.) product. Redshirted in 2010. In '11, appeared in just two games before having surgery on his knees to address patellar subluxation. Saw limited action in 11 games in '12. Started all 27 games at left guard 2013-14. Graduated with an economics degree. Elected not to run or lift at the Combine.

Strengths: Good body and arm length. Plays strong in tight quarters and has outstanding base strength to anchor in pass protection. Very effective matching up with size and power over the top of him. Runs his legs on contact and can generate some movement as a drive blocker. Plays with some vinegar and will seek to root defensive linemen out of the hole. Measured only 14.8 percent body fat at the Combine and is very well conditioned. Very good football character.

Weaknesses: A bit knock-kneed and duck-footed. Had surgery on both knees and long-term durability requires closer scrutiny given the way the surgery appeared to affect his movement. Cannot unlock his hips and play with natural power originating from his lower body. Bends at the waist too much and will fall off blocks. Lumbers to the second level and is often late to the block point. Slow to react to movement.

Future: Upright, stiff-hipped power guard more suited for the right side than the left on which he played in college. Athletic limitations appear to be partly traceable to knee injuries early in his career.

Draft projection: Fourth- to fifth-round pick.

Scout's take: "I liked Kouandjio to a point. I

think he is smart and steady. I wouldn't touch him any time before the middle of (the fourth round). Because he is so smart, I think he will learn it really well. He's just not a great foot athlete. I graded him at the top of the fifth round."

C-OG GREG MANCZ, #75 (Sr-5)

TOLEDO   ▶ GRADE: 5.13

Ht: 6-4 ½ | Wt: 301 | 40: 5.11 | Arm: 32 ⅜ | Hand: 10

History: Lost his father in sixth grade. Won a state title as an Ohio prep. Redshirted in 2010. Started all 26 games at right guard 2011-12. Started all 12 games in '13 — the first three at right tackle and the final nine at ORG. Was voted the Mid-American Conference's top player in '14 when he shifted to center and started all 12 games. Has torn his right labrum three times. Team captain graduated with a degree in finance. Was a medical exclusion from the Combine because of a right shoulder injury.

Strengths: Versatile and has played multiple positions on the line. Good agility to work up a level and fit on linebackers. Experienced, four-year starter. Selfless, team leader. Good football intelligence. Makes the line calls and adjusts well to stunts and loops. Smart, efficient and works at the craft.

Weaknesses: Marginal arm length for the outside. Plays short-armed and lets defenders inside his frame. Struggles with quick gap penetrators. Can be controlled and ragdolled by bigger blockers. Registered 28.6 percent body fat at the Combine and could stand to improve conditioning. Struggled against Missouri and must prove he can match up with better competition and continue honing core strength.

Future: A good-sized, positional zone blocker with limited power in his body, Mancz could compete for a job as a backup in a slide protection scheme. Developmental prospect with a concerning history of shoulder injuries that could affect his draft status.

Draft projection: Late draftable pick

C-OLG ALI MARPET, #55 (Sr-4)

HOBART   ▶ GRADE: 5.49

Ht: 6-3 ⅞ | Wt: 307 | 40: 4.99 | Arm: 33 ⅜ | Hand: 10

History: Lightly recruited high school prospect who weighed 245 pounds out of high school. Was a two-way lineman and also played basketball as a New York prep. As a true freshman in 2011, appeared in six games.

Started all 37 games at left tackle 2012-14 for the Division III Statesmen. As a senior, was voted Liberty League Co-Offensive Player of the Year, becoming the first offensive lineman in league history to earn that honor. Two-year captain graduated with an economics degree. Was the only Division III player invited to the Senior Bowl.

Strengths: Has a solid build and carries his weight very well. Efficient movement skill. Plays with consistent pad level. Strong finisher with good leg drive. Strong run blocker. Good football-playing temperament and intensity. Very good balance, agility and lateral quickness. Very smart and competitive. The game was not too big for him at the Senior Bowl, where he showed he could handle better competition, and worked out extremely well at the Combine. Very diligent, self-motivated and driven to improve.

Weaknesses: Regularly matched up against lesser competition. Was seldom challenged in college. Could do a better job recognizing the blitz and will need to hone his eyes. Inconsistent hand placement and technique — does not reload his hands. Can be overly analytical.

Future: Division III college left tackle with the length and quickness ideally sought on the inside in the pros. Projects to center or guard and possesses the foot quickness and run-blocking grit to emerge as an eventual starter most ideally in a zone-blocking scheme. May have improved his draft standing as much as any player in the draft by proving himself in the postseason and could have an opportunity to contribute readily.

Draft projection: Third- to fourth-round pick.

Scout's take: "He is a climber. From the Senior Bowl to the Combine, he keeps answering any questions. I think he'll go somewhere in the third round, maybe even higher than that. I think it is going to shock you a little bit. It reminds me of the kid from Central Florida (Jah Reid) a few years ago. He got pushed up for dominating at the East-West game. Hobart went to the Senior Bowl and just outclassed all the other offensive linemen. I think I only saw him get beat once or twice in one-on-one's total. I just think the kid doesn't know what he is supposed to know, so he just goes out and competes, and does a really good job. Our (area scout) was not wowed by the tape. He was shocked at the

OFFENSIVE LINE

Senior Bowl, that a kid from Hobart came out and was the no. 1 (lineman) at the game."

OLG-ORT JOSUE MATIAS, #70 (Sr-4)

FLORIDA STATE   ▶ GRADE: 5.38

Ht: 6-5 ½ | Wt: 309 | 40: 5.58 | Arm: 33 ⅛ | Hand: 10

History: Born in the Dominican Republic and moved to the U.S. when he was six. Prepped in New Jersey. Missed his senior season after suffering a right patellar tendon avulsion and bone fracture. Worked at tackle and guard as a true freshman in 2011, appearing in seven games with his first career start against Notre Dame in the Champs Sports Bowl. Took ownership of the left guard spot, starting all 41 games from 2012-14. Will be a 22-year-old rookie. Elected not to lift at the Combine.

Strengths: Outstanding size. Active hands. Solid base strength to handle a charge in pass pro. Is effective working up a level and fitting on linebackers and even capable of hitting the third level on screens. Energetic working down the field and plays faster than he times. Generates some movement at the point in the run game. Is tough, competitive and committed to the game. Takes pride in his job.

Weaknesses: Has stiff ankles with lower-body tightness. Tight in the hips with limited lateral agility. Slow off the ball. Marginal processing speed and blocking instincts. Lacks lead in his anchor and gets driven back too easily when he stands tall. Susceptible to inside counters. Registered the Combine's lowest vertical jump (17 1/2 inches) and broad jump (6 foot, 10 inches). Also tied for the second-slowest 3-cone time (8.21 seconds) and had the slowest short shuttle (5.16 seconds) among guards.

Future: Has enough length and mass that some teams are projecting him to tackle in the pros. However, Matias possesses starting-caliber physical traits more suited for the inside. Will require a patient positional coach and would be best acclimating to the NFL offense employing a streamlined playbook. Has eventual starter potential.

Draft projection: Third- to fourth-round pick.

Scout's take: "I worry about what's upstairs. There are times in games where you are scratching your head wondering what he is doing. It shows up in practice when his coach is standing right behind him instead of the center and pointing out mistake after mistake. He's top heavy and always leaning. I see some

upside, but he scares me."

OLG-C DARRIAN MILLER, #77 (Sr-4)

KENTUCKY   ▶ GRADE: 4.78

Ht: 6-4 ⅞ | Wt: 307 | 40: 5.44 | Arm: 33 | Hand: 9 ¾

History: Kentucky native. As a true freshman in 2011, played all 12 games and started two September contests at right guard. Started all 24 games at left tackle 2012-13. In '14, was suspended for the season opener against Tennessee-Martin before starting the next 11 games at OLT. Played through shoulder pain against Florida. Elected not to lift at the Combine.

Strengths: Good length. Plays on his feet with good balance and is quick into his blocks. Is functional walling off and sealing run lanes. Flashes a mean streak to finish. Very intelligent.

Weaknesses: Does not have a lot of pop. Marginal play strength and hand use. Not strong at the point of attack. Marginal finishing strength. Very underpowered. Lacks weight-room strength. Does not generate power through his lower body. Inconsistent adjusting to targets on the second level. Struggled to handle the speed of Shane Ray off the edge and repeatedly was beat to the block point.

Future: A developmental interior OL prospect that needs to spend time in an NFL strength and conditioning program for a few years before he is ready to challenge for a job. Practice-squad candidate.

Draft projection: Priority free agent.

Scout's take: "He is light framed. He didn't pass the eyeball test for me. The coach introduced me to him when I was there. He was 287 pounds and looked like he has not seen a weight room. … He's going to have to play center or guard."

OLG JOHN MILLER, #70 (Sr-4)

LOUISVILLE   ▶ GRADE: 5.38

Ht: 6-2 ½ | Wt: 303 | 40: 5.28 | Arm: 33 ¼ | Hand: 10 ¼

History: Prepped in Kentucky, where he won a 6A state title. As a true freshman in 2011, started all 10 games played at guard. Missed three games (ankle). In '12, started 11-of-12 games at OLG. Sat out against Pittsburgh and did not start against South Florida (right ankle). Started all 26 games at strong-side guard from 2013-14. Graduated.

Strengths: Has a well-muscled frame and looks the part. Can bend his knees and plays with a good, wide base. Is alert in pass protection. Plays hard and competes through the whistle. Has pop in his punch. Functionally

OFFENSIVE LINE

strong at the point of attack. Solid anchor strength to handle power in pass pro. Showed very well at the East-West Shrine game. Measured only 11.5 percent body fat at the Combine, the second lowest of any offensive linemen at the event, and is well-conditioned. Good football character — has a "grinder" reputation within the program. Experienced, four-year starter. Durable.

Weaknesses: Undersized. Average athlete. Has some heaviness in his body. Marginal lateral agility to slide, shuffle and mirror. Labors to the second level and struggles to connect with linebackers. Could stand to do a better job locking out and keeping defenders off his frame. Average finishing strength.

Future: A gritty, strong-side guard with a powerful base and enough mass to develop into a solid pro. Has eventual starter potential, though size and agility limitations could always be restricting.

Draft projection: Fourth- to fifth-round pick.

Scout's take: "He's a strong mauler with a good base. He's not a good athlete. He's not a fit for us, but I will take him as a backup if he drops. I think I'd rather just go buy a veteran (in free agency). I can find a guy on the street to do what he does."

ORT-C MITCH MORSE, #65 (Sr-5)

MISSOURI ▶ GRADE: 5.32

| Ht: 6-5 ⅜ | Wt: 305 | 40: 5.18 | Arm: 32 ¼ | Hand: 9 ¼ |

History: Prepped in Texas. Redshirted in 2010. Was a reserve in '11, appearing in all 13 games. Started all 11 games played in '12 — eight at center, four at right tackle. Missed the Alabama contest with a sprained left MCL. Started all 14 games at ORT in '13. Shifted to left tackle in '14 (replacing Seahawks '14 second-rounder Justin Britt) and started all 14 games. Broke his left index finger against Texas A&M. Team captain graduated with a hospitality management degree.

Strengths: Very energetic and competes hard. Locks on and mauls defenders in the run game. Productive pass protector — gets the job done (even if he does not look pretty doing it). Has pop in his punch and will recoil his hands. Flashes some nastiness. Takes measured steps and plays under control at the second level. Finished second among offensive linemen with 36 bench-press reps at the Combine and tested well.

Weaknesses: Has the shortest wingspan (76 3/4 inches) of any offensive lineman at the Combine and tends to grab a lot to compensate for lack of length. Gets overextended at the second level and struggles to reach the block point. Can play with better leverage – lets his pads rise and gets up on his toes when engaged.

Future: A big, nondescript, short-armed, zone blocker who is warranting some looks as both a center and guard in the pros and could also fit at right tackle. Offers versatility as a swing backup. Possesses eventual-starter potential, but could always be restricted by athletic limitations and leave teams desiring better.

Draft projection: Third- to fourth-round pick.

Scout's take: "(Morse) graded out pretty well at his Combine workout. He doesn't look very good in his picture — he's soft through the chest and not overly defined. He tested out pretty well athletically, but his (positional) workout was not as good. He was on his heels, (upright) in the shoulders and stiff-looking. His arms were flailing. I was surprised that the athletic numbers were as good as they were. He is a better athlete than given credit for by how he looks and moves around."

ORG ROBERT MYERS, #70 (Sr-5)

TENNESSEE STATE ▶ GRADE: 5.16

| Ht: 6-4 ¾ | Wt: 326 | 40: 5.41 | Arm: 33 ¾ | Hand: 9 ½ |

History: Tennessee native. Redshirted in 2010. Appeared in 10 games in '11, drawing one start at right tackle. Started 8-of-10 games played at ORT in '12. Did not play against Arkansas-Pine Bluff after tearing right thumb ligaments. Started all 14 games at ORT in '13. Started all 12 games in '14, including the season opener at ORT and the rest of the season at right guard. Did not lift at the Combine because of a left pectoral injury.

Strengths: Has a well-proportioned build with a solid base. Very good size. Functional run blocker — creates a push. Can control defenders in close quarters — good grip strength to torque defenders. Solid anchor strength in pass pro — can stop a charge. Athletic enough to reach and scoop. Very durable.

Weaknesses: Inconsistent pad level — rises out of his stance and plays too straight-legged, negating natural leverage. Hands occasionally will shoot wide of target and go outside. Regularly matched up against lesser competition and did not distinguish himself in the Senior Bowl.

Future: Kicked inside as a senior and looked more comfortable. Has the size and physical talent to be groomed.

Draft projection: Late draftable pick.

Scout's take: "I am not a fan. I kept him in

OFFENSIVE LINE

the late fifth (round). The kid last year from there (Kadeem Edwards) went in the fifth. People think this guy is not as good as him. (Myers) is a good-looking kid in person – he has a good body build and length and all that. He does not play to it."

OLT CEDRIC OGBUEHI, #70 (Sr-5)

TEXAS A&M ▶ GRADE: 5.42

Ht: 6-5 ¼ | Wt: 306 | 40: 5.15e | Arm: 35 ⅞ | Hand: 10

History: Last name is pronounced "oh-BWAY-hee." Won a state title at Allen High (TX). Redshirted in 2010 — was part of the same recruiting class as Luke Joeckel and Jake Matthews. Played 10 games in '11, starting six (five at left guard, one at right guard). Suffered an ankle injury against Arkansas and missed three games. In '12, started all 13 games at ORG. Started all 11 games played at right tackle in '13. Did not play against Vanderbilt and UTEP while nursing a groin injury. Started all 13 games in '14 — 11 at OLT, two at ORT — but tore an ACL in the Liberty Bowl against West Virginia. Graduated with a degree in recreation, parks, and tourism sciences. Did not perform at the Combine while still recovering from right knee surgery.

Strengths: Good body structure and build with rare arm length and a very athletic frame. Exceptional athlete — very light on his feet and moves effortlessly. Outstanding body control and lateral agility. Very good recovery speed to handle quick counters and inside moves. Can climb to the second level and cut off linebackers. Three-and-a-half-year starter in the Southeastern Conference.

Weaknesses: Struggled making the conversion to left tackle. Plays too soft-tempered and is not strong at the point of attack. Limited base anchor strength to handle power in pass pro. Does not play strong or aggressive in the run game. Needs to get stronger and learn to use the spring in his legs. Gave up too much pressure and could be walked back. Questionable mental toughness. Plays down to the competition. Is coming off a serious knee injury and likely will not be fully recovered for more than a year.

Future: An extremely athletic left tackle with underachiever traits, Ogbuehi entered his senior season as one of the best blockers in the country. However, after struggling to adapt to the left side and suffering through a season-ending injury, his draft stock plunged, inviting new questions about when he will be ready and what a team will be able to expect on the other end of the draft.

Knee injury could diminish his draft value by several rounds. Will fit best in a zone-blocking scheme where his core-strength deficiency could be best concealed and his athletic ability maximized, and might be best at right tackle or guard.

Draft projection: Second- to third-round pick.

Scout's take: "(Ogbuehi) has left tackle feet. He has all the ability in the world. He needs to get stronger like they all do coming out of (Texas) A&M. They kept all of them light because of the tempo offense. (Jake) Matthews even had to get stronger. Ogbuehi has better athleticism than Matthews or (Luke) Joeckel. They fired their O-line coach there because the unit underachieved so much."

OLT ANDRUS PEAT, #70 (Jr-3)

STANFORD ▶ GRADE: 5.45

Ht: 6-6 ⅞ | Wt: 313 | 40: 5.22 | Arm: 34 ⅜ | Hand: 10 ⅝

History: Father, Todd, was a six-year NFL offensive lineman with the Raiders and Cardinals (1987-93). Andrus was a highly recruited Parade and USA Today All-American out of Arizona, where he won a Division I state title and played basketball. As a true freshman in 2012, appeared in 13 games at left tackle (averaged 20 snaps per game). Did not play against Colorado (hand). Started all 27 games at left tackle from 2013-14. Was medically excluded from lifting at the Combine because of a right elbow injury. Will be a 21-year-old rookie.

Strengths: Has a huge frame with massive thighs, an extremely powerful base and natural brute strength. Can dominate in the run game (when he wants to). Flashes violence in his hands and can jolt defenders to the ground with his punch (see Notre Dame). Plays with outstanding balance and natural knee bend and is rarely on the ground. Can clamp down powerful five-techniques. Controlled kick slide in pass protection. Smart and alert.

Weaknesses: Can improve upper-body strength. Has some heaviness in his legs that gives him trouble with speed and inside counters. Plays with too much complacency and is not a glass-eater. Will play down to the competition and go through the motions. Could do a better job sustaining. Technique could use refinement. Was challenged by the quickness of Utah's Nate Orchard and struggled some vs. the power of Oregon's very talented ends. Could stand to play with more consistency.

Future: Big, strong, powerful, physical

specimen with the raw athletic tools to be special. Has a body type that makes scouts drool and may be as gifted as any offensive lineman to enter the draft in the last decade, with a very unique combination of raw power, brute strength and foot quickness. Is still growing into his body and far from a finished product, yet with technique refinement, has perennial Pro Bowl potential. Extremely talented with an ascending arrow.

Draft projection: Top-10 pick.

Scout's take: "He blocks guys off the screen almost like the character portrayed in The Blind Side, and also has the other side in him like Baby Huey, not wanting to hurt anyone. After he gets embarrassed, it's on and he will dominate the rest of the game. I've never seen anything like it. … I worry a little bit about his makeup, but I think he'll figure it out. The trick with him is figuring out how to get the most out of him. When his fire is lit, look out."

OLG-ORT TERRY POOLE, #79 (Sr-5)

SAN DIEGO STATE ▶ GRADE: 5.05

Ht: 6-4 ¾ | Wt: 307 | 40: 5.12 | Arm: 33 ¼ | Hand: 9 ½

History: California native who considered basketball his primary sport until his senior season when he played tight end and defensive end. Spent two years (2010-11) at Monterey (Calif.) Peninsula College. Redshirted at SDSU in '12. Started all 12 games played at right tackle in '13. Was benched against Ohio State (missed team bus). In '14, moved to left tackle and started all 13 games. Team captain. Graduated with a degree in criminal justice.

Strengths: Thickly built with good overall size. Rolls his hips and can create some push in the run game. Attacks linebackers on the second level. Sets quickly in pass pro and generally seals his man. Flashes a mean streak. Tied for the best broad jump (9-feet, 5-inches) among offensive linemen at the Combine.

Weaknesses: Raw technician — only played one year of high school football and it shows. Rises out of his stance and plays too upright. Hands tend to go wide of the target and will lose sustain. Is stressed by speed and opens up the gate, allowing rushers to cross his face. Uses a shuffle-and-slide technique instead of kick sliding, and footwork will need to be retrained to handle NFL speed rushers.

Future: A big, strong, top-heavy, wall-off blocker who functioned on the left side as a senior, but has the herky-jerky technique and movement skill most ideally suited for the right side or inside in the pros. Developmental

project at least a few years away.

Draft projection: Priority free agent.

ORT JEREMIAH POUTASI, #73 (Jr-3)

UTAH ▶ GRADE: 5.62

Ht: 6-5 ⅛ | Wt: 335 | 40: 5.36 | Arm: 33 ⅞ | Hand: 9 ½

History: Last name is pronounced "po-tah-see." Las Vegas native. As a true freshman in 2012, started 10-of-11 games played at right tackle. Started all 25 games at left tackle 2013-14. Opted to forgo his senior season to support his family against the recommendation of the NFL Draft Advisory Board, that suggested he was best served returning to school for another season. Will be a 21-year-old rookie.

Strengths: Big and powerful with tree trunk legs and natural brute strength. Can move defenders with sheer strength in the run game. Flashes pop in his hands and snap in his hips. Pancakes linebackers when he arrives on time. Matches up well with power (see vs. Oregon's DeForest Buckner). Very good base anchor strength to stop a charge. Has played both right- and left-handed and handled both edges.

Weaknesses: Tends to grab more than punch and needs to learn how to coil and replace his hands. Relies on his upper-body strength too much. Hands and feet do not always work in conjunction — leading to a lack of balance. Does not unlock his hips and use the innate power in his body. Arrives late at the second level and does not consistently finish. Was stressed by speed of UCLA edge rushers and opens up his shoulders too early in pass protection, becoming more susceptible inside. Ran a pedestrian 8.09-second 3-cone time at the Combine. Could require a few extra reps to master a game plan.

Future: A big, strong enough talent to remain outside in the pros, but could be most naturally suited on the right side where he began his college career. Could also be tried inside. Has starter potential.

Draft projection: Second- to third-round pick.

Scout's take: "You better study him closely. He is only 20 years old and has a lot of upside. He is big and athletic with good feet. All his issues are technical. He's a third-year junior who has started from the day he arrived. He has played on both sides and is athletic enough to be a left tackle. He pretty much handled everyone in the three games I watched. I was impressed how he fared against the big boys at Oregon. A lot of teams are playing with worse

OFFENSIVE LINE

at left tackle — trust me on that."

ORT COREY ROBINSON, #53 (Sr-5)

SOUTH CAROLINA ▶ GRADE: 5.31

Ht: 6-6 ⅝ | Wt: 324 | 40: 5.40e | Arm: 35 ⅝ | Hand: 10 ¾

History: Prepped in North Carolina. Redshirted in 2010. Provided depth at defensive tackle in '11 (did not see action). Switched to left tackle in '12 — played 11 games and started nine of the final 10 contests. Started all 27 games at OLT 2013-14. As a senior, played through a lateral meniscus tear before having it surgically repaired in late December. Graduated with a degree in hotel, restaurant, tourism management. Was a medical exclusion from the Combine because of left knee surgery.

Strengths: Exceptional arm length and overall size and body mass. Very long reach to keep pass rushers at bay and has some kick in his legs in pass pro to extend and cut off the edge. Sets and triggers his hands. Does a good job uncoiling and striking with pop in his punch. Bench-pressed 28 reps at the Combine and has good weight-room strength. Physically tough and will play through injuries.

Weaknesses: Plays too straight-legged and stiff and bends from the waist. Pushes more than he drives as a run blocker and is not explosive coming off the ball. Does not handle the speed-to-power conversion very well and can be driven back by leverage rushers. Late to see and react to the blitz. Hits and falls off blocks too much. Lumbers to the second level. Inconsistent game-day intensity.

Future: A mountain of a man with rare arm length. College left tackle who profiles as a right tackle in the pros. Flashes ability to dominate in both phases when he wants to, but too often appears complacent going through the motions.

Draft projection: Fourth- to fifth-round pick.

Scout's take: "He's big, long and athletic. He's not very strong. He will get bulled. He is unusually better in pass protection than he is in the run game. He comes off the snap, and his first movement is up."

ORT-ORG TY SAMBRAILO, #51 (Sr-5)

COLORADO STATE ▶ GRADE: 5.32

Ht: 6-5 ⅞ | Wt: 311 | 40: 5.37 | Arm: 33 | Hand: 10

History: California native. Captained his high school team for three years. Also earned letters in soccer, basketball and baseball and was a standout skier. Redshirted in 2010. Played 11 games in '11, starting seven at left tackle. Hurt his elbow against UNLV. In March

of '12, was involved in a fight at a house party and was stabbed in the back of his shoulder. Started 10-of-12 games on the season — five at left guard, two at left tackle, two at right tackle and one at right guard. Despite tearing his left labrum in Week Three, started all 14 games at OLT in '13. Had post-season surgery that sidelined him for off-season strength and conditioning and '14 spring practice. In the fall, started all 11 games played OLT. Sprained his right MCL against Colorado and did not play against Boise State and UC Davis. Team captain.

Strengths: Good feet, balance and body control. Uses his quickness to reach and seal defenders. Can get positioning and sustain in pass pro. Quick, active hands to sustain. Can bump and steer and control defenders. Quick to pull and locate. Smart and versatile and can play multiple positions. Unselfish, team player.

Weaknesses: Plays small. Average arm length. Limited strength and explosion. Not strong in the core and is too easily knocked off balance and controlled. Plays with too much finesse. Durability has been an issue and shoulders must be evaluated closely.

Future: Underpowered, developmental, finesse college left tackle that will benefit from another year in the weight room and would fit most ideally into a zone-blocking scheme. Has the agility, athletic ability and intelligence to develop into a functional contributor, similar to Eagles 2008 fourth-round pick Michael McGlynn.

Draft projection: Fourth- to fifth-round pick.

Scout's take: "His strength numbers are down from shoulder surgery a few years ago. He has upside though. He's a big, athletic offensive linemen that is smart and could play every position. He likes the weight room. He'll harden up. His body is just underdeveloped. He's a late bloomer. He might be a guard when all is said and done. He's a fourth-rounder for me that probably goes in the third."

OLT-OLG BRANDON SCHERFF, #68 (Sr-5)

IOWA ▶ GRADE: 6.52

Ht: 6-4 ⅝ | Wt: 319 | 40: 5.04 | Arm: 33 ⅝ | Hand: 11

History: High school QB who played tennis and clocked an 85 mph fastball. Iowa native who earned all-state recognition in football (two-way lineman who played QB as a sophomore), baseball (four letters) and track and field (state shot put champion). Redshirted in 2010. Sat out the first two games in '11 (stingers) before appearing in 10 games (three starts at left guard). In '12, started all seven games played at left tackle before suffering a dislocated right ankle and broken right fibula against Penn State. Returned to start all 13 games at OLT in '13. Decided to return for senior season after being told he would not be the top tackle drafted. Was the Outland Trophy winner and Big Ten Offensive Lineman of the Year in '14 when he started all 13 games at OLT. Team captain graduated with degree in leisure studies. Pulled his right hamstring while running the 40-yard dash at the Combine and withdrew from the rest of the on-field workout.

Strengths: Has a thick trunk and torso with a very sturdy frame and huge 11-inch meat hooks, tied for the biggest hands of any player at the Combine. Dominant run blocker. Explosive on contact. Nasty finisher with a reputation for decleating defenders and driving them into the sidelines. Exceptional pulling and locating. Understands angles and leverage. Very sound technician coming from a program run by former NFL OL coach Kirk Ferentz known for its fundamental offensive line play. Has rare power in his body, confirmed by a 480-pound hang-clean. Has a very stable support system and outstanding personal and football character. Smart, tough and accountable. Unselfish, team player. Outstanding football intelligence and blocking awareness to handle a complex playbook.

Weaknesses: Lacks ideal arm length and will let defenders into his frame. Could be challenged by elite speed rushers on the edges in the pros. Has some tightness in his ankles and body. Had a history of injuries early in his college career. Only bench-pressed 225 pounds 23 times.

Future: A powerful, determined, consistent road grader with the toughness, intelligence and competitiveness to earn a spot in the Pro Bowl as a rookie at either guard spot. Lack of ideal length makes most ideally suited for the inside, yet understands angles and positioning and has good enough feet to handle the edges in the NFL. Was born to play football and possesses the highest floor of any player in this year's draft. A can't-miss pick capable of fitting in any type of blocking scheme and will find a way to get the job done at a top level.

Draft projection: Top-15 pick.

Scout's take: "Scherff is one of the best run blockers I have seen in a long time. He gouges and finishes. I don't know if he has the frame you want for a left tackle. I graded him as an immediate starter as an offensive guard. He just doesn't have a lot of length. He can climb to the second and even third level and moves

fine. I'd feel more comfortable with him at right tackle than left. Plug him in at guard and you might have something special."

OG ADAM SHEAD, #74 (Sr-5)
OKLAHOMA ▶ GRADE: 5.07
Ht: 6-3 ⅝ | Wt: 338 | 40: 5.79 | Arm: 33 ¾ | Hand: 10 ⅜

History: Last name is pronounced "SHED." Prepped in Texas. Redshirted in 2010. Played nine games in '11, starting five at left guard. Missed the last two games (MCL sprain). Started all 13 games at OLG in '12. Started the first 10 games at OLG in '13 before a back injury sidelined him the final three games. In '14, started 12-of-13 games played at OLG — did not start against TCU, and missed the Russell Athletic Bowl against Clemson (knee). Strained his left groin during positional drills at the Combine and did not perform jumps or shuttles.

Strengths: Very thickly built. Has a solid base and good anchor strength to hold his ground. Good point-of-attack strength and grip strength to latch on. Can shuffle and mirror in pass pro. Plays physical and can generate some movement in the run game. Three-and-a-half-year starter.

Weaknesses: Heavy-footed and sluggish in his movement. Marginal lateral agility. Late to reach the block point pulling. Tied for the slowest 10-yard split (2.02 seconds) of any player at the Combine and clocked the event's slowest 40 time (5.81). Also registered the highest body fat percentage (29.90) of any offensive linemen at the Combine and has room to improve his conditioning. Has been slowed by back injuries throughout his career, and long-term durability is a concern.

Future: A big-bodied, mauler best in a phone booth where he can mash defenders in short areas. Will be most ideally suited for a power run game. Limited movement skill and durability concerns may leave him undrafted.

Draft projection: Priority free agent.

ORT-ORG AUSTIN SHEPHERD, #79 (Sr-5)
ALABAMA ▶ GRADE: 5.12
Ht: 6-4 ⅜ | Wt: 315 | 40: 5.39 | Arm: 32 ⅞ | Hand: 10

History: Prepped in Georgia. Redshirted in 2010. Had both shoulders (AC joints) repaired after the season. Was a reserve right tackle his first two seasons — appeared in seven games in '11 and 10 games in '12. Dealt with plantar fasciitis in his right foot in '13, but started all 13 games at ORT. Started all 14 games at ORT in '14. Sprained his knee and ankle against Texas A&M. Earned his master's degree in

OFFENSIVE LINE

marketing.

Strengths: Good straight-line, track blocker when defenders are aligned over the top of him. Sets quickly and is patient in pass protection. Solid anchor strength. Can shuffle and slide and mirror his man. Good football character.

Weaknesses: Has short arms. Limited athlete. Is late off the ball and into blocks in the run game. Grabs too much and struggles to handle edge speed. Has a passive playing temperament and catches too much. Could stand to improve his hand use and strike with more pop. Marginal recovery speed.

Future: A good-sized, productive pro that could provide depth at tackle or guard most ideally in a zone-blocking scheme. Has no distinguishable trait, yet is steady and dependable and an ideal role player.

Draft projection: Sixth- to seventh-round pick.

Scout's take: "(Shepherd) is a competitive right tackle. He is not a killer, but he does a nice job getting on blocks. He doesn't have any power to him, and if you want to kick him into guard, he doesn't fit. He doesn't have the (anchor) or mass or power in his body. He might have a chance if you're asking him to zone block. He is solid. He will probably play in this league and be a good backup player."

OLG-ORT DONOVAN SMITH, #76 (Sr-4)

PENN STATE ▶ GRADE: 5.77

Ht: 6-5 ⅝ | Wt: 338 | 40: 5.28 | Arm: 34 ⅜ | Hand: 10 ⅝

History: Did not allow a sack his final two seasons as a Maryland prep. Redshirted in 2011. Started 9-of-10 games played at left tackle in '12. Sustained a sprained ankle against Virginia and missed two games. Started 11-of-12 games at OLT in '13. Did not start against Illinois (coach's decision). In '14, started all 11 games at OLT, though he sat out against Maryland and Indiana (undisclosed injury). Opted to forgo his final year of eligibility, but not before earning a criminology degree.

Strengths: Looks every bit the part with long arms and natural thickness in his body. Can block out the sun with sheer mass. Powerful run blocker who can create a surge in the run game. Comes off the ball flat-backed and moves defenders, making it look easy. Very solid showing at the Senior Bowl. Flashed ability to dominate Ohio State highly-touted DE Joey Bosa. Stuffs pass rushers when they come down his cylinder. Has natural power and explosion in his body. Has a 32-inch vertical jump, the best of any offensive guard at the Combine (despite being the second heaviest).

Weaknesses: Footwork could use refinement — uses a shuffle-slide technique instead of a kickslide. Raw hands and feet. Has some underachiever tendencies with too many inconsistencies showing up in technique and effort. Hands tend to shoot outside and could stand to do a better job with inside placement. Struggles some with speed-to-power conversion when defenders get underneath his pads. Can be late to adjust to the blitz. Late to reach the block point on the second level. Not a strong finisher.

Future: A better run blocker than pass protector, Smith can be challenged by edge speed and needs to clean up his technique. Yet he possesses a unique combination of mass, length, power, strength and movement skill and should be able to contribute readily as a power guard or right tackle.

Draft projection: Top-50 pick.

Scout's take: "(Smith) is talented. He is just an underachiever. Man, he doesn't finish! He will flash and pancake guys and wow you with his ability and other times leave you scratching your head. He is not as fast as the kid from Virginia (2014 66th overall pick Morgan Moses) that went to the Redskins. Smith has way more talent but he reminds me of that kind of player. I think he might be a better guard than tackle. He looks more functional in short areas. … You have to figure out what makes him tick."

OLT TYRUS THOMPSON, #71 (Sr-5)

OKLAHOMA ▶ GRADE: 5.42

Ht: 6-4 ⅞ | Wt: 324 | 40: 5.34 | Arm: 34 ⅞ | Hand: 10 ¼

History: Was born in Germany, where his father was stationed as an Army paratrooper. Tyrus is married with a son and daughter. Redshirted in 2010. Provided depth at tackle in '11, seeing limited action in five games. Played all 13 games in '12, starting five of the final six (three at right tackle, two at left tackle). Sustained a high ankle sprain against West Virginia. In '13, started all 11 games played at OLT. Broke his foot against Kansas State and missed the final two games. Started all 14 games at OLT in '14. Graduated. Strained his left hamstring during the short shuttle at the Combine and did not run run the 40 because of foot injury.

Strengths: Outstanding size with very long arms, big hands and a thick trunk. Is quick into blocks and can reach, scoop and seal. Agile for a big man and can shuffle and mirror in pass pro. Runs speed rushers wide of the pocket and

OFFENSIVE LINE

has fine recovery speed to adjust when he gets beat. Shut down Baylor's highly touted DE Shawn Oakman.

Weaknesses: Looks thin from the knees down and has had multiple injuries to the lower extreminites that could be exacerbated at the pro level. Tends to bend at the waist and get overextended. Plays too upright. Leans more than he drives and is too easily controlled by power. Late climbing to the second level. Does not finish blocks. Could use some more glass in his diet. Lacks core functional strength and point-of-attack strength. Not strong-handed and is more of a grabber than a puncher.

Future: Enormous, pear-shaped, finesse, positional blocker with the agility to be effective in a zone-slide protection scheme. Has enough athletic talent to earn a starting job, though must become functionally stronger. Will require some extra maintenance to maximize his potential.

Draft projection: Second- to third-round pick.

Scout's take: "He plays too soft and has some laziness in his play. He is going to need some hard coaching and will have to be monitored."

ORG LAKEN TOMLINSON, #77 (Sr-5)

DUKE ▶ GRADE: 5.68

Ht: 6-3 ⅜	Wt: 323	40: 5.34	Arm: 33 ⅝	Hand: 10 ⅛

History: Born in Jamaica (moved to the U.S. when he was 10). Commuted an hour by train and bus to attend Chicago's Lane Tech, where he also competed in track and field. Suffered a broken right tibia during his 2010 redshirt year. Did not miss a game in his career — started all 52 games at right guard 2011-14. Team captain will graduate with a double major in psychology and evolutionary anthropology, and aspires to become a neurosurgeon. Named to AFCA Good Works Team.

Strengths: Has a very thick build with shoulders as wide as a refrigerator and good mass through his legs and trunk — is proportionally big. Plays square in pass protection and can shuffle and slide. Explosive on contact and jars defenders. Can steer and control once locked on. Very experienced, four-year starter.

Weaknesses: Average contact balance, body control and recovery speed. Struggles some adjusting when defenders get on his edges and does not consistently finish when matched against speed and working up a level. Could stand to play with more violence in his hands.

Future: A very strong, square-cut, drive blocker with plug-and-play starter potential.

Does his best work in tight quarters where he can use his power and neutralize big bodies.

Draft projection: Second- to third-round pick.

Scout's take: "(Tomlinson) strikes and locks on and controls. I never really saw him fall off a block. ... If they go down the cylinder, he is good. If defenders are on his edge, he struggles more."

ORT-ORG DARYL WILLIAMS, #79 (Sr-5)

OKLAHOMA ▶ GRADE: 5.27

Ht: 6-5 ¼	Wt: 327	40: 5.38	Arm: 35	Hand: 9 ¾

History: Engaged. Prepped in Texas. Redshirted in 2010. Appeared in nine games in '11. Started the first 10 games of the '12 season at right tackle before a sprained MCL sidelined him the final three. Started all 13 games in '13, including the first 12 at ORT before shifting to the left side against Alabama in the Sugar Bowl. In '14, started all 13 games at ORT. Team captain. Did not run the 3-cone drill at the Combine because of lower-body tightness.

Strengths: Very powerfully built base with a thick trunk. Outstanding point-of-attack strength. Stout in pass protection with very good lower-body strength. Very good grip strength to latch on and control defenders. Has a 370-pound power clean, and explosive power to jolt defenders off the line on initial contact. Very focused. Versatile and has played multiple positions on the line.

Weaknesses: Average foot athlete. Struggles to reach linebackers and adjust in space. Tight in the hips and bends at the waist. Posted the slowest short shuttle time (5.21 seconds) of any player at the Combine, demonstrating very limited lateral agility to get off the track and adjust to movement. Can be late to recognize and anticipate the blitz and needs to become more alert in pass pro.

Future: A big, strong, physical mauler ideally suited for a power-blocking scheme, Williams has the makeup to eventually earn a starting job and would be most ideally suited playing inside in the pros, where he has some help on each side of him. Must prove that he can handle the game getting on top of him more quickly inside and sort out pressure packages to earn a starting job.

Draft projection: Fourth- to fifth-round pick.

Scout's take: "He is the bell cow of that offensive line. He is the most likely to be successful. I like the way he is wired. He is not a great athlete, but he is tough. ... He might have to move to guard. He won't be drafted highly, but he will stick in the league. He has exceptionally high character."

OFFENSIVE LINE

DEFENSIVE LINE

DEFENSIVE LINE

JOHN PYLE

Nawrocki's TOP 10

1. **LEONARD WILLIAMS**
2. **Randy Gregory**
3. **Vic Beasley**
4. **Malcom Brown**
5. **Eddie Goldman**
6. **Arik Armstead**
7. **Mario Edwards**
8. **Jordan Phillips**
9. **Carl Davis**
10. **Danny Shelton**

DLE-5T-3T HENRY ANDERSON, #91 (Sr-5)

STANFORD   ▶ GRADE: 5.17

| Ht: 6-6 ¼ | Wt: 294 | 40: 4.99 | Arm: 33 ½ | Hand: 9 ¾ |

History: Also lettered in basketball and track and field as a Georgia prep, winning a shot put state title. Redshirted in 2010. Played all 13 games in '11, scratching together six tackles, zero for loss and zero sacks. In '12, started all 14 games as a defensive end in Stanford's 3-4 defense — recorded 50-16-6 with five batted passes, earning the team's Tommy Vardell Award for excellence in athletics and academics. In '13, managed 19-4-3 in eight starts — missed six games after tearing his left MCL against Army. Started all 13 games in '14, totaling 65-15-8 1/2 with two batted passes. Did not lift at the Combine because of a right pectoral strain.

Strengths: Outstanding length — can make himself skinny, slip through gaps and work half-a-man. Has enough strength to set the edge. Versatile and has worked inside and outside, capable of creating mismatches with his quickness on the interior. Plays with discipline. Smart and hard working and put a lot of extra time in the training room to recover from a knee injury in 2013.

Weaknesses: Thin-framed with average core strength, hip flexibility and power to collapse the corner and play big. Average athlete with limited change of direction. Struggles to disengage from blocks and could stand to improve his hand usage and develop a better pass-rush plan. Tends to play tall and get stymied standing straight up out of his stance. Cannot pierce the double team. Leaves production on the field not wrapping up.

Future: A developmental backup most valuable contributing as a gap penetrator on the inside in a wave role. Could be drafted by a team employing a 30 front, where his unique size and length could offer depth, but will struggle to hold up at the point of attack. Shares similarities with former Oregon and current Eagles DE Brandon Bair, who went undrafted in 2011 and had practice-squad stints with the Chiefs and Raiders before reuniting with his college coach in Philadelphia.

Draft projection: Late draftable pick.

Scout's take: "(Anderson) is very stiff and has no lower-body strength. (Scouts) are going to try to make him a defensive end in a 3-4. He is not strong enough to do it. His legs buckle on contact. He has some sack production at Stanford, but if you watch it closely, it's all schemed. Every one of them. He runs that tackle loop and comes unblocked."

5T-DLE ARIK ARMSTEAD, #9 (Jr-3)
OREGON ▶ GRADE: 6.04
Ht: 6-7 ⅛ | Wt: 292 | 40: 5.11 | Arm: 33 | Hand: 10 ½

History: Older brother, Armond, was a defensive lineman who played at USC, spent one year in the CFL and signed with the Patriots before retiring for health reasons. Arik was a Parade All-American who also played basketball as a California prep. As a true freshman in 2012, played most of the season with a broken right middle finger — played all 13 games (one start) and tallied 26 tackles, two for loss and one-half sack. Played all 13 games in '13 — started the first five at defensive tackle before giving way to DeForest Buckner — and recorded 15-2 ½-1 with two batted passes. Hurt his left shoulder against Tennessee in Week Three then broke his left wrist against Colorado two weeks later. Played five-technique in '14 when he started 13 games and produced 46-5 ½-2 ½ with a forced fumble. Hurt his left ankle against Arizona — sat out against UCLA and tried to come back against Washington but lasted just a few snaps before exiting and sitting out against California, too. Played on the Ducks' basketball team until January '14.

Strengths: Very athletic for his size with an enormous wingspan. Measured the tallest (6-7 1/8) of any defensive lineman at the Combine and looks every bit the part. Is not yet done filling out his frame and could easily be a trim 310 pounds. Plays with a good, wide base and can set the edge. Good swat move. Coordinated and in control of his body. Bends his knees and is ability to flatten down the line. Very good length to disrupt passing lanes and obstruct a quarterback's sight lines.

Weaknesses: Average lateral agility and twitch for an end with minimal closing burst. Is not a well-developed sack artist. Marginal career sack production. Comes off the ball too upright and can be moved off spots by the double team. Lacks a variety of pass-rush moves. Could stand to do a better job protecting his legs — is so tall that he is susceptible to being cut. Needs to play with more consistent leverage. Is too easily fooled by play-action and drawn inside by bootlegs

and could stand to be more disciplined in his approach. Intermittent motor and intensity.

Future: An ideal five-technique in a 30 front, Armstead possesses unique mass and length to stack the corner, yet he is far from a finished product, still very much developing as a pass rusher and his best football is still years away. Has intriguing, raw, physical tools.

Draft projection: Top-40 pick.

Scout's take: "I graded him at the bottom of (the first round). I just think his motor needs to go on a more consistent basis if you're going to pull the trigger and take him earlier. I thought that was the missing factor. … The big knock on him is that he is not a worker, but he hustled a lot in the national championship game. He is a perfect five-technique. For as tall as he is, he can anchor."

DLE TAVARIS BARNES, #9 (Sr-5)
CLEMSON ▶ GRADE: 5.02
Ht: 6-3 ¾ | Wt: 282 | 40: 4.83 | Arm: 33 ⅛ | Hand: 8 ½

History: Married with a daughter. Unexpectedly lost his brother, Gary Tinsley (a Minnesota football player), to an enlarged heart in April 2012 then endured the death of his newborn son in June. Tavaris also played basketball as a Jacksonville, Fla. prep. Redshirted in 2010. Provided depth at the three-technique in '11, appearing in nine games and tallying seven tackles, zero for loss and zero sacks. In '12, was moved to defensive end by new defensive coordinator Brent Venables. On the season, tallied 24-2 ½-1 in 12 games. Did not play against North Carolina State (coach's decision). Wore jersey No. 6 prior to his junior season. Played all 13 games in '13, managing 14-2-1 with a batted pass. In '14, scratched together 14-5-3 with a batted pass and forced fumble in 13 games (one start). Could not crack the starting lineup during his time at Clemson while backing up Falcons '13 fourth-rounder Malliciah Goodman, Vic Beasley and Corey Crawford. One semester shy of his degree in Parks, Recreation and Tourism Management. Did not perform jumps or shuttles at the Combine because of a right hamstring strain.

Strengths: Outstanding height-weight-speed combination. Good athlete. Has active hands and will work up the field to contain. Flashes a quick first step. Has enough size and strength to hold the point and anchor vs. the run. Is athletic enough that he was commanding interest as a Sam linebacker prior to bulking up and could offer some versatility.

Weaknesses: Plays small and lacks pass-

DEFENSIVE LINE

rush instincts. Tends to stand up tall out of his stance and gets washed down the line. Does not understand how to convert speed to power or trim the corner. Lacks a plan as a pass rusher. Is late to locate the ball and does not feel and react to blocking pressure. Hands measured the smallest of any defensive lineman at the Combine. Marginal career production.

Future: Bulked up and has added nearly 30 pounds since the spring of 2013 and has enough size, length and athletic ability to warrant some interest as a five-technique in a 30 front. However, he is a big man who plays small and may have to fend for a job as a rotational base end.

Draft projection: Late draftable pick.

Scout's take: "(Barnes) doesn't make any plays. He backed up an average player in college. He'll get some looks for his size. … He is a good-looking kid. You get intrigued when you see him in person, but when you throw on the tape, you get disappointed so easily. Some (scouts) think he is draftable. We wouldn't take him until after the draft."

DEFENSIVE LINE

DRE-ROLB-PRS **VIC BEASLEY**, #3 (Sr-5)

CLEMSON ▶ GRADE: 6.34

Ht: 6-3 | Wt: 246 | 40: 4.52 | Arm: 32 ½ | Hand: 9 ⅜

History: Father, Vic, played football at Auburn. Beasley also played basketball as a Georgia prep. Redshirted in 2010 after entering the program as a running back. Saw limited action in nine games in '11 (16 snaps), scratching together two tackles, zero for loss and zero sacks. Played all 13 games in '12 and tallied 18-8-8 with two batted passes and a forced fumble. Stepped into the starting lineup in '13 and was a Hendricks Award finalist after producing 44-23-13 with six batted passes and four forced fumbles in 13 starts. In '14, was the Atlantic Coast Conference Defensive Player of the Year (coaches, media), as well as a finalist for the Bednarik, Lombardi and Hendricks Awards — registered 34-21 1/2-12 with three batted passes and two forced fumbles. Also had a 16-yard fumble recovery touchdown. Finished career with 52 1/2 tackles for loss and 33 sacks. Graduated in August '14 with a degree in sociology.

Strengths: Very sudden and explosive off spots with dynamic closing speed. Outstanding foot quickness and agility. Tied for the most bench-press reps (35) and clocked the fastest 40-yard dash (4.50 seconds) and three-cone drill time (6.91 seconds) of any defensive lineman at the Combine. Also recorded a 41-inch vertical jump, indicating rare lower-body explosion. Uses an assortment of moves — rip under, swim, swat, spin and inside counter. Outstanding career sack production. Superb weight-room strength. Unselfish, team player. Has special teams experience.

Weaknesses: Struggles converting speed to power. Average point-of-attack stack. Lacks ideal size to play the run — marginal tackle production. Overly reliant on speed. Has short arms and difficulty fighting through blocks when defenders get their hands on him. Can be drawn in by play-action. Does not consistently play to his timed speed. Measured 220 pounds in April 2014, has a high metabolism and struggled to stack on weight. Looks nearly maxed with a naturally lean frame. Only a two-year starter.

Future: An all-or-nothing, speed rusher who could be most ideally suited for a role as a 'wide-nine' technique in a 40 front or the 'elephant' end role popularized by Charles Haley and Chris Doleman. The more he can be schemed free, the more productive he will be. Will also command attention as a ROLB or "Jack" linebacker in a 30 front, with more prototypical dimensions for an odd front.

Draft projection: First-round pick.

Scout's take: "I think he is a one-trick pony who played better as a junior than he did as a senior. He popped off the film for me last year. I was not as impressed breaking him down more closely this year. He's going to be drafted more highly than where I would take him. I think he is so one-dimensional and that one dimension is not as elite as I thought it was. It's not like he takes the corner all the time. His production comes in spurts. He gets blocked a lot and if he doesn't win at the get-off, he is stuck. He doesn't play the run very well. … He is not as strong or physical as (Seahawks 2012 15th overall pick) Bruce Irvin, who I thought was a reach coming out."

3T **MIKE BENNETT**, #63 (Sr-4)

OHIO STATE ▶ GRADE: 5.54

Ht: 6-2 | Wt: 293 | 40: 5.04 | Arm: 33 ⅝ | Hand: 10 ¼

History: Parents graduated from West Point. Also competed in track and field as an Ohio prep. Played all 13 games as a true freshman in '11, recording 17 tackles, five for loss and three sacks. Missed the first four games of the '12 season (left groin), but played eight games (one start) and notched 11-1-1 with a batted pass and forced fumble. Started all 28 games the next two seasons — totaled 42-11 ½-7 with three forced fumbles in '13 (13 games); and 41-14-7 with three batted passes and three forced fumbles in '14 (15 games) for the national champions. Team captain changed his jersey number from 63 to 53 to honor teammate Kosta Karageorge, who died in late November. Did not lift or work out at all at the Combine because of a right groin injury.

Strengths: Has long arms and big hands. Very good initial quickness off the ball. Throws his hips in the hole and gets underneath blocks. Flattens down the line and can make plays to the sideline. Plays on his feet with fine quickness, balance and agility. Good instincts to react to blocking pressure and sniff out screens. Flashes some violence in his hands. Versatile and has lined up everywhere along the line, inside and outside. Extremely intelligent.

Weaknesses: Undersized and lacks strength at the point of attack. Gets turned too easily and moved off the spot against the double team. Often stands straight up out of his stance. Motor does not always run and plays in spurts. Executives described him as the "smartest guy in the room", "overly analytical" and "different" during interviews.

Future: An undersized, one-gap penetrator with the quickness and burst to be disruptive in gaps and effective rushing the passer from the three-technique in nickel situations. Started senior season slowly, but finished strong for a national championship defense.

Draft projection: Second- to third-round pick.

Scout's take: "He was really missing the first six games of the year and not making any plays. If you grade him early in the year, he looks like a fifth-rounder at best. You watch him later in the year and he was playing a lot better. It's a tale of two players. I'm keeping him in the fourth (round) because of the inconsistency. He might go a round or two sooner, but it's too rich for me. I don't know what I'm getting."

5T-NT ANGELO BLACKSON, #98 (Sr-4)
AUBURN   ▶ GRADE: 5.12
Ht: 6-4⅝ | Wt: 318 | 40: 5.03 | Arm: 33¾ | Hand: 9¾

History: Also played basketball as a Delaware prep. Played all 13 games as a true freshman in 2011, scratching together six tackles, 1 1/2 for loss and zero sacks. Started 10-of-12 games in '12, producing 26-7-1 with two batted passes, two forced fumbles and two blocked kicks. Missed time during '13 spring practice with a shoulder injury. In the fall, played all 14 games, starting four, and managed 16-3-½ with a forced fumble. In '14, recorded 17-5½-3 with a blocked kick in 13

games (five starts). Graduated in December with a degree in sociology.

Strengths: Looks the part and carries his weight well. Good agility for his size and has the tools to flatten down the line. Recorded a 31-inch vertical jump. Has very good body and arm length and has a knack for blocking kicks.

Weaknesses: Very marginal career production. Lacks twitch or explosive power. Marginal instincts — does not feel blocking pressure and is late to locate the ball. Plays too top heavy and struggles to protect his legs and hold the point. Comes off the ball upright and is too easily controlled. Needs to learn how to use his hands better to shed and disengage.

Future: A big, agile, underpowered rotational big body with enough mass, quickness and length to fend for a backup role in a camp. Is best as a space occupier.

Draft projection: Priority free agent.

Scout's take: "I like the way he looks. He looks like you would draw them up. I think he's draftable just based on the visual without seeing the tape. ... I would like to have him as a free agent and let him play nose tackle — see if he could put some weight on. He's a little bit of an underachiever."

3T-NT MALCOM BROWN, #90 (Jr-3)
TEXAS   ▶ GRADE: 6.22
Ht: 6 2⅜ | Wt: 319 | 40: 5.07 | Arm: 32½ | Hand: 10

History: Has two daughters with his wife Faith. Also lettered in basketball and track and field as a prep in Texas, where he was a consensus five-star recruit (signed by then-head coach Mack Brown). As a true freshman in 2012, appeared in 13 games and notched 25 tackles, two for loss and zero sacks. Took over as the Longhorns' three-technique and started all 26 games 2013-14 — totaled 68-12-2 with five batted passes in '13; and 72-15-6 ½ with a batted pass and two forced fumbles in '14. Was a finalist for the Nagurski and Outland Trophies as a junior.

Strengths: Has well-distributed body mass and carries his weight well. Played a variety of techniques (end and tackle). Good eyes and instincts to locate the ball quickly and knife through the backfield. Keeps working to the quarterback. Very good athlete for the position. Impressive 10-yard split (1.71 seconds) for a 320-pounder. Active hands to play off blocks. Very good balance, quickness and movement skill — is seldom on the ground. Plays with violence in his hands. Can dig his heels in the dirt and neutralize the double team. Flattens down the line and makes plays — productive

DEFENSIVE LINE

tackler. Can set the edge and does a fine job sifting through traffic and keeping his feet.

Weaknesses: On the short side with short arms. Lets his pads rise, negating leverage and lower-body power. Needs to become a more consistent finisher and could develop more variety as a pass-rusher.

Future: Strong, versatile, interior presence with the ability to play the piano and move up and down an even or odd front.

Draft projection: First-round pick.

Scout's take: "I couldn't find a fit for him in the 3-4. … He will probably play on the nose, but he is good enough to be a three-technique. He has hip flex. He's one of those guys who (have) played in both schemes. You can play him on a shade. He's just as good as and stronger than (Viking 2013 23rd overall pick) Shariff Floyd coming out."

DLE-DT **ANTHONY CHICKILLO**, #71 (Sr-4)

MIAMI (FLA.) ▶GRADE: 5.26

Ht: 6-3 ⅛ | Wt: 267 | 40: 4.82 | Arm: 33 ½ | Hand: 10 ⅛

History: Third-generation Hurricane. Highly recruited Parade All-American out of Tampa, where he racked up 50 sacks in three years. Suffered a broken collarbone in 2009. As a true freshman in 2011, played 12 games and started eight of the final nine — notched 38 tackles, 6 ½ for loss and five sacks with a forced fumble. Became a fixture in '12 when he started all 12 games and produced 45-6 ½-4 with a batted pass. Had his right ankle scoped after the season. Started all 13 games in '13, recording 46-7 ½-3 ½ with two batted passes. Was bothered by a broken left toe the last two games of the season. In '14, totaled 41-4 ½-3 with a forced fumble and two batted passes in 13 starts. Suffered a minor knee injury against Florida State, but did not miss a start. Team captain graduated with degree in sports administration.

Strengths: Outstanding size. Very active hands. Solid functional strength to set the edge and play square. Can out-quick blockers from the inside. Chases hard from the backside and makes effort plays in pursuit. Uses his hands well to stack and shed and play off blocks. Tough. Has a passion for the game and prepares like a pro. Gym rat — lives in the football facility so much that he needs to be kicked out. Film junkie. Very good football intelligence. Impressed at the East-West Shrine game, where he stood out for his motor and initial get-off. Experienced four-year starter. Versatile and has played inside and outside.

Weaknesses: Below-average athletic ability, short-area explosion and quickness. Limited bend. Lacks ideal functional strength to handle the double team on the inside.

Future: An energetic, blue-collar grinder, Chickilo plays with an infectious energy and is wired right. Plays both inside and outside and has the quickness to work half-a-man and create pressure from the interior. Could contend for a job as a starting base end.

Draft projection: Fourth- to fifth-round pick.

Scout's take: "He is a try-hard, high-motor tough guy that competes and battles. I wouldn't mind having him around as a sixth, seventh or eighth defensive linemen. He's smart and can come in and play. You know exactly what you are getting. He'll bring it every down."

DLE-LOLB **FRANK CLARK**, #57 (Sr-4)

EX-MICHIGAN ▶GRADE: 5.05

Ht: 6-2 ⅞ | Wt: 271 | 40: 4.78 | Arm: 34 ⅜ | Hand: 10 ⅛

History: Spent the first 10 years of his life in the drug-, crime- and gang-infested Crenshaw neighborhood of Los Angeles, where he lived a wandering life with his mother, who had drug problems, per MLive. Separated from his mother in 2003 when he moved to Cleveland, where he was coached by Ted Ginn Sr. at Glenville High. As a true freshman in 2011, tallied 10 tackles, one-half for loss and zero sacks with an interception in 12 games. In the summer of '12, pleaded guilty to felony second-degree home invasion (had a stolen laptop from a neighboring dorm room). Was sentenced to one year of probation and ordered to pay $1,741 in fines. On the season, served a one-game suspension (Alabama) before starting 4-of-11 games played at defensive end and recording 25-9-2 with three batted passes and a forced fumble. Did not play against Nebraska (left ankle). Was UM's top defensive lineman in '13 when he produced 43-12-4 ½ with a batted pass in 13 starts. In '14, started 9-of-10 games played and totaled 42-13 ½-4 ½ with two batted passes. Was kicked off the team in November after he was involved in a domestic violence incident with his girlfriend. Was charged with misdemeanor domestic violence and assault. Entered counseling after the incident.

Strengths: Outstanding arm length. Good strength to hold the point and spill the outside run. Has a feel for blocking pressure. Plays on his feet with good balance and comes underneath blocks. Flashes some violence in his hands. Posted the best short shuttle (4.05 seconds) and 60-yard shuttle (11.22) of any defensive lineman at the Combine. Strong

DEFENSIVE LINE

tackler with knockback body power. Enough athletic ability to fall back into coverage and play on his feet.

Weaknesses: Inconsistent eyes. Lacks variety in his pass-rush arsenal — does not have a plan. Is often a step or two late to arrive and lacks the edge burst and closing speed to finish. Only bench-pressed 19 reps at the Combine. Character and maturity must be investigated carefully — has been removed from NFL draft boards for concerns.

Future: A long-armed, leverage-power rusher with the strength and power in his body to be effective defending the run. Could warrant some interest as an outside linebacker in a 30 front, but is most likely to fit as a base end in 4-3 scheme. Has the talent to become a solid contributor in the pros. However, off-field concerns could force him to prove himself as an undrafted free agent.

Draft projection: Priority free agent.

Scout's take: "He flashes. He has long arms and plays with leverage. But he's only had two sacks in seven games so far. What kind of pass rusher is that? I see more hesitation in his play that I like to see. I just don't see it."

3T-5T XAVIER COOPER, #96 (Jr-5)

WASHINGTON STATE ▶ GRADE: 5.34

Ht: 6-2 ⅞ | Wt: 293 | 40: 4.84 | Arm: 31 ½ | Hand: 9 ⅜

History: Washington native also played basketball in high school. Grayshirted in 2010. Redshirted in 2011 while he was a partial qualifier. Was deployed as a defensive end in WSU's 3-4 defense. In '12, started 9-of-11 games and produced 34 tackles, 8 1/2 for loss and three sacks with a forced fumble. Didn't see action in the season opener against BYU. Started all 25 games the next two seasons — totaled 50-13 ½-5 with two forced fumbles and a 29-yard fumble recovery touchdown in '13 (13 games); and 37-9 ½-5 with a batted pass in '14 (12 games). Was WSU's Defensive Lineman of the Year as a junior.

Strengths: Has enough functional strength to set the edge and hold the point. Plays multiple techniques, inside and outside, and offers scheme versatility. Recorded a 10-yard split (1.65 seconds) that places him second among defensive tackles at the Combine. Good agility and quickness to slant, stunt and play in gaps. Bench-pressed 29 reps at the Combine.

Weaknesses: Has very short arms and small hands. Plays too upright and narrow-based and gets stuck on blocks. Lacks lower-body explosion and power in his body. Does not show a variety of pass-rush moves and gets stalled too easily. Is still learning how to convert his weight-room strength to the field.

Future: An unrefined, gap penetrator with the size, quickness, agility and versatility to warrant interest developing. Has played multiple positions in different schemes, yet is most ideally suited for a role as a one-gap penetrator.

Draft projection: Fourth- to fifth-round pick.

Scout's take: "I like him as a three-technique. He is versatile. You can put him over the nose or line him up as a five-technique. He has some versatility. I know a lot of scouts that don't like him (as a player) and have been beating him up for what he can't do. He is big and he is quick. There's a value on that alone."

3T CHRISTIAN COVINGTON, #1 (Jr-4)

RICE ▶ GRADE: 5.34

Ht: 6-2 ⅜ | Wt: 289 | 40: 5.00e | Arm: 33 ¼ | Hand: 10

History: Father, Grover, is in the CFL Hall of Fame after a standout career as a defensive end for the Hamilton Tiger-Cats (1981-91) — owns the CFL record with 157 sacks. Prepped in British Columbia, where he won a Provincial Championship and was considered the best defensive lineman in Canada. Rice was Covington's only Division I offer. Redshirted in 2011. Started 11-of-12 games played in '12 and recorded 43 tackles, 10 for loss and five sacks. Non-start came was versus SMU, when he gave way to a senior walk-on on Senior Night. In '13, was the first Rice sophomore to earn first-team all-conference honors since the return of two-platoon football — managed 59-14-4 with three batted passes and a forced fumble in 14 starts despite playing the final five games with his right hand in a cast to protect a thumb injury. In '14, totaled 20-4-3 with a batted pass in seven starts before suffering a season-ending dislocated left knee cap injury against Florida International. Medically excluded from performing at the Combine while recovering from the injury. Wore jersey No. 56 prior to senior season when he switched to No. 1 to honor Rice alum N.D. Kalu. On track to graduate in May with a Kinesiology degree.

Strengths: Flashed elite quickness to beat blockers at the snap in 2013, when he was more healthy. Plays with a sense of urgency and times the snap very well to slice gaps. Good swim and rip moves – can work underneath blockers to come free. Enough strength to hold the point of attack. Plays flat-backed and runs to the ball. Has NFL pedigree.

Weaknesses: Tends to play too upright and

DEFENSIVE LINE

flat-footed. Lacks ideal core strength. Limited body control — cannot redirect quickly or change direction. Plays too out of control. Not a consistent wrap tackler and leaves production on the field. Durability has been a lingering issue and likely will continue to be with the reckless style with which he plays.

Future: A quick, undersized gap penetrator who played his best in 2013 before injuries derailed his junior season. Has the quickness and energy to be disruptive when healthy. Durability could affect his draft standing.

Draft projection: Third- to fourth-round pick.

Scout's take: "(Covington) had one good game vs. Notre Dame. Then he got hurt and lost all his power. He is hurt all the time. I don't understand why I am even cross-checking him. I don't want guys that are hurt all the time. He should be off our board. ... Our area (scout) put him in the third (round). He's sitting in the top of six for me. The guy didn't play a full year and even when he was at his best, I just didn't see it."

DLE COREY CRAWFORD, #93 (Sr-5)

CLEMSON ▶ GRADE: 5.17

Ht: 6-5 ¼ | Wt: 283 | 40: 4.94 | Arm: 34 ½ | Hand: 9 ¼

History: Prepped in Georgia and spent 2010 at Hargrave Military Academy (Va.). Played all 14 games in '11, recording 29 tackles, two for loss and zero sacks with two batted passes. Lost his mother to breast cancer in February '12. In the fall, stepped into the lineup and started all 13 games, notching 47-6-1 with a batted pass. In '13, started 12-of-13 games and posted 52-10 ½-3 with four batted passes, two forced fumbles and an interception. Was suspended for the '14 season opener (violation team rules), but started all 11 games played and logged 25-7-2 with a batted pass. Sat out against Georgia State (ankle). Played opposite Vic Beasley the last two seasons. Graduated in December with a degree in parks, recreation and tourism, management. Did not lift at the Combine because of a left shoulder injury.

Strengths: Outstanding size with arms like an anaconda to smother ball carriers. Measured the longest wingspan (85 inches) of any defensive lineman at the Combine. Flashes quickness off the ball. Good mass to anchor down to play the run. Is fairly light on his feet in space to run with backs releasing in the flats and close to the quarterback when he has a free lane. Fluid athlete.

Weaknesses: Disappears too much. Intermittent motor, intensity and effort. Is late off the ball and plays at his own pace.

Does not play with violence in his hands. Not a glass-eater. Average eyes and instincts. Underwhelming career production. Sluggish and heavy changing direction, as evidenced with one of the slowest short shuttle times (4.66 seconds) of any defensive end at the Combine. Opponents were focused on stopping teammate Vic Beasley and received a lot of single blocks.

Future: A talented athlete who has yet to live up to his potential. Moves well enough that some scouts were even considering projecting him to Sam linebacker. Has a big enough frame and the length and mass to consider as a developmental five-technique, yet does play strong or hard enough to make a living battling. Could have to fend for a job as a rotational base end.

Draft projection: Fifth- to sixth-round pick.

Scout's take: "He's a big underachiever. I put him in the sixth round, but really didn't care for the way he plays. I hate non-productive players. I didn't think he made any plays. If they can't be productive in college, how are they going to produce in the pros."

3T-5T CARL DAVIS, #71 (Sr-5)

IOWA ▶ GRADE: 5.72

Ht: 6-4 ⅝ | Wt: 320 | 40: 5.09 | Arm: 34 ⅝ | Hand: 11

History: Also lettered in basketball and track and field as a Detroit prep. Redshirted in 2010. Saw limited action in six games in '11, scratching together two tackles, zero for loss and zero sacks. Appeared in 11 games in '12, logging 14-1 1/2-0. Missed two games because of a sprained right MCL. Started all 26 games at defensive tackle the next two seasons — totaled 42-4-1 1/2 with a batted pass in '13; and 36-9-2 in '14. Received a Coaches Appreciation Award. Opted not to lift at the Combine

Strengths: Has very long arms, a huge frame and is extremely well built with well-distributed mass – looks every bit the part. Tied for the biggest hands (11 inches) of any player at the Combine and also finished among the top performers in the vertical jump (33 inches), 10-yard split (1.70 seconds) and the short shuttle (4.47 seconds). Versatile and has lined up as a three-technique and nose tackle in the Hawkeye's 40 front and is capable of kicking outside in a 30 front. Good strength to stack the corner and anchor. Has a 400-power clean and exceptional power in his body (though he does not often use it)

Weaknesses: Minimal career sack production. Does not play to his measurables and runs like

DEFENSIVE LINE

his feet hurt — is not quick to turn them over and stays tied up on twists, loops and stunts when he is schemed to come free. Very inconsistent pad level – tends to stand straight up out of his stance and negate his leverage. Does not consistently finish. Plays with too much finesse. Only a two-year starter. Did not show as well during team periods in practice at the Senior Bowl as he did in one-on-one's. Scouts question how much he loves football, and if his best will only come out in a contract year.

Future: Big, strong, quick, versatile defensive linemen capable of manning the post in a 30-front or disrupting the inside in a 40-front. Exceptional showing during Senior Bowl one-on-one's moved his name into the first-round discussion, yet performance during the fall left some scouts exiting Iowa stamping free-agent grades on the career underachiever. Can be as good as he wants to be, but immense talent needs to be tempered with disappointing motor, intensity and desire and comes with a 'buyer beware' label.

Draft projection: First-round pick.

Scout's take: "I stuck him in the third round with the underachiever tag. The Senior Bowl showed what he could do when he is motivated. Based on the tape work, I couldn't push him up. He reminded me of the (University of) Minnesota kid (Falcons 37th overall pick Ra'Shede Hageman) last year."

NT-DLE TYELER DAVISON, #92 (Sr-5)

FRESNO STATE ▶ GRADE: 5.17

Ht: 6-1⅝ | Wt: 316 | 40: 5.17 | Arm: 34 | Hand: 10¾

History: Two-way lineman and state wrestling champion as an Arizona prep. Redshirted in 2010. Appeared in all 13 games in '12, logging 16 tackles, one for loss and one sack. Took ownership of the nose guard position by starting all 40 games the next three seasons — totaled 43-7-3 with a batted pass, forced fumble, blocked kick and nine-yard fumble recovery touchdown in '12 (13 games); 41-7 ½-2 with two batted passes and a blocked kick in '13 (13 starts) despite playing through a sprained right MCL and back spasms; and 61-13-8 ½ with two forced fumbles in '14 (14 starts).

Strengths: Has a huge frame with a thick trunk, long arms and big hands. Flattens down the line and shows good playing range for his size. Active and energetic and productive for a nose tackle. Good short-area quickness to close. Flashes some ability to push the pocket. Football is important to him.

Weaknesses: On the short side and plays short-armed. Marginal lateral agility. Does not play to his size or stay square. Runs himself out of plays, gets washed down the line too easily and plays like he is on skates. Has been bothered by a lot of nagging injuries to his back, knee, quad and shoulder.

Future: A finesse, movement nose tackle with enough size, mass and length to provide depth in a rotational role for an aggressive, slanting 30 front.

Draft projection: Late draftable pick.

Scout's take: "(Davison) has long arms. He just doesn't use them. I thought he played better (in 2013) when they were playing with leads more often and he was able to cut it loose and get after the quarterback."

DLE-LOLB RYAN DELAIRE, #56 (Sr-5)

TOWSON ▶ GRADE: 5.18

Ht: 6-4⅛ | Wt: 254 | 40: 4.94 | Arm: 32½ | Hand: 10⅜

History: Played four sports as a Connecticut prep. Began his college career at UMass, where he redshirted in 2010. Wearing jersey No. 55 for the Minutemen, appeared in 10 games in '11 and recorded nine tackles, one for loss and one-half sack. Was suspended for the New Hampshire contest for a personal foul and ejection against Delaware. Appeared in eight games in '12, tallying 19-5-2 ½. Seeking more playing time, transferred to FCS Towson, where he started all 27 games at the "Bull" (defensive end/rush linebacker) position the next two seasons — totaled 68-17 ½-11 ½ with three batted passes and two forced fumbles in '13 (15 games); and 64-14 ½-11 with a batted pass and three forced fumbles in '14 (12 games). Did not perform jumps, shuttles or drills at the Combine because of a right groin injury.

Strengths: Very well-conditioned athlete – measured only 6.9 percent body fat at the Combine. Strong inside move — does a good job setting up blockers hard to the outside, turning their hips and slipping inside. Athletic enough to slip into coverage and buzz the flats. Is tough and plays hard with good energy and urgency. Closes fast to the ball and makes plays in backside chase pursuit. Good sack production. Has a frame to grow into and could easily be 270 pounds.

Weaknesses: Below-average arm length. Could stand to do a better job wrapping up and securing tackles. Plays too upright with marginal explosion and foot quickness. See-and-go reactor — digests what he sees and is not instant off spots. Production is inflated from facing inferior competition and a lot of

DEFENSIVE LINE

it was clear-view where he was uncontested running free from a wide-nine alignment.

Future: Developmental rush linebacker prospect with the urgency and football temperament to warrant developing. Plays faster than his timed speed and has untapped talent to be molded.

Draft projection: Fifth- to sixth-round pick.

DLE B.J. DuBOSE, #11 (Sr-5)

LOUISVILLE   ▶ GRADE: 5.18

Ht: 6-4 | Wt: 284 | 40: 5.04 | Arm: 33 | Hand: 9 ¾

History: Prepped in Florida. Redshirted in 2010. Played all 13 games in '11, starting three at defensive end, and tallied 22 tackles, five for loss and two sacks. In '12, started 4-of-7 games played and managed 15-1-0 with a batted pass, though he spent most of the season in then-head coach Charlie Strong's doghouse. Started four of the first five games before he was left off the travel squad for the Pittsburgh contest ("bad week of practice") then suspended for the final five games of the season. Appeared in 11 games in '13, collecting 16-4-1 1/2. Did not play the final two games. In '14, started all 13 games at right end in the Cardinals' 3-4 front — notched 41-7 1/2-4 with a batted pass. Graduated. Did not perform jumps or shuttles at the Combine because of a right hamstring strain.

Strengths: Good movement skill for a big man. Has enough strength to push the pocket and set the edge. Flashes power in his body and can drive blockers into the backfield. Solid run defender.

Weaknesses: Average instincts – is late to diagnose and locate the ball. Limited body control. Has few pass-rush moves and gets stuck on blocks easily. Overly reliant on bull-rush move. Gets moved off spots by the double team and washed down the line by tight ends. Could stand to do a better job wrapping as a tackler and using his hands to disengage blockers. Does not flatten down the line – minimal backside effort. Marginal career production.

Future: A big-bodied, base end with enough size and strength to hold the point and provide depth in a rotation for an odd front. Lacks the instincts, awareness, rush savvy and discipline desired in a starter.

Draft projection: Late draftable pick.

3T-5T MARIO EDWARDS, #15 (Jr-3)

FLORIDA STATE   ▶ GRADE: 5.87

Ht: 6-2 ⅝ | Wt: 279 | 40: 4.84 | Arm: 33 ¼ | Hand: 10 ⅞

History: Texas prep was rated the No. 1 recruit in the nation by multiple services. Was named USA Today Defensive Player of the Year and Parade All-American. Was slated to redshirt in 2012 before Brandon Jenkins was injured. On the season, appeared in 11 games (one start) and tallied 17 tackles, 2 1/2 for loss and 1 1/2 sacks with a batted pass. Started 11-of-12 games in '13, producing 28-9 1/2-3 1/2 with a batted pass, an interception, a forced fumble and a 37-yard fumble recovery touchdown. Played with a cast on his right hand early in the season to protect an injury that required surgery and kept him out of the Bethune-Cookman and Boston College games. Played the "Jack" linebacker in '14 — registered 44-11-3 with five batted passes and two forced fumbles in 13 starts. Sustained a concussion against Clemson and did not play against North Carolina State then sprained his MCL against Syracuse.

Strengths: Big, strong and powerful enough to stack the corner in an odd front. Locates the ball quickly and will play off blocks and make plays at him. Can drive single blocks deep into the backfield and collapse the pocket. Good bull strength to press off blockers and anchor. Can work half-a-man and take an edge from the inside — is quick off the ball and disruptive flushing the quarterback from the pocket.

Weaknesses: Has a smooth-muscled body and does not look the part. Weight has fluctuated (312 at one point). Plays too upright. Cut too easy and can do a better job protecting his legs. Limited pass-rush skill as a base end — cannot win with speed or quickness. Does not make many plays. Effort is up and down and will play down to the level of competition. Must prove more motivated.

Future: Classic underachiever more ideally suited for a role on the inside slanting, stunting and playing in gaps than stacking the corner and playing square as he was primarily asked to do in 2014. Has some similarity to Packers 2013 first-round pick (26th overall) Datone Jones and has boom-or-bust potential. Will not be able to get away with coasting in the pros and must ratchet up the intensity to realize his potential.

Draft projection: Top-40 pick.

Scout's take: "(Edwards') stock has fallen this year. He won't get out of the first (round). … He is a very average pass-rusher outside. He is a power player who can set the edge and will be hard to knock around because of his size. He is better when he is kicked down as a defensive tackle in a 4-3. He is very intriguing as a three-technique. I don't think his value is as great as a defensive end where he has no pass-rush ability. … I thought he played a lot better (in 2013)."

DLE **TREY FLOWERS**, #86 (Sr-4)

ARKANSAS ▶ GRADE: 5.26

Ht: 6-2 ⅛ | Wt: 266 | 40: 4.89 | Arm: 34 ¼ | Hand: 10

History: Also played basketball as an Arkansas prep. Was recruited by then-head coach Bobby Petrino. As a true freshman in 2011, played all 13 games (three starts at defensive end as an injury replacement) and recorded 28 tackles, 5 ½ for loss and one sack with two batted passes. Started all 12 games in '12, notching 50-13-6 with three batted passes. Started all 11 games played in '13, totaling 44-13 ½-5 with two batted passes, three forced fumbles and an interception. Did not play against Samford (knee). Was voted team co-MVP in '14 after starting all 14 games and amassing 68-15 ½-6 with six batted passes and a forced fumble. Team captain graduated in December with an economics degree. Will be a 22-year-old rookie.

Strengths: Flashes the ability to set the edge. Plays hard. Assignment sound and disciplined with run reads. Keeps his outside arm free and maintains good block-to-ball relationships and contain. Very underrated production.

Weaknesses: Stiff-legged. Limited pass-rush savvy and quickness. Is often a step or two late to the mark and lacks finishing speed. Gets washed out of the hole when he is reduced inside, lacking ideal bulk strength to hold the point (see LSU and Alabama). Limited twitch and explosion. Lacks the burst to trim the corner.

Future: Is not a flashy, productive, sack artist, but is a very functional base end with enough power, length, discipline and effort to defend the run. Lacks ideal size to stack the corner for a 30 front, but could compete for a role as a two-down run defender within a 40 front.

Draft projection: Fourth- to fifth-round pick.

Scout's take: "I don't know where to put the guy. He has 34-inch arms and an 85-inch wingspan. He can rush the passer. Is he a speed-rusher — no, but I can move him inside. I have got to find a spot for a football player. They had him at rush linebacker at the Senior Bowl."

DLE-LOLB **MARKUS GOLDEN**, #33 (Sr-5)

MISSOURI ▶ GRADE: 5.53

Ht: 6-2 ⅜ | Wt: 260 | 40: 4.84 | Arm: 31 ⅛ | Hand: 10 ½

History: Highly productive linebacker-running back as a St. Louis prep — totaled 276 tackles and 26 sacks with 3,400 yards and 46 touchdowns his final two seasons. Was a non-qualifier coming out of high school, so headed to Hutchinson (Kan.) Community College. In 2010, recorded 85 tackles, 25 ½ for loss and 9 ½ sacks with a batted pass, two interceptions and five forced fumbles in 12 games. Redshirted in '11. Joined the Tigers in '12 and was used primarily on special teams, tallying 10-0-0 with a forced fumble. With '14 draftees Kony Ealy (Panthers, second round) and Southeastern Conference Defensive Player of the Year Michael Sam (Rams, seventh) entrenched in the starting lineup, Golden played all 14 games (nearly 40 percent of the snaps) in '13, registering 55-13-6 ½ with a forced fumble and 70-yard interception touchdown against Toledo. Started opposite Shane Ray in '14 — amassed 78-20-10 with two batted passes, three forced fumbles and a 21-yard fumble recovery score. Sat out against Indiana (left hamstring). Team captain. Graduated in December, becoming the first in his family to earn a college degree. Did not lift at the Combine because of a right hand injury and did not perform jumps or shuttles after straining his left hamstring in positional drills.

Strengths: Good functional core strength. Plays hard and competes — makes a lot of plays in pursuit running down ball carriers from the backside. Opportunistic — steps up in the clutch and is a respected team leader willing to do what it takes. Outstanding football-playing temperament. Flashes some violence in his hands. Plays disciplined. Aggressive special teams performer. Very good 10-yard splits (1.63 seconds) indicative of short-area burst. Solid personal and football character.

Weaknesses: Has very short arms and gets tied up in tight quarters and struggles to disengage. Lacks ideal burst and acceleration at the top of his rush to close to the quarterback. Only a one-year starter. Could be challenged by complex assignments initially and take a little extra time to get acclimated.

Future: A high-effort, leverage-power rusher with the strength to warrant interest as a strong-side rush linebacker in an odd front or as a base end in a 40 front. Will require a short adjustment period but will work to exceed expectations once he settles in.

Draft projection: Third- to fourth-round pick.

Scout's take: "(Golden) might be a poor man's Courtney Upshaw. Upshaw was more physical, powerful and nasty coming out. Golden is a tough kid. He has a good motor. He plays hard. There are some positives to like."

DEFENSIVE LINE

NT-5T EDDIE GOLDMAN, #90 (Jr-3)

FLORIDA STATE ▶ GRADE: 6.20

Ht: 6-3 ⅞ | Wt: 336 | 40: 5.20e | Arm: 33 ⅛ | Hand: 10 ⅛

History: USA Today and Parade All-American and consensus five-star recruit out of Washington, D.C. As a true freshman in 2012 (wore jersey No. 81), recorded eight tackles, one for loss and zero sacks in 10 games. Started all 13 games at left end in '13, recording 19-3-2. Was suspended against Bethune-Cookman (violation team rules). Was a defensive tackle in '14 when he posted 35-8-4 with a batted pass and a forced fumble in 14 starts. Sprained his left ankle in Week Two against The Citadel, but had two weeks to heal before the 'Noles' next game. Played for three defensive coordinators in three years: Mark Stoops, Jeremy Pruitt and Charles Kelly. Opted not to lift at the Combine and did not work out because of a right ankle injury.

Strengths: Extremely strong and plays with physicality. Can stack the point. Is powerful enough to collapse the pocket and walk defenders back to the quarterback. Regularly plays on the other side of the line of scrimmage and seldom is inverted. Digs his heels in the dirt vs. the double team. Can press blockers off his frame and create extension to play off blocks. Good movement skill for a big man. Locates the ball quickly. Is quick to discard blockers and run to the ball. Very strong club move — swats blockers. Made opportunistic plays at critical times and plays big in the clutch (see Clemson). Terrific game-day competitor.

Weaknesses: Has some body stiffness. Stands tall out of his stance and plays a bit upright. Average lateral agility to redirect . Average behind-the-line production. Is still learning how to work half-a-man, get skinny and play in gaps.

Future: Played various techniques under three defensive coordinators in a national championship program and showed he could make an impact at multiple positions. More strong than explosive, Goldman plays big in a big man's game and has enough athletic talent to warrant looks in even or odd fronts.

Draft projection: First-round pick.

Scout's take: "(Florida State) lost their defensive coordinator (Jeremy Pruitt) last year. Go back and watch this kid in 2013 and there's a big difference. If you have any questions or doubts, that will help. … I think he can play as a three technique. He didn't work out at the Combine. I know he is going to have a good workout. I don't need to see it."

DRE-ROLB RANDY GREGORY, #4 (Jr-4)

NEBRASKA ▶ GRADE: 6.60

Ht: 6-4 ⅞ | Wt: 235 | 40: 4.62 | Arm: 34 | Hand: 10

History: Comes from a military family. Also starred on the hardwood as an Indiana prep. Originally committed to Purdue (liked then-head coach Danny Hope and admired Indiana native and Purdue alum Ryan Kerrigan), but failed to qualify academically. Instead, attended Arizona Western Community College. Broke his wrist playing pickup basketball before the season, but recorded 82 tackles, 21 for loss and nine sacks with a batted pass and three forced fumbles in 2011 (12 games). Scratched together 5-1-1 with a batted pass in the first game of the '12 season before suffering a season-ending broken left fibula in practice. Interested schools cooled on Gregory after the injury, and once Hope was fired from Purdue, Gregory opted to sign with Nebraska and then-head coach Bo Pelini. Made an immediate impact in '13, garnering Team MVP honors — started 10-of-13 games at defensive end, producing 66-19-10 1/2 with five batted passes, an interception and a forced fumble. Battled through an injury-riddled, redshirt-junior season to start 10-of-11 games played and post 54-10-7 with three batted passes, an interception, forced fumble and two blocked kicks. Played through turf toe; hurt his left knee in the season opener against Florida Atlantic, had arthroscopic surgery and missed the McNeese State contest; and sat out against Iowa (concussion, ankle). Did not start in the Holiday Bowl vs. USC. Did not perform shuttles at the Combine because of leg cramps.

Strengths: Very loose-hipped, flexible athlete with a unique combination of length, bend and explosion. Can so deftly cross the face of a lineman without even a hand being placed on him, indicative of his rush instincts and ability to beat blocks. Often commands double- and triple-teams and still is able to weave in and around blockers. Extremely nimble and light on his feet. Uses his terrific length to create leverage and play with strength. Can convert speed to power and create movement and still get an inside arm bar and hold the point. Produced the fastest 10-yard split (1.50 seconds) of any defensive lineman at the Combine. Can even kick inside, line up over a guard and be effective slipping and avoiding blocks because of his bionic hips and rare body control.

Weaknesses: Narrow-hipped and very lean with an underdeveloped frame. Measured the lightest (235 pounds) of any defensive

Randy Gregory

lineman at the Combine and has had difficulty maintaining weight. Measured only 4 percent body fat at the Combine and does not have enough armor on his body to withstand a pounding — could be more prone to injury and had numerous injuries in college. Needs to add bulk and get stronger. Won't be able to hold up vs. double teams, wham and mash blocks in the NFL. Underwhelming sack production. Scouts say he appeared to be playing not to get hurt in bowl game vs. USC. Disappears for stretches where he does not impact the game. Will require maintenance and needs to be monitored closely.

Future: A very long, fluid, flexible, gangly edge rusher with very similar athletic and rush talent as Browns 2013 sixth overall pick Barkevious Mingo, who also recorded underwhelming sack production in college. Also reminds scouts of Dion Jordan, who was selected third overall by Miami in 2013 and has been slow to develop in part because of off-the-field issues. Gregory has a rare combination of burst, bend, balance and body control that allows him to beat any blocker from any side with grace, and a frame to grow into a feared sack artist. However, he will need a very strong support structure to blossom. Has boom-or-bust potential and could require patience. Injury-prone past must be considered.

Draft projection: First-round pick.

Scout's take: "Gregory is smooth and dynamic. He looks pretty making moves rushing the passer. Some of the stuff he does cannot be taught. You can put his cut-ups in a coaching clinic for how to set up moves. It's just pure rush instincts and exactly what you are looking for in the way of bend and slide and adjust and motor. Gregory does a lot of things very, very good. He is the most natural pass rusher in the draft."

DRE-PRS OBUM GWACHAM, #86 (Sr-6)

OREGON STATE ▶ GRADE: 5.10

| Ht: 6-5 ⅞ | Wt: 246 | 40: 4.69 | Arm: 34 ⅜ | Hand: 10 |

History: Name is pronounced "oh-BOOM GWAH-chem." Born in Nigeria and moved to the United States at the age of seven. Captained the football and track teams as a California prep — played receiver and excelled as a high, triple and long jumper. Missed the 2007 football season with a broken collarbone. Was recruited as a receiver. Grayshirted in 2009 then redshirted in '10. Played 12 games in '11, recording eight catches for 147 yards (18.4-yard average) and zero touchdowns. Was supposed to compete for a slot position in '12, but a nagging ankle injury made him a non-factor — scratched together 2-12-1 (6.0) in 13 games. Was a reserve split end in '13 when he grabbed 1-6-0 (6.0). Tallied nine special-teams tackles his first three seasons. After struggling mightily to become the receiver the coaching staff envisioned, was converted to defensive end in '14. Responded with 28 tackles, 5 ½ for loss and four sacks with a forced fumble in 12 games, as he was used primarily as a pass-rush specialist. Also competed as a track and field athlete at OSU. Will be a 24-year-old rookie.

Strengths: Is a very good athlete with long arms and good movement skill. Fluid mover. Buzzes the deep zone and shows good range in coverage. Tested well at the Combine and has the size and athletic ability to play linebacker or end.

Weaknesses: Very lean with limited bulk and bulk strength. Is late to diagnose or sort out what he sees. Marginal eyes, instincts and anticipation.

Future: A converted receiver who is still learning to understand the game from the defensive point of view. Has clear athletic talent that could be best suited for a pin-your-ears-back-and-go, pass-rush specialist or wide nine-technique role. Will require time for the game to slow down. Developmental pass rusher with enough upside to warrant a camp invitation.

Draft projection: Late draftable pick.

Scout's take: "He has zero instincts. (The coaching staff) couldn't find a spot for him. There were a lot of scouts buzzing about his length and measurables during the fall. I never understood it. He can't find the ball. He is a late-rounder on measurables alone. That's it."

5T-3T MARCUS HARDISON, #1 (Sr-4)

ARIZONA STATE   ▶ GRADE:5.38

Ht: 6-3 ⅛ | Wt: 307 | 40: 4.91 | Arm: 33 ½ | Hand: 10 ⅜

History: Prepped in Florida, where he played quarterback early in his career. Attended Dodge City (Kan.) Community College for two years — recorded 46 tackles, 12 for loss and three sacks with a forced fumble in 2011 (10 games); and 38-9-4 with two forced fumbles

and two blocked kicks in '12 (nine games). A reserve with the Sun Devils in '13, had 5-1-1 in 13 appearances. Shifted from tackle to end in late September. Did not play against UCLA. Gained traction as a senior when he started all 13 games and produced 53-15-10 with two batted passes, two interceptions and three forced fumbles. Medically excluded from testing at the Combine because of a left knee injury.

Strengths: Surprising first-step quickness and agility for his size. Plays on his feet with good balance and flashes pop and power in his hands. Has the strength to press blockers off his chest and lock out with good extension. Is active and keeps working to the quarterback. Very good sack production. Versatile and has played inside and out and made noticeable strides as a senior. Is coachable.

Weaknesses: Tight in the hips with limited lower-body explosion. Motor runs hot and cold. Could stand to do a better job using his hands to disengage from blockers. Green instincts and football intelligence. Struggled learning the defensive audibles his first year at ASU and could be challenged by complex defensive assignments. Lacks discipline and will lose gap integrity freelancing.

Future: A former prep quarterback and hoops standout with unique athletic traits for the position. Is a thickly built, compact 300-plus pounder still learning to translate his talent to the field. Could warrant interest as a five-technique in a 30 front where he played heavily as a senior, or as a developmental three-technique, with intriguing speed to pierce gaps and disrupt from the interior.

Draft projection: Fourth- to fifth-round pick.

DRE-PRS DANIELLE HUNTER, #94 (Sr-3)

LSU   ▶ GRADE: 5.36

Ht: 6-5 ⅛ | Wt: 252 | 40: 4.56 | Arm: 34 ¼ | Hand: 10 ½

History: Prepped in Texas. As a true freshman in 2012, tallied 12 tackles, zero for loss and zero sacks in 12 appearances. Did not see action against South Carolina. Played all 13 games in '13, starting the final 10 at right end, and produced 57-8-3 with two batted passes and a forced fumble. In '14, started all 13 games at DRE and registered 73-13-1 ½ with six batted passes, a forced fumble and a 25-yard fumble recovery touchdown. Was honored with LSU's post-season award for performance, leadership and commitment to the team. Does not turn 21 until late October. Did not perform jumps, shuttles or positional drills at the Combine because of a right

DEFENSIVE LINE

hamstring injury.

Strengths: Looks the part with a chiseled physique (only 6.4 percent body fat) and exceptional timed speed. Very good hustle and pursuit effort — runs down the ball from behind and leaves everything on the field. Lines up inside at times and creates mismatches slipping and circling around overmatched guards. Intense and competitive. Very solid character.

Weaknesses: Has a thin base and can be run at. Average eyes, instincts and anticipation. Lacks a plan as a pass-rusher. Segmented movement skills — too herky jerky and tight-hipped. Gets hung up easily on blocks. Cannot keep his cleats in the ground coming around the corner and does not show the natural bend and leverage to trim the corner. Has too much body stiffness. Shut down by better competition (see vs. Notre Dame's Ronnie Stanley and Mississippi's Laremy Tunsil). Only has 4 ½ career sacks and marginal overall production in two years as a starter. Much of tackle production comes downfield chasing.

Future: A linear, high-effort, speed rusher in a similar mold as 49ers 2013 third-round pick Corey Lemonier and Buffalo Bills 2009 11th overall pick Aaron Maybin, Hunter looks like a superstar on paper and plays hard, but he has not figured out how to convert his immense physical talent into the field and will require time to be developed as a pass rusher.

Draft projection: Third- to fourth-round pick.

Scout's take: "He can't set the edge. He is not a very instinctive football player. If it doesn't flash in front of him, he can't figure it out. I thought he should have stayed in school to refine his skills. When he decided to depart, it was a 'wow.' After meeting with him in the interview process, it was a bigger 'wow.' He doesn't know what he doesn't know. Football does not come natural to him. He is an athlete — not a football player."

3T-DLE MARTIN IFEDI, #97 (Sr-5)

MEMPHIS ▶ GRADE: 4.92

Ht: 6-3 ⅛	Wt: 275	40: 4.94	Arm: 33 ⅞	Hand: 10

History: Houston native posted 85 tackles and 17 sacks as a high school senior. Redshirted in 2010. Appeared in all 12 games in '11, recording 13 tackles, one for loss and one sack with a batted pass, a forced fumble and a fumble recovery score. Was moved from tackle to end in '12 — started 10-of-12 games and tallied 46-11-7 1/2 with two batted passes. Sustained a sprained left ankle in the season

opener against UT Martin, costing him two starts. Started all 12 games in '13, producing 52-14 1/2-11 ½ with a batted pass and a forced fumble. Recognized as the university's Zach Curlin Award winner, given annually to the top male student-athlete. In '14, started all nine games played and managed 29-9 ½-2 ½ with two batted passes. Missed four games after hurting his left knee in the season opener against Austin Peay. Owns Memphis' career sacks record (22.5). Graduated in May '14 with a degree in health promotion and lifestyle management. Will be a 24-year-old rookie.

Strengths: Very good size and arm length. Flashes strength to hold the point. Versatile and has played inside and outside. Good career sack production. Plays hard and competes.

Weaknesses: Tight-hipped. Average athlete. Ordinary Combine workout. Bench-pressed merely 16 reps and needs to get stronger. Limited lower-body explosion. Late to locate the ball. Marginal foot speed, bend and balance. Cannot take the corner.

Future: Nondescript plodder with no distinguishable trait. Has enough strength, mass and length to warrant interest as a developmental five-technique in a 30 front.

Draft projection: Priority free agent.

NT GRADY JARRETT, #50 (Sr-4)

CLEMSON ▶ GRADE: 5.28

Ht: 6-0 ¾	Wt: 304	40: 5.08	Arm: 32 ⅜	Hand: 10

History: Father is former Falcons LB Jessie Tuggle. Refers to former Ravens LB Ray Lewis as an uncle (though not biological). Three-sport standout as a Georgia prep — posted 198 tackles, 63 for loss and 27 ½ sacks his last two seasons, and captured state titles in wrestling and shot put. As a true freshman in 2011, scratched together 2-0-0 in nine appearances (61 snaps). Was named the Tigers' co-defensive MVP in '12 — started 11-of-13 games at nose tackle in '12, notching 49-8 ½-2 with a batted pass. Started all 26 games at NT the next two seasons — totaled 83-11-2 in '13; and 45-10-1 ½ with two forced fumbles in '14. Played with a torn left labrum as a junior. Team captain graduated in December with a management degree. Will be a 22-year-old rookie.

Strengths: Comes off the ball low with natural leverage. Has a very strong lower body. Can squat 600-plus pounds. Tough and intrinsically motivated. Very good motor — plays hard and competes. Disruptive slanting in the backfield. Recorded the best 10-yard split (1.64 seconds) among defensive tackles at the Combine. Very good functional football-playing instincts. Locates the ball quickly and runs to it. Feels blocking pressure and reacts. Very workman-like in his approach. Outstanding weight room worker. Vocal leader.

Weaknesses: Measured the shortest (6-0 3/4) of any defensive lineman at the Combine. Too compact and falls off some tackles — unable to secure and wrap. Anchor can be moved — can be washed down and overpowered at the point of attack. Has a maxed-out frame.

Future: Tweener who lacks the ideal quickness, agility and explosion sought in a three-technique and the mass desired on the nose. A poor man's version of Brandon Mebane, Jarrett plays with the natural leverage , effort and instincts that are best suited playing on a shade in the middle of a defense. A solid football player capable of overcoming his height and length deficiency.

Draft projection: Third- to fourth-round pick.

Scout's take: "I'm just looking at all the PFA (priority free agent) grades I stamped that someone in our building gave a draftable grade to. Jarrett was one of them. He plays hard. He really does. He just doesn't fit for us (in a 30 front). … You have to look away from the measurables and view him as a football player. He's a pretty good one."

5T-3T DERRICK LOTT, #91 (Sr-6)

TENNESSEE-CHATTANOOGA ▶ GRADE: 5.26

Ht: 6-4 | Wt: 314 | 40: 4.96 | Arm: 33 ⅝ | Hand: 9 ⅛

History: Prepped in Georgia and began his college career at the University of Georgia, where he redshirted in 2009 after tearing a right ankle ligament. Saw limited action in three games in '10 (wore jersey No. 85), scratching together 7-1-0. Saw limited action in two games in '11, tallying 3-½-0. Looking for more playing time, transferred to FCS UTC, where he started all 11 games at nose tackle in '12, producing 57-4-2. In '13, managed 17-2 ½-0 in four games (two starts at NT, one at left end) before suffering a season-ending torn left ulnar collateral ligament. Was granted a sixth year of eligibility, enabling him to play all 14 games and post 41-13 ½-6 with forced fumble in '14. Graduated in August with a degree in integrated studies.

Strengths: Outstanding size. Good point-of-attack strength. Flashes pop and power in his hands to control blockers. Good movement skills and closing speed to the ball. Has an active presence behind the line of scrimmage. Bench-pressed 30 reps at the Combine.

Weaknesses: Durability has been an issue throughout his career. Average football intelligence. Is late to feel blocking pressure and freelances too much. Relies too much on bull-rush move. Has some underachiever tendencies.

Future: Developmental three-technique with enough length and mass to line up as a five-technique in an odd front. Does not play with the explosion, quickness or savvy desired in a penetrator and best asset is as a plugger against the run. Has the physical talent to be molded into a solid contributor with a patient, demanding position coach.

Draft projection: Third- to fourth-round pick.

NT JOEY MBU, #92 (Sr-4)

HOUSTON ▶ GRADE: 5.14

Ht: 6-2 ⅞ | Wt: 313 | 40: 5.53 | Arm: 35 | Hand: 9 ¼

History: Last name is pronounced "EM-boo." Texas native. As a 355-pound true freshman in 2011, was credited with four tackles, one for loss and zero sacks in 12 appearances. Started 8-of-12 games in '12, producing 27-1 ½-1 with a batted pass and an interception. Started all 26 games the next two seasons and totaled 29-3 ½-½ with three batted passes in '13; and 32-4 ½-2 ½ with four batted passes and an interception in '14. Team captain. Had three different position coaches. Medically excluded from lifting at the Combine because of a left pectoral strain.

Strengths: Arms measured the longest (35 inches) of any defensive lineman at the Combine. Has good pop in his punch to jolt blockers and control the line. Very good base strength. Active, plays hard and runs to the ball. Good balance and body control. Outstanding work ethic – reshaped his body since he arrived and dropped more than 40 pounds. Is tough, competitive and respected for his work ethic.

Weaknesses: Has very small hands. Limited athlete and playing range. Spins too much in place and gets caught at the line hand-fighting. Could stand to do a better job disengaging from blocks. Can be moved by the double team. Posted the lowest vertical jump (22 ½ inches) of any defensive lineman at the Combine. Needs to develop a greater array of pass-rush moves. Thud tackler – does not strike with explosion.

Future: A heavy-footed, long-armed plugger with athletic talent best suited for a one-gap scheme. Could provide depth in a rotation as a nose tackle or shade in a 4-3 front.

Draft projection: Late draftable pick.

DEFENSIVE LINE

NT-OG ELLIS McCARTHY, #90 (Jr-3)

UCLA ▶ GRADE: 4.97

Ht: 6-4⅝ | Wt: 338 | 40: 5.22 | Arm: 34⅛ | Hand: 9⅞

History: Highly recruited USA Today All-American from California. Missed part of 2012 fall camp after having surgery to repair a torn left meniscus. Dealt with lingering effects of the injury in the fall when he was credited with 10 tackles, one for loss and one sack with a batted pass in nine appearances (wore jersey No. 93). Played sparingly the last five games before having right knee surgery in December. Started 8-of-13 games in '13 — seven at five-technique, one at nose tackle — and produced 31-4-2 with two batted passes. Was a backup/rotational player in '14 when he totaled 21-3-3 with a forced fumble in 13 games. Will be a 21-year-old rookie.

Strengths: Has rare size to occupy space and clog running lanes. Outstanding arm length. Can generate some push and hold the double team. Can close to the ball (when he wants to).

Weaknesses: Does not have a defensive temperament. Plays too sluggishly and is late to move at the snap. Stands tall out of his stance. Marginal instincts – see-and-go reactor who takes time to digest. Weight and conditioning have been issues — was pulled out of fall camp for a week just to get in shape. Been slowed by knee issues with both knees, and long-term durability is a concern, especially given his size and weight fluctuation. Marginal production.

Future: A mountain of a man with surprisingly light feet. Has struggled to play up to his potential since he arrived and has been slowed by knee injuries, weight issues and underachiever tendencies. Size prospect only. Should have a chance to compete in a camp and will require a very demanding DL coach. Best opportunity in the pros might come as an offensive guard conversion.

Draft projection: Priority free agent.

NT RAKEEM NUNEZ-ROCHES, #97 (Jr-4)

SOUTHERN MISSISSIPPI ▶ GRADE: 5.19

Ht: 6-2¼ | Wt: 307 | 40: 5.04 | Arm: 32⅝ | Hand: 10⅛

History: Born and raised in Belize and emigrated to the United States in 2000 — lived in five different states, enduring periods of homelessness. Also played basketball and baseball as an Alabama prep. Appeared in six games as a true freshman 2011, tallying two tackles, 1 ½ for loss and zero sacks. Started 11-of-12 games in '12 and produced 37-6-1 with a batted pass, forced fumble and blocked kick. Non-start was against UTEP on Senior Night.

In '13, managed 8-1/2-1 in two starts before suffering a season-ending injury. Started all 11 games played in '14, notching 58-14-3 with a blocked kick. Did not play against Texas-San Antonio. Will be a 22-year-old rookie.

Strengths: Has a well-distributed frame and is naturally thick and big-boned. Quick off the ball. Flashes the ability to stack, locate and shed. Bends his knees and redirects efficiently. Has some explosive power in his body. Recorded the best vertical jump (34 inches) among defensive tackles at the Combine. Moves well for a 300-pounder and flows well laterally.

Weaknesses: Has short arms and needs to quicken his hands to disengage. Stays blocked too long. Raw counters. Does not dominate single blocks and gets knocked around by double teams. Limited two-gap ability. Can improve snap anticipation.

Future: An agile, well-built, tilted nose in a 40 front that would be most effective slanting and playing in gaps. Has the tools to pique the interest of aggressive, one-gapping 3-4 fronts such as the Ravens and Steelers. Developmental talent with traits to mold.

Draft projection: Late draftable pick.

5T-NT LEON ORR, #8 (Sr-5)

EX-FLORIDA ▶ GRADE: 5.18

Ht: 6-4⅞ | Wt: 323 | 40: 5.11 | Arm: 34⅛ | Hand: 9⅜

History: Had a poor, single-parent upbringing (father in prison). Was used primarily as a tight end as a Florida prep, though he suffered a fractured left ankle in 2009. Was recruited by then-head coach Urban Meyer and enrolled at UF in January '10, though he did not fully heal from his high school injury, and the wear and tear of spring practice led to a torn right meniscus, an overcompensation injury, according to Orr. Ultimately redshirted as an offensive lineman. The following year, was converted to defensive tackle by new head coach Will Muschamp — appeared in all 13 games in '11, recording 10 tackles, one for loss and one sack with a batted pass. Was arrested in January '12 for possession of less than 20 grams of marijuana and possession or use of narcotic equipment — a search of his dorm room revealed a baggy of marijuana, a pipe and rolling papers. Ultimately received deferred prosecution (fined $50 and ordered to serve 12 1/2 hours community service or pay additional $150 fine). However, Orr violated the terms of his deferred prosecution in May when he was cited — for the second time in

DEFENSIVE LINE

15 months — for knowingly driving with a suspended license. In the fall, tallied 15-5 ½-1 in the first nine games before missing the final four contests (kidney infection). Played through a (misdiagnosed) broken left wrist in '13 — started 8-of-12 games at nose tackle, notching 21-4 ½-2 ½. Hurt his left shoulder against Tennessee in Week Three. Had his wrist repaired after the season and missed '14 spring practice. Graduated in May. Wore jersey No. 44 prior to his senior season. Played four games (two starts), managing 16-2-0 with a forced fumble. After Week Three, had surgery to repair lateral meniscus and cartilage damage, which cost him three games. Returned in early November to play against Georgia, but did not start and was not slated to start the following week against Vanderbilt, prompting him to confront Muschamp and leave the team (was sent back to Gainesville from Nashville on a Greyhound bus before the game) with five games remaining. Within days, was remorseful of his decision, tweeting that it will haunt him forever. Then penned 2,200-word public letter apologizing for "how everything ended," saying, "At the end of the day, I acted irrational and went with the gut feeling in my heart instead of breaking down what was going on. I could have made a better decision, but to say that I quit on my team is a lie. Personally, I feel like the coach quit on me."

Strengths: Outstanding size and arm length. Good strength to stack the line of scrimmage and hold the point. Shows some violence in his hands to strike and press blockers. Fine balance and body control – carries his weight well. Versatile and has played multiple positions, including time on the offensive line.

Weaknesses: Tends to play tall. Pad level is inconsistent. Marginal lateral agility. Registered the slowest three-cone drill (8.28 seconds) of any defensive lineman at the Combine. Is late to diagnose plays and locate the ball. Marginal career production. Immature. Needed to be coached during the Combine about where to start his 40 and will require a lot of maintenance.

Future: A massive, pear-shaped big body with the frame ideally suited to line up as a five-technique in a 30 front. Arrived in the program as an offensive tackle and might even have better tools to be converted back to offense.

Draft projection: Priority free agent.

Scout's take: "(Orr) was dealt a bad hand. He had a lot of (adversity) to work through in his life. Maybe some things could have been handled better, but when you look at everything

he was dealing with and see that he was just trying to support his family, you appreciate the situation a little more. … He has talent."

NT DAVID PARRY, #58 (Sr-4)

STANFORD   ▶ GRADE: 5.18

Ht: 6-1 ¼ | Wt: 308 | 40: 5.32* | Arm: 31 | Hand: 9 ⅞

*Pulled hamstring while running 40.

History: Two-way lineman as an Iowa prep. Redshirted in 2010. Appeared in all 13 games in '11, recording six tackles, 1 ½ for loss and zero sacks. Played all 14 games in '12, starting the final three at nose tackle, and posted 28-3-2 with two batted passes. Played through lower abdominal pain in '13 when he started 10-of-14 games at NT and managed with 23-5-0. In '14, started 11-of-12 at NT, logging 34-7 ½-4 ½. Missed the Oregon State game after hurting his knee against Arizona State. Did not run shuttles or perform skill drills at the Combine after pulling his right hamstring in the 40.

Strengths: Very energetic and competitive — plays hard and stands out for his effort. Bench-pressed 34 reps at the Combine and has enough functional strength to burrow and win with natural leverage.

Weaknesses: Has a very compact frame. Arms are tied for the shortest (31 inches) of any defensive lineman at the Combine. Gets hung up on blocks too easily and is often a tick late to the spot. Misses tackles. Has been nicked a lot with nagging injuries and only been a part-time player.

Future: A stocky, compact plugger who anchored the middle of The Cardinal's 30 front and slid to a three-technique in sub-packages. Lacks the stature and bulk desired in the middle of a 30 front and is best suited for one-game scheme in a similar mold as Bills 2006 fifth-round pick Kyle Williams.

Draft projection: Late draftable pick.

NT JORDAN PHILLIPS, #80 (Jr-3)

OKLAHOMA   ▶ GRADE: 5.84

Ht: 6-5 ¼ | Wt: 329 | 40: 5.19 | Arm: 34 ¾ | Hand: 9 ⅜

History: Defensive tackle-tight end who also played basketball as a prep in Kansas, where he was the consensus top recruit in the state. Redshirted in 2011. Appeared in 11 games in '12, collecting 12 tackles, zero for loss and zero sacks. In '13, managed 7-2-1 ½ with a batted pass in four starts at defensive tackle before undergoing season-ending back surgery. Returned to start all 13 games in '14, posting 39-7-2 with a batted pass.

Strengths: Outstanding size and arm length.

DEFENSIVE LINE

Has grown man strength and can control blockers (when he wants to). Very good anchor strength. Unique athlete for his size — can do a standing backflip in his pads and two-hand slam a basketball. Athletic enough to zone drop. Neutralizes the double team and holds his ground.

Weaknesses: Back needs to evaluated thoroughly by medical staff — reportedly bothered him progressively before surgery and still flares up post-surgery. Tends to stand too tall out of his stance, negating his power, and does not cut it loose. Limited sack production. Tired easily playing in a rotation and stamina was an issue. Led all players at the Combine with 30.9 percent body fat and has considerable room to improve his conditioning.

Future: An exceptionally athletic big man ideally suited for a role as a slanting nose tackle in a movement 30 front such as those employed by Baltimore, Buffalo or New Orleans. Has the quickness, athletic ability and strength to become a disruptive force, if he can stay healthy and motivated and improve his playing stamina.

Draft projection: Top-50 pick.

Scout's take: "I really like his size and he plays with some strength. I don't see a lot of pass-rush skill. He didn't play with a consistent motor. That was the reason they didn't play him every down — stamina and intelligence. … If he played hard, he is a first rounder. And I would say middle of the first. That is where he should go on talent. But he shuts it down too much."

3T DARIUS PHILON, #91 (Soph-3)

ARKANSAS ▶ GRADE: 5.37

Ht: 6-1⅜ | Wt: 298 | 40: 4.92 | Arm: 32⅜ | Hand: 9½

History: Last name is pronounced "FIE-lahn." Prepped in Alabama. Originally verballed to Auburn before committing to Alabama. However, when Alabama asked him to grayshirt, Philon signed with the Razorbacks. Redshirted in 2012. Played all 12 games in '13, starting the final five at defensive tackle, and was credited with 46 tackles, nine for loss and three sacks with two forced fumbles. Started all 13 games in '14 and notched 46-11 1/2-4 ½ with two batted passes and a forced fumble. Will be a 21-year-old rookie. Did not complete shuttles at the Combine because of a left knee injury.

Strengths: Very good initial quickness and short-area burst – can be disruptive slicing gaps and playing behind the line of scrimmage. Good playing range to chase down runs to the perimeter. Active hands. Has some savvy as a pass rusher to spin, rip and come underneath blocks. Very young and best football is still ahead of him.

Weaknesses: Lacks bulk and bulk strength. Has some struggles pressing off blocks once he is engaged. Tends to get stalled and play a bit flat-footed. Is not a glass-eater and effort wanes.

Future: A very quick, agile three-technique still filling out his frame. Has intriguing potential to factor as a sub-package pass rusher on passing downs until he is ready to become an every-down player.

Draft projection: Third- to fourth-round pick.

Scout's take: "I put (Philon) in the fourth round. I thought he had some upside. He played defensive tackle, but I thought he could be a five-technique for us (in a 3-4 scheme). He has some pass-rush skill."

DLE-5T CEDRIC REED, #88 (Sr-4)

TEXAS ▶ GRADE: 5.14

Ht: 6-5¼ | Wt: 269 | 40: 4.95e | Arm: 33⅜ | Hand: 9¾

History: Defensive end-tight end who earned all-Texas honors in football and basketball and placed second in state in the shot put. As a true freshman in 2011, was credited with three tackles, zero for loss and zero sacks with a batted pass in seven appearances. Played all 13 games in '12, starting the final six at "Buck" end in place of Jackson Jeffcoat (Redskins) — posted 46-8-2 ½ with a batted pass. Playing opposite Jeffcoat in '13, produced 79-19-10 with four batted passes and five forced fumbles in 13 starts. Started all 13 games at strong end in '14, registering 73-10 1/2-5 ½ with two batted passes and a forced fumble. Graduated in December with a degree in physical culture and sports. Medically excluded from workouts at the Combine because of a left knee injury.

Strengths: Very good size with long limbs. Has enough strength at the point to constrict the edge. Uses his hands well to rip under and swim through blocks. Has experience kicking inside, where he can create mismatches over the top of guards and win with quickness.

Weaknesses: Limited athlete. Tight in the hips. Long strider. Marginal change of direction. Lacks explosion and suddenness. Only shows one speed. Does not play with a sense of urgency. Not a fiery competitor. Little variety in his pass-rush arsenal.

Future: A long-limbed, heavy-footed strider who could compete for a job as a base end, yet might offer more intrigue as a developmental

DEFENSIVE LINE

three-technique if he could pack on some weight and get stronger.

Draft projection: Late draftable pick.

5T BOBBY RICHARDSON, #95 (Sr-4)

INDIANA ► GRADE: 5.10

Ht: 6-2 ⅝ | Wt: 283 | 40: 5.19 | Arm: 34 ⅝ | Hand: 11

History: Florida native who played his senior season at Tampa Plant. As a true freshman in 2011, sustained a concussion during fall camp, but came on later in the year — started 6-of-9 games played at left end, recording 27 tackles, four for loss and three sacks with a batted pass and a forced fumble. Appeared in all 12 games in '12, collecting 28-5-2 ½ with a batted pass and a forced fumble. Despite being dinged up, played all 12 games in '13, starting the final 10 at defensive tackle, and produced 39-3 ½-0 with three batted passes. Had off-season hernia surgery. In '14, started 11-of-12 games at defensive end, tallying 35-9 1/2-5 ½ with a batted pass. Team captain. Medically excluded from the Combine with a right shoulder injury.

Strengths: Has very long arms and tied for the biggest hands of any player at the Combine. Versatile and has played inside and out in even and odd fronts. Plays on his feet with good balance and flashes a burst to close.

Weaknesses: Underpowered upper body. Lacks bulk to hold the point of attack. Average first-step quickness and burst. Does not play big. Late to locate the ball. Slow to disengage from blocks. Limited two-gap potential. Struggles to clear one-on-one blocks and defeat the double team.

Future: Developmental five-technique lacking ideal bulk, length and foot speed to match up with NFL offensive tackles. Made strides as a senior but strength and instinct deficiencies still were restricting.

Draft projection: Late draftable pick.

DLE-LOLB RYAN RUSSELL, #95 (Sr-4)

PURDUE ► GRADE: 5.32

Ht: 6-4 ¼ | Wt: 269 | 40: 4.76 | Arm: 33 ⅜ | Hand: 10 ¼

History: Prepped in Texas. Redshirted in 2010. Played all 13 games in '11, starting 11 at defensive end, and recorded 33 tackles, 4 ½ for loss and one sack with three forced fumbles. Started all 13 games at defensive end in '12, producing 37-8 ½-4 with a batted pass. In '13, was used as a defensive end/"Jack" linebacker — started 11-of-12 games and tallied 35-5 ½-2. Started all 12 games at defensive end in '14, totaling 44-6 ½-3 with a batted pass and forced fumble.

Team captain played under two head coaches and three defensive coordinators. Graduated in December.

Strengths: Looks the part. Good size. Outstanding arm length. Flashes strength and power. Squats 600-plus pounds and has a very strong base. Is quick off spots and athletic enough to bend and take the edge. Four-year starter in the Big Ten. Very durable. Comes from a program with a strong track record of producing NFL pass rushers.

Weaknesses: Has some tightness in his hips and plays too out of control, missing tackles in the open field. Could stand to play with more discipline. Eyes, anticipation and instincts are not as fine-tuned as would expect from a 48-game starter. Motor runs hot and cold. Marginal sack production. Does not respond well to hard coaching and did not respond well to coaching turnover.

Future: A big, strong power rusher with the physical talent to step into a starting job in the pros as a base end. Could also warrant interest as a developmental rush linebacker. Inconsistencies in effort and with mental toughness have affected his performance. Would be best in a simple scheme where he could be turned loose.

Draft projection: Fourth- to fifth-round pick.

Scout's take: "(Russell) has more potential than production. His best football is ahead of him."

NT DANNY SHELTON, #55 (Sr-4)

WASHINGTON ► GRADE: 5.72

Ht: 6-2 ⅛ | Wt: 339 | 40: 5.62 | Arm: 32 | Hand: 10 ¼

History: Two-way lineman also wrestled and won a Washington state 4A shot put title. As a true freshman in 2011, was credited with 11 tackles, zero for loss and zero sacks with two batted passes in 13 games (one start). Started all 40 games at nose tackle the next three seasons — totaled 45-4-½ with a blocked kick in '12 (13 games); 59-3 ½-2 with three batted passes and two blocked kicks in '13 (13 games); and 93-16 ½-9 in '14 (14 games). Broke his right hand against Stanford in late September '12. Played through a torn left rotator cuff in '13 (hand off-season surgery). As a senior, was voted the team's most inspirational player. Also became the first Husky named to the Academic All-American team since 1991, and was the only player in the country named first-team All-America and first-team Academic All-America.

Strengths: Very stout. Can block out the sun with sheer size and measured the heaviest

(339 pounds) of any defensive lineman at the Combine. Has the girth and exceptional strength to plant blockers in the backfield and re-establish the line of scrimmage. Improved intensity and stamina as a senior, when he bought in to the program. Can keep his feet through traffic and was not on the ground a lot. Flashes the ability to dominate vs. the run and can steer, control and ragdoll blockers. Can collapse the pocket. Strong tackler with knockback power. Very good sack production. Has a knack for blocking kicks.

Weaknesses: Has very short arms — gets tied up and stuck on blocks. Tied for the slowest 10-yard split (2.02 seconds) and recorded the slowest 20-yard split (3.31) of any player at the Combine, as well as posting the slowest 40-yard dash (5.73) of any defensive lineman. Lacks the quickness to rush the passer. Inconsistent motor.

Future: Mammoth wide body capable of stacking the middle of an odd front and occupying blockers. A physical run stuffer who made his senior year his best and emerged as a difference-maker.

Draft projection: First-round pick.

Scout's take: "I've heard the hype. I don't see top-15 personally. I see more late first (round). I actually gave him a second-round grade coming out of the school. There are no stud guards in the Pac-12. He beat up on a bunch of undersized guards. Look where he got his sacks. That is where his production comes from. He's really not a pass-rusher. He is a nose tackle. ...(Star) Lotulelei was way more athletic with better range and movement skill. So was (Haloti) Ngata and even Phil Taylor for that matter. ... Louis Nix was supposed to go in the first round last year — Shelton is not much better. My scouts love him though."

NT-5T DEON SIMON, #99 (Sr-6)

NORTHWESTERN STATE   ▶ GRADE: 5.27

Ht: 6-4 ⅜ | Wt: 321 | 40: 5.17 | Arm: 33 | Hand: 10 ½

History: Baton Rouge native who also competed in track and field. Missed time in 2007 because of an ankle sprain. Committed to Central Florida (also had an offer from Kentucky), but suffered a severe right leg injury (torn right ACL and MCL, hamstring avulsion) in '08. Graduated in '09, but failed to qualify academically, spent time at prep school and wasn't eligible to join the Demons until 2011. That season (wore jersey No. 76), saw limited action in six games and was credited with six tackles, zero for loss and zero sacks. Appeared in eight games in '12,

managing 14-1-1 with a batted pass. Did not play against Texas Tech, Mississippi Valley State and Southeast Louisiana. Started all 12 games in '13 and recorded 38-6-4 ½ with three batted passes. In '14, managed 24-5 ½-1 with two forced fumbles in seven starts before a grade two MCL sprain ended his season. Team captain. Became the first in his family to graduate college when he earned his criminal justice degree in December. Will be a 24-year-old rookie.

Strengths: Has rare size with a very thick build and a huge power base. Can generate power from his lower half. Exceptional weight-room strength. Tied for the most bench-press reps (35) of any defensive lineman at the Combine and has a 650-pound squat. Can ragdoll blockers and beat the double team. Moves well for his size. Showed well vs. better competition (see Baylor). Does the extras and is always looking to work.

Weaknesses: Overaged. Fatigues easily and technique fades – will stand straight up out of his stance. Only shows one gear and does not play fast or consistently finish. Does not drive through ball carriers. Is late to see and react to misdirection. Minimal career production against lesser competition. Limited pass-rush arsenal.

Future: A gargantuan, power player with the versatility to play anywhere along the line. Is still very much a developmental project and has a lot to learn, but is willing to put the work in and has unique size, strength and movement skill to mold.

Draft projection: Fourth- to fifth-round pick.

DLE-5T-3T PRESTON SMITH, #91 (Sr-4)

MISSISSIPPI STATE   ▶ GRADE: 5.52

Ht: 6-4 ⅞ | Wt: 271 | 40: 4.73 | Arm: 34 | Hand: 10 ⅝

History: Daughter, Lauren Marie, was born New Year's Eve 2013. Preston is a Stone Mountain, Ga. native — played at Stephenson High, which produced 17 FBS signees his final two seasons. As a true freshman in '11, was credited with seven tackles, zero for loss and zero sacks with a batted pass and forced fumble in eight games. Backed up at defensive end in '12, tallying 35-5 ½-4 ½ with a forced fumble in 13 appearances. Started 11-of-12 games played in '13 when he produced 44-6 ½-2 ½ with three batted passes and a forced fumble. Did not start against Auburn in September and sat out the October Bowling Green contest because of a sprained right MCL. Was named Most Outstanding Defensive Player of the Liberty Bowl. In '13, started all 13 games and totaled 48-15-9 with three batted passes, two interceptions, two forced fumbles and two blocked kicks.

Strengths: Has a long first step and good initial take-off speed. Solid strength at the point of attack. Active hands. Can jar tackles off balance with his hands. Regularly disrupts the backfield, pushes the quarterback off spots and flushes production to his teammates. Tough and will play through pain.

Has been very durable. Versatile and can play inside or outside. Rushes inside in sub-packages and can disrupt.

Weaknesses: Average athlete and lateral agility with stiffness in his body. Too often his first move is up — plays too upright and narrow-based. Does not convert speed to power or generate a lot of power from his lower body. Plays a bit out of control.

Future: A long-limbed, leverage base end with the ability to win with strength and savvy off the edge and to win quickness inside. Similar to Titans 2008 second-round pick (54th overall) Jason Jones, Smith's most natural position is left end in a 40 front with the potential to move inside as a nickel rusher in passing situations. Has received some looks as a rush linebacker.

Draft projection: Second- to third-round pick.

DLE-5T ZA'DARIUS SMITH, #94 (Sr-4)

KENTUCKY ▶ GRADE: 5.42

Ht: 6-4 ½	Wt: 274	40: 4.78	Arm: 32 ⅝	Hand: 10

History: Brother, Bob Meeks, had a cup of coffee with the Broncos in 1993, and a cousin, Davern Williams, was drafted by the Dolphins in 2003. Za'Darius prepped in Alabama, where he played basketball only until his senior year. Attended East Mississippi Community College, where he was part of a national championship in '11 — logged 19-7-4 ½ with a batted pass in 12 games. A starter in '12, he recorded 46-11-6 ½ with two batted passes, an interception and four forced fumbles in 10 games. Chose UK over offers from Florida State, Miami and Texas A&M, among others. Stepped right into the lineup and started all 24 games the next two seasons — totaled 59-6 ½-6 with a batted pass in '13; and 61-7 ½-4 ½ with two batted in '14. Missed time during '13 fall camp with a high left ankle sprain. Hurt his ankle against Georgia in '14, but did not miss a start. Team captain. Graduated in December with a degree in community and leadership development.

Strengths: Good size. Plays tough and physical with a lot of energy. Uses his hands

well to leverage the edge, displaying an assortment of moves (swipe, rip and swim). Can cross the face of blockers on inside moves and stunts and flush the pocket. Anchors well against power and is stout enough to handle the double team. Good base strength. Kicks inside and can out-quick guards on passing downs. Well-conditioned athlete with only 11.4 percent body fat. Consistently won one-on-one battles and created pressure at the East-West Shrine game and showed well at the Senior Bowl.

Weaknesses: Has short arms. Shows some tightness in his hips. Is not a great foot athlete coming off the ball. Is not explosive. Posted the slowest 60-yardest shuttle (12.70 seconds) of any defensive lineman at the Combine and registered the second slowest short shuttle (4.66 seconds) among defensive ends. Average sack production. Could require some extra reps.

Future: An energetic power rusher with the strength and base to defend the run and potentially be groomed as a five-technique in a 3-4 front. Could also factor inside and warrant consideration as a base end in a 40-front, with eventual starter potential. Late bloomer whose best football is still ahead of him.

Draft projection: Third- to fourth-round pick.

Scout's take: "(Smith) does not have a lot of twitch or the great foot speed for the outside. I am not sure what to do with him. He is probably a five-technique for us. That's where he would have to play. … I met him while I was at the school. He seemed like a very respectful, down-to-earth, likable personality."

DT J.T. SURRATT, #97 (Sr-5)

SOUTH CAROLINA ▶ GRADE: 5.12

Ht: 6-1	Wt: 304	40: 5.14	Arm: 32	Hand: 10 ⅛

History: Also played basketball as a South Carolina prep. Redshirted in 2010 after dislocating his right shoulder in August. Saw limited action in three games in '11, scratching together two tackles, zero for loss and zero sacks. After serving a three-game suspension (academics) to begin the '12 season, played the final 10 games (including one start against Florida when the Gamecocks opened in goal-line personnel) and recorded 14-2 ½-½. In '13, started all 13 games at defensive tackle and produced 33-4-1 ½. Notched 30-4 ½-1 with a batted pass and blocked kick in 12 starts in '14, though he missed the Independence Bowl with stomach illness. Team captain. Graduated in December with a degree in hotel, restaurant and tourism management.

Strengths: Competes hard and makes plays

DEFENSIVE LINE

flattening down the line. Slippery to squeeze through gaps and runs to the ball. Solid anchor vs. the run. Bulls blockers into the backfield.

Weaknesses: Short and short-armed and gets engulfed. Gets stuck on the line easily and does not play with much violence in his hands to disengage. Could stand to play with more consistent leverage. Average football IQ. Not a secure, wrap tackler. Marginal sack production — is not a pass rusher. Will require some extra maintenance.

Future: A squatty, strong, fairly athletic plugger most ideally suited for a rotational role as a movement nose in a 40 front.

Draft projection: Late draftable pick.

DLE-LOLB-TE **LYNDEN TRAIL**, #7 (Sr-5)

NORFOLK STATE ▶ GRADE: 4.85

Ht: 6-6 ⅝ | Wt: 269 | 40: 4.94 | Arm: 34 ⅞ | Hand: 10 ½

History: Prepped at Booker T. Washington in Miami, where he also ran track and was considered a D1-caliber basketball player. As a senior, lost one of his best friends and teammates when the young man was shot and killed at a party Lynden's mother forbade him from attending. Began his college career at Florida (recruited by then-head coach Urban Meyer), where he redshirted in 2010 and didn't see the field in '11. Felt overlooked and underappreciated at Florida, opting to transfer to FCS NSU rather than play for Will Muschamp. In '12, tallied 70 tackles, 17 for loss and six sacks with four batted passes and a forced fumble in 11 games (three starts at outside linebacker in the Spartans' 3-4 defense). Also worked at defensive end and as a "gunner" on the punt coverage team. In '13, was the College Football Performance Awards National FCS Defensive Player of the Year, NSU Male Athlete of the Year and the Spartans' Defensive MVP — started all 12 games at OLB and registered 94-12 ½-8 ½ with 10 batted passes, five forced fumbles and two blocked kicks. Started all 12 games in '14 (started at DE against North Carolina Central), totaling 91-11 ½-5 with four batted passes, two forced fumbles and two blocked kicks. Two-time Buck Buchanan Award finalist. Team captain earned his mass communication degree in December. Will be a 24-year-old rookie.

Strengths: Has rare length with a frame to continue growing into. Disrupts a quarterback's vision with his long vines. Eats up ground with his long strides and closes to the ball. Versatile and has played a number of positions, including OLB, DE, TE and gunner on special teams.

Weaknesses: Overaged with an underdeveloped body. Lacks power in his body. Limited pop or strength in his hands to discard blockers. Rigid in his movement. Soft anchor. Easily controlled by double teams. Has a passive playing temperament. Limited agility to handle slot receivers (where he aligns at times to cover).

Future: Raw, long-limbed, thin-framed developmental project who was tried at tight end during the Senior Bowl and might be better served on the offensive side of the ball given his style of play. Could also compete for a role as a backup base end.

Draft projection: Priority free agent.

3T **LOUIS TRINCA-PASAT**, #90 (Sr-4)

IOWA ▶ GRADE: 5.06

Ht: 6-1 | Wt: 290 | 40: 4.99 | Arm: 31 ⅞ | Hand: 10 ⅛

History: Born to Romanian parents, and is the only one of his four siblings born in America. Last name is pronounced "TRIN-kuh puh-sot." Also lettered in basketball and track and field as a Chicago prep. Redshirted in 2010 and appeared in just one game in '11. Nearly quit football after the season. Rejuvenated in '12, Trinca-Pasat played through a torn left rotator cuff, producing 40-4-0 with a batted pass. Had rotator cuff surgically repaired after the season and missed '13 spring practice. In the fall, started all 13 games and collected 38-8-1 with two batted passes. Started all 13 games in '14 when he led Big Ten defensive linemen in tackles with 69-11 ½-6 ½ with three batted passes. Hurt his left ankle against Iowa State. Team captain graduated with a sports studies degree, and is pursuing a master's in educational leadership. Will be a 24-year-old rookie. Opted not to lift at the Combine.

Strengths: Smart, competitive and tough. Battles and scraps to produce and generates a lot of effort production. Good lateral agility, as confirmed in his 4.30-second short shuttle time that paced all defensive tackles at the Combine. Effective slanting – runs tight stunts to come free.

Weaknesses: Very undersized with short arms. Marginal strength to hold the point. Is easily pinballed and struggles to win one-on-one matchups vs. size (see Senior Bowl). Limited power. Marginal contact balance. Gets waylaid and washed down the line by the double team. Struggles to play square.

Future: Intense, try-hard overachiever

DEFENSIVE LINE

lacking ideal size and length for the NFL game, yet possesses the motor and makeup to win the heart of coaches and fight for a roster spot.

Draft projection: Priority free agent.

DRE-ROLB **ZACK WAGENMANN**, #37 (Sr-5)

MONTANA ▶ GRADE: 5.22

Ht: 6-3 ⅛ | Wt: 247 | 40: 4.82 | Arm: 33 ½ | Hand: 9 ½

History: Captained the football and basketball teams as a Montana prep. Redshirted in 2010, earning Scout Team Player of the Year recognition. Appeared in 13 games in '11 and was credited with 13 tackles, one for loss and zero sacks. Became a fixture at defensive end in '12 when he started all 11 games played and produced 50-13-11 ½ with four batted passes and two forced fumbles. Played through a labrum tear in his right shoulder late in the season. In '13, started all 13 games and totaled 64-16 ½-8 ½ with two batted passes and three forced fumbles. Started all 14 games in '14, racking up 74-22 ½-17 ½ with four batted passes, six forced fumbles and a safety. Two-year captain wore jersey No. 58 prior to '13 when he was given the Grizzly legacy No. 37. Owns Montana's career records for sacks (37 ½), tackles for loss (53) and forced fumbles (11). Graduated with a communications degree. Donated his signature long hair to Locks of Love in December, his first hair cut in over four years.

Strengths: Very good motor and intensity. Plays disciplined and with energy. Tied for the fastest 3-cone drill time (7.07 seconds) of any defensive end at the Combine. Has a 37 1/2-inch vertical jump. Extremely productive. Outstanding football character. Extremely smart. Film junkie. Lives in the football facility. Has special teams experience.

Weaknesses: Lacks bulk and will struggle to stack the point vs. NFL offensive linemen. Average hip flexibility and closing speed. Pads tend to rise running the arc. Not a natural bender. Produced the fewest bench-press reps (14) of any defensive lineman at the Combine and needs to get stronger. Production is inflated from facing lesser competition.

Future: A light-framed, small-school standout pass rusher lacking the requisite bulk and burst desired in the pros. Will warrant interest as a developmental rush linebacking prospect or Sam linebacker, though must improve his strength levels to leverage the edge.

Draft projection: Late draftable pick.

5T-NT **LETERRIUS "L.T." WALTON**, #58 (Sr-5)

CENTRAL MICHIGAN ▶ GRADE: 5.20

Ht: 6-4 ⅞ | Wt: 319 | 40: 5.24 | Arm: 32 ¼ | Hand: 10 ¼

History: Earned letters in football (two), baseball (four) and basketball (two) as a Michigan prep. Redshirted in 2010. Appeared in four games in '11 — scratched together seven tackles, two for loss and one-half for loss, but missed the final eight games of the season after tearing his left meniscus. In '12, started 7-of-10 games played at defensive tackle and collected 32-3 ½-2 ½ with a batted pass. Missed three games because of a herniated disk. Started all 25 games at nose tackle the next two seasons — totaled 34-9 ½-1 with a forced fumble in '13 (12 games); and posted 33-3 ½-2 with two batted passes and a forced fumble in '14 (13 games).

Strengths: Exceptional size. Good functional strength to create some push. Flashes some power in his hands. Very solid showing at the East-West Shrine game.

Weaknesses: Has short arms. Very inconsistent pad level — tends to play tall and lock his legs. Could stand to do a better job pressing off blocks and controlling linemen. Limited pass-rush ability — does not have a rush plan. Marginal initial quickness and closing burst to finish.

Future: Played on a shade in a 40 front in college and projects as a developmental five technique in the pros. A raw size prospect whose best football is at least three years away. Could provide depth on a roster.

Draft projection: Fifth- to sixth-round pick.

3T-5T **LEONARD WILLIAMS**, #94 (Jr-3)

USC ▶ GRADE: 7.20

Ht: 6-4 ⅝ | Wt: 302 | 40: 4.94 | Arm: 34 ⅝ | Hand: 10 ⅝

History: Has a two-year-old daughter named Leana, who lives with her mother in Florida. Father, Clenon, is incarcerated until November 2019 for multiple crimes, including armed robbery. Leonard, who spent nights in homeless shelters growing up, was born in California and lived in Bakersfield, Sacramento, Michigan and Arizona before putting down roots in Daytona Beach, Fla., where he attended Mainland High. Was persuaded to spurn Southeastern powers for USC thanks to an eleventh-hour sales pitch from then-Trojans assistant Ed Orgeron. Was the Pac-12 Defensive Freshman of the Year in 2012 — started 9-of-13 games at the three-technique in Monte Kiffin's defense, producing 64-13 ½-8 with four batted passes and an interception. In '13, was deployed as a defensive end in Clancy Pendergrast's 5-2

DEFENSIVE LINE

124

scheme — totaled 74-13 ½-6 with two forced fumbles in 13 starts despite playing through a torn right labrum. Aggravated the shoulder injury against Oregon State and sat out against California. Had post-season surgery and missed '14 spring practice. In the fall, played DE in Justin Wilcox's 3-4 multiple front — was a Hendricks Award finalist and the Trojans' MVP after racking up 80-9 ½-7 with three batted passes, an interception and three forced fumbles in 13 starts. Was named the Holiday Bowl Defensive MVP. Sustained a high ankle sprain prior to the Trojans' Week-Two contest against Stanford. Became USC's first two-time first-team All-American defensive end in 55 years. Team captain will be a 21-year-old rookie. Did not lift at the Combine because of a right shoulder injury. Has never had a driver's license.

Strengths: Can play the piano and line up anywhere along a defensive front and be disruptive, mismatching offensive guards with quickness and tackles with power and athletic ability. Was scheme diverse and was productive despite three different schemes caused by coaching changes. Moves extremely well for a big man and plays with outstanding balance and body control to slip through gaps. Strong and powerful to rip, tug and cross the face of blockers. Terrific instincts to feel blocking pressure. Alert to sniff out screens. Outstanding grip strength to lock out, press and control blockers. Consistently barrels into the backfield and corrals backs with his long arms. Gets underneath the pads of blockers and can generate speed to power. Plays with abandon and keeps working to the quarterback, fighting through congestion and displaying a multitude of pass-rush moves. Chases down backs to the perimeter. Opportunistic clutch player with outstanding all-around production. Is physically and mentally tough and will play through injuries.

Weaknesses: Will play tall at times and could stand to play with more consistent knee bend and hip roll. Is a bit underdeveloped in the upper body and has a history of shoulder injuries. Could stand to continue refining his pass-rush repertoire and understanding the art of the rush. Motor does not always run hot.

Future: A big, strong, disruptive interior force with the ability to dominate wherever he lines up. Is coveted as an interior disruptor and power end and could give a creative coordinator a very versatile mismatch piece to feast on opposting offensive lines. Is capable of fitting in a one-gap or two-gap scheme and his best football is still ahead of him. Has immediate impact potential, instantly upgrades a defensive line and should be a Pro Bowl regular in short time. Is the highest graded player in this year's draft and worthy of the top overall pick.

Draft projection: Top-10 cinch.

Scout's take: "Leonard Williams is hands down the best player in the draft. He is Reggie White. He can play anything and dominate. Watch the bowl game. When he could have shut it down, he dominated Nebraska. He will be a perennial Pro Bowler – no and's, if's or but's. If I am Lovie Smith, I'm not taking a chance on a quarterback. I'm taking the sure thing."

3T-5T GABE WRIGHT, #90 (Sr-4)

AUBURN ▶ GRADE: 5.09

Ht: 6-2¾ | Wt: 300 | 40: 5.07 | Arm: 32⅝ | Hand: 10¾

History: Engaged to be married. Prepped in Georgia. As a true freshman in 2011, played all 13 games (three starts) and recorded 12 tackles, three for loss and one sack with a forced fumble. Suffered a broken left foot during '12 spring practice. Played all 12 games in the fall, starting the final six, and had 19-4 ½-1 with two batted passes. In '13, logged 31-8 ½-3 in 14 games (11 starts). Started 7-of-13 in '14, including the first two at defensive end (played DE in Auburn's "rhino" package), and totaled 24-4 ½-1. Sprained his left foot during Senior Bowl practice. Team captain.

Strengths: Flashes some quickness and burst to shoot gaps and create some penetration. Good upper-body strength. Led all defensive tackles with 34 bench-press reps at the Combine. Plays with emotion.

Weaknesses: Has short arms. Lacks explosive body power and lower-body strength. Marginal tackler. Freelances too much. Limited sack production. Recorded a 26 ½-inch vertical jump, indicative of limited athletic ability. Questionable focus and football character. Had to be re-taught a drill at the Combine after sitting at the back of the line.

Future: Top-heavy, knock-kneed rotational one-gap penetrator who lacks the consistency, lower-body power and focus desired in a front-line defender. Could compete for a role in a rotation.

Draft projection: Fourth- to fifth-round pick.

Scout's take: "(Wright) is intriguing and inconsistent at the same time. Someone is going to buy in and get enamored like happened with (Packers 2012 second-round pick) Jerel Worthy. What is he on now – his third team in three years? I expect the same trajectory with this kid. That's who he reminds me of, from a personality and football player standpoint."

DEFENSIVE LINE

LINEBACKERS

JAY METZ / FLORIDA

Nawrocki's TOP 10

1. **DANTE FOWLER**
2. Eli Harold
3. Shane Ray
4. Bud Dupree
5. Eric Kendricks
6. Shaq Thompson
7. Benardrick McKinney
8. Hau'oli Kikaha
9. Owa Odighizuwa
10. Stephone Anthony

WLB-SS KWON ALEXANDER, #4 (Jr-3)

LSU ▶ GRADE: 5.28

Ht: 6-0 ¾ | Wt: 227 | 40: 4.57 | Arm: 30 ¼ | Hand: 9 ¼

History: Prepped in Alabama, where he racked up 144 tackles, 17 sacks and six forced fumbles as a junior. Tore his right ACL four games into his senior season. Played seven games as a true freshman in 2012 — earned two starts at "Sam" linebacker and tallied 11 tackles, one for loss and zero sacks with one pass breakup and one forced fumble. Started 9-of-13 games at "Sam" in '13, posting 65-6 ½-0 with four pass breakups. In '14, shared the Tigers' Outstanding Defensive Player award after leading the team in tackles — started all 12 games playing on the weak side and notching 90-7 ½-1 ½ with one pass breakup and two forced fumbles. Sat out against Louisiana-Monroe (stinger). Team captain will be a 21-year-old rookie.

Strengths: Outstanding range, recovery speed and short-area burst, as confirmed in his LB-best 1.53-second 10-yard split at the Combine. Flashes play-making ability (see Mississippi State). Can beat blockers to the block point and efficiently slip and avoid. Gets good fits in the run game. Dynamic shooting gaps and blitzing.

Weaknesses: Short and short-armed and struggles sorting out traffic and disengaging from blockers inside the tackle box. Average eyes and anticipation — takes false steps and is a tick late to trigger. Plays too narrow-based and tall (and it showed up in Combine drills). Lacks functional core strength and knock-back striking power — easily sealed and walled off and runs himself out of plays. Much of his production comes in lateral pursuit and downfield.

Future: A fast-flowing, run-and-chase "Will" linebacker lacking ideal every-down size to hold up physically in the pro game, yet could find a niche as nickel or dime linebacker and profile as a core special teamer. Could even warrant some interest as a box safety. Needs to be schemed free where he can run to the ball to produce.

Draft projection: Fourth- to fifth-round pick.

Scout's take: "Alexander is a stiff, straight-line speed guy. He will be a good (special) teamer."

MLB STEPHONE ANTHONY, #42 (Sr-4)

CLEMSON ▶ GRADE: 5.62

Ht: 6-2 ⅝ | Wt: 243 | 40: 4.56 | Arm: 32 ½ | Hand: 10 ⅜

History: Has a daughter with long-time girlfriend. Also played basketball and baseball as a prep in North Carolina, where he was a USA Today and Parade All-American, Gatorade Player of the Year and a consensus five-star recruit. As a true freshman in 2011, recorded 32 tackles, six for loss and two sacks with a pass breakup and two forced fumbles in 13 games (started three of the final four at middle linebacker). Did not play against Boston College (left foot sprain). Played through a broken left wrist in '12 — started 6-of-13 games at MLB in '12, producing 77-4 ½-1 with three pass breakups, an interception and a forced fumble. Had off-season surgery to repair his wrist. Switched from jersey No. 12 in '13 when he started all 13 games at MLB and totaled 131-13 ½-4 to lead the team in tackles with five pass breakups and an interception. In '14, started 12-of-13 games at MLB and notched 75-10 ½-2 ½ with four pass breakups and two forced fumbles. Was suspended for the first half of the Russell Athletic Bowl against Oklahoma because he incurred a targeting penalty against South Carolina. Team captain graduated in December with a sociology degree.

Strengths: Outstanding size with a muscled, well-proportioned frame, broad shoulders and trim physique — looks how a linebacker was meant to be drawn up. Good take-on strength to step downhill and knock back fullbacks. Plays with physicality. Quick to fill vs the run and see and pick up backside crossers in coverage. Strikes with thump. Underrated in coverage. Very good effort and on-field energy. Produced the second-best 20-yard shuttle time (4.03 seconds) of any linebacker at the Combine.

Weaknesses: Has some tightness in his body and is a bit straight-linish and has some difficulty opening up his hips and changing direction in coverage. Will overrun the ball at times and miss some tackles in space. Does not beat blockers easily. Could do a better job using his hands to disengage from blockers and slicing through the line of scrimmage as a blitzer.

Future: A stiff, strong, tough, energetic "Mike" linebacker capable of playing in either a 3-4 or 4-3 front. Can close fast to the ball in a straight-line, but rigidity could always create issues tackling in the open field. Will be most effective in a defense where he is schemed to be protected and could run free to the ball.

Draft projection: Second- to third-round pick.
Scout's take: "Anthony struggles in space. He might be a two-down 'backer when all is said and done. He will hit you. ... I graded him in the late third (round)."

SLB NEIRON BALL, #11 (Sr-5)

FLORIDA ▶ GRADE: 4.95

Ht: 6-2 ½ | Wt: 236 | 40: 4.70e | Arm: 33 ⅝ | Hand: 9 ⅝

History: Played defensive end as a Georgia prep. Was used primarily on special teams as a true freshman in 2010, recording 10 tackles, one for loss and zero sacks. Had off-season surgery to repair a sports hernia. Did not play in '11 after it was discovered he incurred a busted brain vessel resulting from an arteriovenous malformation, a hereditary condition which abnormally tangles arteries and veins. Returned to play 11 games in '12 (two starts at strong-side linebacker), tallying 10-½-0 with a pass breakup and an interception. Did not play against Jacksonville State and Florida State (right ankle sprain). Started 7-of-12 games — four on the weak side, three on the strong side — and collected 25-1 ½-1 with a pass breakup. Missed '14 spring practice with a sprained left MCL. In the fall, started 7-of-9 games at "Sam" and had 49-3-2 with two pass breakups and a forced fumble. Missed the final three games and was medically excluded from the Combine (micro fracture/meniscus). Graduated in May '14 with a sport management degree.

Strengths: Fluid athlete with clean movement skills. Flies to the ball and has very good range to the sideline to contain the outside run. Good closing speed to the perimeter. Natural knee bender with loose hips. Good upfield burst off the edge. Dependable open-field tackler. Good effort and pursuit. Versatile and has played multiple positions in both fronts. Hard-working and the game is important to him.

Weaknesses: Has a narrow bone structure and plays small. Limited point-of-attack strength and knock-back body power. Not strong in the core. Exits the game in nickel situations. Overmatched by tight ends in the run game. Overruns the ball and plays a bit recklessly in pursuit. Has been dinged a lot with a history of knee, ankle, groin and head injuries and is coming off very serious knee surgery. Limited special teams experience.

Future: Lined up mostly at "Sam" linebacker in college, yet is more suited for a role on the weak side in the pros and will have to prove he can make a mark on special teams to stick.

LINEBACKERS

Best suited for a fast-flowing, 4-3 front, though must clear medically to warrant an opportunity. Has overcome a lot of adversity in his life to beat the odds and is the type you root for.

Draft projection: Priority free agent.

Scout's take: "A linear player with length who lacks power and strength. He looks like more of a slip-and-avoid type with lateral chase. He has adequate cover skills in man and zone, but very limited to no ball production. I don't know if he has the frame to hold up at our level."

SLB YANNIK CUDJOE-VIRGIL, #51 (Sr-5)

MARYLAND   ▶ GRADE: 4.87

Ht: 6-2 ⅛ | Wt: 248 | 40: 4.75e | Arm: 32 ⅝ | Hand: 9 ¾

History: Born in Trinidad. Two-year football captain also ran track as a Maryland prep. Began his college career at Division II Seton Hill (wore jersey No. 15). As a true freshman in 2010, sat out the season opener against Bowie State before collecting 14 tackles, zero for loss and zero sacks in 10 games. In '11, played defensive end in a 3-3-5 — produced 44-8-5 with a batted pass, a forced fumble and a single-season school record six blocked kicks. Also served as a team captain. Transferred to Maryland and walked on, sitting out the '12 season. In '13, managed 18-3 ½-3 in six games (one start at outside linebacker) before suffering a season-ending torn pectoral muscle injury. Missed the first three games of the '14 season (left foot) before recording 21-2 ½-2 with four pass breakups in 10 games (three starts at OLB). Was a member of the Terps' leadership council. Did not work out at the Combine because of a right knee (patella) injury.

Strengths: Very good body mass and physical stature for a strong-side backer. Enough strength to hold the point and constrict running lanes. Good weight-room worker. Tied for most bench-press reps (25) among outside linebackers at the Combine. Good football intelligence. Plays with emotion and has a passion for the game. Good effort and energy. Kicked inside and showed on third downs and showed some rush savvy (see Iowa).

Weaknesses: Small-handed with average arm length to lock out and press. Has some heaviness in his movement and is not quick to change direction and redirect. Can be late to locate and react to the ball.

Future: A big, strong "Sam" 'backer relegated to a situational role following injury and the emergence of sophomore Yannik Ngakoue. Could provide depth in a training camp, but lacks the movement skill desired on special teams to stick.

Draft projection: Priority free agent.

ILB AARON DAVIS, #37 (Sr-4)

COLORADO STATE   ▶ GRADE: 4.75

Ht: 5-11 ⅝ | Wt: 225 | 40: 4.99 | Arm: 31 | Hand: 9

History: Cousins with the Tuiasosopo family, including Marques and Matt, who played in the NFL and Major League Baseball, respectively. Aaron prepped in Orange County, Calif. Originally committed to Washington, but his scholarship offer was pulled weeks before Signing Day. As a true freshman in 2011, was credited with 23 tackles, zero for loss and zero sacks in 11 appearances. Took ownership of the Rams' weak-side linebacker position and started all 37 games the next three seasons — totaled 84-5-0 with two pass breakups in '12 (12 games); 120-7-0 with three pass breakups and three forced fumbles in '13 (14 games); and 118-6 ½-0 with five pass breakups, an interception and a forced fumble in '14 (13 games). Was the team's leading tackler as a sophomore and senior. Team captain.

Strengths: Very good eyes, instincts and anticipation — quick to diagnose and run to the ball. Active and energetic. Plays with intensity. Always around the ball. Rolls his hips and explodes through contact. Outstanding production. Exceptional football character. Has a special teams personality — tough, competitive and will sacrifice his body around piles. Football smart and coachable. Alert in coverage.

Weaknesses: Undersized with short arms and small hands. Bench-pressed only 16 reps at the Combine and lacks core strength to stack and shed. Is overpowered and engulfed at the point. Lunges and leaves his feet too early and will miss some open-field tackles. Too much wasted motion transitioning in space (and confirmed in movement at Combine).

Future: Will be rejected by measurables on paper, yet has the scrappy football temperament to make a living on special teams.

Draft projection: Priority free agent.

ILB-WLB PAUL DAWSON, #47 (Sr-4)

TCU   ▶ GRADE: 5.46

Ht: 6-0 ⅛ | Wt: 235 | 40: 4.91 | Arm: 31 ½ | Hand: 9 ½

History: High school receiver also played basketball and ran track at Dallas Skyline. Was a qualifier out of high school but was not heavily recruited, so began his college career at Trinity Valley Community College (TX) in 2011 — posted 52 tackles, eight for loss and four sacks with a pass breakup, an interception and two forced fumbles in 11 games. With the Horned Frogs in '12, had 14-1-0 with one forced fumble in 13 appearances. Tested positive for Adderall as a sophomore, but later got a prescription for it. Played 12 games in '13, starting the final seven at middle linebacker, and produced 91-10-½ with three pass breakups and an interception. In '14, was the Big 12 Defensive Player of the Year after leading TCU in tackles for the second straight year — started 11-of-13 games at strong-side linebacker, amassing 136-20-6 with five pass breakups, four interceptions and two forced fumbles. Was benched in the first half against SMU after reportedly breaking a team rule at the hotel. Also did not start against West Virginia (coach's decision). Did not run the 3-cone drill at the Combine and did not provide a reason why.

Strengths: Extremely instinctive — good eyes, anticipation and foot fire before the snap. Very good lateral agility to flow fast and fill alleys. Attacks the ball square. Very sudden off spots. Field fast and plays much faster than his timed speed because of instant reaction. Has a great feel for the game and knifes through running lanes before blockers can react. Exceptional production. Very good awareness in zone coverage. Tough and durable.

Weaknesses: Registered the lowest vertical jump (28 inches) and slowest recorded 40 time (5.03 seconds) of any inside linebacker at the Combine. Marginal 20-yard shuttle time (4.51 seconds). Has a 28-inch vertical jump, the lowest of any linebacker at the Combine, and lacks lower-body explosion. Does not always bring his feet with him and drive through contact — lunges too much. Has short arms and can be engulfed in tight quarters once blockers get their hands on him. Has had issues with punctuality and accountability.

Future: More sleek and silky than Bengals LB Vontaze Burfict but has similar traits and accountability issues. Could still prove to be a very productive pro and possibly the best bubble linebacker in this draft because of his instincts and short-area quickness. Could excel as an inside linebacker in a 30 front or as a weak-side linebacker in a 40 front and is scheme-diverse.

Draft projection: Third- to fourth-round pick.

Scout's take: "(Dawson) is going to need structure and a lot of maintenance. He has not figured out what it means to work and is not accountable. Teammates will not respect him if the light bulb does not come on."

ILB TREY DePRIEST, #33 (Sr-4)

ALABAMA   ▶ GRADE: 5.10

Ht: 6-0 ⅜ | Wt: 254 | 40: 4.93 | Arm: 31⅝ | Hand: 9

History: Has a daughter. Highly recruited out of Ohio, where he was the Division I Defensive Player of the Year. Was a reserve/special-teams player in 2011, collecting 25 tackles, 1 ½ tackles for loss and zero sacks in 13 games. In '12, started 13-of-14 games at the "Mike" linebacker and produced 59-4-0 with two pass breakups. Did not start against Western Carolina because the Tide opened the game with six defensive backs. Had surgery in spring '13 to repair a stress fracture in his right foot then served a one-week suspension during fall camp (violation team rules). Started all 13 games at the "Mike" in the fall, totaling 65-7 ½-2 with a pass breakup, an interception and two forced fumbles. Was suspended for the '14 season opener against West Virginia (NCAA rules violation) before starting all 13 games at the "Mike" and registering 88- 4 ½-0 with three pass breakups, a forced fumble and a safety. Played all season on a torn left meniscus, which he had repaired after the season (medically excluded at the Combine). Graduated in December with a degree in fashion retail.

Strengths: Solid tackler. Will step downhill and fill and has functional playing range between-the-tackles. Can beat blocks to the spot in a short area. Face-up tackler with some strike in his body to knock ball carriers back.

Weaknesses: Has short arms. Marginal athlete. Short stepper with heaviness in his feet. Has limitations in coverage, as he has very minimal production on the ball and is tight in his hips to open up and drop. Can be exposed by backs in man coverage, unable to carry wheel routes down the field. Marginal take-on ability. Not explosive thru contact. Takes some bad angles and plays undisciplined. Weight has fluctuated and body fat measured the second-most (19.1 percent) of any linebacker at the Combine. Needs to improve conditioning.

Future: A strong-side inside linebacker with limited foot quickness, agility and cover instincts to be trusted on passing downs, DePriest brings the most value as a short-area, two-down run plugger in the pros.

Draft projection: Late draftable pick.

Scout's take: "(DePriest) looks overweight. He's stiff, tight and sloppy in his movement. He's not a great athlete, but he's good when action is right on the line for him. I thought he looked better (in 2013). He has off-field issues. He's immature. I don't think he'll get drafted before the seventh (round) if he does."

LINEBACKERS

SLB-DLE XZAVIER DICKSON, #47 (Sr-4)

ALABAMA　　　　　　　　▶ GRADE: 5.07

Ht: 6-3 ½ | Wt: 260 | 40: 4.76 | Arm: 33 ½ | Hand: 10

History: Prepped in Georgia. As a true freshman in 2011, was credited with three tackles, 1 ½ for loss and one-half sack in seven appearances. Played all 14 games in '12, starting six at the "Jack" linebacker, and tallied 33-5-3 ½ with one pass breakup and one forced fumble. Had patella tendon surgery during '13 fall camp. On the season, started 6-of-12 games played at the "Jack," managing 13-2-1. Was suspended for the Sugar Bowl against Oklahoma. In '14, totaled 41-12 ½-9 with two pass breakups in 14 games (nine starts at the "Jack").

Strengths: Outstanding size, arm length and foot speed. Has a solid base with good lower-body strength. Flashes some power to disrupt on stunts. Solid senior sack production.

Weaknesses: Lacks discipline in his play. Does not have a pass-rush arsenal and gets hung up on blocks easily and stalled at the line. Inconsistent effort. Plays small. Cannot convert speed to power and most of his sack production was schemed, not created. Recorded a 29 ½-inch vertical jump and 8-foot-4-inch broad jump, the least explosive of any linebacker at the Combine. Bench-pressed only 19 reps at the Combine. Marginal football character. Turned off executives during interviews at the Combine.

Future: Career underachiever with limited strength, explosion and desire to contribute in the pros. Has enough length and speed to compete for a job as a "Sam" linebacker and may be more ideally suited for a role as a base end in a simple scheme. Limited special-teams, value and immaturity could hinder opportunity.

Draft projection: Priority free agent.

Scout's take: "I thought he could be a "Sam" linebacker. I put him in the fifth round, but I'm taking my grade back after hearing him talk at the Combine. Everything was monotone and it was like he didn't care to be there."

ROLB-DRE ALVIN "BUD" DUPREE, #2 (Sr-4)

KENTUCKY　　　　　　　　▶ GRADE: 6.12

Ht: 6-4 | Wt: 269 | 40: 4.63 | Arm: 32 ⅝ | Hand: 9 ¾

History: High school tight end/linebacker (had 1,000 yards receiving as a senior) who also won a state basketball championship as a Georgia prep. Was recruited by then-head coach Joker Phillips. Played all 12 games as a true freshman in 2011, starting the final three at strong-side linebacker, and notched 21 tackles, 2 ½ for loss and 2 ½ sacks with two pass breakups. Started all 12 games on the weak side in '12, registering 91-12½- 6 ½ with a pass breakup. Moved to defensive end in '13 when he produced 61-9 ½-7 with a batted pass and two forced fumbles in 11 starts. Did not play against Alabama (pectoral strain). Started all 12 games at DE in '14, totaling 74-12 ½-7 ½ with a batted pass, an interception and two forced fumbles. Team captain. Medically excluded from lifts at the Combine because of a left pectoral strain and did not perform shuttles or skill drills because of a groin injury.

Strengths: Excellent size and athletic ability. Natural knee bender with outstanding recovery speed and closing burst. Can pin his ears back and go. Shocks and torques weak tackles off the ground. Recorded a 42-inch vertical jump to pace all linebackers at the Combine and has rare explosion in his legs. Highly competitive and disruptive. Enough strength to hold the point vs. the double team and set the edge. Flattens and chases down the line and plays with good pursuit effort. Lassoes ball carriers in the open field and is a reliable open-field tackler. Long, fast and athletic enough to carry receivers in man coverage. Strong football character and personal character.

Weaknesses: Average arm length. Has to digest what he sees and takes time to sort it out. Not a savvy or refined pass rusher and needs to develop a greater assortment of moves. Does not consistently convert speed to power or roll his hips. Lacks awareness in coverage.

Future: An explosive edge rusher at his best with his hand in the dirt when turned loose to pin his ears back and attack the quarterback. Has the physical traits to become a mismatch piece and offers unique versatility for a creative coordinator. Would fit most ideally as a 3-4 weak-side or outside linebacker, and could also command interest as a speed-rushing, 4-3 right defensive end. Instinct issue still gives reason for pause.

Draft projection: First-round pick.

Scout's take: "I'm not sure he is all there instinctually. He's kind of a basketball player playing football. He is good-looking, yoked up and put together. Dallas would love him. He's kind of like (Cowboys 2007 first-round pick) Anthony Spencer. ... They asked (Dupree) to do too much and he was not playing as well this year, but he's too big and too fast and too strong and productive to last very long in the draft. Although he graded as a fourth-rounder in one of the games I did. ... I don't see how he gets out of the first (round)."

LINEBACKERS

LOLB-DLE KYLE EMANUEL, #53 (Sr-5)

NORTH DAKOTA STATE　▶ GRADE: 5.22

Ht: 6-3 ¼ | Wt: 255 | 40: 4.76 | Arm: 31 | Hand: 9 ⅜

History: Linebacker/running back that also competed in basketball, soccer and track and field as a Nebraska prep. Redshirted in 2010. Played all 15 games in '11, starting seven (first six, FCS national championship) at defensive end, and recorded 41 tackles, four for loss and 3 ½ sacks with a batted pass, forced fumble and three-yard fumble recovery touchdown. Started 10-of-15 games at DE in '12, collecting 49-12-5 with a forced fumble. Started all 15 games at right end in '13, logging 47-10-7 ½ with a forced fumble and two blocks. Was the Buchanan Award winner (top defensive player in FCS) in '14 after leading the Missouri Valley Conference in sacks and tackles for loss — racked up 97-32 ½-19 ½ with three batted passes, an interception and three forced fumbles. Played all 61 games of his career, winning four FCS national titles. Team captain graduated in December with a degree in construction management.

Strengths: Active and energetic — much of his production results from effort and running to the ball. Functional short-area speed and burst coming off the edge. Flashes suddenness to turn the corner and wins with quickness. Plays with discipline and good backside pursuit. Has a good feel for locating the ball.

Weaknesses: Has short flappers and plays small. Cannot convert speed to power and runs into a wall. Gets bounced around against the run and will be pinballed by NFL base blockers. Measured the shortest arms (31 inches) and wingspan (74 ⅝ inches) of any defensive lineman at the Combine. Production is inflated from regularly facing inferior competition.

Future: Similar to Eagles 2008 sixth-round pick Andy Studebaker, Emanuel emerged as a dominant edge rusher against lesser, small-school competition and has developmental potential as a 3-4 rush linebacker. However, his lack of length and body power could always be restricting. Should make a mark on special teams while adapting to the NFL and might be best as a bubble linebacker, where he is more unencumbered to run free to the ball in a 40 front.

Draft projection: Fifth- to sixth-round pick.

ROLB-DRE DANTE FOWLER, #6 (Jr-3)

FLORIDA　▶ GRADE: 7.15

Ht: 6-2 ⅝ | Wt: 261 | 40: 4.59 | Arm: 33 ¾ | Hand: 9 ½

History: Highly recruited Florida prep that also competed in the shot put. Originally verballed to Florida State, but switched his commitment on National Signing Day. As a true freshman in 2012, recorded 30 tackles, eight for loss and 2 ½ sacks in 13 games, including one start at the "Buck" position. Toggled back and forth from defensive end and "Buck" in '13 when he started all 12 games and notched 30-8-2 ½. Was the Gators' MVP in '14 — started all 12 games at the "Buck" and registered 60-15-8 ½ with a batted pass and two forced fumbles. Team captain.

Strengths: Very good arm length with a well-distributed, athletic frame and a strong base. Outstanding football-playing temperament. Very tough, physical and competitive. Plays with violence in his hands and jolts blockers and ball carriers on contact. Motor runs hot and chases down ball carriers to the sideline from behind. Is very fluid and loose-hipped for as big as he is and shows a very good closing burst to the quarterback on loops and stunts. Showed improved ability to convert speed to power and walk blockers back to the quarterback. Produced the fastest 20-yard split (2.51 seconds) of any defensive lineman at the Combine. Has an explosive get-off and an efficient spin move. Plays with emotion. Has a passion for the game and it shows.

Weaknesses: Has a 32 ½-inch vertical jump and bench-pressed only 19 reps at the Combine, tied for third-fewest among defensive ends. Could have been more consistently productive, with 13 ½ career sacks. Freelances at times and plays outside the scheme of the defense. Is not a nuanced or crafty pass rusher and still must add more moves to his arsenal. Could do a better job timing up the blitz.

Future: A strong, fast, physical leverage rusher who can win with speed or power, Fowler made the most of a final season in Gainesville that went off track for the program and made his final game his best, dominating the Birmingham Bowl and playing with more determination and discipline than he had all season following Will Muschamp's departure. Has been moved around the defense throughout career, showing the versatility to rush from anywhere along the front, and could be a better pro than college player. Has only scratched the surface of what he could do rushing the passer, having yet to develop an arsenal of pass-rush moves and the best is still ahead of him. Has as much upside as any pass-rusher in the draft and has impact potential. Top-10 cinch.

Draft projection: Top-10 pick.

Scout's take: "Watch the East Carolina game at about the 10:30 mark and see what he does to the pulling guard. You watch that play and

LINEBACKERS

say 'wow'. He hits the pulling guard so hard he looks like he is out cold for a second. The kid goes down like a boxer hit with a roundhouse. (Fowler) is very violent in the way he plays the game. To me, he might be the best player in the draft. He's fun to watch."

SLB ALANI FUA, #5 (Sr-5)

BYU ▶ GRADE: 5.09

Ht: 6-4 ¾ | Wt: 238 | 40: 4.69 | Arm: 32 | Hand: 10 ⅛

History: Has two sons — Jrae and Malaki — with his wife Malaysia. Brother, Sione, was a defensive tackle with the Browns last year, and cousin, Kyle Van Noy, was a BYU teammate before he was drafted by the Lions (second round, 2014). Alani attended Oaks Christian in California, where he also played volleyball. Chose BYU over offers from Ohio State, Arizona State and Washington, among others. Redshirted in 2010. Played eight games in '11 (wore jersey No. 36) and was credited with six tackles, two for loss and two sacks with a pass breakup. Collected 13-0-0 with an interception in '12 (appeared in all 13 games). In '13, started 9-of-13 games at strong-side linebacker in the Cougars' 3-4 defense — produced 65-5-3 with 10 pass breakups and two interceptions, including a 51-yard touchdown against Georgia Tech. Started 9-of-10 games played at SLB in '14, managing 42-7 ½-4 with four pass breakups, two interceptions and a forced fumble. Sustained an ankle injury against Utah State, costing him four mid-season games.

Strengths: Very good body length. Recorded the best short shuttle (4.15 seconds) and 3-cone drill time (6.83 seconds) of any outside linebacker at the Combine. Is athletic enough to line up in the slot and match up with some receivers. Plays on his feet with good balance.

Weaknesses: Marginal functional strength and weight room strength with an underdeveloped frame. Has short arms for as long as he is and tends to play too upright. Bench-pressed only 18 reps at the Combine and needs to get stronger. Has a soft, passive playing temperament. Marginal football character. Does not play to timed speed and is not quick to come off spots. Not a finisher.

Future: A big man who plays small and lacks power in his body. Could intrigue coaches with his triangle numbers on paper and will disappoint with his performance on tape. Developmental "Sam" linebacker lacking physicality and play strength to consistently match up with tight ends in the trenches.

Draft projection: Late draftable pick.

Scout's take: "I don't know where you play him. He's not strong or instinctive. He's going to be a project."

LOLB-DLE-3T GENEO GRISSOM, #85 (Sr-5)

OKLAHOMA ▶ GRADE: 5.33

Ht: 6-3 ⅜ | Wt: 262 | 40: 4.82 | Arm: 33 ⅜ | Hand: 10 ¼

History: First name is pronounced "GEE-no." Prepped in Kansas. Redshirted in 2010. Was a reserve defensive end in '11, scratching together five and ½ tackles for loss and zero sacks in five appearances. In '12, was suspended for the season opener versus UTEP (violation teams rules) before tallying 4-0-0 in 12 appearances. Suffered stress fractures in both feet ('10 fall camp, '12 spring). Played all 13 games in '13, starting five at DE, and recorded 40-9-4 ½ with four batted passes and an interception (54-yard touchdown against Texas). Moved to right outside linebacker in '14 — started 7-of-10 games and managed 39-6 ½-3 ½ with four pass breakups, one interception (38-yard TD against Tulsa) and two forced fumbles before suffering a season-ending right MCL injury against Texas Tech. Graduated in the fall of '14 with a degree in African-American studies.

Strengths: Very good athlete with unique versatility, having lined up as a DE, DT, OLB and TE throughout his career. Has a 37-inch vertical jump and is explosive through the lower body. Good strength to set the edge. Athletic enough to drop into coverage and buzz the flats (see pick-six vs. Tulsa). Has a strong, powerful stride and strong hands and is capable of disrupting with his hand in the dirt. Looked unblockable at times as a light-framed three-technique as a junior. Good closing speed. Strong tackler.

Weaknesses: Average career production. Shows some tightness in his hips and is a bit straight-linish, struggling to change directions quickly and make sudden reactionary cuts to the quarterback fleeing the pocket. Average lateral agility. Needs to do a better job coming to balance in the open field and finishing. Never settled on a position in college.

Future: An athletic pass rusher who flashed the ability to win one-on-one matchups from the interior as a junior, Grissom converted to a hybrid rush outside linebacker role as a senior. May be best suited for a role as a base end and sub-package rusher as a pro.

Draft projection: Fourth- to fifth-round pick.

Scout's take: "He was 260 and lining up as a

defensive tackle in a 30 front as a junior. Watch the Alabama game when he had two sacks in the bowl game and two fumble recoveries in the end zone as a 260-pound three-technique. He has talent. … He is a man without a home. They tried him all over — TE, DE, LB — and couldn't find a place for him."

ILB BRYCE HAGER, #44 (Sr-5)

BAYLOR ▶ GRADE: 5.22

Ht: 6-0 ¾ | Wt: 234 | 40: 4.59 | Arm: 31 ¾ | Hand: 9

History: Father, Britt, was an All-American linebacker at Texas before enjoying a nine-year NFL career with the Eagles, Broncos and Rams (1989-97). Younger brother, Breckyn, is set to join Texas next year. Bryce was a lightly recruited linebacker/running back out of Austin Westlake. Redshirted in 2010. Was a reserve/special-teams player in '11, collecting 13 tackles, zero for loss and zero sacks with a forced fumble in 13 appearances. In '12, started 10-of-13 games at middle linebacker and produced 124-9 ½-4 with one pass breakup and two forced fumbles. Started the first nine games at MLB in '13 — totaled 71-2 ½-1 with three pass breakups, though he suffered a groin injury against Kansas State in Week Five — played through it until he was shut down for the final four games. Underwent off-season surgery to repair an abdominal tear and an abductor tear, sidelining him for '14 spring practice. In the fall, returned to start all 13 games at MLB, registering 114-12-2 with one pass breakup, two forced fumbles and one interception. Graduated in December with a degree in health, human performance and recreation studies.

Strengths: Very competitive. Plays with a lot of energy and is around the ball a lot. Good weight-room strength and functional play strength to drive through tackles. Is football smart and makes all the calls. Good durability (despite small frame).

Weaknesses: Has short arms and plays short-armed with small hands and a smallish bone structure. Lacks bulk and bulk strength. Gets caught up in the wash and is late getting over the top. Does not strike with pop and power and often catches on contact. Average lateral agility. Limited in coverage and has marginal production on the ball.

Future: A speedy, flow-and-scrape "Mike" linebacker with coverage limitations and a frame not desirable for the rigors of the pro game. Has the mentality of a core teams player and could make a living covering kicks and providing depth at linebacker.

Draft projection: Fifth- to sixth-round pick.
Scout's take: "He's a little guy. I wouldn't draft him, but someone might take him in the seventh (round). He is a (special) teamer."

ROLB-DRE ELI HAROLD, #7 (Jr-3)

VIRGINIA ▶ GRADE: 6.32

Ht: 6-3 ⅛ | Wt: 247 | 40: 4.59 | Arm: 33 | Hand: 9 ⅜

History: Virginia Beach native who played defensive end, quarterback, running back and receiver as a prep. Chose UVA over offers from LSU, Florida, Ohio State and Miami, among others. Grew up without a father then lost his mother to pancreatic cancer in January 2011. As a true freshman in '12, recorded 36 tackles, seven for loss and two sacks with a forced fumble and an interception in 12 games. Started all 24 games at defensive end the next two seasons — totaled 51-15-8 ½ with a batted pass and two forced fumbles in '13; and 54-14 ½-7 with two batted passes, an interception and a forced fumble in '14. Opted not to lift at the Combine, and bench-pressed 24 reps at pro day.

Strengths: Looks the part with a very athletic frame and good arm length. Has a frame to grow into and good musculature with 10 percent body fat. Outstanding speed and athletic ability. Rises to the occasion vs. better competition (see Miami and Pittsburgh). Uses his hands well to come up and underneath blocks and is efficient working the edge. Athletic enough to fold into coverage. Terrific game-day competitor. Brings energy to the field and is a defensive tempo-setter. Confident and competitive.

Weaknesses: Light by NFL OLB standards and could stand to add some bulk and improve weight-room strength. Lacks lower-body strength and struggles some at the point of attack vs. big bodies. Still learning how to gauge his body power and can learn to play with more consistent knee bend. Did not record double-digit sacks in any given year.

Future: Very quick, athletic, smooth speed rusher with the ability to leverage the edge. Has a sleek, silky rushing style and is able to bend around bigger blockers and disrupt the backfield. Should only continue to get better as he fills out his frame and has the physical tools to contribute readily as a rookie.

Draft projection: Top-40 pick.
Scout's take: "Harold is going to be an outside linebacker, but he plays with his hand in the ground most of the time. That's what he will be. He'll get to 255-260 easy. He's big-boned. I think he is the third-best pass-rusher in the class."

LINEBACKERS

ILB BEN HEENEY, #31 (Sr-4)

KANSAS ▶ GRADE: 5.05

Ht: 6-0 ¼ | Wt: 231 | 40: 4.59 | Arm: 30 ¾ | Hand: 9

History: Kansas native who starred as a linebacker and running back in high school — rushed for 2,083 yards and 39 touchdowns as a senior. Was charged with DUI and racing on a highway in July 2011 (ultimately granted diversion). Was a reserve/special-teams player as a true freshman in the fall when he recorded eight tackles, zero for loss and zero sacks with a blocked kick. Stepped into the lineup in '12 — started all 12 games at middle linebacker and produced 112-12-1 with two pass breakups and a forced fumble. Was cited for misdemeanor battery in January '13 when he was asked to leave a bar and did not go peacefully. In '13, totaled 88-11 ½-2 with six pass breakups and three interceptions in 10 starts at MLB. Missed two games (Oklahoma, Baylor) after suffering a partially torn right MCL against TCU. Started all 12 games at MLB in '14, registering 127-12-1 ½ with one pass breakup, one interception and two forced fumbles. Led the NCAA and Big 12 in solo tackles (7.3 per game). Three-time leading tackler for the Jayhawks. Two-year captain. Expected to graduate in May.

Strengths: Good functional football-playing instincts. Posted the best short shuttle time (4.00 seconds), 60-yard shuttle (11.06 seconds) and 3-cone drill time (6.68 seconds) of any linebacker at the Combine and among the best at the event, demonstrating very good lateral agility and burst.

Weaknesses: Smallish frame with very short arms and small hands. Struggles to wrap and secure tackles in space — allows ball carriers to step out of grasp. Tight-skinned with a nearly maxed-out frame and does not have much room to get bigger. Lacks functional play strength and gets hung up on blocks a lot. Limited coverage skills.

Future: A try-hard overachiever with size and tackling deficiencies. Best chance will come with a fast-flowing Cover 2 scheme such as Dallas' or Tampa Bay's that places greater premium on speed than size. Will have to make a mark on special teams to stick.

Draft projection: Late draftable pick.

ILB AMARLO HERRERA, #52 (Sr-4)

GEORGIA ▶ GRADE: 5.14

Ht: 6-0 ⅝ | Wt: 244 | 40: 4.84 | Arm: 32 ¾ | Hand: 9 ⅝

History: Georgia native. Played 3-4 weak inside linebacker for the Bulldogs. As a true freshman in 2011, started 8-of-14 games and recorded 37 tackles, three for loss and zero sacks with two pass breakups and one forced fumble. Started 9-of-14 games in '12, notching 70-3-0 with two pass breakups, one interception and one forced fumble. Was the team's defensive MVP in '13 when he piled up 112-5-½ with six pass breakups, one interception and one forced fumble. Also recognized for his dedication to strength and conditioning. Was the team's leading tackler in '14 when he totaled 115-10-3 with one pass breakup, one interception and one forced fumble. Was named defensive captain and received a coaches leadership award at the team's postseason awards banquet. Will be a 24-year-old rookie.

Strengths: Very thickly built with good bulk. Superb tackle production. Good football smarts — calls the defense and understands football concepts. Has an edge to him and plays with emotion. Tough and competitive. Experienced four-year starter in the Southeastern Conference.

Weaknesses: Too straight-linish, as confirmed in 7.37-second three-cone time. Has tight hips and struggles to open up, flip his hips and run — could be very limited in coverage. Liability in coverage and in space. Struggles to come to balance and tackle in space. Not explosive. Takes time to digest what he sees.

Future: An active, compactly built, between-the-tackles linebacker whose production is heavily funneled to him in the Bulldogs' defense, Herrera could fit best as a weak-side inside linebacker in a 30 front. Hip tightness and limited agility could make it difficult to operate in space on special teams and could limit opportunities to earn a roster spot.

Draft projection: Late draftable pick.

Scout's take: "(No.) 52 can step and fill, but he has limitations to him as far as his lateral ability and outside in coverage. He does a nice job inside. He's limited outside the box. ... I'm not sure what he can give me on special teams."

ILB-WLB JORDAN HICKS, #3 (Sr-4)

TEXAS ▶ GRADE: 5.32

Ht: 6-1 ⅜ | Wt: 236 | 40: 4.66 | Arm: 32 | Hand: 10

History: Born in Colorado and lived in Indiana, South Carolina and Ohio, where he was a Parade and USA Today All-American, high school Butkus Award winner and the state's Gatorade Player of the Year. Captained the football and basketball teams. Was recruited to UT by then-head coach Mack Brown. As a true freshman in 2010, was credited with 23 tackles, one for loss and one sack in 12 appearances. Broke his right foot during '11 spring practice. In the fall, started 8-of-13 games at strong-side linebacker (non-starts were nickel/dime personnel), tallying 65-4-1 with four pass breakups. In '12, managed 23-3-0 with one pass breakup in three starts at weak-side linebacker before suffering a season-ending hip flexor injury against Mississippi. Was suspended and sent home a day before the Alamo Bowl for breaking team rules. In '13, posted 41-3-0 in four starts at WLB before suffering a season-ending ruptured left Achilles tendon against Kansas State. Missed some time in the spring with a hamstring injury. Was the Longhorns' leading tackler in '14 when he started all 13 games at WLB and registered 147-13-3 ½ with two pass breakups and two interceptions. Had 12 career special-teams tackles. Graduated in December '13 with a sports management degree.

Strengths: Very good speed to run down ball carriers to the sideline — good playing range to the perimeter. Is often around the ball. Has a 38-inch vertical jump and a 6.78-second short shuttled, both tied for second-best among inside linebackers at the Combine. Good football character and intelligence. Plays hard and competes.

Weaknesses: Lacks functional take-on strength and is not a drive-through tackler, often looking for a backside angle to lasso. Instincts are off — can be fooled by misdirection. Bench-pressed only 20 reps at the Combine. Has some limitations in coverage. Only a one-year, full-time starter. Has been slowed by ankle, hip and foot injuries throughout career and durability has been an issue.

Future: A career marred by injuries and disappointment took a turn for the better in 2014 for Hicks, when he made his senior season his best. Has the physical talent to start readily in the pros but has never been able to shake injuries and proven sturdy enough to handle the rigors of the NFL.

Draft projection: Fourth- to fifth-round pick.

Scout's take: "They have him playing outside, and he's not playing as well. He might be more natural inside. I'm not sure he has been the same guy since he hurt his hamstring. He has some snap to him. He might be a "Mike". I'm not sure he is that explosive outside guy."

ROLB-DRE ZACK HODGES, #99 (Sr-5)

HARVARD ▶ GRADE: 5.17

Ht: 6-2 ½ | Wt: 250 | 40: 4.68 | Arm: 34 ¼ | Hand: 9 ⅞

History: Born in Queens, N.Y. Lost his father as a young child and his grandfather when he was 14. Moved with his mother to North Carolina, where he spent two-plus years at Charlotte Independence High. Zack grew up poor, as his mother, Barbara, worked three jobs to provide the bare essentials before she died suddenly during Zack's junior year. Soon after, moved to Atlanta to live with his grandmother and aunt. Was dominant as a senior, racking up 21 sacks and 10 forced fumbles in nine games. Spent a postgraduate year at Phillips Exeter Academy (N.H.) before joining the Crimson in '11. On the season, tallied 20 tackles, 3 ½ for loss and two sacks with a batted pass and forced fumble in nine games (two starts). Suffered a torn left labrum and did not play against Dartmouth. Started all 10 games at left defensive end in each of the next three seasons — totaled 32-16-9 in '12; 40-11 ½-6 ½ with two batted passes, four forced fumbles and an interception in '13; and 26-10-8 ½ with two batted passes in '14. Two-time Ivy League Defensive Player of the Year was a Buck Buchanan Award finalist as a senior. Owns Harvard's career sacks record (26). Double majored in government and sociology, and is on pace to graduate in May. Did not lift at the Combine because of a left shoulder injury and did not perform the 3-cone drill because of bone bruise in his left knee.

Strengths: Has very long arms and a projectable frame and looks the part. Flashes the ability to convert speed to power. Opens up his stride in space and tracks ball carriers down from behind. Athletic enough to drop into coverage, flip his hips and drive on the ball. Recorded a 10-foot, 4-inch broad jump, second-best among outside linebackers at the Combine. Has overcome a lot of adversity in his life. Very durable.

Weaknesses: Underdeveloped upper body. Average eyes and instincts. Gets hung up on blocks too much and needs to learn how to use his hands better and develop a pass-rush plan. Recorded a 4.66-second short shuttle at the Combine, the slowest of any linebacker at the NFL. Turned off teams with arrogance in the interview process at the Combine. Had a lot of clear-view production. Regularly matched up against lesser Ivy League competition and was not often challenged. Inconsistent motor and intensity. Needs to get stronger. While Harvard book smart, his football IQ is not great.

Future: An underdeveloped football player with the speed, athletic ability and bend to warrant an opportunity as an outside linebacker in a 30 front. Has overcome a lot of adversity in his life to get where he is and would be best paired with a strong, nurturing father figure

LINEBACKERS

in the program who could provide emotional support, guidance and direction.

Draft projection: Fourth- to fifth-round pick.

Scout's take: "The Harvard guy wouldn't stop talking in the (interview) room when we brought him in. He didn't understand football techniques. He was far out there, talking about being the best player in the Ivy League. He could have a hard time fitting in a locker room."

MLB MIKE HULL, #43 (Sr-5)

PENN STATE ▶ GRADE: 5.22

Ht: 5-11 ⅞ | Wt: 237 | 40: 4.72 | Arm: 30 ½ | Hand: 9 ⅜

History: Father, Tom, played on the undefeated 1973 PSU team before playing 25 games with the 49ers and Packers (1974-75). Mike was a linebacker/running back who captained the football, baseball and wrestling teams as a Pennsylvania prep. Redshirted in 2010. As a reserve/special-teams player in '11, was credited with 18 tackles, five for loss and three sacks with two pass breakups and one forced fumble in 13 games. Played all 12 games in '12 — including his first career start in the season finale against Wisconsin in place of injured weak-side linebacker Michael Mauti ('13 seventh round, Vikings) — and logged 58-5-4 with four pass breakups, one interception and one blocked kick. Started 8-of-10 games played at WLB in '13, totaling 78-4 ½-½ with two pass breakups and one forced fumble. Sprained his right MCL in the season opener versus Syracuse — did not play against Eastern Michigan and Kent State and was limited/did not start against Syracuse and Central Florida. Moved to middle linebacker in '14 — was the Big Ten's leading tackler and the Nittany Lions' team MVP after registering 140-10 ½-2 with three pass breakups, one interception and one forced fumble in 13 starts (injuries to teammate forced him to WLB against Michigan State). Team captain graduated with a finance degree. Had his left knee scoped after the season — tried to participate the Senior Bowl, but was sidelined by swelling. Also did not perform jumps at the Combine because of the injury. Will be a 24-year-old rookie.

Strengths: Very alert and urgent. Quick-footed and agile. Triggers quickly and is around the ball a lot. Terrific production. Outstanding football character and work habits. Led all inside linebackers with 31 bench-press reps at the Combine and is very strong in the upper body. Good football intelligence. Understands the game. Respected team leader and tempo-setter.

Weaknesses: Lacks ideal height and arm length and gets caught up on blocks and struggles to disengage. Benefited from playing behind a solid defensive line that kept him free to roam. Struggles to match up with tight ends in coverage.

Future: A very productive, undersized, run-and-hit "Mike" linebacker with the toughness, determination and grit to make a living on special teams.

Draft projection: Fourth- to fifth-round pick.

Scout's take: "Hull is a good, little college football player and flies around and makes a lot of plays. I'm not sure how it is going to translate (to the pros). When I graded the guy, I felt like he was the next Casey Matthews. He is a backup. He is an undersized guy and you can only keep six linebackers. The next thing you know, someone gets hurt and you are worrying about how you are going to cover this guy up because the coaches are not going to want to cut him. Once you get him in the building, you're not going to be able to get him out, so the way I'm looking at it, I don't want to bring him in. What you see is what you get. But he does show up on tape."

ILB A.J. JOHNSON, #45 (Sr-4)

TENNESSEE ▶ GRADE: 5.09

Ht: 6-2 | Wt: 244 | 40: 4.85e | Arm: 32 ⅛ | Hand: 10 ⅞

History: Prepped in Georgia, where he earned all-state honors three times and was named the state's AAA Defensive Player of the Year as a senior. Amassed 464 tackles, 52 for loss and 18 sacks his final three high school seasons, including 12 forced fumbles his last two seasons. Started 10-of-12 games on the weak side in 2011, producing 80-4 ½-0 with a forced fumble. In '12, shifted to middle linebacker and was the Southeastern Conference's leading tackler — piled up 138-8 ½-1 with one pass breakup. Was also used on offense in short-yardage situations ("Beast" formation), rushing 12 times for 21 yards (1.8-yard average) and six touchdowns. Sustained a high right ankle sprain during '13 spring practice. Was the Vols' leading tackler in the fall when he registered 106-8 ½-0 with three pass breakups (12 starts at MLB). In '14, notched 101-9-2 with two pass breakups, an interception and two forced fumbles in 10 starts — was suspended for the duration of the season after he was identified as a suspect in the alleged rape of a 19-year-old woman. Was indicted in February, at which time the NFL rescinded Johnson's Combine

LINEBACKERS

invitation. Johnson, who was released on $40,000 bond, pleaded not guilty. Trial is set for Aug. 24. Played for two head coaches and three defensive coordinators. Graduated in December with a degree in sociology.

Strengths: Very thickly built with big hands and broad shoulders and looks the part. Aggressive coming downhill and striking. Hits with some explosion and thump. Very good strength at the point of attack. Faces up ball carriers and drives them backwards on contact. Exceptional career production. Earned a reputation as one of the hardest workers in the program and has been an alpha dog leader in the locker room. Highly competitive. Has a passion for the game. Has been very durable and never missed a game to injury.

Weaknesses: Is tight in the hips and struggles transitioning and making plays to the sideline. Has limitations in man coverage, lacking the agility to run with tight ends and backs. The more ground he has to cover, the more he struggles. Is facing very serious litigation calling his personal character into question and training camp availability will be affected.

Future: A very physical, downhill inside linebacker with enough talent to compete for a starting job in the pros. Was forced to learn three defenses in four years and at times was processing too much, yet consistently found ways to make plays and affect the game. Off-field concerns will limit his opportunities in the NFL and could force him to prove himself in a developmental league if he clears litigation. A middle-round talent whose draft stock was deflated when charges were filed against him.

Draft projection: Priority free agent.

Scout's take: "I didn't think he was instinctive to locate and you hear it talked about, but he seems to find the ball. You chart it and he makes 12 plays per game. He has a knack to find the ball. … He was one of the couple guys I have seen be able to take on (Georgia RB Todd) Gurley and stand him up or at least knock him backwards. He is a tough, competitive kid who makes plays. I put a solid fourth-round grade on him before serious legal issues came to light."

ILB **TAIWAN JONES**, #34 (Sr-4)

MICHIGAN STATE ▶ GRADE: 5.19

Ht: 6-2 ⅝	Wt: 245	40: 4.94	Arm: 34	Hand: 10

History: Two-way standout also played basketball as a Michigan prep. Missed all but two games of his junior (2009) season because of an injury. As a true freshman in 2011, was credited with 18 tackles, one-half tackle for

loss and one-half sack with one pass breakup in 14 appearances. Played all 13 games in '12, starting four at the "Star" linebacker position, and tallied 38-5 ½-1 with three pass breakups. Started 13-of-14 games at the "Star" in '13, posting 67-7-0. Was hurt against Youngstown State and did not start the following week against Notre Dame. Was hobbled by an ankle injury during '14 spring practice when he shifted to "Mike" linebacker. In the fall, totaled 60-12 ½-4 with two pass breakups and an interception in 13 starts. Does not turn 22 until December.

Strengths: Has outstanding size with very long arms and bulk strength. Is strong at the point of attack and can knock back lead blockers on contact and re-route tight ends. Tough and physical. Runs hard to the ball. Drive-through tackler. Versatile and has played inside and on the strong side. Solid East-West Shrine showing. Was a core special teams player early in his career.

Weaknesses: Very tight-hipped and plays too upright. Mechanical and robotic in his movement. Limited bend and lateral agility to come to balance and tackle in space. Too straight-linish. Marginal foot quickness and long speed. Lacks discipline in his approach — does not fill with the correct shoulder and eyes may require re-training to read cross-keys. Slow digester — has to process what he sees in front of him.

Future: An old-school, downhill thumper who struggles to unlock his hips and lacks range outside the tackle box. Lacks ideal foot quickness to match up with tight ends in coverage but could provide depth as a backup "Mike" and "Sam" linebacker. Must refine his eyes and hone his instincts to ascend in the pros and may always be restricted by rigidity and lack of foot speed.

Draft projection: Fifth- to sixth-round pick.

Scout's take: "He looks the part. The coaches love the guy. He plays too close to the line and gets caught up in a lot of trash because he is too slow. He played outside last year. It took him time to adjust to playing inside this year. He runs like a duck with his feet pointed outward."

ILB-WLB **ERIC KENDRICKS**, #6 (Sr-5)

UCLA ▶ GRADE: 5.86

Ht: 6-0 ¼	Wt: 232	40: 4.61	Arm: 31	Hand: 9 ⅝

History: Father, Marv, led the Bruins in rushing (1970-71). Brother, Mychal, is a starting linebacker for the Philadelphia Eagles after winning Pac-12 Defensive Player of the

LINEBACKERS

Year and being selected in the second round of the 2012 draft. Eric was raised by a single mother after his father became addicted to cocaine (has since cleaned up and become present in Eric's life, per LA Times). Prepped in California, where he played linebacker, quarterback, running back and kicker while captaining the team for two years. Also captained the basketball team and played baseball. Was recruited to UCLA by then-head coach Rick Neuheisel. Redshirted in 2010. Played all 14 games in '11 (wore jersey No. 30), starting the final three (two at strong-side linebacker, one at weak-side linebacker in the Bruins' 3-4 defense), and recorded 77 tackles, 4 ½ for loss and two sacks with three pass breakups. Took ownership of the right inside linebacker position in '12 when he started all 14 games and piled up 149-6-2 with four pass breakups, one interception, two forced fumbles and a blocked kick. Dealt with a right ankle injury in the spring of '13 — had surgery in July to remove "loose bodies," but discomfort lingered through the season. Started all 11 games played at RILB, notching 106-4-2 with two pass breakups, one interception, one forced fumble and one blocked kick. Left the Stanford game with kidney pain. Sprained his right AC joint against Oregon and sat out against Colorado. Had his right ankle surgically repaired in December — was sidelined for the Sun Bowl against Virginia Tech and '14 spring practice. Posted a historic season in the fall when he became UCLA's first Butkus Award winner, took home the Lott IMPACT Trophy and was honored as team MVP and Jerry Long "Heart" Award winner — led the Bruins in tackles for the third straight season, registering 149-11 ½-4 with two pass breakups, three interceptions (one touchdown) and a forced fumble. Two-time captain finished his career as UCLA's all-time leading tackler (481). Played for two head coaches, three defensive coordinators and three position coaches. Graduated with a political science degree. Pulled his hamstring on his first 40 attempt at the Combine and did not perform shuttles.

Strengths: Exceptional eyes, anticipation and angles. Outstanding pre-snap recognition — thinks and reacts 4.4 and is often moving at the snap. Field fast. Covers a lot of ground in pursuit and chases down ball carriers from behind. Extremely competitive with a non-stop motor. Outstanding football intelligence — knows the responsibilities of everyone on defense and can get everyone lined up. Serves like a coach on the field. Very good lateral agility. Has a 38-inch vertical jump. Terrific awareness in coverage reading the quarterback and anticipating throwing lanes. Record-setting production. Has NFL pedigree and understands what it takes to play at a high level. Highly respected team leader. Outstanding personal and football character.

Weaknesses: Has an unassuming build with short arms and does not look the part. Lacks ideal take-on strength and does not play with explosion in his body. Struggles to match up with big bodies and can be overwhelmed in tight quarters. Could stand to do a better job of running through contact.

Future: A scrappy, football-smart tackling machine that compensates for his lack of size and length with superb instincts. Record-setting production is indicative of his playmaking ability and is every bit as advertised as a respected locker room leader, on-field commander and defensive heartbeat. Will make an immediate impact upon his arrival in the pros despite physical shortcomings and emerge as a very consistent, productive pro.

Draft projection: First-round pick.

Scout's take: "He has the best instincts of any player in this year's draft. He is a quarterback on the field, with the smarts and intelligence to line people up. You see him doing it. …He is all over the field. The dude is instinctive. Very, very instinctive. It's just his size that worries you. It's kind of like Larry Foote or Jonathan Vilma, those types. Vilma hit with more explosion."

LOLB-DLE HAU'OLI KIKAHA, #8 (Sr-5)

WASHINGTON ▶ GRADE: 5.74

Ht: 6-2 ⅜ | Wt: 253 | 40: 4.95e | Arm: 32 ½ | Hand: 9 ⅝

History: Name is pronounced "ha-OH-lee key-KAH-hah," and his first name means "happy" in Hawaiian. Hau'oli is a native Hawaiian of Polynesian descent. Legally changed his last name in 2013, taking Kikaha from his mother's side of the family (previously went by Jamora). Didn't know his father until he was 16, grew up poor and lived in Ohio, Texas and California before settling back on the island his freshman year. Also competed in wrestling and judo as a prep in Hawaii, where he played defensive end and tight end, went to two state championship games and was named the state's defensive player of the year. Was recruited by then-head coach Steve Sarkisian. Played all 13 games as a true freshman in 2010, starting the final seven at

Eric Kendricks

GREG TURK

defensive end, and recorded 49 tackles, eight for loss and three sacks with a batted pass and forced fumble. In '11, managed 15-3-1 in four starts at DE before suffering a season-ending torn left ACL injury. Missed the '12 season after re-tearing the ACL. Wore jersey No. 52 prior to '13, when he rebounded with 70-15 ½-13 with three batted passes and three forced fumbles in 13 starts. Was given permission to miss two months of the winter conditioning program to attend a cultural anthropological study of French Polynesia ("Certain guys get certain privileges," explained head coach Chris Peterson to the school's official website). After playing 4-3 DE his first four years, switched to "Buck" linebacker in the new coaching staff's 3-4 system in '14. Was a finalist for the Lombardi, Butkus, Hendricks, Lott IMPACT and Polynesian Player of the Year awards after establishing UW single-season records for sacks and tackles for loss — racked up 72-25-19 with two pass breakups and three forced fumbles in 14 starts. Team captain owns UW's career sacks record (36). Is scheduled to graduate with a degree in anthropology and ethnic studies. Did not lift at the Combine after training was affected by the flu and opted not to work out.

Strengths: Plays faster than his timed speed. Good initial quickness. Plays hard and competes. Fires into the backfield and is disruptive. Extremely intelligent — described as "brilliant" by college professors. Understands angles, leverage and rush technique and is very savvy working edges, displaying an assortment of moves (rip, club, swim). Works his hands and feet in coordination. Shows a burst at the top of his rush and closes. Good sack production.

Weaknesses: Is a bit of a tweener, lacking the size of a true defensive end and the burst of an outside linebacker. Average arm length and bulk. Limited foot speed and lower-body explosion. Misses some tackles in the open field. Is not a strong, physical run defender and can be moved by big bodies. Durability has been an issue during his career — tore the ACL in his left knee twice and does not move with fluidity.

Future: A highly productive edge rusher in the same mold as Steelers 2012 first-round pick Jarvis Jones, Kikaha has natural pass-rush ability to earn a starting job as a strong-side outside linebacker in a 30 front. A better football player than athlete. Long-term durability evaluations could affect draft status.

Draft projection: Second- to third-round pick.

Scout's take: "(Kikaha) is a 3-4 OLB all day. He played well vs. the Stanford tackle (Andrus Peat) who (should) be a top-10 pick. I wrote him as a starting OLB. He's not a true defensive end. The measurables will scare (scouts) away. He ran a 5-flat in the spring (of 2014). I don't care. He is a good football player."

LOLB-DRE **LORENZO MAULDIN**, #94 (Sr-4)
LOUISVILLE ▶ GRADE: 5.44
Ht: 6-3 ⅝ | Wt: 259 | 40: 4.84 | Arm: 33 | Hand: 9 ⅞

History: Lived in 16 foster homes growing up. Originally committed to South Carolina, but was a victim of oversigning and landed at UL with then-head coach Charlie Strong. As a true freshman in 2011 (wore jersey No. 86), played all 12 games (two starts at defensive end) and had six tackles, one-half for loss and zero sacks. Started 6-of-11 games played at DE in '12, tallying 22-6 ½-4 ½ with one batted pass and one forced fumble. Missed two games because of a left MCL sprain. Started all 13 games at weak-side DE in '13, totaling 40-12-9 ½ with four batted passes and three forced fumbles. Had surgery after the season to repair a torn left labrum. Started 11-of-12 games played at the "Will" OLB spot in the new 3-4 scheme installed by defensive coordinator Todd Grantham in '14, producing 51-13-6 ½ with three batted passes and one forced fumble. Did not play against Boston College (hamstring). Team captain. Graduated with a communications degree.

Strengths: Has prototype size for a rush linebacker with very good arm length. Has a long first step and plays with good balance. Tough competitor. Matches up well with tight ends. Functional strength against the run. Has a passion for the game and lives in the football facility. Outstanding football character.

Weaknesses: Tends to play a bit upright and is mechanical in his movement. Does not play with power or show variety in his pass-rush arsenal. Only has a 32-inch vertical jump, indicating average athletic ability. Has some tightness in his hips, as confirmed in 4.63-second short shuttle at the Combine, the slowest time of any outside linebacker. Also ran a pedestrian 7.49-second 3-cone drill time.

Future: A weak-side college defensive end who converted to outside linebacker as a senior, Mauldin lacks the burst and explosion desired to rush the passer. However, he is very

active, plays hard and brings energy to the field. Has overcome a lot of adversity in his life and is the type of player you root for.

Draft projection: Second- to third-round pick.

Scout's take: "I like Mauldin. He's not great, but I will go to bat for him. He'll probably be a 3-4 rush backer when all is said and done. … I think he is a starting "Sam" linebacker."

ILB **BENARDRICK McKINNEY**, # (Jr-3)
MISSISSIPPI STATE ▶ GRADE: 5.74
Ht: 6-4 ⅛ | Wt: 246 | 40: 4.64 | Arm: 33 | Hand: 9

History: Linebacker/quarterback who also played basketball as a Mississippi prep. Redshirted in 2011. Played all 13 games in '12, starting the final 10 at outside linebacker, and produced 102 tackles, 4 ½ for loss and one sack with four pass breakups. Started all 26 games at middle linebacker and was the Bulldogs' leading tackler the next two seasons — totaled 71-7-3 ½ in '13; and 71-8-3 with four pass breakups and a forced fumble in '14.

Strengths: Outstanding size and straight-line speed. Looks the part. Very good take-on strength to step downhill and fill. Good striking ability and pop in his hands. Paced all inside linebackers at the Combine with a 40 ½-inch vertical jump and has explosive talent in his body.

Weaknesses: Tends to play too upright and is not quick to flip his hips and transition. Does not consistently play to his timed speed. Straight-linish and tight and is limited in man coverage. Struggles to make plays outside the tackle box. Tied for the fewest bench-press reps (16) among inside linebackers at the Combine.

Future: A fast, explosive two-down "Mike" linebacker who is often used as a situational edge rusher or gap-shooting blitzer on passing downs to conceal his coverage limitations and turn him loose to disrupt the quarterback. Is at his best moving forward and could fill a Brandon Spikes-type role in the pros.

Draft projection: Top-50 pick.

Scout's take: "(McKinney) has snap and pop — he will whack you. He has enough speed to go outside the tackle box, but not enough to be able to consistently go sideline to sideline. He's a 3-4 "Mike" linebacker. He cannot cover in space at all — not with the way they are spreading everyone out these days. … He could be a better college player than pro. He's high-hipped in coverage and can't change direction fluidly — all of that makes for a slower reactionary athlete. He's a good college player."

LINEBACKERS

WLB **MARK NZEOCHA**, #21 (Sr-4)

WYOMING   ▶ GRADE: 5.19

Ht: 6-2 ⅜ | Wt: 232 | 40: 4.52 | Arm: 33 | Hand: 10

History: Last name is pronounced "en-ZAH-chuh." Born in Germany, where he played club football and was recruited to Wyoming by then-head coach Dave Christensen. As a true freshman in 2011, played 10 games, starting five at the "Leo" linebacker, and collected 15 tackles, one-half for loss and zero sacks with two pass breakups and one interception. Did not play (coach's decision) against UNLV, Air Force or New Mexico. Moved to strong safety in '12 when he played 11 games (started first two) and tallied 32-0-0 with a forced fumble. Did not play against Cal Poly (concussion). Played strong-side linebacker in '13, registering 101-10-1 with two pass breakups and two forced fumbles in 12 starts. In '14, managed 59-3-2 with five pass breakups and two forced fumbles in seven starts at SLB (also shifted to middle linebacker in nickel) before suffering a season-ending torn right ACL injury against San Jose State. Was medically excluded from running at the Combine. Will turn 26 in January. Graduated in December with a finance degree.

Strengths: Very good athlete with loose hips and exceptional timed speed to run and cover. Is agile and light enough on his feet to run with backs, tight ends and slot receivers. Very quick to arrive on the blitz, with outstanding closing speed. Secure, wrap tackler. Very intelligent.

Weaknesses: Overaged. Green football-playing instincts — slow digester still learning the game. Takes time to sort out what he sees. Too many tackles come down the field.

Future: A fast-flowing converted safety with the speed and cover skill to match up in the slot. Is still very new to the game and will require time to develop into a more complete, reactionary football player. However, he has the talent to contribute readily on special teams and could become a niche cover player if assignments are kept simple. Intriguing developmental project with versatility to contribute in multiple areas.

Draft projection: Late draftable pick.

LOLB- DLE-PRS **OWA ODIGHIZUWA**, #94 (Sr-5)

UCLA   ▶ GRADE: 5.64

Ht: 6-3 ½ | Wt: 267 | 40: 4.59 | Arm: 33 ¾ | Hand: 11

History: Name is pronounced "Oh-wuh-MAH-bay Oh-DIGGY-zoo-wuh." USA Today and Parade All-American who also lettered in basketball and track and field as an Oregon prep. Did not see the field in two of the first three games in 2010, but wound up starting 6-of-10 games played at defensive end and recording 10 tackles, four for loss and three sacks. Backed up Packers '13 first-rounder Datone Jones the next two seasons. Played all 14 games in '11 (one start), collecting 21-3-0 with a blocked kick. Played all 14 games in '12 (one start at nose tackle), notching 44-6-3 ½ with three batted passes. Sat out the '13 season after he needed two surgeries to repair a torn hip labrum. Returned to start all 13 games at five-technique in '14 — registered 61-11 ½-6 with five batted passes. Team captain graduated in June with a philosophy degree. Father, Peter, is serving three life sentences for a 2002 triple murder shooting at Appalachian School of Law.

Strengths: Looks like he was dropped down on earth by the football gods, with the most sculpted, picture-perfect physique of any player in the draft. Tied for the biggest hands (11 inches) of any player at the Combine and has very long arms. Very good strength to set the edge and cave the corner. Outstanding competitor — keeps working to come free. Flashes power and strike in his hands (see Stanford and USC). Explodes off the edge and can be a disruptive edge rusher. Good open-field tackler. Exceptional weight-room strength — can squat 600-plus pounds, bench-press 400-plus and power-clean 350 pounds. Has a 39-inch vertical jump. Outstanding personal and football character. Respected team leader.

Weaknesses: Unrefined pass rusher. Overanalyzes the game and does not consistently play fast or cut it lose. Will rise out of his stance to process what he is seeing, negating his natural speed, leverage and power. Does not have a great feel for blocking pressure or use his hands well to play off blocks. Struggles to hold the point and split the double team. Durability must be carefully evaluated following hip surgery that kept him out as a junior.

Future: Looks like the prototype of how a rush linebacker would be drawn up and might have as much physical talent in his body as any player in the draft. However, for as rare of an athletic specimen as he is, he is still developing as a football player. Has lined up inside and outside on the defensive line throughout his career and has intriguing traits to be tried as a pin-your-ears-back, fly-at-the-snap edge rusher. Was utilized as a base, power end in college and may fit best as a power-leverage left outside linebacker in a 30-front in the pros.

Draft projection: Second- to third-round pick.

LINEBACKERS

ROLB- DRE NATE ORCHARD, #8 (Sr-4)

UTAH ▶ GRADE: 5.57

Ht: 6-3 ¼ | Wt: 250 | 40: 4.84 | Arm: 33 ¾ | Hand: 10 ⅛

History: Full name is Napaa Lilo Fakahafua Orchard, but goes by Nate Orchard. Never knew his biological father. Grew up in Los Angeles (Inglewood), where he witnessed his older brother fail to maximize the opportunities sports provide, vowing to make the most of his own athletic prowess. When Nate was 10, moved to Utah to live with his brother's family, but with his mother unable to provide from California and his brother facing eviction, Nate asked to move in with the family of his AAU basketball coach. Believed that turning to Dave and Katherine Orchard — instead of moving back to California — was the only way to continue playing organized sports and avoid a life destined for prison or early death. The Orchards became Nate's legal guardians when he was 12. Had his first child, Lily, as a high school freshman (Lily was given up for adoption, but Nate remains part of her life and maintains a journal for her). Temporarily quit football during his sophomore year because he wasn't targeted enough as a receiver. Matured gradually and came to embrace the Orchards' support and stability. Married his high school sweetheart, Maegan, in 2013, at which time he asked to legally change his last name to Orchard (explained the decision in a TV interview with the Pac-12 Network, saying the Orchards "molded me, made me the man I am today. So I pay all my respects to them, and they're blood to me."). In August, the newlyweds named their daughter Katherine Mae in honor of Katherine Orchard, whom Nate said is the only person who never gave up on him. As a Utah prep, Nate earned four letters in football (receiver), basketball and track — captained the football and basketball teams and won state titles in both sports (had 10 receptions for a state-record 200 yards and three scores in the championship game). Was Utah's 4A MVP as a senior. Committed to the Utes as a sophomore. Upon arriving, was quickly converted from receiver to defense — saw action at defensive end, linebacker and on special teams as a true freshman in 2011, collecting four tackles, zero for loss and zero sacks with two batted passes in 13 games. Started 11-of-12 games at left end in '12, recording 48-8 ½-3 with four batted passes and two forced fumbles. Started all 12 games at LDE in '13, notching 50-9-3 ½ with a batted pass and three forced fumbles. At right end in '14, paced defensive linemen nationally in sacks — started all 13 games (including one at "Stud" linebacker) and piled up 84-21-18 ½ with three batted passes and three forced fumbles. Won the Hendricks Award and was named most outstanding defensive lineman in the Pac-12. Team captain. Medically excluded from lifting at the Combine because of a left shoulder injury. On pace to graduate with an economics degree in May. Will be a 22-year-old rookie.

Strengths: Has long arms. Flashes the ability to convert speed to power and play with violence in his hands — has a powerful six-inch punch. Understands how to create leverage getting underneath the pads of blockers and win inside. Notched 3 ½ sacks against Stanford, showing well vs. better competition. Very good motor. Plays hard with good effort and makes a lot of plays with second effort. Had a strong showing at the Senior Bowl and stood out in one-on-one's. Outstanding career production.

Weaknesses: Underpowered body. Lacks bulk strength to dig his cleats in the dirt and play big — is not a strong edge-setter. Can be engulfed when big-bodied maulers get their hands on him. Could stand to add more moves to his pass-rush arsenal. Has a 31 ½-inch vertical jump and is not an elite athlete. Lacks explosive edge rush potential. Did not look natural dropping in LB drills at the Combine.

Future: A quick, undersized, high-effort pass rusher who blossomed as a senior with newfound stability and motivation in his life. Is not the biggest, strongest or fastest, but will win a lot of matchups with savvy and effort and has the heart to become a solid producer in the pros.

Draft projection: Second- to third-round pick.

Scout's take: "(Orchard) is a good football player. He is a 3-4 rush backer. He is not an elite athlete. I think he'll fall in the third round. That's where his value is."

MLB DENZEL PERRYMAN, #52 (Sr-4)

MIAMI (FLA.) ▶ GRADE: 5.46

Ht: 5-10 ¾ | Wt: 236 | 40: 4.71 | Arm: 31 ⅞ | Hand: 9 ½

History: Has a one-year-old daughter named Ella Grace. Coral Gables native. As a true freshman in 2011, recorded 69 tackles, 6 ½ for loss and one sack with two forced fumbles in 12 games (three starts at weak-side linebacker, one at middle linebacker). Started 6-of-9 games played in '12 (five at MLB, one at WLB), totaling 64-6-0 with two pass breakups, one interception and one forced fumble. Missed three games with a high right ankle sprain. Started all 13 games at outside linebacker in '13, posting 108-5-1 ½ with three pass breakups and a forced fumble. Moved to middle linebacker in '14. Was a Butkus finalist, as well as the Hurricanes' defensive MVP and leading tackler for the second straight season, as he registered 110-9 ½-2 with five pass breakups, one interception and three forced fumbles in 13 starts. Team captain. Did not play in the Senior Bowl (abdominal strain). Did not perform shuttles at the Combine because of left hip flexor injury.

Strengths: Violent striker with knockout body power. Plays with intent and tackles with authority. Good base and balance. Takes direct paths to the ball and understands angles. Steps up and fills quickly. Extremely instinctive. Drives through contact. Good burst to close. Defensive tempo-setter. Alpha-leader in the locker room and trusted to run warm-ups and meetings. Very football smart.

Weaknesses: Tight in the hips and has some limitations in coverage with a height deficiency matching up against tight ends and average agility to carry backs on wheel routes. Could do a better job using his hands to protect his legs and play off blocks through congestion — is late to shoot his hands and does not have a lot of pop in his punch to separate. Man coverage deficiencies kept him off the field in some passing situations and third downs.

Future: Has drawn comparisons from scouts to Zach Thomas and Lance Briggs and has the twitch, hammer and instinct to carry on a strong tradition of Miami linebackers. However, he is a short-legged, short-strider with tight hips and coverage limitations that could restrict him to more of a two-down role.

Draft projection: Second- to third-round pick.

Scout's take: "Perryman is a stud. He has snap. Jiminy Christmas is he put together. He is just short, but he hits like a truck. He is athletic enough to be a "Will" — often that is where you wind up having to play guys with limited length. He is a little fire hydrant. He's strong enough to stay in the middle. He's a lot like Jon Beason."

ILB **HAYES PULLARD**, #10 (Sr-5)

USC   ▶ GRADE: 5.23

Ht: 6-0 ½ | Wt: 240 | 40: 4.74 | Arm: 31 ¼ | Hand: 9 ⅝

History: Parade All-American who also played basketball and ran track at Crenshaw High in Los Angeles, where he played with Chiefs 2014 fourth-rounder De'Anthony Thomas. Hayes lost his father during his junior year in high school. Was competing for playing time at strong-side linebacker as a true freshman in '10 before he hurt his knee during fall camp, had arthroscopic surgery and redshirted. In '12, started all 12 games at weak-side linebacker and produced 81 tackles, 6 ½ for loss and four sacks with two pass breakups and two forced fumbles. Started all 13 games in '12 (10 at WLB, three at middle linebacker), posting 107-8-2 with one pass breakup, one interception (27-yard touchdown) and one forced fumble. Played the "Mike" inside linebacker in a 5-2 defensive front in '13 — amassed 94-5 ½-0 with six pass breakups and one interception in 14 starts. Was the Trojans' leading tackler in '14 — anchored the "Mike" position in a 3-4 scheme, registering 95-5 ½-0 with eight pass breakups and one interception in 13 games (12 starts). Was suspended for the first half against Boston College after he was ejected for targeting against Stanford. Dealt with a knee bruise prior to the Utah contest. Two-year captain. Experienced inordinate coaching turnover — was originally recruited to USC by then-head coach Pete Carroll and assistant coach Ken Norton Jr., but they left for the Seattle Seahawks three weeks before Signing Day, and Hayes played under two head coaches, three defensive coordinators and four linebacker coaches. Graduated in May '14 with a degree in policy, planning and development.

Strengths: Active and energetic and flows to the ball. Is alert in coverage and showed improvement reading the quarterback and playing the ball as a senior. Can mirror backs and keep stride with tight ends. Experienced four-year starter. Versatile and has played in the middle and on the weak side.

Weaknesses: Short and has short arms. Instincts are off and eyes will require re-training. Does not play with much physicality or thump or drive his legs through contact. Lacks take-on strength. Average athlete. Has a 31-inch vertical jump. Falls off some tackles and could stand to become more secure.

Future: A compact, undersized, fluid-moving run-and-hit linebacker with the cover skill and range most ideally suited for a weak-side role in the pros.

Draft projection: Fourth- to fifth-round pick.

ROLB-DRE-PRS SHANE RAY, #56 (Jr-4)

MISSOURI ▶ GRADE: 6.32

Ht: 6-2 ⅝ | Wt: 245 | 40: 4.68 | Arm: 33 ⅛ | Hand: 9

History: Father, Wendell, also played at Missouri and was drafted by the Vikings in 1981. Shane lived in a part of Kansas City known as "Murder Factory." Won a state title as a junior. Redshirted in 2011. Appeared in 12 games in '12, recording 16-2 ½-0. Was used to spell starters Kony Ealy and Michael Sam in '13, contributing 39-9-4 ½ with two forced fumbles and a 73-yard fumble recovery score. His 11 pressures ranked second on the team. Was the Southeastern Conference Defensive Player of the Year in '14 when he set an Missouri single-season sacks record — registered 65-22 ½-14 ½ with a batted pass and three forced fumbles in 14 starts. Led the SEC in sacks and tackles for loss. Was ejected for targeting vs. Alabama in the SEC Championship game after drilling Blake Sims in the helmet after he had released the ball. Medically excluded from working out at the Combine because of right foot injury.

Strengths: Explosive take-off speed. Wins a very high percentage of one-on-one blocks from the inside and outside with his trademark dip-and-rip move. Very effective shooting gaps. Plays with a sense of urgency and is extremely competitive. Snaps his hips on contact and drives through ball carriers. Plays hard and competes. Has an edge to his game.

Weaknesses: Has a narrow lower body and a small frame, small hands and a sleigh back. Lacks bulk and bulk strength to hold the point of attack. Plays short-armed and gets engulfed in the run game. Struggles to set the edge — can be run at. Straight-linish and stiff. Not fluid changing directions and transitioning. Only a one-year starter. Is not built to be an every-down player.

Future: An explosive, undersized edge rusher ideally suited for a role as a wide nine-technique, where he could scream off the edge. Though he has deficiencies in the run game, Ray will make his living in the NFL terrorizing quarterbacks on third downs and will need to be creatively schemed to maximize his rush potential. Could warrant looks as a "Sam" or "Leo" linebacker in a 40 front.

Draft projection: First-round pick.

Scout's take: "I would love to have this guy if I had to play against Tom Brady and Aaron Rodgers and Peyton Manning with regularity. You have to use stunts and move (Ray) around — you can't expect him to line up and take on tackles are that are 6-7. I would bring him in on third downs and once in a while on first and second downs to keep them guessing. Don't tell me he has to go toe-to-toe and two-gap and play against a tight end in a closed area. If I were the GM and you did that to my player, I would fire the coach the next morning."

WLB EDMOND ROBINSON, #30 (Sr-5)

NEWBERRY ▶ GRADE: 5.00

Ht: 6-2 ⅝ | Wt: 245 | 40: 4.61 | Arm: 34 | Hand: 10 ¼

History: Also played basketball as a South Carolina prep. Redshirted in 2010 after breaking his right ankle during fall camp. Played outside linebacker in a 4-4 scheme for the Division-II Wolves. Played 10 games in '11, starting four, and was credited with 22 tackles, one for loss and zero sacks with one pass breakup and one forced fumble. Started 5-of-8 games played in '12, collecting 41-2 ½-0 with one pass breakup. Suffered a separated left shoulder against Wingate, causing him to miss three games. Started all 12 games in '13, posting 69-12-2 ½ with five pass breakups, one interception and one forced fumble. Led the team in tackles for the second straight season in '14 when he started 9-of-11 games and totaled 68-7 ½-0 with five pass breakups. Two-year captain. Was one of two Division II players invited to the combine, and is trying to become the first Newberry player drafted in 41 years. Graduated in December with a business administration degree.

Strengths: Has long arms and big hands. Very good size-speed ratio with excellent timed speed. Has a 37-inch vertical jump. Good playing range to chase the ball down across the field — good backside chase pursuit. Unselfish team player.

Weaknesses: Very leggy and underdeveloped lower body and limited lower-body power. Does not play strong or use his hands well to disengage. Lacks take-on strength and pop in his hands. Turns down some contact and left production on the field. Regularly faced lesser competition and did not rack up much production.

Future: A lean, leggy strider with unique speed, Robinson did not show well at the East-West Shrine game against better competition. Dropped 12 pounds from the Shrine game to the Combine, yet still lacks ideal fluidity and transitional skills to cover the slot in the pros. Developmental "Will" linebacker who must prove tough enough to handle NFL competition.

Draft projection: Late draftable pick.

Scout's take: "He's 6-2 and 250 pounds

and he is spending half his time outside the numbers covering a 5-9, 170-pound slot receiver. And he does a decent job, but I didn't understand why they did not play him more in the box or use him more as a pass rusher. You ask the coaches and they tell you he is their best cover guy. I think a lot of scouts will want to dismiss him because you don't get oohed and awed on tape against small-school competition, but that was the same reaction to the receiver (Corey Washington) there last year. Everyone said, 'he can't run, he can't catch, he won't play.' It didn't stop him from making the Giants' roster."

ILB **JAKE RYAN**, #47 (Sr-5)

MICHIGAN   ▶ GRADE: 5.52

Ht: 6-2 ⅝	Wt: 240	40: 4.66	Arm: 31	Hand: 9 ⅜

History: Prepped in Ohio. Redshirted in 2010. Started 11-of-13 games — 10 at "Sam" linebacker, one at defensive end — and recorded 37 tackles, 11 for loss and three forced fumbles. In '12, racked up 88-16-4 ½ with three pass breakups and four forced fumbles in 13 starts (11 at "Sam," two at DE). Tore his right ACL during '13 spring practice, but made it back to the field in Week Six — started 5-of-8 games played, managing 30-4 ½-0 with one pass breakup. Was the Wolverines' team MVP and leading tackler from the middle linebacker spot in '14, piling up 112-14-2 with three pass breakups, one interception and two forced fumbles in 12 starts. Two-time captain. Graduated in May '13 with a sociology degree. Was elected a team captain at the East-West Shrine game and the winner of the Pat Tillman Award, which is presented to the player who best exemplifies intelligence, sportsmanship and service.

Strengths: Has a good feel for the game. Outstanding football temperament. Versatile and scheme-diverse, having played inside and outside. Uses his hands well to shed and play off blocks. Good closing burst to the ball. Strong at the point of attack. Secure, wrap tackler. Field fast. Takes good angles. Plays relentlessly and motor is always revving. Very good production. Tough and competitive. Film junkie. Outstanding football character. Terrific work ethic. Experienced four-year starter. Respected team leader. Solid showing at the East-West Shrine game.

Weaknesses: Has short arms and at times gets velcroed on blocks. Has some athletic limitations that showed up in Combine drills. Is still honing his eyes from the inside after lining up outside the first three years in college. Has some tightness in his hips and is not fluid opening up and turning in coverage. Will overrun the ball. Loses some separation covering tight ends in man coverage.

Future: A throwback "Mike" linebacker with the grit, energy and attitude desired in the middle of a defense, Ryan could also line up at strong-side linebacker. Adapted well to playing off the line as a senior and has the focus, football character and mental toughness to walk into a starting job. May not be destined for the Hall of Fame, but has one of the highest floors of any player in the draft and could show more twitch next season in his second year removed from ACL surgery.

Draft projection: Second- to third-round pick.

Scout's take. "I love him. He was a standup outside linebacker before this year. Now he is playing behind the ball, which he has never done before, and he shows up. I feel very good about him as a football player. You know what you are getting. He's not a pass rusher to me. It took him a little time to figure it out, but you could see him get more comfortable later in the year the more he played inside. He has some upside. He'll keep getting better."

WLB **MARTRELL SPAIGHT**, #47 (Sr-4)

ARKANSAS   ▶ GRADE: 5.22

Ht: 5-11 ⅞	Wt: 236	40: 4.84	Arm: 32 ¾	Hand: 9 ⅛

History: Arkansas native. Missed his sophomore high-school season after he sliced his toe in a lawn mower accident. Was lightly recruited out of high school — was headed to Southern Oregon before he changed his mind and attended Coffeyville (Kan.) Community College, where he played weak-side linebacker. In 2011, recorded 121 tackles, 11 for loss and three sacks with two pass breakups in nine games. In '12, the Jayhawk Community College Conference Defensive Player of the Year was an All-American for the second time — totaled 127-14 ½-1 ½ with two pass breakups, one forced fumble and a blocked kick in nine games. Committed to Kansas State, but signed with Arkansas — his dream school — when new head coach Brett Bielema offered a scholarship. With the Razorbacks in '13, tallied 22-1-1 in nine games, including two starts (one at WLB, one at strong-side linebacker). Was the Southeastern Conference's leading tackler and Arkansas' co-MVP in '14 — started all 13 games at WLB and racked up 128-10 ½-1 with three pass breakups, one interception and two forced fumbles.

Strengths: Is quick in short areas. Plays

LINEBACKERS

145

with good leverage. Hits with some thump — good striking ability. Takes good angles. Fills fast and plays downhill. Secure wrap, open-field tackler. Good production. Film junkie. Good football intelligence — plays smart and anticipatory.

Weaknesses: Lacks ideal height and has small hands. Leaves his feet too early and lunges — side, lasso tackler. Does not have elite speed to the outside. Could be outmatched in man coverage.

Future: Emerged as Razorbacks' best defensive player in his first year as a full-time starter and has the eyes and anticipation to be a productive tackler. Could make a mark on special teams readily.

Draft projection: Late draftable pick.

OLB J.R. TAVAI, #58 (Sr-4)
USC   ▶ GRADE: 5.14

Ht: 6-1 ¾ | Wt: 249 | 40: 4.89 | Arm: 31 ½ | Hand: 9 ⅛

History: Full name is John Robert Tavai. Defensive lineman/fullback who also competed in track and field (throws) as a California prep. As a true freshman in 2011, was credited with four tackles, zero for loss and zero sacks in seven appearances as a reserve defensive tackle. Did not suit up against Minnesota (right hamstring) or UCLA (right ankle). Played 10 games in '12, starting three (two at defensive end, one at defensive tackle), and tallied 17-2 ½-0 with one batted pass. Missed three games after suffering an injury (undisclosed) against Syracuse in Week Two. Broke his left foot in the Sun Bowl against Georgia Tech. Played 12 games in '13, notching 56-8-3 ½ in 12 games — started eight of the final nine as a stand-up rush linebacker in place of the injured Morgan Breslin (learned the position in practice for the Week-Six contest against Arizona). Missed September games against Washington State and Boston College (right ankle). In '14, started 9-of-11 games played at rush linebacker and totaled 53-13 ½-7 with two batted passes and three forced fumbles. Did not play against Washington State and Cal (strained left knee ligaments). Won the Trojans' courage award. Opted not to run shuttles at the Combine. On pace to graduate with a sociology degree this spring.

Strengths: Versatile and has lined up at DT, DE and OLB during college career. Very good motor and hustle. Tough and will battle through injuries. Strong for his size and plays with physicality.

Weaknesses: Average athlete. Plays with a reckless abandon that often results in injury.

Falls into sack production that was flushed to him playing alongside Leonard Williams. Not a creative pass rusher. Has coverage limitations.

Future: Undersized, high-motor overachiever with the desire to emerge as a functional role player. Dropped from 270 pounds to play linebacker and has make-it qualities. A solid football player limited by a lack of size, length and foot speed. Late bloomer.

Draft projection: Late draftable pick.

Scout's take: "I don't question his instincts — just his foot speed. He moved from outside to inside and 'Will' to 'Mike' so it's a little bit different. He'll be a good role player."

WLB-RB-SS SHAQ THOMPSON, #7 (Jr-3)
WASHINGTON   ▶ GRADE: 5.78

Ht: 6-0 ⅛ | Wt: 228 | 40: 4.59 | Arm: 33 | Hand: 9 ½

History: Older brother, Syd'Quan, was a 2010 seventh-round pick of the Broncos (played 13 games before tearing his right Achilles tendon and being released prior to the '12 season). Shaq was a blue chipper out of Sacramento, where he was a Parade and USA Today All-American and a finalist for U.S. Army National Player of the Year. Despite not playing baseball from sixth grade until his senior season, was drafted by the Boston Red Sox in the 18th round of the 2012 MLB draft and played rookie-level ball that summer (went hitless in 39 at-bats with 37 strikeouts). Also was a sprinter and long jumper in high school. Was recruited by then-head coach Steve Sarkisian. As a true freshman in '12, was used in a nickel/hybrid role — started all 13 games and recorded 74 tackles, 8 ½ for loss and two sacks with three pass breakups, three interceptions and a blocked kick. Also returned two kickoffs for 46 yards (23.0-yard average) and two punts for eight yards (4.0). Started 12-of-13 games at outside linebacker in '13 (gave way to an extra defensive back against Washington State), posting 78-4-½ with four pass breakups and an 80-yard interception touchdown against Oregon State. Won the Paul Hornung Award (nation's most versatile player) in '14 — started all 14 games at weak inside linebacker, though he was deployed all over the field, and totaled 81-2 ½-1 with four pass breakups, a 36-yard INT TD, three forced fumbles and three fumble recovery scores covering 184 yards. Was also called upon to start a pair of games at running back (Colorado, UCLA) — rushed 61 times for 456 yards (7.5-yard average) and two touchdowns and had four receptions for 56 yards (14.0-

yard average).

Strengths: Very quick and active. Natural bender with outstanding closing burst and speed. Flies around the field and beelines to the ball. Shows good awareness in coverage. Plants and drives quickly. Explosive hitter. Chases runners down to the perimeter with ease and looks like he is moving at another gear. Great pursuit. Is effective slipping and avoiding blocks. Can break down in the open field and wrap up as a tackler. Very competitive. Has playmaking ability. Unique versatility as a two-way star and could warrant consideration as a running back. Is football smart. Outstanding special teams player.

Weaknesses: Lacks ideal bulk. Has small hands. Is a bit undisciplined and will run himself out of some plays freelancing. Can get engulfed by bigger blockers. Average take-on strength. Could stand to do a better job shooting his hands to get off blocks. Can lose a step trying to cover slot receivers. Does not time up the blitz very well and could do a better job slicing through gaps.

Future: An extremely athletic, run-and-hit linebacker with the closing speed, short-area burst and acceleration to make a living in a fast-flowing 40 front such as the Cowboys, Cardinals, Jets or Buccaneers. Fits a similar mold as former second-round picks Lavonte David (Tampa, 58th overall, 2012) and Darryl Washington (Arizona, 47th overall, 2010) and could be an immediate impact performer able to match up with backs, tight ends and slot receivers in a pass-first league. Could add additional value as a short-yardage running back and may receive some consideration as a projected strong safety.

Draft projection: Second-round pick.

Scout's take: "He's a "Will" linebacker. That's where he will play. He has a frame to get a little bigger. He was 224 (pounds) when I went through in the fall and will be 235 pounds before long. He has long arms and is strong and fast and instinctive. There will be a lot of discussions about where to play him, but I think he will wind up being a "Will"."

SLB-DRE DAVIS TULL, #90 (Sr-5)
TENNESSEE-CHATTANOOGA ▶ GRADE: 5.20
Ht: 6-2 ⅝ | Wt: 246 | 40: 4.57 | Arm: 31 ¼ | Hand: 9 ¾

History: Knoxville native suffered a broken right femur two games into his senior season in 2009. Redshirted in 2010. Started all 48 games of his career (played left end his first three seasons before switching to right end as a senior) — totaled 30 tackles, eight for loss

and five sacks with a forced fumble in '11 (11 games); 56-19-12 ½ with three forced fumbles in '12 (11 games); 52-15-9 with a batted pass and four forced fumbles in '13 (12 games); and 58-18-10 ½ with two forced fumbles and a blocked kick in '14 (14 games). Owns the Southern Conference career sacks record (37). Three-time AFCA All-American and two-time Buchanan Award finalist. Three-time SoCon Defensive Player of the Year — the first three-peat honoree since Dexter Coakley (1994-96). Team captain graduated in December with a degree in health and human performance. Did not run at the Combine because of a left hamstring strain.

Strengths: Quick to flatten down the line of scrimmage and make effort plays. Posted the best vertical jump (42 ½ inches) and broad jump (11 feet) of any defensive lineman at the Combine, indicating rare lower-body explosion. Outstanding weight-room worker — has a 400-pound power clean. Showed well vs. Tennessee. Football smart. Highly decorated, four-year starter and three-time, conference player of the Year. Extremely motivated and driven to succeed.

Weaknesses: Marginal size. Has very short arms and struggles matching up against offensive tackles. Struggles to press off blocks and create separation. Is seldom asked to drop into coverage. Drag-down tackler. Production is inflated from facing Southern Conference competition.

Future: A small-school college defensive end with rare explosive power that must prove he can translate it to the field against better competition. Projects to "Sam" linebacker in the pros. Developmental project capable of earning a roster spot and providing depth.

Draft projection: Fifth- to sixth-round pick.

Scout's take: "He'll be a late consideration for us in the sixth (round) as a 'Jack' linebacker."

SLB-LOLB MAX VALLES, #88 (Soph-3)
VIRGINIA ▶ GRADE: 5.34
Ht: 6-4 ⅝ | Wt: 251 | 40: 4.87 | Arm: 32 ⅝ | Hand: 9 ⅜

History: Played defensive end, safety and receiver as a prep in New Jersey, where he won three state titles. Also played baseball. Attended Fork Union (Va.) Military College in 2012. With the Cavaliers in '13, played the final 10 games, starting four (three at strong-side linebacker, one at weak-side linebacker) — recorded 23 tackles, 5 ½ for loss and four sacks with four pass breakups and a forced fumble. Started all 12 games at SLB in '14, notching 55-12 ½-9 with eight pass breakups,

LINEBACKERS

one interception and three forced fumbles. Did not lift at the Combine because of a left A/C (shoulder) sprain.

Strengths: Has a long, rangy frame with room to grow. Good hand-eye coordination — has a knack for batting balls at the line (see Louisville) and disrupting the quarterback's vision. Plays strong with good leverage and can control the edge. Natural knee-bender. Overpowers tight ends and does a good job disrupting their release. Has pass-rush ability. Very good production.

Weaknesses: See-and-go reactor who needs some time to digest what he sees. Lacks ideal foot speed and is not explosive off the edge. Much of his production is clear-view and comes from beating tight ends. Plays too much on his heels. Takes some plays off on the backside. Movement skill, change of direction and closing speed are average. Marginal transitional quickness. Did not follow direction well repeatedly through Combine drills and could require some additional reps to acclimate to an NFL playbook.

Future: Compares favorably to Steelers 1996 seventh-round pick Carlos Emmons, who enjoyed an 11-year career in the NFL, and has the length, agility and athletic ability to play a long time in the league.

Draft projection: Third- to fourth-round pick.

Scout's take: "I think he is a starting 'Sam' linebacker. I really like his length. The position is not as valuable as it once was with the way the league has changed to a pass-first league. That affects his value. I think he could start for us."

MLB ZACH VIGIL, #53 (Sr-5)

UTAH STATE ▶ GRADE: 5.05

| Ht: 6-2 | Wt: 236 | 40: 4.68 | Arm: 32 ½ | Hand: 10 |

History: Younger brother, Nick, is also a linebacker for the Aggies. Safety-receiver who also wrestled as a Utah prep. Walked on and redshirted in 2010. Appeared in four games in '11, recording four tackles, one for loss and zero sacks. Missed four games early in the season after having his right knee scoped and played through a torn rotator cuff injury in his left shoulder. Started all 41 games at inside linebacker the next three seasons — totaled 105-9 ½-5 ½ with one pass breakup, one forced fumble and one blocked kick in '12 (13 games); 124-12 ½-2 with one pass breakup, one interception and two forced fumbles in '13 (14 games); and team-high 156-20 ½-9 with four pass breakups, one

interception (35-yard touchdown) and a forced fumble in '14 (14 games). Had his left knee scoped following the '12 season. Was named Mountain West Defensive Player of the Year as a senior. Team captain. Graduated in spring '14 with a degree in interdisciplinary studies and is pursuing a second bachelor's degree in business administration.

Strengths: Good size and play speed. Plays with intensity and makes plays across the field. Is tough and will play through injuries. Very competitive. Experienced three-year starter. Good football intelligence. Makes all the line calls.

Weaknesses: Has a narrow bone structure. Durability needs to be examined closely after multiple knee and shoulder injuries — does not have a frame to hold up. Has not faced top competition.

Future: Former walk-on linebacker who ascended to become a decorated achiever and has the competitiveness and mental toughness ideally suited for a role on special teams.

Draft projection: Priority free agent.

Scout's take: "He doesn't look the part when you see his body in person, but he's a good football player."

SLB TONY WASHINGTON, #91 (Sr-5)

OREGON ▶ GRADE: 5.03

| Ht: 6-3 ⅝ | Wt: 247 | 40: 4.94 | Arm: 33 | Hand: 9 ½ |

History: Prepped in California. Lost his father to a heart attack in late August 2009. Redshirted in '10. A reserve/special-teams player in '11, tallied 18 tackles, one for loss and one sack with a pass breakup and a forced fumble in 10 games. Missed three games with a dislocated left elbow. Backed up Dolphins '13 No. 3 overall pick Dion Jordan in '12 — had 20-1-0 in 13 games (two starts at a defensive end/outside linebacker hybrid position). Started all 13 games at defensive end in '13, producing 60-12-7 ½ with four forced fumbles. Was deployed as an outside linebacker in '14 when he logged 60-11 ½-6 with two pass breakups and three forced fumbles in 15 starts. Showed up at East-West Shrine practices the day after the national championship game. Graduated as a double major in psychology and sociology.

Strengths: Good length and bend. Fluid mover with good agility, change of direction and short-area burst. Has a long second step to get up field and challenge the edge. Very book smart.

Weaknesses: Developing instincts. Is not a nuanced pass rusher. Posted the slowest 60-

yard shuttle (12.87 seconds) of any player at the Combine. Also bench-pressed only 17 reps, the fewest of any outside linebacker. Lacks weight-room strength and functional football-playing strength. Soft anchor — can be rooted out of holes. Measured 21.40 percent body fat at the Combine, the highest of any linebacker.

Future: A long-limbed, flexible, smooth pass rusher who looks like he is gliding coming off the edge. His game and body are still very underdeveloped but has enough pass-rush talent to warrant a developmental opportunity.

Draft projection: Priority free agent.

ILB **DAMIEN WILSON**, #5 (Sr-4)

MINNESOTA   ▶ GRADE: 5.09

Ht: 6-0 | Wt: 245 | 40: 4.79 | Arm: 33 ¾ | Hand: 9 ⅜

History: Cousin of Gophers running back David Cobb, also a member of the 2015 draft class. Wilson began his college career at Alcorn State — was the Braves' leading tackler in '11 when he started all 10 games at defensive end (wore jersey No. 90) and recorded a team-high 69 tackles, 16 for loss and 6 ½ sacks with a batted pass and two forced fumbles. In '12, was at Jones County Community College (Miss.), where he totaled 122-6-2 with two pass breakups and a blocked kick in nine games. With the Gophers in '13, started 12-of-13 games and produced 78-5 ½-1. Did not start against Indiana (nickel personnel). Suffered a right meniscus tear against Penn State, but had the benefit off an off week and did not miss a start. Was honored as the Gophers' Outstanding Defensive Player in '14 after logging a team-high 119-10 ½-4 with three pass breakups, one interception and one forced fumble. Was benched to begin the Iowa contest ("Gotta be on time, gotta do some things, so you always send a little message," explained head coach Jerry Kill on TwinCities.com). Sprained his left ankle against TCU.

Strengths: Good athlete. Very active and runs to the ball. Does a good job slipping blockers. Good playing range. Will face up ball carriers. Times up the blitz well and knifes into the backfield. Has a 37-inch vertical jump.

Weaknesses: Is not strong to take on blocks. Could stand to do a better job of using his hands to disengage and ward off cut blockers. Takes some bad angles and gets hung up in traffic. Football does not come natural and lacks discipline being on time and following assignments. Marginal football character. Is easily fooled by play-action. Limited cover skills.

Future: A more quick than fast, compact-built "Mike" linebacker ideally suited for a fast-flowing defense such as Dallas, Tampa Bay or Carolina. Needs to learn what it means to be a pro to make it.

Draft projection: Late draftable pick.

ILB-WLB **RAMIK WILSON**, #51 (Sr-4)

GEORGIA   ▶ GRADE: 5.36

Ht: 6-1 ¾ | Wt: 237 | 40: 4.74 | Arm: 33 | Hand: 10 ⅝

History: First name is pronounced "ra-MEEK." Prepped in Florida, where he played linebacker and tight end. As a true freshman in 2011, missed two spring practices following the death of his father. On the season, saw limited time in eight games and recorded four tackles, zero for loss and zero sacks. Appeared in 10 games in '12, collecting 6-1-0 with a forced fumble. In '13, led the Southeastern Conference in tackles — started 12-of-13 games at inside linebacker, racking up 133-11-4 with three pass breakups. Non-start was against Missouri (equipment issue). Dealt with a knee contusion leading up to the Vanderbilt contest. Sustained a concussion during '14 fall camp. In the fall, started all 13 games at the "Mike" linebacker, notching 110-7-2 with a pass breakup and a forced fumble. Opted not to run the 3-cone drill at the Combine.

Strengths: Very good size with big hands and long arms. Looks the part. Good playing range — covers a lot of ground. Matches up well with tight ends. Plays faster than his timed speed. Secure open-field tackler. Can slip and avoid. Very good career production. Measured only 4.6 percent body fat at the Combine, the lowest of any linebacker. Well-conditioned athlete. Three-year starter in the Southeastern Conference.

Weaknesses: Average core strength and striking power. Tight in the hips and loses phase in coverage. Gives ground to get off blocks. Does not play with consistent intensity or effort.

Future: A very productive college football player, Wilson should provide immediate help as a core special-teams player and sub-package defender and has starter-caliber traits to earn a job as a "Will" in either a 30 or 40 front.

Draft projection: Third- to fourth-round pick.

Scout's take: "He's not a smashmouth (hitter). They stack him over the tight end and use him a lot split outside over no. 2 in the slot. It sets up No. 52 to have more production. Wilson makes enough tackles in the box. I like him because of the versatility."

LINEBACKERS

DEFENSIVE BACKS

MICHIGAN STATE ATHLETICS

Nawrocki's TOP 10

1.	**TRAE WAYNES**
2.	Marcus Peters
3.	Landon Collins
4.	Kevin Johnson
5.	Jalen Collins
6.	Senquez Golson
7.	Doran Grant
8.	Byron Jones
9.	Ronald Darby
10.	Charles Gaines

FS ADRIAN AMOS, #4 (Sr-4)

PENN STATE   ▶ GRADE: 5.20

Ht: 6-0 ½ | Wt: 218 | 40: 4.49 | Arm: 32 ¼ | Hand: 9 ⅛

History: Baltimore native. As a true freshman in 2011, collected 13 tackles, four pass breakups and one interception in 13 games (one start). Started all 37 games the next three seasons — totaled 44-3-2 with 2 ½ tackles for loss and one-half sack in '12 (12 games); 50-5-1 with four tackles for loss and 2 ½ sacks in '13 (12 games); and 42-7-3 with 2 ½ tackles for loss in '14 (13 games). Graduated in 3 ½ years with a degree in recreation parks and tourism management. Opted not to lift at the Combine.

Strengths: Outstanding size-speed com–bination. Good movement skills, range and ball skills. Zone aware. Football smart. Has played cornerback and safety. Three-year starter.

Weaknesses: Lukewarm intensity. Incon–sistent run fits. Struggles to break down in the open field, come to balance and secure tackles. Pile inspector. Turns down contact. Grab-and-drag tackler.

Future: Possesses an intriguing size-speed combination and enough range to interchange on the back end, but lack of physicality, toughness and tackling prowess could limit opportunities.

Draft projection: Late draftable pick.

Scout's take: "I have him written as a practice-squad player. I don't like the way he tackles. He doesn't help us."

FS DETRICK BONNER, #8 (Sr-5)

VIRGINIA TECH   ▶ GRADE: 5.09

Ht: 5-11 ¾ | Wt: 207 | 40: 4.68 | Arm: 31 ¼ | Hand: 8 ⅞

History: First name is pronounced "DEE-trick." Prepped in Georgia. Redshirted in 2011. Played all 13 games in '11, starting

DEFENSIVE BACKS

three (two at cornerback, one at nickel), and tallied 27 tackles, four pass breakups and one interception with 3 ½ tackles for loss. Started all 39 games at free safety the next three seasons — totaled 60-10-1 with three tackles for loss and one sack in '12; 48-5-2 (one touchdown) with two tackles for loss in '13; and 72-4-1 with 6 ½ tackles for loss, 3 ½ sacks and one forced fumble in '14. Named team captain at East-West Shrine Game. Graduated with a degree in human development. Medically excluded from working out at the Combine and was not able to perform at Virginia Tech's pro day because of injuries to both feet.

Strengths: Looks the part. Handled a variety of assignments — was deployed at deep safety, in the box and over slot receivers. Fluid movement and transition. Covers ground and shows recovery speed. Takes the game seriously and works hard.

Weaknesses: Needs to get stronger. Smoother than sudden — not an explosive mover or striking tackler. Inconsistent open-field tackler. Questionable eyes — late to trigger. Loses phase in man coverage. Measured 15.1 percent body fat at the Combine.

Future: Versatile safety prospect whose cornerback background is evident in his movement skills, which enable him to be used as a sub-package player capable manning up inside receivers, working underneath/ in the box or blitzing the quarterback. Draft stock could be affected by missing out on the chance to work out for scouts. Versatility could help him earn a roster spot if he can prove his worth on special teams.

Draft projection: Late draftable pick.

Scout's take: "He looks like Tarzan, plays like Jane. He is body beautiful, but he can't tackle. He didn't have a lot of opportunities, but when he did, he was catching ghosts."

SS IBRAHEIM CAMPBELL, #24 (Sr-5)

NORTHWESTERN ▶ GRADE: 5.29

Ht: 5-11 ⅜ | Wt: 208 | 40: 4.56 | Arm: 30 ⅜ | Hand: 10 ¼

History: First name is pronounced "E-bruh-heem." Three older brothers played college football. Safety-running back that also ran track as Pennsylvania prep. Redshirted in 2010. Started 12-of-13 games at strong safety in '11, producing 100-4-2 with 3 ½ tackles for loss. Was benched against Penn State. Started all 25 games at SS the next two seasons — totaled 89-12-2 with one-half tackle for loss and two forced fumbles

in '12; and 73-5-4 with 2 ½ tackles for loss and one sack in '13. Suffered a broken jaw during '14 spring practice. In the fall, started all eight games played at SS, managing 54-3-3 with one tackle for loss. Missed four mid-season games with a hamstring injury. Team captain graduated with an economics degree. Medically excluded from working out at the Combine because of a left hamstring injury.

Strengths: Good muscularity. Reads and reacts quickly. Controlled mover who plays with balance. Good agility. Usually initiates — uncoils on contact. Physical player with a healthy disregard for his body. Opportunistic seeking turnovers — flashes playmaking ability. Measured only 4.5 percent body fat. Has special-teams experience. Intelligent player who studies the game. Solid character. Loves football. Does a lot of extras. Film junkie. Experienced, four-year starter.

Weaknesses: Short arms. Tight hips. Builds to top speed. Not an explosive athlete. Below-average leaping ability. Limited man-coverage skills. Lacks speed and burst to recover. Durability could be a continued issue given body tightness and history of nagging injuries. Tackle production diminished every season.

Future: Good-sized, assignment-sound, aggressive box safety with the smarts, physicality and special-teams ability to stick as a no. 3 or no. 4 safety. Has the toughness and physicality to eventually earn a starting job in the box.

Draft projection: Fourth- to fifth-round pick.

Scout's take: "I think the safety does some good things, but he's a straight-line guy. He is smart as a whip, takes really good angles and understands the game."

RCB ALEX CARTER, #25 (Jr-3)

STANFORD ▶ GRADE: 5.38

Ht: 6-0 ⅛ | Wt: 196 | 40: 4.52 | Arm: 32 ⅛ | Hand: 9 ⅛

History: Has plans to marry Ariana Alston in July. Father, Tom, was a 1993 Washington Redskins first-round pick and a nine-year NFL cornerback with the Redskins, Bears and Bengals (1993-2001). Alex was a Parade All-American as a prep in Virginia, where he won a state championship and was the Gatorade Player of the Year. Also ran track and was a finalist for the Watkins Award, presented to the nation's top African-American male high school scholar athlete. Lost his sister, Cameron, to diabetes during his senior year. Played all 14 games as a true freshman in

'12, earning starts at right cornerback the final eight weeks — recorded 46 tackles, one pass breakup and zero interceptions with three tackles for loss and three forced fumbles. Added five kickoff returns for 110 yards (22.0-yard average). Started 12-of-13 games in '13, logging 59-7-1 with two tackles for loss and one forced fumble. Did not start against California (concussion). Missed '14 spring practice with a hip injury. Was cleared to practice just weeks before the season opener against UC Davis (lone non-start), but posted 41-9-1 with one forced fumble in 13 games (12 starts at left cornerback).

Strengths: Looks the part with excellent size, including the longest wingspan (79 5/8 inches) of any defensive back at the Combine. Has a 40-inch vertical. Good press strength. Uses his length to play off blocks. Strong in run support. Measured only 4.4 percent body fat. Has NFL bloodlines.

Weaknesses: Long strider with some hip tightness that negates transitional quickness. Gives up separation at the break point, loses phase downfield and struggles with his back to the ball. Limited ball skills. Not a playmaker — recorded two interceptions in three seasons. Will shoot low and miss some tackles in space.

Future: Long-armed press corner best utilized to the boundary. Is likely to be overdrafted for measurables, yet can function very well as a short-area, zone corner.

Draft projection: Third- to fourth-round pick.

Scout's take: "Carter has no ball skills or instincts, and his hands are terrible. Someone will get infatuated with his size and take him in the third round because of the way he can run in a straight line. I'm not sure he has any career interceptions."

RCB DONALD CELISCAR, #34 (Sr-4)
WESTERN MICHIGAN ▶ GRADE: 5.10
Ht: 5-10 ⅞ | Wt: 194 | 40: 4.59 | Arm: 31 ⅜ | Hand: 9 ¼

History: Born in Haiti and moved to the United States when he was eight. Prepped in Florida, and was recruited by then-head coach Bill Cubit's staff. Played 11 games as a true freshman in 2011, starting the final four (three at field corner, one at nickel), and recorded 45 tackles, five pass breakups and one interception with two forced fumbles. Was deployed as a rover back in '12 when he registered 79-14-2 with three tackles for loss, one forced fumble and a safety. In '13, started 11-of-12 games at FCB, collecting 60-9-3.

Did not start against Eastern Michigan. Tied for the national lead with 21 passes defended in '14 — tallied 63-17-4 with one sack in 13 starts. Sustained a concussion in the season opener against Purdue. Also had 23 career kickoff returns for 489 yards (21.2-yard average). Did not lift at the Combine because of right pectoral surgery and did not perform the vertical jump or shuttles because of a left knee injury.

Strengths: Very good size. Strong at the line of scrimmage to re-route receivers. Anticipatory and with good route recognition. Will lay out and sacrifice his body to make plays (also did during Combine drills). Excellent ball production with 45 career pass breakups and 10 interceptions. Plays bigger than his size and tackles well.

Weaknesses: Plays on his heels. Below-average speed — short-stepper who covers little ground in his pedal. Hip tightness shows in transition. Struggles to mirror quicker receivers and can be late out of breaks. Registered the slowest 10-yard split (1.69 seconds) of any defensive back at the Combine and lacks the short-area quickness to keep pace with NFL receivers. Measured 13.2 percent body fat at the Combine and could stand to improve conditioning. Did not regularly face top competition.

Future: A better football player than athlete, Celiscar could fend for a job as a short-area zone corner where some of his athletic limitations could be concealed and he could maximize his ball skills.

Draft projection: Priority free agent.

NCB IMOAN CLAIBORNE, #18 (Sr-5)
NORTHWESTERN STATE ▶ GRADE: 5.24
Ht: 5-9 ⅝ | Wt: 189 | 40: 4.50e | Arm: 30 | Hand: 9 ⅛

History: Has a daughter (Addison) with his fiancée Ashlee England, and the couple plans to marry in June. As a Louisiana prep, only played two years of football (played receiver until his senior season, when he was deployed as a rover defender who shadowed the offense's best player). Also earned all-state recognition as a kick returner and ran track. Saw limited action in five games in 2010. Redshirted in '11 while on academic suspension (poor grades). Started 6-of-9 games played at right cornerback in '12, recording 18-2-1 (28-yard touchdown). Started 10 of 11 games at RCB again in '13, notching 36-3-2, missing the Central Arkansas game. Started 11 games at RCB spot in '14, recording 46-7-4 with two tackles for loss and a sack. Did not play vs.

McNeese State.

Strengths: Feisty and confident cover man – aggressive attacking the ball in the air. Very good athlete with fluid transitional skill out of his breaks. Clings to receivers in man coverage and is alert in zones. Showed well at the Senior Bowl matching up against top competition.

Weaknesses: Average size. Will struggle matching up with bigger receivers outside and could be challenged to support in the run game. Can be overaggressive jumping the ball and play with a bit of a riverboat gambler mentality.

Future: Quick, light-footed, athletic nickel corner with the cover skill to earn a job in the slot and contribute on special teams.

Draft projection: Fifth- to sixth-round pick.

Scout's take: "He had a real good week at the Senior Bowl. He was not intimidated at all. He's a good little football player."

NCB **JUSTIN COLEMAN**, #27 (Sr-4)

TENNESSEE ▶ GRADE: 5.11

Ht: 5-10 ⅝ | Wt: 185 | 40: 4.54 | Arm: 31 ¼ | Hand: 9 ⅜

History: Also ran track as a Georgia prep. Played all 12 games as a true freshman in 2011, starting four — first two at left cornerback and two November games at right cornerback — and recorded 10 tackles, two pass breakups and zero interceptions. Played all 12 games in '12, starting the final nine at strong safety, and totaled 59-3-0 with 3 ½ tackles for loss. Back at corner in '13, started all 12 games and logged 46-7-1 with one tackle for loss. Started all 13 games in '14 (seven at nickel, six at CB), posting 42-5-4 with four tackles for loss. Graduated in December with a degree in Communication Studies.

Strengths: Posted the quickest three-cone drill time (6.61 seconds) of any player at the Combine. Good zone awareness. Willing in run support — quick to read and react, comes to balance and takes down receivers in one-on-one situations. Showed well at the East-West Shrine Game.

Weaknesses: Lacks top-end speed to carry receivers down the field on the outside. Misses open-field tackles and needs to become more dependable filling. Struggles to keep pace with burners outside.

Future: Quick, agile, instinctive, short-area zone cornerback with a chance to fend for a job as a nickel or dime defender.

Draft projection: Late draftable pick.

Scout's take: "He is a nickel. I thought he had too many limitations to draft him. Some (scouts) in our room disagreed with me."

LCB **JALEN COLLINS**, #32 (Jr-4)

LSU ▶ GRADE: 5.97

Ht: 6-1 ½ | Wt: 203 | 40: 4.49 | Arm: 32 ⅛ | Hand: 9 ⅜

History: Prepped in Mississippi. Redshirted in 2011. Played all 13 games in '12 (one start as nickel back), recording 30 tackles, six pass breakups and two interceptions. Played all 13 games in '13 (started first two at right cornerback), tallying 22-2-0. In '14, started 7-of-13 games — first three and final four at left cornerback — and collected 38-17-1 with three tackles for loss. Opted not to lift at the Combine. Had foot surgery following the Combine and was not able to work out before the draft.

Strengths: Excellent length and overall size. Very good recovery speed and closing burst (see Wisconsin, chasing down Melvin Gordon). Solid technician — good footwork and hand placement in press coverage. Uses his long arms, body length and leaping ability to take away passing lanes. Strong tackler. Matched up well vs. Amari Cooper. Smart, mature and hard working. Served as a gunner on special teams.

Weaknesses: High-hipped and a bit tight in transition. Questionable ball skills. Marginal hands were evident in gauntlet drill at the Combine, where he dropped three balls and let several into his body. Could become more patient with the jam and be more physical supporting the run. Was never a full-time starter and has only 10 career starts.

Future: A rangy, long-limbed press corner who was relegated to a no. 3 cornerback role in a talented secondary early in the season, yet possesses the length, short-area burst and press skills to earn a job as a starter in the pros.

Draft projection: Top-50 pick.

Scout's take: "I don't like drafting players that don't start. Collins is a big corner that can run. The history of LSU cornerbacks has been pretty good, but it has started to fade lately. Patrick Peterson has been very good. Morris Claiborne has not. I wish (Collins) tackled better."

SS **LANDON COLLINS**, #26 (Jr-3)

ALABAMA ▶ GRADE: 6.23

Ht: 6-0 | Wt: 228 | 40: 4.48 | Arm: 31 ½ | Hand: 9 ⅜

History: Safety-running back who garnered Parade and USA Today All-American honors coming out of New Orleans, where he was an elite recruit. As a true freshman in 2012, backed up Packers 2014 first-rounder Ha-

Ha Clinton-Dix, recording 17 tackles, zero pass breakups and zero interceptions with a blocked kick in 14 games. Started 9-of-13 games in '13 (six at strong safety, three as dime defender) — posted 70-6-2 (one touchdown) with four tackles for loss and two forced fumbles, as he moved into the starting lineup when Vinnie Sunseri was injured. Was a finalist for the Nagurski, Thorpe and Lott IMPACT awards in '14 — started all 14 games at strong safety and registered a team-high 103-7-3 with 4 ½ tackles for loss and one forced fumble. Also returned three kickoffs for 55 yards (18.3-yard average). Dealt with cramps against Tennessee. Hurt his right shoulder against Ohio State in the Sugar Bowl. Team captain. Opted not to lift at the Combine (shoulder).

Strengths: Outstanding straight-line speed. Fills quickly and is strong on contact — attacks like a linebacker in the box and is an enforcer in the run game. Very tough and competitive. Outstanding special teams performer. Efficient matching up with backs and tight ends in man coverage. Good zone instincts to read the quarterback and make plays on the ball in front of him.

Weaknesses: Bulked up and carried too much weight as a junior, negating lateral agility and reactive quickness. Not a natural catcher. Hip tightness showed up at the Combine in his inability to transition quickly. Recorded the slowest three-cone drill time (7.41 seconds) of any defensive back at the Combine. Measured 12.8 percent body fat and could stand to improve conditioning. Marginal pro day workout — scouts said he looked heavy and out of shape.

Future: Bulked up as a junior and lost some of the range and burst he displayed in 2013. Will make the most impact in the box filling and dropping the hammer in the run game. Has the toughness and physicality to become an immediate starter in the pros, though would be best playing close to the line of scrimmage. Could stand to benefit from shedding some weight and improving his agility.

Draft projection: First-round pick.

Scout's take: "The player who has the most pub who I was not oohed and awed by is Landon Collins. He will come down and run the alleys and be a really good support player. He has some physicality to him. In coverage, he is okay. I thought he was supposed to be a 'wow'. I didn't see a 'wow'. To me, wow's jump off tape when you are not looking for

Landon Collins

them. I think I saw one pick in the games I did. He had some good, solid tackles."

FS-CB JUSTIN COX, #9 (Jr-4)
MISSISSIPPI STATE ▶ GRADE: 5.20

Ht: 6-0 ⅝	Wt: 191	40: 4.32	Arm: 31 ¼	Hand: 9

History: Mississippi native who won a pair of state titles and was a finalist for the state's Mr. Football award. Spent two years at East Mississippi Community College, where he won a NJCAA national championship in 2011 — recorded 67 tackles, nine pass breakups and five interceptions with eight tackles for loss and one sack. In '12, tallied 52-9-6 with five tackles for loss in 10 games. With the Bulldogs in '13, notched 31-3-1 with one-half tackle for loss in 13 games (one start at right cornerback). Moved to free safety in '14 when he started 8-of-9 games played and had 21-4-1 with one-half tackle for loss. Did not play against South Alabama and did not start against LSU while dealing with a hamstring injury. Was suspended for the final three games of the season — was arrested in November and charged with burglary of a dwelling and aggravated domestic violence. Police responded to a burglary at a Starkville apartment complex in the wee hours, at which time they found a female victim with a head injury. Ultimately the domestic violence charge was dropped at the request of the victim, as Cox pled guilty to a misdemeanor charge of trespassing.

Strengths: Very good length. Outstanding straight-line speed. Explosive out of his speed turns with terrific closing burst.

Weaknesses: Tends to play tall and is too upright in his pedal, negating some transitional quickness. Does not have a balanced pedal or come out of his breaks smoothly. Tweener – has a narrow frame for a safety and is very tight for a cornerback. Has a history of off-field issues that require closer scrutiny.

Future: A lean, speedy defensive back with corner-safety versatility who could be most ideally suited for a role as a press-man corner in the pros. Will need to make an impact on special teams and could stick as a No. 4 or No. 5 corner.

Draft projection: Late draftable pick.

LCB RONALD DARBY, #3 (Jr-3)

FLORIDA STATE ▶ GRADE: 5.74

Ht: 5 10 ⅝ | Wt: 193 | 40: 4.38 | Arm: 31 ⅜ | Hand: 8 ⅝

History: Prepped in Maryland, where he starred on the field and the track — highly recruited USA Today All-American who played six positions as a senior. Won state championships in the 100 and 200 meters, and was a member of the gold medal-winning USA medley relay team at the 2011 World Youth Championships. Decommitted from Notre Dame to sign with FSU. Was the Atlantic Coast Conference Defensive Rookie of the Year in '12 when he recorded 22 tackles, eight pass breakups and zero interceptions with one forced fumble in 14 appearances. Had sports hernia surgery after the season. Started 9-of-14 games for the national champions in '13, collecting 14-4-2. Dealt with a lingering hamstring pull in '14 when he started all 14 games, posting 43-4-0 with one tackle for loss and one forced fumble. Suffered an arm injury against Georgia Tech.

Strengths: Excellent straight-line speed and striking ability. Quick to support the run. Good man and man-off coverage skills. Has a 41 ½-inch vertical jump. Good short-area quickness, acceleration and burst — anticipates well with good route pattern recognition and at times will hit break points jumping routes before receivers. Outstanding short-area quickness — recorded a blazing 1.50-second 10-yard split at the Combine. Extremely well-conditioned athlete — measured only 4 percent body fat at the Combine, the lowest of any defensive back. Smart and football smart.

Weaknesses: Average size with small hands. Has a tendency to clutch and grab. Stays blocked too long and could be more physical and eager in run support. Shows some tightness in transition. Though he has not been charged with any crimes and was cleared of any wrongdoing in Jameis Winston's sexual assault case, he was at the scene and was a passenger in the car for P.J. Williams' hit-and-run accident — has received some negative marks from scouts for personal character.

Future: A fast, straight-linish, explosive press-man cover corner with starter-caliber traits, Darby was overshadowed by teammate P.J. Williams in college, yet brings a more pro-ready skill set and should be able to step into a starting lineup readily.

Draft projection: Second- to third-round pick.

Scout's take: "He is physical. He can play press coverage. He has good long speed. He is not as sudden or good to read and react. He will make a lot of great flash plays. ... There are some negatives on his character, but nothing criminal. He's always around trouble, but never gets pinched himself."

NCB-PR QUANDRE DIGGS, #6 (Sr-4)

TEXAS ▶ GRADE: 5.23

Ht: 5-9 ⅛ | Wt: 196 | 40: 4.53 | Arm: 29 ⅝ | Hand: 9 ⅝

History: Brother, Quentin Jammer, starred as a cornerback at Texas before being drafted fifth overall in 2002 and having a 12-year NFL career, 11 with the Chargers (2002-13). Also ran track and played basketball as a prep in Texas, where he produced all over the field in four varsity seasons. Totaled 8,265 all-purpose yards and 83 touchdowns; 237 tackles, 52 pass breakups and 10 interceptions (four TDs) with 19 tackles for loss, six sacks, 11 forced fumbles and seven blocked kicks; and 11 kick return scores. Was the Big 12 Defensive Freshman of the Year in 2011 — started 11-of-13 games and recorded 51-15-4 with four tackles for loss and two forced fumbles. Started all 13 games in '12, logging 59-7-4 with four tackles for loss and one sack. Started 12-of-13 games in '13 — seven at CB, five at nickel — and had 58-10-0 with four tackles for loss, 2 ½ sacks and one forced fumble. Did not start against Kansas State. Started all 13 games in '14 — eight at nickel, five at CB — and produced 73-5-3 with five tackles for loss, two sacks and one forced fumble. For his career, returned 29 punts for 326 yards (11.2-yard average) and 20 kickoffs for 392 yards (19.6). Graduated in December with a degree in physical culture and sports (with a minor in social work).

Strengths: Very experienced, four-year starter with good instincts, eyes and anticipation. Quick-footed and agile. Balanced in his pedal. Sees the quarterback and the ball and is aggressive playing it in front of him. Bench-pressed 17 reps at the Combine and has good functional press strength. Solid, wrap tackler. Has NFL pedigree.

Weaknesses: Short and very short-armed and gets stuck on blocks too much. Average speed — is challenged to keep stride with receivers vertically. Lacks home-run speed in the return game and can be tracked down from behind.

Future: Thickly built, squatty Cover 2 corner with the toughness desired in the slot. Lacks the size and speed to match up with outside receivers and the top-end speed desired in the return game, yet could still factor on special teams.

Draft projection: Late draftable pick.

Scout's take: "He's short. He's barely 5-10. He is a nickel. He gets beat outside a lot."

NCB LORENZO DOSS, #6 (Jr-3)
TULANE ► GRADE: 5.34
Ht: 5-10 ⅝ | Wt: 182 | 40: 4.49 | Arm: 29 ¾ | Hand: 9

History: Brother, Lee, played receiver at Southern before signing with the Redskins as an undrafted free agent and spending time on the Browns' practice squad last year. Lorenzo was a high school receiver who also played baseball and ran track as a New Orleans prep. Chose Tulane over offers from Kansas State, among others, because he desired to remain close to home. Manned right cornerback for the Green Wave. As a true freshman in 2012, started 9-of-12 games and tallied 44-2-5. Started all 15 games the next two seasons — totaled 34-9-7 (two touchdowns) with 1 ½ tackles for loss in '13 (13 games); and 48-9-3 with five tackles for loss and one sack in '14 (12 games). Suffered a hyperextended elbow against Texas-San Antonio as sophomore. Missed a week during '14 spring practice with a minor knee injury. Also ran track at

Tulane, competing in the 100 meters, 4X100 and 4X400. Ran a 10.81 100 meters in April '14. Will be a 21-year-old rookie.

Strengths: Very good eyes to see receivers and the quarterback and anticipate where the ball will be thrown. Outstanding ball skills and hands. Natural interceptor, as confirmed at the Combine when he caught the ball with ease in drills. Recorded 15 interceptions in three seasons. Efficient in his movement and explodes out of breaks. Smart, tough and hard working at his craft.

Weaknesses: Has short arms and small hands. Does not play physical and struggles to match up against size. Bench-pressed only 9 reps at the Combine. Can be overaggressive at times playing the ball, loose positioning and get beat. Especially vulnerable to double moves. Has a 33 ½-inch vertical jump — is not an elite athlete. Limited in run support and Durability could be more concerning given lack of size.

Future: Lean, active, competitive man cover corner who flashed playmaking ability during his career and has the twitch and feistiness to contribute readily in sub-packages.

Draft projection: Fourth- to fifth-round pick.

Scout's take: "He is a very wiry guy. He is only 180 pounds. I'm not sure how well he'll hold up at our level."

FS KURTIS DRUMMOND, #27 (Sr-5)
MICHIGAN STATE ► GRADE: 5.24
Ht: 6-0 ⅝ | Wt: 208 | 40: 4.64 | Arm: 32 ¼ | Hand: 10 ⅜

History: Safety-receiver who also played basketball as an Ohio prep. Redshirted in 2010 after having surgery to repair a torn labrum. In '11, was a backup free safety to Trenton Robinson (Redskins) and contributed as a nickel back — recorded 17-0-2 with one sack and one forced fumble in 12 games (started against Georgia in the Outback Bowl). Missed two November contests (concussion). Played all 13 games in '12, starting the final seven at FS when Jairus Jones was lost for the season — notched 53-4-2 with 4 ½ tackles for loss and one forced fumble. Sustained a concussion and a stinger against Nebraska. Started all 14 games at FS in '13, producing 91-6-4 (one touchdown) with 3 ½ tackles for loss and one forced fumble. Was the Big Ten Defensive Back of the Year in '14 after registering a team-high 72-11-4 with five tackles for loss in 13 starts at FS. Team captain graduated in December with a psychology degree. Did not lift at the

Combine because of right shoulder surgery.

Strengths: Good size with long arms and big hands. Very good ball skills to range off the hash and make plays to the sideline. Outstanding hands, as he confirmed at the Combine in the gauntlet drill. Recorded a 39 ½-inch vertical jump at the Combine, best among all safeties, and also had the biggest hands of any defensive back at the event. Plays the ball well in front of him.

Weaknesses: Does not play to his size and misses too many tackles in the open-field. Pile inspector with a passive approach to the ball. Does not like to be the first at the scene. Too leggy, resulting in extra steps, slow foot turnover and too much wasted motion. Takes long strides and has marginal transitional quickness. Marginal timed speed, clocking as high as 4.71 seconds in the 40-yard dash. Recorded a 4.35-second short shuttle time at the Combine, the slowest of any free safety and it showed up in speed turns at the event when his arms flailed and he stumbled in his turns.

Future: Ballhawking back-end defender lacking the toughness, physicality and secure tackling desired in the box and the range desired in center field. Will need to show more willingness in run support and improve as a tackler to be more than a spot backup. Temperament may not be suitable for special teams.

Draft projection: Fourth- to fifth-round pick.

Scout's take: "I went to practice, and he looks the part and has length. You can double-move him all day, though. He gets double-moved to death. He takes poor angles to the ball. ...He grabbed an interception and had a whole wall set up to score and he cut back into traffic. I shut the tape off after I saw it. I was done."

NCB **IFO EKPRE-OLOMU**, #14 (Sr-4)

OREGON ▶ GRADE: 5.37X

Ht: 5-9 ⅛ | Wt: 192 | 40: 4.50e | Arm: 30 ⅞ | Hand: 9 ⅝

History: Pronounced "ee-fo eck-pray-olo-moo." Born to Nigerian parents. Prepped in California, where he played safety and running back. Hurt his right shoulder during an October 2010 contest. Recruited by then-head coach Chip Kelly. As a true freshman in '11, recorded 33 tackles, three pass breakups and two interceptions with 3 ½ tackles for loss and two sacks in 14 games (two starts at right cornerback). Started all 13 games at RCB in '12, producing 63-16-4 (one touchdown) with six forced fumbles. Played with torn left thumb

ligament then had off-season surgery to repair a torn right shoulder. Started all 13 games at RCB in '13, logging 84-3-0 with five tackles for loss and one forced fumble. In '14, posted 63-9-2 with one tackle for loss and one forced fumble in 13 starts before suffering a torn left ACL. Also had seven career punt returns for 51 yards (7.4-yard average). Was medically excluded from Combine workouts (knee). Graduated with a social science degree.

Strengths: Very good athlete with loose hips and good quickness, agility and balance. Is tough and physical for his size and more than willing to support the run. Plays physical at the line disrupting the release of receivers. Good eyes and awareness to sort out combo routes and switch off receivers passing through his zone. Good production. Carries a swagger.

Weaknesses: Small-framed. Will have difficulty matching up with the size of NFL receivers on the outside and be height-challenged in man coverage. Is coming off a serious knee injury and will not be fully recovered in time for training camp. Long-term durability is concerning given his size and aggressive style of play.

Future: An instinctive, undersized ballhawk who could prove to be a tremendous value pick once he returns to full health. A second-round talent likely to last until the fourth round due to injury, Ekpre-Olomu is most ideally suited to play in the slot, where he has starter potential when healthy. Should contribute readily on special teams.

Draft projection: Third- to fourth-round pick.

Scout's take: "He is a good corner, but he plays small. He really struggles in the run game. He was wearing a walking boot in practice (when I was just there). He is just small-boned. Maybe I am being hard on him, but I'm worried about how he will hold up. If you are a 5-foot-9 corner when all is said and done, you better be flying. ... Everyone in the league is going to big receivers ... . Small corners get beat up."

FS **DURELL ESKRIDGE**, #3 (Jr-4)

SYRACUSE ▶ GRADE: 5.09X

Ht: 6-2 ⅞ | Wt: 208 | 40: 4.59 | Arm: 32 ⅜ | Hand: 9 ⅝

History: Has a daughter named Khloe. Grew up in gang- and drug-infested part of Miami, where he developed a tight bond with Devonta Freeman (Falcons). Safety-receiver won a state championship at Miami Central. Redshirted in 2011 when an NCAA eligibility issue kept him off the field. Appeared in 12 games in '12, recording 36 tackles, three pass breakups and zero interceptions with three tackles for loss, two sacks, one forced fumble and one blocked kick. Had surgery in spring '13 to repair a fractured right wrist and torn ligament in his ring finger. Played with a cast in the fall when he started all 12 games played at free safety and produced a team-high 78-1-4 with four tackles for loss, one-half sack and one forced fumble. Sustained concussions against Maryland and Boston College and did not play against Minnesota in the Texas Bowl. Underwent off-season hernia surgery. In '14, started all 12 games at FS and totaled 68-3-1. Did not lift at the Combine because of right shoulder surgery.

Strengths: Very good body and arm length, measuring the tallest of any defensive back at the Combine. Has a good feel for the game and takes good angles. Has enough length and range to get protect the top of the field.

Weaknesses: Is a tick late to diagnose and a step late to make plays on the ball. Tends to pedal tall and rise in transition. Recorded the lowest vertical jump (31 inches) of any defensive back at the Combine. Not a reliable, open-field tackler. Tends to lead with his helmet and has had multiple concussions during his career. Long-term durability is a concern.

Future: A tall, back-end safety that does not show desirable feet, eyes or anticipation for the position. The greatest concern facing teams, however, is his inability to stay healthy, with a scary concussion history. Medical concerns could leave him undrafted and forced to win a roster spot with little upright risk.

Draft projection: Priority free agent.

Scout's take: "The medical concerns will be too big of an issue for us to deal with him. Concussions are a scary subject right now, especially when you're talking about multiple. I don't know many teams that want to deal with brain issues right now."

NCB-KR CHARLES GAINES, #3 (Jr-4)
LOUISVILLE ▶ GRADE: 5.72
Ht: 5-9 ⅞ | Wt: 180 | 40: 4.38 | Arm: 31 ⅜ | Hand: 8 ¾

History: Played receiver and defensive back at Miami Central, where he won a state championship. Missed part of his junior season with a shoulder injury. Recruited as a receiver. Had shoulder surgery and redshirted in 2011. Appeared in seven games in '12, recording 11 receptions for 172 yards (15.6-yard average) and one touchdown. Switched to cornerback in '13 — started

6-of-13 games and tallied 22-7-5 (70-yard touchdown against Central Florida) with a blocked punt he turned into a score against UCONN. Started 12-of-13 games at right cornerback in '14, logging 36-10-2 with one sack and one forced fumble. Non-start was against Kentucky when UL opened with three safeties. Also had 12 career kickoff returns for 339 yards (28.3-yard average), including a 93-yard score against Florida International as a junior. Team captain graduated with a justice administration degree. Opted not to lift at the Combine and did not perform the 60-yard shuttle because of hamstring tightness.

Strengths: Very good movement and cover skill, with loose ankles and good recovery speed. Is quick to support vs. the run. Looked extremely fluid and natural in reverse and transitioning during positional drills at the Combine. Very balanced in his pedal and patient with pattern recognition. Has a natural feel for routes and at times runs them for receivers, anticipating break points. Adjusts very easily to the ball downfield and can track it over his shoulder. Carries a swagger and plays with confidence.

Weaknesses: Lacks ideal height. Has very small hands and is not a natural-handed interceptor. Catches like his hands are made of stone. Can be overaggressive and lose phase biting on double moves. Lacks stature and physicality as a tackler and will be more vulnerable to be run at in the pros.

Future: Smart, aware, instinctive field corner lacking ideal height for the outside, but has the cover skill to be a no. 2 and kick inside in sub-packages. May be the finest pure cover corner in the draft, though tackling deficiencies could diminish his draft value.

Draft projection: Second- to third-round pick.

Scout's take: "He plays the ball as well as anyone. Ball skills have nothing to do with interceptions. His problem is not ball skills. It's his hands. He is aggressive and he can tackle."

SS CLAYTON GEATHERS, #26 (Sr-5)
CENTRAL FLORIDA ▶ GRADE: 5.31
Ht: 6-1 ⅝ | Wt: 218 | 40: 4.49 | Arm: 31 ⅝ | Hand: 9 ⅛

History: Nephew of Robert Geathers Sr. and Jumpy Geathers, and cousin of Robert Jr., Clifton and Kwame. Clayton prepped in South Carolina, where he was all-state as a defensive back and running back. Suffered a broken right ankle during his senior season. In 2010, saw action in one game before a sprained right MCL caused him to redshirt. Took ownership of the strong safety position and started all 52 games over four seasons — totaled 67-6-0 with three tackles for loss in '11 (12 games); 117-5-0 with four tackles for loss and two forced fumbles in '12 (14 games); 100-10-2 with 4 ½ tackles for loss and two forced fumbles in '13 (13 games); and 97-9-1 with 6 ½ tackles for loss, one sack and one forced fumble in '14 (13 games). Had surgery to repair broken right thumb following his junior season. Team captain graduated with a degree in sports and fitness.

Strengths: Field fast and plays hard. Attacks the ball in the air and goes up to highpoint it. Sifts through traffic and fills hard vs. the run. Very good tackle production — is always around the ball. Strikes with thump and will drive ball carriers backward on contact. Led all strong safeties at the Combine with a 37-inch vertical jump. Great motor and on-field intensity. Takes good angles. Technique- and assignment-sound. Has the speed to match up with tight ends in man coverage. Experienced four-year starter. Does extra film work and works at his craft. Takes the game very seriously. Leader by example and also an emotional on-field, game-day leader. Strong Senior Bowl showing.

Weaknesses: Very tight in the hips and pedals a bit tall. Recorded the slowest 60-yard shuttle (12.60 seconds) of any player at the Combine. Average range to get over the top from center field. Limited ball skills.

Future: An excellent-sized, thickly built box safety with very good skill to drop down in the box and enforce the run. Could be very effective if used primarily near the line of scrimmage and has starter-quality traits.

Draft projection: Fourth- to fifth-round pick.

Scout's take: "I gave a late-round grade to Geathers. He has size, is a tough kid and ran well. I just didn't see him as being a really good athlete. I didn't think he ran well or showed a lot of range in the pass game. I thought he was a downhill, fill-the-alley guy. I know I beat up on him (in my report) more than I should have."

RCB JACOBY GLENN, #12 (Soph-3)

CENTRAL FLORIDA ▶ GRADE: 5.28

Ht: 6-0 | Wt: 179 | 40: 4.64 | Arm: 31 ¼ | Hand: 8 ⅝

History: Also played basketball as an Alabama prep. Redshirted in 2012. Started all 12 games played in '13, logging 52 tackles, 15 pass breakups and two interceptions with three tackles for loss, two sacks and two forced fumbles. Sat out against Temple (ankle).

Was the American Athletic Conference Co-Defensive Player of the Year in '14 after tallying 48-11-7 with one tackle for loss and one forced fumble in 13 starts. Did not lift at the Combine because of a right hand sprain.

Strengths: Good production on the ball. Excels in off coverage. Attacks the ball well in the air and goes up to get it. Natural interceptor — very aggressive to break points and knows how to use his body to post up and shield receivers. Plays faster than he tests. Competes hard and plays with energy. Functional in run support (despite lack of size).

Weaknesses: Very small hands. Very thinly built and is tightly wound for as lean as he is. Average transitional quickness — pedals too tall and plays on his heels. Lacks the quickness, short-area burst and athletic ability to match up with NFL receivers. Did not regularly face top competition in the American Athletic Conference.

Future: A squatty, instinctive, short-area corner with a chance to contend for a job in a scheme that likes to employ a two-deep look such as the Cowboys, Buccaneers or Saints. Compensates for his athletic limitations with very good eyes, anticipation and ball skills and could be drafted more highly than he grades on tape because of his playmaking skills. Is still very young and best football is ahead of him.

Draft projection: Third- to fourth-round pick.

Scout's take: "We already have a guy like him on our roster that we found after the draft. He was the same type of guy. (Glenn) can play in the league, but with the way he is built and the way he ran, it didn't help him. ... I've heard other teams that have him stacked in the second- and third round. That was the buzz when he declared. We wouldn't think about him until the fifth (round), and he fits what we do."

NCB SENQUEZ GOLSON, #21 (Sr-4)

MISSISSIPPI ▶ GRADE: 5.83

Ht: 5-8 ⅝ | Wt: 176 | 40: 4.47 | Arm: 29 ¾ | Hand: 9 ⅜

History: Three-sport start as a Mississippi prep. Won the 6A 100-meter dash state championship, and was a baseball All-American — was drafted by the Boston Red Sox in the eighth round of the 2011 MLB draft. Turned down a $1.1 million contract to join the Rebels. Played all 12 games as a true freshman in '11, starting four (one at right cornerback, final three at left cornerback), and had 16 tackles, one pass breakup and one interception. Started 6-of-12 games played in '12 — four at boundary corner, two at field corner — and tallied 36-3-3 with one-half tackle for loss. Did not play against Georgia (concussion). Started 10-of-12 games played at FCB in '13, notching 41-3-2 with 2 ½ tackles for loss. Did not start against Vanderbilt or Idaho, and was suspended against LSU for a violation of team rules. Was arrested in June '14 and charged with disorderly conduct — was found on foot at 4:50 in the morning and refused to identify himself to police. Charges were eventually dropped. In the fall, led the Southeastern Conference in interceptions — started all 13 games at FCB and produced 43-8-10 (57-yard touchdown against Louisiana-Lafayette, game-saving pick versus Alabama) with three tackles for loss and one-half sack. Won the College Football Performance Awards Elite Defensive Back Trophy, honoring the top career DB performance over the past four seasons. Had three different position coaches. Gave up baseball after his freshman season. Did not run the 60-yard shuttle at the Combine because of a bilateral big toe sprain.

Strengths: Feisty, tough, physical and instinctive. Plays bigger than his size and is aggressive supporting the run. Strong tackler. Shows a contagious confidence and carries an intense swagger that appears to energize the secondary. Exceptional agility and leaping ability. Rabbit-quick switching off receivers and jumping routes in zone coverage. Outstanding eyes and anticipation – has an innate feel for routes developing and appears to bait quarterbacks. Makes big plays in critical situations (see game-clinching interception in the end zone vs. an undefeated Alabama team). Outstanding closing speed, short-area burst and explosion. Can carry receivers deep and make plays with his back to the ball. Very natural hands with terrific hand-eye coordination and ball skills.

Weaknesses: Lacks ideal height, measuring the shortest of any defensive back at the Combine, and will struggle to match up with and climb the ladder against long receivers. Limited experience in press coverage and tends to use a bail technique and rise in his pedal. Can be overaggressive jumping routes, bite on double-moves and take some overly aggressive angles in the run game. Durability could be an issue given his small frame and aggressive style of play. Jaw runs in overdrive, can be overly emotional and on-field body language will rub some the wrong

way and challenge mild-mannered coaches. Better game-day performer than practice player and will need to learn what it means to consistently prepare like a pro. Struggled to learn the defense early as a sophomore and had to be challenged by Hugh Freeze. Baseball could be an offseason distraction.

Future: An opportunistic, ball-hawking, big-play cornerback in the same mold as Chargers 2014 first-round pick Jason Verrett, Golson really emerged as a senior and plays cornerback like he was born to play the position. Fits most ideally as a nickel cornerback in the pros, yet possessed the instincts, toughness and swagger to handle top assignments in college and won't back down from a challenge in the pros. Playing style and passion for the game is reminiscent of Cardinals 2013 third-round pick (69th overall) Tyrann Mathieu.

Draft projection: Top-50 pick.

RCB DORAN GRANT, #12 (Sr-4)

OHIO STATE ▶ GRADE: 5.82

Ht: 5-10 ¼ | Wt: 200 | 40: 4.44 | Arm: 30 ¼ | Hand: 9 ⅜

History: Receiver-cornerback who prepped at Akron St. Vincent-St. Mary, where he was a USA Today All-American and 110-meter hurdles and 60-meter hurdles state champion. Also played basketball. As a true freshman in 2011, collected six tackles, zero pass breakups and zero interceptions in 13 appearances. Backed up Broncos '14 first-rounder Bradley Roby in '12, tallying 19-1-1 with one tackle for loss in 12 games (one start). Started all 29 games the next two seasons — totaled 58-10-3 with two tackles for loss in '13 (14 games); and 63-9-5 with one tackle for loss in '14 (15 games) for the national champions. Team captain. Sustained a head injury against Indiana as a junior. Suffered a minor hand injury during Senior Bowl practice and sat out the game. Did not complete shuttles at the Combine because of a right calf strain.

Strengths: Has a strong, muscular build. Very good anticipation in zone coverage. Football smart to switch off receivers on combo routes. Can keep stride with receivers in man coverage and plays well with his back to the ball. Good recovery speed. Is quick to read run and support downhill. Physical tackler — takes on blocks with abandon and plays bigger than his size. Shows no fear filling vs. big backs. Outstanding open-field tackler. Exceptional upper-body strength — bench-pressed 21 reps at the Combine, second-best among cornerbacks at the Combine, and is stronger up top than linebackers. Very natural catcher, as he confirmed at the Senior Bowl with soft hands. Gunner on special teams.

Weaknesses: Has short arms. Is tight in the hips and some stiffness in his body that will allow some separation in transition. Plays into the boundary. Gives up some back-shoulder throws — can open his hips too early and be a tick late to plant and drive. Could stand to improve pattern recognition and feel for routes developing. Inconsistent tracking the deep ball.

Future: A strong, physical, tough cover man with the strength and aggressive football-playing temperament to start readily in the pros and make an impact covering on special teams. Is one of the best tackling cornerbacks in the draft, which could drive up his draft value.

Draft projection: Second- to third-round pick.

Scout's take: "I have studied two games. He only gave up a TD vs. Clemson in the bowl game, but it was a tough play at the top of the stem on a switch route. He is supposed to run like a deer. He looks long, but he is only 5-10. He can run. He can hit. He will tackle. I don't know how he gets out of the second round."

RCB LADARIUS GUNTER, #37 (Sr-5)
MIAMI (FLA.) ▶ GRADE: 5.23

Ht: 6-1 ½ | Wt: 202 | 40: 4.69 | Arm: 31 ½ | Hand: 9 ⅝

History: Prepped in Alabama, but failed to qualify academically and spent two years at Fort Scott (Kan.) Community College. Redshirted in 2010. In '11, recorded 24 tackles, two pass breakups and a 100-yard interception touchdown with three tackles for loss and two forced fumbles in seven games. Played all 12 games with the Hurricanes in '12, starting five of the final six at cornerback, and collected 27-6-1 with one tackle for loss. Started all 12 games played in '13, logging 46-6-3 with two tackles for loss and one forced fumble. Suffered a neck injury against Virginia and did not play against Pittsburgh. Had off-season surgery to repair a torn left labrum and sat out '14 spring practice. In the fall, started all 13 games and posted 28-6-2.

Strengths: Very good body length and overall size to match up with big receivers and compete in the red zone. Disruptive re-routing receivers. Willing tackler. Experienced, 30-game starter. Has safety experience.

Weaknesses: Too upright in his pedal and

technique and footwork need refinement — does not play with balance in his feet and it negates his transitional quickness. Ran the slowest short shuttle (4.45 seconds) and 60-yard shuttle (12.44 seconds) of any cornerback at the Combine. Average leaping ability — has a 33 ½-inch vertical jump. Lacks explosion, burst and closing speed to recover. Limited playing range. Marginal top-end speed to stick with receivers down the field. Drag-down tackler — could stand to be more physical in run support.

Future: A long-limbed, tight-hipped, press corner most ideally suited for a defense that likes to employ a lot of press coverage such as the Seahawks, Jaguars, Eagles or Patriots. Could be effective in short zones and near the goal line, but will be nickel-and-dimed with quick outs and double moves and exposed if asked to run down the field. Unique length is his most intriguing trait.

Draft projection: Fifth- to sixth-round pick.

FS CHRIS HACKETT, #1 (Jr-4)
TCU ▶ GRADE: 5.07

Ht: 6-0 ¼ | Wt: 195 | 40: 4.77 | Arm: 31 ½ | Hand: 9 ⅞

History: Parade All-American who also played basketball as a Texas prep. Redshirted in 2011. Played all 13 games in '12, starting the final 10 at weak safety in the Horned Frogs' 4-2-5 scheme, and recorded 61 tackles, five pass breakups and two interceptions with 1 ½ tackles for loss and one forced fumble. In '13, started 11-of-12 games at WS and produced 88-5-3 with 4 ½ tackles for loss, two sacks and three forced fumbles. Did not start against Kansas State. Started all 13 games at free safety in '14, totaling 75-6-7 with 3 ½ tackles for loss and a forced fumble.

Strengths: Plays with urgency. Very good job reading the quarterback on the back end and reacting to the thrown ball. Anticipatory, opportunistic and zone-instinctive. Johnny on the spot — has a knack for being in the right place at the right time. Good career interception (12) production. Flashes play-making ability.

Weaknesses: Has a lean frame. Side-lasso, drag-down and ankle-biting tackler — seldom faces up or knocks defenders back. Will be challenged more by the speed of the NFL against backs that will be able to step out of his tackle attempts. Recorded the slowest 10-yard split (1.71 seconds) and 40-yard dash (4.82) of any defensive back at the Combine. Limited foot speed. Late to transition out of breaks and lacks the range to get over the top

DEFENSIVE BACKS

and leverage the field from the middle. Was not asked to man cover much in college and will have man coverage limitations matching up with bigger, faster NFL tight ends.

Future: A better football player than tester, Hackett plays faster than his timed speed and has the coverage instincts and ball skills to warrant and opportunity as a nickel safety. However, physical limitations are glaring and disappointing Combine performance could keep him from being drafted. Could prove worthy of a late-round flier if his role were restricted to short-area zone/curl/flat responsibilities for a heavy zone cover team.

Draft projection: Priority free agent.

FS-CB ANTHONY HARRIS, #8 (Sr-4)

VIRGINIA ▶ GRADE: 5.42 (TOP 3)

Ht: 6-0 ⅝ | Wt: 183 | 40: 4.55e | Arm: 32 | Hand: 9 ¼

History: Also played basketball as a Virginia prep. Suffered a broken leg in 2009. Was a reserve/special teams player as a true freshman in '11 (wore jersey No. 28) when he tallied 14 tackles, zero pass breakups and zero interceptions in 13 games. Started all 12 games at free safety in '12, producing 87-3-1 with one-half tackle for loss and one forced fumble. Started 11-of-12 at strong safety in '13, amassing 80-6-8 with 3 ½ tackles for loss, one sack, one forced fumble and one blocked punt. Was suspended for the first half of the season finale against Virginia Tech after he was ejected for targeting against Miami. In '14, started all 12 games at SS and piled up 108-10-2 with two forced fumbles and one sack. Team captain graduated with a sociology degree. Medically excluded from the Combine because of right shoulder surgery.

Strengths: Very good eyes and anticipation — has a knack for reading the quarterback and seeing routes developing. Very technique-sound — has a smooth, controlled, balanced pedal and is very efficient transitioning on his plant and drive with no wasted motion or extra steps. Outstanding hands and ball skills. Very willing tackler — sacrifices his body and seeks to face-up running backs in the box and on the perimeter, waiting for the cavalry to arrive. Unselfish, team player. Has been an effective special teams contributor.

Weaknesses: Very thin-hipped, skinny-legged and a bit tight. Limited hip flexibility. Pedals tall. Can be overaggressive supporting the run and get pulled in by play-action (see TD allowed vs. Louisville). Not a strong or physical tackler (though he is willing to fill).

Long-term durability is concerning given his slight frame and willingness to throw his body around.

Future: Rangy, athletic interchangeable safety with a body type more suitable at cornerback. Has the football intelligence, play-making ability and toughness to compete for a job as a nickel safety and factor immediately on special teams. A full conversion to cornerback could be in his future. Needs to add some bulk and continue getting stronger. Is at his best in zone coverage jumping routes.

Draft projection: Third- to fourth-round pick.

Scout's take: "I like the kid. He is a smart player. He really is. He is just light – he weighed a-buck-eighty-eight. But he is very smart. He lines everyone up. He has a lot of what you are looking for. He doesn't have great flexibility. I have him in the mid-round range right now."

NCB TROY HILL, #13 (Sr-6)

OREGON ▶ GRADE: 5.10

Ht: 5-10 ½ | Wt: 182 | 40: 4.51 | Arm: 29 ½ | Hand: 8 ¾

History: Youngstown, Ohio native, though he played his high school ball at St. Bonaventure in California. After the fact, his high school team had to forfeit an 11-2, league-championship season when it was discovered Hill was an ineligible fifth-year senior as a result of failing grades in 2005-06. Was cleared by the NCAA to join the Ducks in 2010, his redshirt season. Played 14 games in '11 (wore jersey No. 2), starting six (four at right cornerback, two at left cornerback), and recorded 43 tackles, six pass breakups and one interception with one tackle for loss. Took a back seat to Ifo Ekpre-Olomu and Cowboys 2014 seventh-rounder Terrance Mitchell the next two seasons. Tallied 26-4-1 (29-yard touchdown against Arizona) with one tackle for loss in '12 (10 games). Did not play against Tennessee Tech, Colorado or California. Appeared in 11 games in '13, managing 29-4-0 with one-half for loss and one forced fumble. Was suspended for the final two games after a December domestic violence arrest — was charged with menacing and felony fourth-degree assault and strangulation. Ultimately pleaded guilty to lesser charges of menacing and was sentenced to 36 months of probation, $200 in fines and 70 hours of community service. Was also ordered to attend a six-month anger treatment program, as well as steer clear of

DEFENSIVE BACKS

"offensive contact" with the victim. Stepped in for Mitchell in '14 when he started all 14 games opposite Ekpre-Olomu and logged 71-18-1 with four tackles for loss and two forced fumbles. Did not play against Wyoming (knee). Did not lift at the Combine because of a left wrist injury.

Strengths: Fluid and smooth in his pedal with sewing machine footwork. Very good zone awareness. Outstanding ball production. Opportunistic making plays on the ball — good peripheral vision. Plays with a passion and it shows.

Weaknesses: Very thin-framed and lacks functional strength to re-route receivers. Shoestring, low-cut tackler. Has small hands and is not a natural catcher. Has only three career interceptions. Arms measured the shortest of any defensive back at the Combine. Was also tied for the lowest vertical jump among DBs — 32 ½ inches. Durability and personal character are concerns that require careful vetting.

Future: Smallish, short-armed, nickel corner blossomed in the absence of the injured Ifo Ekpre-Olomu, yet lacks size, strength, tackling and overall athletic ability that coupled with character, intelligence and durability concerns, could leave his draft card in the Moscow May Day category. Drastically improved, competitive senior season is an indication that he may be ready to put the past behind him.

Draft projection: Late draftable pick.

FS GEROD HOLLIMAN, #8 (Jr-4)

LOUISVILLE ▶ GRADE: 5.40

Ht: 5-11 ¾ | Wt: 218 | 40: 4.62 | Arm: 32 | Hand: 9 ½

History: Has a twin sister. Miami native recorded 12 interceptions as a high school senior. Attended Milford Academy (N.Y.) in 2011. Appeared in three games in '12 before having season-ending surgery to repair a torn left labrum. Played 11 games in '13, starting two (one at corner, one at free safety), and tallied 16 tackles, three pass breakups and zero interceptions with one tackle for loss. In '14, was moved to free safety full-time by new defensive coordinator Todd Grantham — played all 13 games, starting the final 11, and registered 44-3-14 (one touchdown) with three tackles for loss and one forced fumble. Won the Thorpe Award after tying an FBS single-season record for interceptions. Did not work out at the Combine because of a left hamstring strain, which he was still feeling at his March pro day. Will be a 21-year-old rookie.

Strengths: Very productive interceptor –

had 14 career interceptions, with a knack for positioning himself on the back end. Very good coverage instincts, ball skills and hands. Terrific hand-eye coordination. Has a good feel for routes developing and outstanding wide-eyed, peripheral vision to see the quarterback and receiver. Very good reactive quickness. Attacks the ball in the air like a receiver.

Weaknesses: Steps downhill too gingerly and does not play with physicality in the box or sacrifice his body. Wraps too tentatively in run support and lets ball carriers step out of tackles. Shies from and turns down contact. Not dependable dropping down from deep to short and making open-field tackles. A 60/40 tackler. Posted a 27-inch vertical jump at pro day. Measured 15 percent body fat at the Combine. Only a one-year, full-time starter.

Future: An opportunistic, Cover 2 safety with a knack for being in the right spot at the right time, Holliman has good ball skills and enough range to produce on the back end and would be most ideal in a defense such as Tampa Bay's or Kansas City's. However, a noticeable lack of physicality, in-the-box toughness and secure tackling could be exposed and could drive down his draft value.

Draft projection: Third- to fourth-round pick.

Scout's take: "A lot of his picks came on lucky overthrows. I don't care if he has 14 interceptions if he cannot play the run. He's the kind of safety I like to play against — all you need to do is just run right at him."

SS-PR KYSHOEN JARRETT, #34 (Sr-4)

VIRGINIA TECH ▶ GRADE: 5.29

Ht: 5-9 ⅞ | Wt: 200 | 40: 4.56 | Arm: 31 | Hand: 9 ¾

History: Brother, 21-year-old Daishawn, has cerebral palsy and often Kyshoen often cared for him with his two older brothers growing up. First name is pronounced "KY-shawn." Prepped in Pennsylvania. As a true freshman in 2011, had seven tackles, zero pass breakups and zero interceptions in 14 appearances. Added two punt returns for 12 yards (6.0-yard average). Stepped into the lineup in '12 and started all 13 games at rover, producing 83-4-0 with 4 ½ tackles for loss and one forced fumble. Returned punts 18-250 (13.9), including a 94-yard score against Pittsburgh. Started all 13 games at rover in '13, logging 71-2-2 with one tackle for loss and 26-139 (5.3) on punt returns. Tore his left labrum against Boston College in early November (underwent surgery after the season and missed '14 spring practice). In the fall, started 12-of-13 games at rover (lined up at "Whip" linebacker against Georgia Tech) and totaled 88-5-3 with three tackles for loss, one-half sack and one forced fumble. Returned punts 6-62 (10.3). Did not start against Western Michigan (coach's decision). Graduated in December with a human development degree.

Strengths: Very thickly built with good musculature. Tough and physical. Aggressive supporting the run. Plays with physicality. Good football IQ. Very active and energetic field presence. Drops the hammer and hits through contact. Strikes with bad intent and has knock-out body power. Alert in zones. Very good reacting to the thrown ball in front of him. Has enough range to make some plays on the back end. Can match up with tight ends in man coverage.

Experienced, three-year starter. Mentally tough and will battle through injuries. Outstanding personal and football character. Good run strength and balance as a punt returner.

Weaknesses: Short. Has some man-coverage limitations Plays a bit flat-footed and is often used more like another linebacker in the box with limited coverage responsibility. Average recovery speed and burst to range over the top and roam center field.

Future: A hammering box safety that can bring an intimidating presence to a defense and has more coverage ability than strictly a box safety. Is not as big or explosive, but plays the game similar to Steelers 2013 fourth-round pick (111th overall) Shamarko Thomas and should make an immediate impact on special teams.

Draft projection: Fourth- to fifth-round pick.

RCB-FS ANTHONY JEFFERSON, #23 (Sr-5)
UCLA　　　　　　　　　　　▶ GRADE: 5.03

| Ht: 6-0 ⅞ | Wt: 198 | 40: 4.69 | Arm: 31 ½ | Hand: 8 ½ |

History: Los Angeles native. Saw action in three games in 2010 before suffering a season-ending Lisfranc fracture in his left foot (granted medical hardship). Sat out the '11 season after having back surgery. Was a reserve/special-teams player in '12, collecting five tackles, zero pass breakups and zero interceptions. In '13, started all 13 games at free safety and produced 89-5-2 with one tackle for loss. Started all 12 games played in '14, logging 72-8-1 with three tackles for loss. Did not play against Texas (knee/flu). Graduated. Did not run the 60-yard shuttle at the Combine because of hamstring tightness.

Strengths: Very good size and length for a cornerback to match up against big receivers and tight ends. Good instincts and route recognition. Plays the ball well in front of him. Functional tackler. Versatile — has played cornerback and safety.

Weaknesses: Loses a step in transition and lets receivers get on top of him too quickly. Does not have the long speed to carry receivers down the field and will be challenged over the top in the pros. Lacks range to leverage the field as a safety. Has a 33 ½-inch vertical jump. Did not catch the ball well at the Combine or look relaxed and confident in his pedal. Durability needs to be evaluated carefully given two surgeries early in career.

Future: Tall, stiff, straight-linish, zone corner with limited transitional quickness and athletic ability for the CB position and average range and feet for a safety. However, he offers enough versatility to contribute at multiple spots and on special teams to warrant a chance. Durability concerns could affect his draft status.

Draft projection: Priority free agent.

LCB KEVIN JOHNSON, #9 (Sr-5)
WAKE FOREST　　　　　　　▶ GRADE: 6.12

| Ht: 6-0 ¼ | Wt: 188 | 40: 4.47 | Arm: 31 | Hand: 8 ⅜ |

History: Cornerback-running back who spent four years on varsity at powerhouse River Hill High (MD), where he was part of a team that won two state championships, went 47-3 and posted 21 shutouts over three seasons. High school teammate of Ravens 2014 seventh-round receiver Michael Campanaro. Played right cornerback his first three seasons. Played 11 games in '10, starting the final five, and totaled 31 tackles, two pass breakups and zero interceptions with one tackle for loss. Was academically ineligible in '11. Started all 24 games the next two seasons — produced 58-15-3 with 3 ½ tackles for loss, one-half sack and two forced fumbles in '12; and 58-12-3 with one forced fumble in '13. Playing under a new coaching staff in '14, manned the field corner and posted 44-6-1 with 3 ½ tackles for loss and a recovered blocked punt for touchdown against Louisiana-Monroe. Was ejected from the Louisville contest (targeting). Graduated with a communication degree. Opted not to lift at the Combine. Has served as a gunner on special teams and dabbled with punt returns.

Strengths: Outstanding length. Smooth and fluid in his movement skill. Good man-cover skills. Matches up well vs. length of

DEFENSIVE BACKS

tight ends and can climb the ladder to make plays. Has a 41 ½-inch vertical jump, tied for the second-best among cornerbacks at the Combine. Confident and competitive. Was often assigned to opponent's No. 1 receiver and showed he could keep stride vertically and shadow and mirror. Good ball skills — attacks it in the air. Instinctive and football smart. Good press skill. Plays off. Mirrors and jumps routes with very good closing speed. Reads receiver and the quarterback – very good eyes and anticipation. Has loose hips and thin, flexible ankles, translating to very good reactionary quickness. Ran a 3.89-second short shuttle and 6.79-second 3-cone drill time at the Combine, demonstrating superb agility. Very willing and aggressive in run support. Solid open-field tackler.

Weaknesses: Very lean, wiry build with narrow shoulders and very small hands. Lacks weight-room strength and could benefit from more time in the weight room, choosing not to lift at the Combine or his pro day. Plays into boundary. Can be too handsy down the field. Not as comfortable in off coverage. Can still become a more secure tackler.

Future: One of the cleanest evaluations in this year's draft, Johnson is a very polished press cover man who has consistently matched up with some of the best receivers in football the last three years and showed well. A more confident version of Patriots 2009 second-round pick (41st overall) Darius Butler.

Draft projection: First-round pick.

Scout's take: "I think Kevin Johnson is a helluva football player. He will come downhill and play the run. He is physical. He already got ejected one time for targeting. He is really good in coverage. …I think he has a really good skill set. He is really intriguing. I was surprised how much I liked the tape."

LCB-FS BYRON JONES, #16 (Sr-5)

CONNECTICUT   ▶ GRADE: 5.76
Ht: 6-0 ⅝ | Wt: 199 | 40: 4.40e | Arm: 32 | Hand: 10

History: Also played basketball and ran track as a Connecticut prep. Redshirted in 2010. Started 8-of-12 games at free safety in '11, booking 51 tackles, four pass breakups and two interceptions with a fumble recovery touchdown. Started all 12 games at FS in '12, logging 88-2-1 with 1 ½ tackles for loss. Following the departure of '13 draftees Dwayne Gratz (third round, Jaguars) and Blidi Wreh-Wilson (third round, Titans), switched to left cornerback in '13 — produced 60-8-3 with two tackles for loss in

12 starts. In '14, managed 24-6-2 (including a 70-yard touchdown against South Florida) at LCB again before undergoing season-ending surgery to repair a torn left labrum (medically excluded from lifting at the Combine). Team captain. Graduated with a double major in economics and political science.

Strengths: Outstanding size and length with long arms and big hands — looks every bit the part. Has rare lower-body explosion. Posted the most explosive broad jump (12-feet, 3-inches) and fastest 60-yard shuttle (10.98 seconds) of any player at the Combine, along with the best vertical jump (44 ½ inches) of any defensive back at the event. Rare leaping ability. Plays the ball well with his back to it. Strong, efficient tackler in run support — discards blockers and leverages the sideline. Natural ball skills. Has unique versatility — equal starting experience at corner and free safety. Very intelligent, nuanced three-and-a-half-year starter. Has been very durable throughout his career.

Weaknesses: Average short-space quickness. Rare workout numbers do not always translate to the field. Does not have elite recovery speed. Has room to improve in route recognition — appears to be overprocessing at times. Tends to clutch and grab down the field. Average ball skills — late to find the ball. Was not heavily challenged in the American Athletic Conference.

Future: An exceptionally sized, explosive bump-and-run corner with the length, speed and agility to match up with big receivers in zone or man coverage. Has the intelligence and experience to line up at free safety, and versatility is a plus.

Draft projection: Top-50 pick.

Scout's take: "Jones is a smooth athlete. You watch him in practice — he is very smooth. I would like to see him play vs. better competition, but he shows you everything you want to see. He plays off, he plays press. He is smart. Is he a playmaking machine? No. He plays the wide side of the field vs. average quarterbacks and average receivers and really doesn't get contested."

LCB CRAIG MAGER, #25 (Sr-5)

TEXAS STATE   ▶ GRADE: 5.33
Ht: 5-11 ½ | Wt: 201 | 40: 4.43 | Arm: 29 ¾ | Hand: 9 ¼

History: Grew up without a father and lost his mother when he was 15. Played running back as a prep in Texas, where he also played basketball and ran track. Redshirted in 2010. Started all 12 games at field corner in '11,

DEFENSIVE BACKS

recording 51 tackles, 12 pass breakups and one interception with 1 ½ tackles for loss and one forced fumble. Suffered a dislocated right elbow during '12 spring practice. In the fall, started all 12 games at boundary corner and tallied 48-8-4 with one tackle for loss and a 79-yard punt return touchdown. Started all 24 games at FCB the next two seasons — totaled 49-9-0 with one tackle for loss, one forced fumble and a 44-yard fumble recovery touchdown in '13; and 63-10-3 with six tackles for loss, two sacks and 10 punt returns for 123 yards (12.3-yard average). Started every game of his career.

Strengths: Has a well-proportioned build with a shredded physique. Very clean footwork with loose hips and fluid transitional skills. Natural man cover skills. Does a good job re-routing receivers. Good career production on the ball. Solid showing during the East-West Shrine week. Has a 38-inch vertical jump. Posted an exceptional 1.50-second 10-yard split at the Combine, tied with three others for the best DB time. Good personal and football character. Experienced, four-year starter. Very durable.

Weaknesses: Has very short arms. Played into the boundary. Can be overaggressive jumping routes. Struggles with some zone concepts and handling combo routes. Could do a better job discarding blocks. Did not regularly face top competition.

Future: A good-sized, small-school, man-cover corner with the feistiness, ball skills and confidence to compete for a starting job in the pros. Showed he could match up against better competition at the Shrine game, showed well at the Combine and has continued to answer any level-of-competition concerns. Ascending talent with upside.

Draft projection: Third- to fourth-round pick.

FS DEAN MARLOWE, #16 (Sr-5)

JAMES MADISON ▶ GRADE: 5.06

Ht: 6-1 ½ | Wt: 203 | 40: 4.57 | Arm: 31 | Hand: 8 ¾

History: Safety-quarterback who also ran track as a New York prep. Redshirted in 2010. Started all 13 games at strong safety in '11, booking 71 tackles, six pass breakups and four interceptions with 2 ½ tackles for loss. Started all 36 games at free safety the next three seasons — totaled 82-4-3 with five tackles for loss, one forced fumble and a safety in '12 (11 games); 77-7-1 with one-half tackle for loss in '13 (12 games); and 96-5-4 with 5 ½ tackles for loss and one sack

in '14 (13 games). Also had 21 career punt returns for 173 yards (8.2-yard average). Team captain. Graduated in December with a degree in sports and recreation management.

Strengths: Good height. Lines up all over the field. Very active supporting the run. Chases hard and gives good pursuit effort. Experienced, four-year starter.

Weaknesses: Very small hands. Underdeveloped — lacks bulk and functional football-playing strength. Not a strong or forceful tackler — and is not aggressive in his approach. Pedals tall. Undisciplined technique. Average foot speed. Could struggle matching up with the speed and agility of NFL receivers.

Future: A raw, college free safety lacking the back-end range desired to play center field and the physicality and secure tackling desired in the box. Will have to prove he could contribute on special teams to earn a job as a backup safety.

Draft projection: Priority free agent.

LCB-QB NICK MARSHALL, #14 (Sr-4)

AUBURN ▶ GRADE: 5.26

Ht: 6-1 ½ | Wt: 207 | 40: 4.53 | Arm: 32 ⅛ | Hand: 9 ¼

History: Also played basketball (averaged 28 points per game) as a prep in Georgia, where he won a state title as a junior, was named Class A Offensive Player of the Year, and set GHSA career record with 103 touchdown passes. Began his college career with Georgia, where he was recruited as a cornerback and played all 13 games in 2011, tallying five tackles, zero pass breakups and zero interceptions. Was dismissed the following February, reportedly for stealing money from teammates. Played quarterback at Garden City (Kan.) Community College in '12 — completed 196-of-343 pass attempts (57.1 percent) for 3,142 yards with 18 touchdowns and 20 interceptions. Added 171 carries for 1,095 yards (6.4-yard average) and 19 touchdowns. Transferred to Auburn to play in Gus Malzahn's offense. In '13, started all 13 games played and passed 142-239-1,976-14-6 (59.4) with 172-1,068-12 (6.2) rushing. Did not play against Western Carolina (right knee). Started 12-of-13 games played in '14, totaling 178-293-2,532-20-7 (60.8) through the air and 153-925-11 (5.2) on the ground. Was suspended the first half of the season opener against Arkansas as punishment for a July citation for marijuana possession. Also had three career receptions for 51 yards (17.0-

yard average) and zero touchdowns.

Strengths: Very good athlete with exceptional size for the cornerback position. Has a 37½-inch vertical jump and outstanding agility, as reflected in 4.15-second short shuttle and 6.96-second 3-cone drill time. Showed great confidence at the Senior Bowl adjusting to playing cornerback and has shown he could handle the pressure of playing on big stages at quarterback. Very competitive, football smart and versatile — could provide an emergency quarterbacking and offensive specialty weapon.

Weaknesses: Technique is very unrefined and will require work. Looks choppy and tall in his pedal at the Senior Bowl. Eyes and instincts need honing. Has run into repeated trouble off the field. Registered 25 fumbles in three years as QB.

Future: A very good-sized, developmental cornerback prospect with rare length and a unique perspective from having played the QB position. Will require some time to get adjusted to the defensive side of the ball but has the size, length and foot quickness to make the transition if he proves he could contribute on special teams. Developmental project with additional value as an offensive utility weapon.

Draft projection: Fourth- to fifth-round pick.

Scout's take: "(Marshall) comes across as just a guy as a quarterback. He is a wildcard as a cornerback. He's big and competitive. He ran well enough that he is going to get a chance to show he can play. I think the Senior Bowl went a long way with teams. How many guys would jump in the way he did and change positions on the fly. It says a lot about him as a person."

NCB-KR BOBBY McCAIN, #21 (Sr-4)

MEMPHIS ▶ GRADE: 5.36

Ht: 5-9 ½ | Wt: 195 | 40: 4.48 | Arm: 30 ½ | Hand: 9

History: Also played baseball (catcher) as an Alabama prep. Chose Memphis over offers from Auburn, Mississippi State and Tennessee, among others. As a true freshman in 2011, played 11 games (started final nine) and tallied 29 tackles, four pass breakups and one interception (79-yard touchdown against Tulane) with one tackle for loss and one forced fumble. Started all 12 games in '12, recording 36-3-0 with 3 ½ tackles for loss, 1 ½ sacks and a 61-yard reception. Had off-season surgery to repair a torn right meniscus. Started all nine games played in '13, accumulating 25-4-6 (75-yard TD against Duke, 36-yard

TD against South Florida) with one tackle for loss. Tore his right meniscus against Central Florida, requiring arthroscopic surgery which sidelined him for three weeks. Returned to start all 13 games in '14, logging 46-4-5 (15-yard TD against Tulane) with one tackle for loss and one fumble recovery score. Had 42 career kickoff returns for 1,061 yards (25.3-yard average). Graduated in December with a degree in sport and leisure management.

Strengths: Quick and explosive in his movement to plant and drive on the ball — good acceleration out of his breaks. Sinks in zones and plays with awareness vs. combo routes. Recorded the best short shuttle time (3.82 seconds) of any player at the Combine. Flashes play-making ability and notched 12 career interceptions. Bench-pressed 17 reps at the Combine and is strong for his size. Is willing in run support. Good tackler. Plays with a sense of urgency and showed well against better post-season competition. Stood out at the East-West Shrine practices for burst, aggressive jumping routes and man cover skills. Experienced, four-year starter.

Weaknesses: Lacks ideal height to match up with bigger NFL receivers on the perimeter. Can be outmatched in jumpball situations. Could stand to do a better job knocking receivers off their routes in press coverage. Drag-down tackler. Did not regularly match up with elite receivers in the American Athletic Conference. Right knee could require closer evaluation.

Future: Lacks the length and physicality desired on the outside and fits most ideally into the slot, where his short-area explosion and plant-and-drive quickness could be impactful. Kickoff return ability adds to his potential.

Draft projection: Fourth- to fifth-round pick.

SS TEVIN McDONALD, #7 (Sr-5)

EASTERN WASHINGTON ▶ GRADE: 5.02

Ht: 5-11 ⅜ | Wt: 195 | 40: 4.61 | Arm: 29 ¾ | Hand: 9

History: Father, Tim, was a 13-year NFL safety with the 49ers and Cardinals (1987-99), and brother, T.J., is a starting safety for the Rams. Tim, who coached Tevin as a California prep, currently serves as the Bills' defensive backs coach. Tevin began his college career at UCLA, where he redshirted in 2010. Missed time during '11 fall camp with an ankle injury. Played all 14 games in the fall, starting the final 11 at free safety, and produced 56 tackles, nine pass breakups and three interceptions with 4 ½ tackles for loss and one forced fumble. Started all 13 games at FS in '12, logging 79-9-1 with one forced fumble. Was suspended for the Holiday Bowl against Baylor after his third failed drug test. Was dismissed in March '13 over what was called a violation of team rules. Transferred to EWU, one of the top FCS programs, and started 8-of-9 games played at FS in '13, totaling 43-2-1 with 2 ½ tackles for loss and one forced fumble. Started all '14 games in '14 and registered 78-7-3 (73-yard touchdown against Portland State) with four tackles for loss, three forced fumbles and a blocked kick. Team captain.

Strengths: Active in run support. Plays downhill fast and can tackle in the open field. Good football intelligence. Experienced, four-year starter. Has NFL pedigree.

Weaknesses: Marginal size with a smooth-muscled frame, short arms and small hands. Idling motor that too often runs hot and cold. Takes inconsistent angles being overaggressive in run fills. Limited foot speed to keep stride with NFL receivers in man coverage. Measured 15.3 percent body fat at the Combine and could stand to pay closer attention to his nutrition and conditioning. Carries some entitlement. Personal character invites closer scrutiny.

Future: Hype has yet to live up to his billing, as he was bounced from UCLA and did not show well in the East-West Shrine game against better competition. Lack of size and history of underachieving could force him to make a team after the draft.

Draft projection: Priority free agent.

LCB STEVEN NELSON, #2 (Sr-4)

OREGON STATE　　　　　　▶ GRADE: 5.32

Ht: 5-10 ⅛	Wt: 197	40: 4.47	Arm: 30 ⅝	Hand: 9 ¼

History: Has a son, Steven III. Was a cornerback and exceptional punt returner as a Georgia prep, though he was a non-qualifier — on the advice of his cousin K.J. Morton, headed to College of Sequoias (Calif.). Played nine games in 2011, recording 29 tackles, six pass breakups and two interceptions with 2 ½ tackles for loss and five kickoff returns for 107 yards (21.4-yard average). Played 10 games in '12, tallying 21-4-3, while returning kickoffs 5-90 (18.0) and punts 10-126 (12.6). Also ran the 4X100 at Sequoias. Originally committed to Georgia, but signed with OSU, where he played all 13 games in '13 — initially contributed as a nickel back before starting the final nine at left cornerback, producing 62-8-6, including a 16-yard

touchdown against San Diego State. Started all 12 games at LCB in '14 and posted 60-8-2 with two tackles for loss.

Strengths: Has good feet and can carry receivers down the field. Feisty and competitive. Good man-off coverage skills. Solid in run support — gets good run fits, quick to trigger and chops down big backs. Bench-pressed 19 reps at the Combine and is strong pound-for-pound. Attacks the line and hits with explosion. Solid career production on the ball. Flashes play-making ability. Experienced, four-year starter. Is coachable and the game is important to him.

Weaknesses: Tight in the hips and it shows when he transitions and gets stuck. Struggles to escape stalk blocks and can be overwhelmed by size. Plays a bit recklessly. Too grabby. Average football intelligence. Limited recovery speed.

Future: Good-sized, classic Cover-2 corner with intriguing ball skills and toughness to tackle. Could be very effective as a short-area zone corner and would be best on the outside with simple one-on-one responsibilities. Has starting-caliber traits if the game slows down for him.

Draft projection: Fourth- to fifth-round pick.

Scout's take: "Nelson has twitch and can run. He is short and yoked up and has trouble when big receivers get on top of him. Every game I've done — this is my fourth game — he has struggled to get off blocks. People post up on him. He is really handsy down the field. He panics a little bit. He is going to get called for a lot of penalties. He can't be a nickel. He's not smart enough."

RCB GARRY PETERS, #26 (Sr-5)

CLEMSON　　　　　　▶ GRADE: 5.19

Ht: 5-11 ¾	Wt: 191	40: 4.59	Arm: 31 ½	Hand: 10

History: Born to Jamaican parents. Also played basketball as a Georgia prep. Missed four games as a senior with a sprained ankle. Redshirted in 2010. Missed time during '11 fall camp with a bruised calf. Played special teams in the fall, booking six tackles, zero pass breakups and zero interceptions in 11 appearances. Played 12 games in '12, drawing five starting assignments, and recorded 20-8-1. In '13, tallied 28-4-0 with 4 ½ tackles for loss. Missed three mid-season games with a broken foot. Was suspended for the '14 season opener against Georgia (violation team rules) before logging 45-12-1 with eight tackles for loss, two sacks and one forced fumble in 12 starts. Scheduled to graduate in May with a

DEFENSIVE BACKS

sociology degree.

Strengths: Good length and overall size with big hands that he uses well to disrupt receivers at the line of scrimmage and knock them off routes. Good zone awareness. Plays the ball well in front of him. Willing in run support. Tough and competitive.

Weaknesses: Pedals too upright. Average foot speed to match up with receivers down the field. Gathers to cut and is not quick out of transition — takes extra steps and is late to plant and drive on the ball. Does not play fast. Passive playing temperament. Marginal functional strength. Plays passively. Tied for the fewest bench-press reps (7) of any player at the Combine. Tied for the lowest vertical jump (32 ½ inches) among cornerbacks at the Combine. Has only two career interceptions.

Future: Good-sized, Cover 2 corner with the size to match up in the red zone and compete with big-bodied receivers. Ability to contribute on special teams will likely determine his roster fate.

Draft projection: Late draftable pick.

LCB **MARCUS PETERS**, #21 (Jr-4)

EX-WASHINGTON ▶ GRADE: 6.23

Ht: 5-11 ⅞ | Wt: 197 | 40: 4.49 | Arm: 31 ½ | Hand: 8 ⅜

History: Had a son, Carson, with his girlfriend Jayla in October (morning of the Huskies' loss to Oregon). Cornerback-receiver who picked off seven passes and returned six kicks for scores as a high school senior in Oakland, Calif., where he also ran track. Is close with Seahawks running back and fellow Oakland native Marshawn Lynch, whom Peters thinks of as a cousin. Was recruited by then-head coach Steve Sarkisian. Failed a drug test (marijuana) during his 2011 redshirt season (earned Scout Team MVP). Played all 13 games in '12, starting the final eight, and recorded 44 tackles, eight pass breakups and three interceptions (21-yard touchdown against Portland State) with two tackles for loss and a blocked kick. Started 12-of-13 games in '13, tallying 55-9-5 with 3 ½ tackles for loss, one sack and one forced fumble. Was suspended the first quarter of the bowl game against BYU (and banned for four weeks from off-season training) after he was late turning in a final for a class. In '14, managed 30-7-3 with four tackles for loss in eight games (seven starts) before he was dismissed from the team for repeated behavioral issues (withdrew from classes and returned home). Against Eastern Washington, was flagged for unsportsmanlike conduct after head-butting

an opposing player — was benched by head coach Chris Peterson, inciting a "hissy fit" from Peters, who argued with coaches and threw his helmet. As a result, was suspended against Illinois, which preceded a two-series benching against Stanford as punishment for being late to team meetings. According to a quote from Marcus' father in USA Today, "things like the music Marcus listened to, the body language in meetings" contributed to Peterson's decision to kick Peters off the team for an accumulation of incidents, including missing practice the day before his dismissal because he was in court for driving on a suspended license.

Strengths: Outstanding size. Very good press strength to disrupt receivers at the line of scrimmage and knock them off routes. Maintains good positioning and stays in phase in coverage. Smooth and fluid in transition. Good ball skills and instincts. Is aggressive playing the ball in the air and baits quarterbacks to throw his way. Very solid supporting the run. Plays with confidence and carries a swagger. Took accountability for his mishaps in college during the interview process with teams at the Combine and eliminated many concerns resulting from his team dismissal.

Weaknesses: Has very small hands. Is not technique-sound and often freelances and plays outside the structure of the scheme. Could do a better job of shedding blocks — at times gets driven out of the play (see Stanford). Could stand to be a more dependable tackler. Mental toughness could improve — had issues controlling his emotions. Does not respond well to hard coaching and was dismissed from the team after repeated issues co-existing with a new coaching staff. Could be defiant at times and has been removed from some NFL draft boards for character concerns.

Future: The most talented pure cornerback in the draft, Peters has the playmaking ability, ball skills and toughness to factor readily in the pros, though he must mature and realize that he will not be able to coast on his natural talent in the pros. Would benefit from a demanding structure

Draft projection: First-round pick.

Scout's take: "All these players have issues, especially the really talented ones. You have to be able to accept them for what they are and manage them. That's the big question with all of them. (Steve) Sarkisian recruited (Peters) and knew how to handle the kid. Nick Saban gets the most of his players. So does Bill Belichick and Pete Carroll. When you

DEFENSIVE BACKS

get star players, you have to treat them a little differently. … Sarkisian knew how to handle Peters. Chris Petersen came in with a button-down approach. He has a box, and if you don't fit in it and conform, you're not going to be around. That kid didn't fit in the box with the Boise way at all. He's as talented as any corner I have seen. He can be a shutdown corner. But he is not a square-cut, button-down, Petersen-conform-type guy. That was the problem."

SS **CODY PREWITT**, #25 (Sr-4)

MISSISSIPPI ▶ GRADE: 5.25

Ht: 6-2 | Wt: 208 | 40: 4.59 | Arm: 32 ⅝ | Hand: 9 ⅛

History: Raised by his grandmother. Also starred in track as a Mississippi prep — captured Class A state championships (and records) in the 100 meters (10.83 seconds), 200 meters (21.56) and triple jump (46 feet, four inches). Was a backup "Spur" as a true freshman in 2011 when he tallied 32 tackles, zero pass breakups and one interception with one-half tackle for loss in 12 games (started final four at strong safety). Broke his right hand in an off-field accident in October. Started all 13 games at free safety in '12, recording 80-4-2 with five tackles for loss, 1 ½ sacks and two forced fumbles. Started 11-of-13 games at FS in '13, notching 71-7-6 with 4 ½ tackles for loss and two forced fumbles. Was benched for a quarter against Troy as punishment for missing a class during the week. Was benched for a quarter against Georgia Tech in the Music City Bowl (violation team rules, reported to be curfew/missed class issue) then sustained a concussion during the game. Started all 13 games in '14 and notched 64-2-3 with a forced fumble. Team captain.

Strengths: Outstanding football intelligence. Sharp zone eyes to see route combos and anticipate the thrown ball. Zeroes in on the quarterback's eyes and is quick to jump routes. Had the longest arms of any defensive back at the Combine and has very good overall body length. Good production on the ball. Good hands and hand-eye coordination. Experienced, three-and-a-quarter year starter.

Weaknesses: Too upright, stiff and choppy in his pedal. Struggles to match up against speed and quickness in the slot and is a liability carrying vertical receivers in man coverage. Lacks physicality and plays small in the run game. Bench-pressed only 11 reps at the Combine, the fewest of any safety.

Future: A stiff, tightly wound boundary safety with good ball skills, football intelligence and awareness to function as an interchangeable safety. Lacks the physicality desired in the box and ideal range and cover skill on the back end and would be most ideally suited for a backup role.

Draft projection: Fourth- to fifth-round pick.

Scout's take: "I was expecting a lot better. I thought he was slow and heavy-legged and did not make plays."

NS-CB-RS **DAMARIOUS RANDALL**, #3 (Sr-5)

ARIZONA STATE ▶ GRADE: 5.64

Ht: 5-10 ⅞ | Wt: 196 | 40: 4.42 | Arm: 30 ¼ | Hand: 8 ⅝

History: Won a state title at Pensacola (Fla.) High. Played baseball (second base, outfield) at Butler Community College (Kan.) in 2010, but had shoulder surgery which prompted a return to football. Redshirted at Mesa (Ariz.) Community College in '11. Was an NJCAA All-American and the Arizona Community College Athletic Conference Defensive Player of the Year in '12 — recorded 73 tackles, six pass breakups and nine interceptions (one touchdown) with 2 ½ tackles for loss, one forced fumble and one blocked kick in 11 games. Also returned 19 kickoffs for 536 yards (28.2-yard average) and 15 punts for 312 yards (20.8), including two scores. With the Sun Devils in '13, started 9-of-12 games at free safety and contributed 71-3-3 (64-yard TD against Arizona) with 5 ½ tackles for loss and two forced fumbles. In '14, played boundary safety and was ASU's leading tackler after registering 106-9-3 (59-yard TD against Notre Dame) with 9 ½ tackles for loss, one sack and two forced fumbles. Had his right ankle spatted vs. Notre Dame.

Strengths: Very smooth in transition and has the movement skill of a cornerback with ability to cover receivers in the slot. Has a 38-inch vertical jump. Notched the best 3-cone drill time (6.83 seconds) of any free safety at the Combine and tied for the best short shuttle (4.07 seconds) in line with times of cornerbacks. Good man-cover skills. Plays with confidence. Aggressive tackler with good hip snap and explosion. Good hands. Flashes play-making ability. Has return ability.

Weaknesses: Has small hands and lacks the bone structure and bulk to hold up at safety. Is not disciplined with his technique and footwork could stand to improve — tends to pedal on his heels too much. Measured 14.9 percent body fat at the Combine (after adding 14 pounds since the end of the season). Will take some chances shooting low to cut as a tackler and misses in the open field.

Future: Fluid, athletic, small-framed, nickel safety capable of making a living in the slot if he could refine his cover skills and footwork. Ascending talent who has some similarities to 49ers 2014 first-round pick Jimmie Ward in his future role and dimensions, though Ward was smarter with better cover skills, ball skills and instincts.

Draft projection: Second- to third-round pick.

SS JORDAN RICHARDS, #8 (Sr-4)

STANFORD ▶ GRADE: 5.25

Ht: 5-10 ¾ | Wt: 211 | 40: 4.61 | Arm: 32 ½ | Hand: 9 ⅜

History: Won a state championship as a prep in California, where he also played basketball. Backed up strong safety Delano Howell as a true freshman in 2011 when he tallied 31 tackles, one pass breakup and zero interceptions in 13 games (three starts). Stepped into the lineup and started all 41 games the next three seasons — totaled 68-12-3 with 6 ½ tackles for loss, one sack and one forced fumble in '12 (14 games); 69-3-3 (30-yard touchdown against Washington) with four tackles for loss and one forced fumble in '13 (14 games); and 79-5-3 with 2 ½ tackles for loss and three forced fumbles in '14 (13 games). Team captain. Is one class short of a public policy degree, and intends to obtain a master's. Was named one of 17 National Football Foundation Scholar-Athletes, recognizing his excellence in academic, athletic and leadership.

Strengths: Good size with long arms. Very intelligent and football smart. Can line everyone up on the defense. Solid technician. Understands angles and route concepts. Competitive and tough. Will step downhill, take on blocks and force contain. Reliable, wrap tackler. Very good all-around character and will represent an organization with class. Extremely focused.

Weaknesses: Recorded the shortest broad jump (8-feet, seven inches) of any player at the Combine — limited explosion and athletic ability. Recorded a 32-inch vertical jump, the lowest of all strong safeties at the Combine. Limited recovery speed, body control, balance and burst. Cannot match up with slot receivers in man coverage in man coverage.

Future: A consistent, super-smart and dependable box safety lacking ideal foot speed and athletic ability to match up with NFL receivers, yet smart and tough enough to get by playing angles. Fits best in the box where he is not asked to cover much ground

and profiles as a backup.

Draft projection: Fifth- to sixth-round pick.

Scout's take: "(Richards) is going to play a long time in the league because he is so smart. He'll probably be a (No.) 3 (safety) for someone. He could be a 10-year veteran — the type of guy (Bill) Belichick would like. (Richards) has decent range. He plays faster than his 40-time. He is so smart and efficient in his movement (that) he could be a (No.) 2 (safety) eventually."

RCB-FS QUINTEN ROLLINS, #2 (Sr-5)

MIAMI-OHIO ▶ GRADE: 5.58

Ht: 5-11 ⅛ | Wt: 195 | 40: 4.54 | Arm: 30 ¼ | Hand: 9

History: Quinten was raised by his mother and grandmother, as his father was incarcerated until Quinten was 15. Was a three-year football captain (receiver-running back) and two-year basketball captain as an Ohio prep. Played basketball his first four years in Oxford (2010-14) — point guard started 106 games, racking up 214 steals and 391 assists. Two-year captain. With one year of NCAA eligibility remaining, joined the football team. Was named Mid-American Conference Defensive Player of the Year in 2014 after starting all 12 games and producing 72 tackles, nine pass breakups and seven interceptions (27-yard touchdown against Ohio) in 12 starts. Graduated with a degree in sport studies.

Strengths: Outstanding ball skills and hands. Strong, physical tackler. Very efficient with his movement and does not waste steps in transition. Does not gather himself to cut or jump and can sky for the ball. Plays the ball very well in front of him. Plays very well balanced, stays in phase and is always in position to recover. Can come downhill in the open field and make secure tackles. Plays with enough physicality and climbs the ladder well enough to match up with flexed tight ends. Offers position versatility, with traits that apply well to the safety position.

Weaknesses: Only played one year of college football and is still honing his eyes and technique. Did not match up against top competition in the Mid-American Conference. Lacks elite top-end speed and acceleration and struggled some matching up with quicker, sudden slot receivers at the Senior Bowl.

Future: A big, athletic, ball-hawking cornerback with a four-year basketball history that transferred very seamlessly to the football field. An ascending cover man whose best football is still in front of him, Rollins already

DEFENSIVE BACKS

showed remarkable improvement in his first year and ability to play cornerback or safety can enhance his draft status.

Draft projection: Second- to third-round pick.

Scout's take: "He is a four-year basketball player for Miami. He played running back in high school. He never played corner. That is what amazes me. How does a kid just line up and play? He has a skill set playing press defense on the hard wood. He actually looks like a running back when you see him in person. Quickness, knee bend, fight – he is a football player. I wasn't sure what I was going to see. I'm glad I made the trip to see him."

RCB-FS ERIC ROWE, #18 (Sr-4)

UTAH ▶ GRADE: 5.34

Ht: 6-0 ¾ | Wt: 205 | 40: 4.41 | Arm: 31 ½ | Hand: 9 ½

History: Lived in six cities in four states growing up. Also played basketball and ran track as a Texas prep. Learned both safety spots as a true freshman in 2011 when he started all 13 games (10 at free safety, three strong safety) and had 69 tackles, nine pass breakups and one interception with 2 ½ tackles for loss and one sack. Sustained a minor MCL sprain against California. In '10, started all 10 games at FS and tallied 64-5-1 with one-half tackle for loss. Missed two games after pulling his right hamstring in Week Two. Started all 12 games at FS in '13, logging 69-7-0 with one tackle for loss and one-half sack. Moved to cornerback in '14 when he started 10-of-12 games played (one at FS) and collected 59-13-1 (11-yard touchdown against Washington State) with three tackles for loss and a blocked kick. Did not play against Arizona State and did not start against Oregon. After the season, acknowledged a right LCL sprain and Achilles soreness. Graduated with a business degree.

Strengths: Exceptional size for a cornerback and very good speed. Clocked as low as 4.37 seconds in the 40-yard dash at the Combine, with a 3.97-second short shuttle and 6.77-second 3-cone drill time, both among the best of times at the CB position. Zone aware with good anticipatory skill. Has safety versatility. Has a 39-inch vertical jump. Experienced, four-year starter. Good football character. Coachable and competitive. Productive, four-year starter.

Weaknesses: Undisciplined eyes. Not a natural catcher. Supports the run recklessly and will miss some open-field tackles. Does not play strong or to his size. Struggles with his back to the ball and clutches too much downfield — limited downfield ball skills.

Marginal recovery speed. Too much of a tweener.

Future: Intriguing press-man corner with the length ideally sought at the cornerback position. A tweener lacking ideal toughness, range and downfield ball skills for a safety and lacking the agility and recovery speed to function at corner outside short areas. Has some similarities Vikings 2007 third-round pick Marcus McCauley.

Draft projection: Second- to third-round pick.

Scout's take: "Big corners who can run historically don't last beyond the second round. He'll probably fit in the second somewhere. ... I don't think he should. But that's probably where he goes."

SS JAMES SAMPLE, #2 (Sr-4)

LOUISVILLE ▶ GRADE: 5.44

Ht: 6-2 ⅛ | Wt: 209 | 40: 4.51 | Arm: 32 | Hand: 9 ½

History: Sacramento native was a high-school teammate of Shaq Thompson. Suffered a torn labrum in high school which was misdiagnosed as a deep bone bruise — was limited to two games as a true freshman in 2011 before having surgery. Was buried on the depth chart in '12, seeing limited action in three games. Facing a position change to linebacker and an uphill battle for playing time, left UW and spent a year at American River College in Sacramento. Landed at UL thanks to the recommendation of grad assistant Cort Dennison, who was with Sample at UW. Arrived in the summer of '14 and won a camp battle for the job vacated by Jets '14 first-rounder Calvin Pryor — posted a team-high 90 tackles, eight pass breakups and four interceptions with two tackles for loss in 13 starts at free safety. Opted not to lift at the Combine.

Strengths: Outstanding size. Rocked with muscled and looks every bit the part. Has a powerful stride and good knock-back power in his body. Fills fast and is aggressive in run support. Steps downhill and can secure open-field tackles. Is tough, sacrifices his body and will deliver some jarring hits. Can buzz the flats and handle hook-curl responsibilities — is best when the ball is in front of him.

Weaknesses: Is tightly wound and too rigid and upright moving in reverse. Average coverage instincts and zone awareness. Can be lured by play-action — plays run-first and is susceptible to quick-hitting routes behind him. Only a one-year, full-time starter.

Future: A tough, hard-hitting, in-the-box banger with starter quality traits as a run

DEFENSIVE BACKS

defender. However, coverage limitations can be exposed the farther he is asked to travel and could be challenged on third downs if passing-game responsibilities are not very streamlined.

Draft projection: Third- to fourth-round pick.

Scout's take: "He has size and toughness. He is a box safety. That's what he really is — a plug-and-play box safety. He's kind of like the safety out of Washington State (Deone Bucannon) that the Cardinals took in the first round. He's really a nickel or dime linebacker. Sample is the same kind of guy. He's not smart enough to play the back half."

LCB-FS JOSH SHAW, #6 (Sr-5)

USC ▶ GRADE: 5.36

Ht: 6-0 ½ | Wt: 201 | 40: 4.39 | Arm: 30 ¾ | Hand: 9

History: Highly recruited Parade All American/do-it-all player from California. Began his college career at Florida, where he appeared in one game in 2010 before redshirting with a knee injury. Played 10 games in '11, drawing one starting assignment at safety, and tallied 22 tackles, one pass breakup and zero interceptions with one tackle for loss. Transferred to USC in '12 in order to be closer to home, where family members were having health and financial difficulties. Was granted a hardship waiver enabling him to play right away. Missed time during spring practice with a rib injury. In the fall (wore jersey No. 26), played all 13 games and started the final seven at cornerback, booking 30-6-2 with two forced fumbles. Started all 14 games in '13 — 11 at cornerback, three (Hawaii, Arizona, Notre Dame) at free safety — and logged 67-7-4 with 5 ½ tackles for loss. Suffered high ankle sprains in August '14 when he jumped off a balcony — fabricated a story about rescuing his drowning nephew because he didn't want to tell the coaching staff the truth about his injuries. In reality, Shaw was running from police who were called when an argument between Shaw and his longtime girlfriend got loud. When asked directly about the incident, Shaw lied to head coach Steve Sarkisian. The tale of his "heroism" was publicized by USC and went national before the weight of Shaw's guilt prompted him to come clean. The school and law enforcement looked into the domestic incident, but no charges resulted (Shaw and his girlfriend insist the argument never became physical). After being stripped of his captaincy and forced to the sidelines while the situation played out, Shaw played in the final three games of the season, starting the final two at cornerback against Notre Dame and

Nebraska and scratching 11-0-0. Graduated in December with a sociology degree.

Strengths: Very long-armed with outstanding body length for a cornerback. Won the weigh-in at the East-West Shrine game with his shredded physical physique and had a solid showing in the game nabbing an interception on an underthrown ball. Is aggressive jamming receivers at the line and attacking the ball in the air. Has corner-safety versatility. Produced the most bench-press reps (26) of any defensive back at the Combine. Extremely well-conditioned athlete — measured only 4.2 percent body fat at the Combine. Has special teams experience.

Weaknesses: Average hip flexibility. Lacks discipline in coverage and loses positioning too often free-lancing. Does not play to his timed speed or show the acceleration and burst to carry receivers down the field. Lets receivers get on top of him too quickly and is late to transition and recover. Marginal production. Does not come to balance in the open field and misses tackles.

Future: Looks like Tarzan, plays like Jane. A big, fast, strong press corner that looks like a first-round talent on paper and has immense physical talent, yet did not play to it as a senior and still has much to prove. Has starter potential if he can return to junior form and could warrant as much interest as a safety as he does at cornerback.

Draft projection: Third- to fourth-round pick.

Scout's take: "Shaw only played in two games this year and when he did come in, he did not play well. The one game he played the most was the Notre Dame game. He got beat three times. He was jogging and not working hard. The consensus in the scouting community is negative."

RCB JaCOREY SHEPHERD, #24 (Sr-4)

KANSAS ▶ GRADE: 5.44

Ht: 5-10 ⅞ | Wt: 199 | 40: 4.55e | Arm: 30 ⅜ | Hand: 8 ⅝

History: Also played basketball as a Texas prep. Was recruited as a receiver. Played 10 games as a true freshman in 2011 (two starts), tallying three catches for 107 yards (35.7-yard average) and two touchdowns. Switched to defense in '12 when Charlie Weis' staff arrived. Did not see action in the first four games, but produced 15 tackles, three pass breakups and zero interceptions with one tackle for loss in the last eight games, including three starts as a nickel back. In '13, started all 12 games at corner and put up 45-13-2 (32-yard touchdown against TCU) with two tackles for loss, one sack and one forced fumble. Manned the right cornerback spot in '14 when he led the Big 12 in passes defended with 30-16-3 in 12 starts. For his career, returned 63 kickoffs for 1,350 yards (21.4-yard average). Received the Lee Roy Selmon Community Spirit Award and was a finalist for the senior CLASS Award. Did not run at the Combine after straining his left hamstring in a DB turn drill. Scheduled to graduate in May with a degree in management and leadership with an emphasis in entrepreneurship.

Strengths: Very good size. Maintains good positioning and stays in phase. Fluid hips. Smooth transitioning out of his pedal and shows very good awareness to stay on top of routes. Terrific hand use. Superb pattern recognition and ball skills, as evidenced in career production on the ball. Plays the ball like a receiver and makes some acrobatic interceptions (see Iowa State). Very good football intelligence. Outstanding work habits. Is a student of the game and it shows.

Weaknesses: Short arms and small hands. Lacks ideal foot speed and is not a blazer. Below-average recovery speed on double-moves. Not explosive out of his breaks. Could struggle keeping stride with receivers down the field in man coverage.

Future: An underrated, natural cover man with the ball skills, anticipation and instincts to contribute readily as a No. 3 corner and make a living in the slot. Has enough length and physicality to play outside. Has been very well technically refined by Kansas defensive coordinator and DBs coach Dave Campo and made big strides

Draft projection: Third- to fourth-round pick.

Scout's take: "Shepherd is a converted receiver. He has only played the position a few years and keeps getting better and better. If you start from the back and watch every game from the end of the season, you'll notice it. …He had a bunch of flash plays vs. TCU. He leads the team in PBUs and not because he can't catch. He reads playing indicators and times up the ball really naturally. You can be taught to read indicators. They coached him up very nicely."

FS DERRON SMITH, #13 (Sr-5)

FRESNO STATE ▶ GRADE: 5.39

Ht: 5-10 | Wt: 200 | 40: 4.55e | Arm: 29 ¾ | Hand: 9

History: Safety/quarterback also played basketball as a California prep. Appeared in all 13 games as a true freshman in 2010,

recording 29 tackles, one pass breakup and zero interceptions with one tackle for loss. In '11, managed 16-2-1 with one tackle for loss and one forced fumble in three games before suffering a season-ending broken left arm injury (received medical hardship). Returned to start all 40 games the next three seasons at strong safety — totaled 79-2-6 with one tackle for loss and one forced fumble in '12 (13 games); 87-6-7 (41-yard touchdown against USC) with eight tackles for loss and four sacks in '13 (13 games); and 93-7-1 with 2 ½ tackles for loss and nine punt returns for 99 yards (11.0-yard average) in '14 (14 games). As a junior, suffered an ankle injury against San Diego State and had it repaired shortly after the season. Team captain. Graduated with a communications degree. Medically excluded from working out at the Combine because of hernia surgery.

Strengths: Good instincts and anticipation — fine pattern recognition. Alert in zones. Takes good angles. Quick-footed and agile. Good movement skill. Smart and instinctive. Plays hard and competes. Motor runs hot. Strong tackler — hits with force. Very productive — has 15 career interceptions. Experienced, four-year starter. Strong personal and football character. Coachable. Football is very important to him.

Weaknesses: Undersized with short arms and small hands. Lacks the length to match up with big receivers in man coverage. Plays too recklessly in run support and is not a secure, dependable, open-field tackler. Measured 14.2 percent body fat at the Combine and could stand to improve his conditioning. Durability needs to be examined.

Future: A compact, well-built, smart free safety with a well-balanced skill set to run, cover and tackle. Has the instincts and desire to earn a starting job.

Draft projection: Third- to fourth-round pick.

NCB D.J. SMITH, #21 (Sr-4)

FLORIDA ATLANTIC ▶ GRADE: 5.31

Ht: 5-10 | Wt: 187 | 40: 4.44 | Arm: 30 ⅜ | Hand: 8 ⅛

History: First name is pronounced "De-Jawn." Also ran track as a Miami prep. Was suspended four games as a junior for a personal foul penalty (illegal hit). Appeared in all 12 games as a true freshman in 2011, tallying 10 tackles, zero pass breakups and zero interceptions. Added 23 kickoff returns for 480 yards (20.9-yard average). Started 9-of-11 games played in '12, recording 25-8-

1 with one tackle for loss and 10-214 (21.4) on kickoff returns. Was benched the final three games of the season because of poor practice habits. Was the Owls' MVP in '13 when he started all 12 games and collected 35-13-7 (75-yard touchdown against South Florida) with two tackles for loss, one sack and two forced fumbles. Was the Owls' Defensive MVP in '14 when he started all 11 games played and posted 53-8-1 (23-yard TD against Tulsa) with 2 ½ tackles for loss and one forced fumble. Added 14-235 (16.8) on kickoff returns. Did not play against Alabama (shoulder). Team captain.

Strengths: Patient in his pedal with good man cover skills. Transitions cleanly and shows excellent long speed to keep stride with receivers. Good body control to mirror his man and ride the hip pocket. Good hands — natural catcher. Willing to fill in run support.

Weaknesses: Thin-framed and lacks the size to match up with big receivers. Hands measured the smallest of any player at the Combine. Could stand to play with more eye discipline. Low cut tackler. Could require some extra reps to assimilate a game plan.

Future: A quick-footed, speedy corner lacking ideal size to match up outside, yet possesses the athletic ability, ball skills and movement ideally desired in the slot. Must prove he could stay healthy.

Draft projection: Fourth- to fifth-round pick.

LCB TYE SMITH, #24 (Sr-4)
TOWSON ▶ GRADE: 5.00

Ht: 6-0 ⅛ | Wt: 195 | 40: 4.56 | Arm: 32 | Hand: 8 ¾

History: Also played basketball and ran track as a North Carolina prep. As a true freshman in 2011 (wore jersey No. 39), recorded 49 tackles, three pass breakups and two interceptions with two tackles for loss, one sack and one forced fumble in 11 games (four starts). Was the Tigers' leading tackler in '12 — recorded 75-5-1 with four tackles for loss, 2 ½ sacks and two forced fumbles in 11 starts. In '13, started 15-of-16 games as the Tigers advanced to the FCS national championship — totaled 103-12-2 with 4 ½ tackles for loss, one sack, two forced fumbles and one blocked kick. Did not start vs. Fordham because of a foot injury and missed some time in the spring while recovering from a procedure on his injured foot. Started all 12 games in '14, logging 85-8-1 with 2 ½ tackles for loss and

one forced fumble. Team captain.

Strengths: Good short-area quickness and burst. Registered a 3.96-second short shuttle and 6.97 3-cone drill time, indicating very good agility and change of direction. Was assigned to cover the opponent's top receiver each week and matched up well at the East-West Shrine game.

Weaknesses: Has small hands and is not a natural catcher. Regularly faced small-school competition and seldom was challenged. Does not play physical or like to support the run. Too thin-framed, underpowered and soft as a tackler.

Future: A lean, long-limbed, press corner most ideally suited for a press cover team such as the Eagles or Seahawks, Smith must show more toughness and willingness as a tackler to earn a roster spot.

Draft projection: Priority free agent.

RCB DAMIAN SWANN, #5 (Sr-4)
GEORGIA ▶ GRADE: 5.08

Ht: 6-0 | Wt: 189 | 40: 4.48 | Arm: 31 | Hand: 8 ⅞

History: Four-year two-way starter (safety-receiver) as a Georgia prep. Played 11 games as a true freshman in 2011 (one start), tallying five tackles, zero pass breakups and zero interceptions with one tackle for loss. Missed two September contests with a hip flexor injury. In '14, started all 14 games and logged 53-5-4 with two tackles for loss, two sacks and two forced fumbles. Missed time during '13 fall camp (hip flexor/groin strain) before starting all 13 games and accumulating 57-8-0 with one tackle for loss. Started all 12 games played in '14 — seven at the "Star," four at corner and one (Missouri) at free safety — and totaled 65-8-4 with 4 ½ tackles for loss, two sacks, four forced fumbles and a 99-yard fumble recovery score against Georgia Tech. Sat out against Troy (headache). Also had 14 career punt returns for 65 yards (4.6-yard average). Team captain. Opted not to lift at the Combine and did not run shuttles because of a right hamstring strain.

Strengths: Good height to tighten throwing windows. Versatile and has lined up at cornerback and safety. Functions well in zone coverage, anticipating underneath routes. Willing run defender.

Weaknesses: Has small hands. Tight-hipped and upright in his pedal — does not play to his timed speed. Lacks coordination and balance in his feet when flipping his hips and is late to transition. Has some underachiever

DEFENSIVE BACKS

tendencies.

Future: A tall, thin-framed, bump-and-run corner who struggles clinging to his man in coverage, yet offers intriguing length and straight-line speed to continue trying to develop.

Draft projection: Late draftable pick.

Scout's take: "I wouldn't draft him, but he is the type of player that I think could make our team as an undrafted free agent because he is a good football player."

FS JAQUISKI TARTT, #6 (Sr-5)

SAMFORD ▶ GRADE: 5.64

Ht: 6-1 ⅜ | Wt: 221 | 40: 4.51 | Arm: 32 ⅜ | Hand: 9 ⅞

History: Alabama native and high school basketball player who didn't play football until his senior season, when he teamed with 49ers '14 first-rounder Jimmie Ward. Redshirted in 2010 while dealing with a right shoulder bruise. Appeared in 10 games in '11, collecting 23 tackles, zero pass breakups and zero interceptions. Did not play against Furman (right knee). Was the Bulldogs' leading tackler in '12 — totaled 94-10-4 (65-yard touchdown against Georgia Southern) with three tackles for loss, one forced fumble and an 80-yard fumble recovery score in 11 starts at free safety. Wore jersey No. 27 prior to junior season. Played through torn right labrum in '13 when he started all 12 games at FS and piled up 98-9-1 (33-yard TD against Georgia State) with one-half tackle for loss. Did not play against Florida A&M. In '14, had 62-1-1 with three tackles for loss in 11 starts at FS. Two-time Buck Buchanan Award finalist graduated in December with a degree in geography with a specialty in geographic systems (computer mapping). First Samford player invited to the Senior Bowl. Opted not to lift at the Combine.

Strengths: Sculpted and looks every bit the part with the build of a small linebacker. Impactful hitter with knockback body power. Intimidating hitter and back-end presence. Stones defenders in the hole. Good instincts. Confident and competitive. Secure, wrap open-field tackler. Quick to diagnose run/pass and sort out routes. Fills the alley with urgency. Good hands. Surprisingly agile and light on his feet for his size. Has a 37-inch vertical jump.

Weaknesses: Gives up some plays in coverage. Measured 16.8 percent body fat at the Combine, the highest of any defensive back and could stand to improve his conditioning.

Can be stressed by athletic tight ends and quick slot receivers.

Future: Big, strong, fast, physical FBS impact performer with a skill set that translates to the NFL. Shows some semblance to Jaguars 2013 second-round pick Johnathan Cyprien and could make an impact readily.

Draft projection: Second- to third-round pick.

Scout's take: "The coach said he hurt his shoulder in Week 2 and had surgery at the end of the year but never took himself out of any games. He was always in constant pain. I didn't know until I went in there. I liked that kid. ... A lot of (scouts) were comparing him to the Georgia Southern safety (Cowboys 2013 third-rounder J.J. Wilcox) that shined at the Senior Bowl a few years ago. (Tartt) compares himself all the time to Wilcox and thinks he is better than him. That is what he was saying at the school in the fall when I was in there."

LCB TRAE WAYNES, #15 (Jr-4)

MICHIGAN STATE ▶ GRADE: 6.37

Ht: 6-0 ⅛ | Wt: 186 | 40: 4.26 | Arm: 31 | Hand: 8 ¼

History: Also played baseball and ran track as a Wisconsin prep. Broke his fibula and ankle and tore ligaments as a senior in 2010. Redshirted in '11. Was a reserve/special-teams player in '12, scratching five tackles, zero pass breakups and zero interceptions and one-half sack in nine appearances. Started all 14 games at field corner in '13, producing 50-5-3 with 1 ½ tackles for loss. Manned the boundary corner in '14, notching 46-8-3 with two tackles for loss and one sack in '14 (13 starts). Did not run the 60-yard shuttle because of cramps.

Strengths: Rare speed to handle one-on-one assignments. Had the fastest 20-yard split (2.40 seconds) of any player at the Combine and the fastest recorded 40-yard time (4.23) of any defensive back at the event. Extremely well-conditioned athlete — measured only 4.2 percent body fat at the Combine. Plays very clean-footed and coordinated, with good balance in his feet. Has a measured, controlled pedal and transitions seamlessly out of his breaks. Can accelerate to top gear in a blink and has exceptional closing burst. Very good recovery speed. Functional tackler — will wrap and drive to drive down.

Weaknesses: Upright in his pedal. Played into the boundary. Very small hands and may be too lean. Tends to grab and hold too much and could benefit from honing his technique

DEFENSIVE BACKS

in off coverage. Gets on top of receivers with his rare speed and gets back-shouldered by quarterbacks sensing how much Wayne overcommits. Recorded a 4.40-second short shuttle, the second-slowest of any cornerback at the Combine, and lateral agility could stand to improve.

Future: A sleek, confident, wiry, sticky press corner with rare speed to keep stride with receivers down the field. Questions still exist about his willingness to tackle, though he is willing enough in run support to be effective and has all the athletic traits. Rare speed will allow him to compensate for his shortcomings and should become a very solid pro.

Draft projection: Top-20 pick.

Scout's take: "He looks a lot like (Tampa Bay 2013 43rd overall pick) Johnathan Banks. (Waynes) has a puny, tiny waist and a tiny bubble on him. He is real wiry lean. He is a cross between Banks and (Cincinnati 2012 17th overall pick) Dre' Kirkpatrick. … I like him. I wish he would start wrapping up (ball carriers) better. His arms hang down to his knees. He is my top corner."

NCB KEVIN WHITE, #25 (Sr-5)

TCU ▶ GRADE: 5.09

| Ht: 5-9 ⅛ | Wt: 183 | 40: 4.61* | Arm: 30 ⅛ | Hand: 8 ⅜ |

*STRAINED HIS RIGHT HAMSTRING WHILE RUNNING.

History: Texas native. Redshirted in 2010. Played 12 games in '12, starting three, and tallied 18 tackles, zero pass breakups and zero interceptions with 2 ½ tackles for loss. Did not play against BYU. Started 12-of-13 games in '12, notching 37-8-1. Did not start against Oklahoma State (coach's decision). Started all 25 games the next two seasons — totaled 40-8-3 in '13 (12 games); and 51-11-2 with four tackles for loss and one sack in '14 (13 games). Was sent a message during the team's off week in September when head coach Gary Patterson temporarily demoted him to the second team for not playing up to standard. Did not run shuttles at the Combine after pulling his right hamstring in first 40 attempt.

Strengths: Light on his feet. Tied with three others for the fastest 10-yard split (1.50 seconds) among defensive backs at the Combine — good short-area burst. Very strong pound-for-pound — bench-presses twice his weight. Plays hard and competes. Good football character.

Weaknesses: Very small hands. Had the shortest wingspan (70 ⅝ inches) of any defensive back at the Combine. Could stand to improve eyes and anticipation. Plays small

— struggles to shed blocks and adequately support the run. Exposed by vertical speed at the Senior Bowl.

Future: A quick, agile, short-area corner, White made big strides as a senior when he replaced his mentor Jason Verrett, yet lacks the size and foot speed desired outside and ideal physicality for the slot. Could contend for a job as a No. 4 or 5 cornerback.

Draft projection: Priority free agent.

Scout's take: "He is tiny with limited speed. He'll have a hard time holding up at our level."

FS-CB JERMAINE WHITEHEAD, #35 (Sr-4)

AUBURN ▶ GRADE: 5.04

| Ht: 5-11 | Wt: 197 | 40: 4.56 | Arm: 31 | Hand: 9 ⅜ |

History: Was valedictorian as a Mississippi prep. Played all 13 games as a true freshman in '11 (wore jersey No. 32) — recorded 31 tackles, three pass breakups and one interception (25-yard interception touchdown against Florida Atlantic) with 1 ½ tackles for loss in 13 games (made first career start at nickel back against Alabama). Started all 12 games at strong safety in '12, producing 90-4-0 with four tackles for loss and one sack. Started all 14 games at free safety in '13, notching 65-6-2 with 2 ½ tackles for loss. In '14, managed 36-1-6 with one tackle for loss in nine games (six starts at FS) — beginning in Week Three, served a four-game suspension (Kansas State, LSU, Mississippi State and South Carolina) after getting into a verbal altercation with his position coach. Was demoted to special-teams duty (requiring him to change his jersey from No. 9 to No. 35 in order to be on the field with the Tigers' return man Roc Thomas) and did not get back into the starting lineup until Nov. 15 at Georgia. Graduated in August with an accounting degree.

Strengths: Good size-speed combination. Adjusts well to the ball in the air. Plays smart and can line up the defense. Versatile and has played every position in the secondary and contributed on special teams.

Weaknesses: Not a strong tackler — leaks yardage. Does not have ideal range to get over the top. Struggles matching up with quickness and speed in man coverage — tends to get back on his heels too much. Football character has come into question following clash with coaches, with some saying he is too smart for his own good.

Future: An intriguing developmental talent that did not see eye-to-eye with the coaching staff, yet possesses the football smarts and

DEFENSIVE BACKS

versatility to contend for a roster spot and contribute on special teams.

Draft projection: Priority free agent.

Scout's take: "(Whitehead) was suspended for the first two games after getting in an altercation with his position coach for the second year in a row. I thought he was intriguing. There will be an investigation. The coaches wanted him back, but the head coach did not."

RCB **P.J. WILLIAMS**, #26 (Jr-3)

FLORIDA STATE ▶ GRADE: 5.69

Ht: 6-0 | Wt: 194 | 40: 4.54 | Arm: 31 | Hand: 8 ⅝

History: Florida native. As a true freshman in 2012, appeared in all 14 games and booked 14 tackles, one pass breakup and zero interceptions with one tackle for loss. Missed the '13 season opener against Pittsburgh, but played 13, starting the final 11, and produced 35-7-3 (20-yard touchdown against Boston College) with 1 ½ tackles for loss. Was Defensive MVP of the national championship against Auburn. In '14, started all 13 games played and totaled 74-10-1 with 6 ½ tackles for loss, one sack and one forced fumble. Pulled a hamstring during fall camp and lingering soreness nagged him into the season (sat out against the Citadel). Was involved in a hit-and-run in the wee hours of Oct. 5, when the car Williams was driving (belonging to his grandmother) turned into the path of an oncoming car. Williams (along with teammate Ronald Darby) fled the scene on foot. Returned 20-30 minutes later, but was not subjected to an alcohol test or charged for leaving the scene. Ultimately, Williams (who was driving on a suspended license) received just two traffic tickets.

Strengths: Uses his hands well to redirect receivers. Can shadow and mirror in man coverage. Good leaping ability. Has a 40-inch vertical jump and tied with three others for the fastest 10-yard split (1.50 seconds) of any cornerback at the Combine. Smart and aware. Solid tackler — uses his size well.

Weaknesses: Has short arms and very small hands. Upright and tight in his pedal. Not a confident catcher. Average twitch, short-area burst and long speed. Struggled recovering from the trail position on vertical routes. Gives up too many plays, unable to recover when he gets beat. Tends to clutch and grab when challenged vertically. Leaves too much production on the field. Not a finisher.

Future: A long, instinctive, bump-and-run corner with the length to match up with big receivers yet lacking desirable speed. Will be best in a predominantly zone scheme where he could work short areas and play the ball in front of him.

Draft projection: Second- to third-round pick.

Scout's take: "(Williams) has decent quickness. He lacks speed. He is polished and makes a lot of steady plays, but he does not have a lot of juice and does not finish a lot. Some of our (scouts) like him a lot more than I do. There are (scouts) that have first-round grades on him. I have him in the third (round). There are receivers that can set him up and get on top of him. He struggled catching up in trail and finding the ball."

RCB-FS **JULIAN WILSON**, #2 (Sr-5)

OKLAHOMA ▶ GRADE: 5.12

Ht: 6-2 | Wt: 205 | 40: 4.53 | Arm: 32 ⅜ | Hand: 9 ¼

History: Oklahoma native also ran track in high school. Redshirted in 2010. Scratched two tackles, zero pass breakups and zero interceptions in '11 (11 appearances). Played all 13 games in '12, drawing two starting assignments, and booked 31-5-0 with two tackles for loss. Started 11-of-13 games in '13, logging 26-3-3 with 4 ½ tackles for loss. Played 11 games in '14, starting the first nine, and totaled 39-7-1 (100-yard touchdown against Tennessee) before breaking his left thumb against Baylor — did not play or was limited in the final four contests, and did not lift at the Combine. Team captain graduated with a human relations degree.

Strengths: Outstanding body and arm length. Good straight-line speed. Functional zone cover skills. Versatile and has played corner, safety and in the slot. Coachable and works at his craft.

Weaknesses: Very stiff. Is leggy in his movement and takes too many extra steps in his transition. Looks out of place in man coverage with limited route awareness. Average closing speed and recovery burst. Soft, leaky tackler.

Future: A very long-limbed, smooth, Cover 2 press corner with intriguing length to warrant late-round consideration. Lacks the size and toughness desired at safety.

Draft projection: Late draftable pick.

Scout's take: "He's a safety that converted to corner. He is long. He doesn't have short-area quickness, but he can run for a 6-foot, 200-pound corner. He has straight-line speed. He misses a lot of open-field tackles."

DEFENSIVE BACKS

SPECIALISTS

P WIL BAUMANN, #36 (Sr-4)
NORTH CAROLINA STATE ▶ GRADE: 4.90
Ht: 6-5 ⅝ | Wt: 187 | 40: 5.00e | Arm: 32 | Hand: 9 ⅛

History: Prepped in North Carolina. As a true freshman in 2011, punted 65 times for an average of 37.5 yards with a long of 62 and 21 dropped inside the 20-yard line. Sat out the Georgia Tech game after straining his groin during pregame. In '12, punted 74-38.9-L60-16 with one blocked. Booted 67-42.1-L66-19 in '13. Led the Atlantic Coast Conference in punt average in '14, logging 60-45.4-L67-23. Holds NC State career records for punts (266) and punting yards (1,868).

Future: Long-levered, right-footed punter who shows good leg strength and ability to drop punts deep inside opponent territory. Could compete for a job as a rookie.

Draft projection: Priority free agent.

PK KYLE BRINDZA, #27 (Sr-4)
NOTRE DAME ▶ GRADE: 4.95
Ht: 6-0 ⅝ | Wt: 236 | 40: 5.05e | Arm: 33 ¼ | Hand: 10

History: Also played soccer (goal keeper) and threw shot and discus as a prep in Michigan, where he set a state record with 19 field goals as a senior, including six from beyond 50 yards. As a true freshman in 2011, kicked off 71 times for an average of 65.3 yards with 12 touchbacks. In '12, made 23-of-31 field goal attempts (74.2 percent) with a long of 52, while booting kickoffs 71-62.6-26. Connected on 20-of-26 FG attempts (76.9) with a long of 53 in '13. Also kicked off 75-62.6-35 and punted 43 times for a 41.1-yard average with a long of 56, seven inside the 20-yard line and one bocked. Struggled in '14 — notched 14-24-L48 (58.3) on FGs; 81-63.3-52 on kickoffs; and 51-41.5-L55-21 on punts (one blocked). Capped his career with a game-winning, 32-yard field goal to defeat LSU in the Music City Bowl. For his career, made 117-of-119 extra points.

Future: Hardworking, right-footed kicker with leg strength to latch on thanks to his 64 percent touchback rate. Must prove his up-and-down senior season was an abberation.

Draft projection: Priority free agent.

LS JOE CARDONA, #93 (Sr-5)
NAVY ▶ GRADE: 4.85
Ht: 6-1 ⅝ | Wt: 242 | 40: 4.89 | Arm: 31 ½ | Hand: 9 ⅝

History: Also played lacrosse as a California prep. Just the second freshman to start at long snapper in program history. Played all 51 games 2011-14, tallying a total of seven tackles and one forced fumble. Participated in the Senior Bowl and was the only long snapper invited to the Combine.

Future: Talented, high-character long snapper who consistently fires the ball back with velocity and accuracy. Works hard at his craft and has the chops to make an NFL living, as he routinely registers snap times under 0.70 seconds.

Draft projection: Priority free agent.

P KYLE CHRISTY, #4 (Sr-4)
FLORIDA ▶ GRADE: 5.00
Ht: 6-2 ¼ | Wt: 202 | 40: 5.10e | Arm: 30 ¼ | Hand: 8 ¾

History: Prepped in Indiana, drawing offers from UF and LSU out of high school. As a true freshman in 2011, stepped into the lineup the last seven games of the season and had 30 punts for a 40.9-yard average with a long of 67 and 10 inside the 20-yard line. Was a Ray Guy Award finalist in '12 when he booted 66-45.8-L62-27 (one blocked). Sat out '13 spring practice while recovering from labrum surgery — tore it in a scooter accident. In the fall, totaled 21-39.6-L53-7 with a 14-yard completion before he was demoted midway through the season. Reclaimed his job in '14, producing 64-44.2-L66-22 (one blocked). Finished his civil engineering degree in four and a half years, graduating cum laude.

Future: Strong-legged, right-footed punter with ability to flip the field. Drives punts with distance and hang time, enabling his coverage team to get down the field. Rebounded from a disappointing junior season to re-establish himself as a pro prospect.

Draft projection: Late draftable pick.

PK SAM FICKEN, #97 (Sr-4)
PENN STATE ▶ GRADE: 4.85
Ht: 6-1 ½ | Wt: 191 | 40: 5.05e | Arm: 31 | Hand: 9

History: Cousin, Robbie Hummel, plays for the NBA's Minnesota Timberwolves. Prepped in Indiana. As a true freshman in 2011, hit 1-of-2 field goals (50.0 percent) with a long of 43 (one blocked). Kicked off four times for a 65.2-yard average and zero touchbacks. Handled field goals and kickoffs for the Nittany Lions the next three seasons — kicked field goals 14-21-L38 (66.7) and kickoffs 68-61.9-27 in '12; 15-23-L54 (65.2) and 67-60.9-18 in '13; and 24-29-L50 (82.8) and 62-60.0-21 in '14. In his career, made 108-of-111 extra points. Had eight career field goal attempts blocked. Special-teams captain graduated in December with a finance degree.

Future: Mentally tough player who overcame very public struggles as a young player to put himself on the NFL radar. Will go as far as his accuracy and success in the clutch takes him.

Draft projection: Priority free agent.

P WILL JOHNSON, #38 (Sr-4)

TEXAS STATE   ▶ GRADE: 5.00

Ht: 6-2 | Wt: 206 | 40: 4.82 | Arm: 31 ½ | Hand: 9

History: Texas native also played baseball in high school. As a true freshman in 2011, connected on 13-of-24 field goal attempts (one blocked) while kicking off 63 times for 65.5-yard average and 17 touchbacks. In '12, punted 22 times for a 41.0-yard average with a long of 59 and nine inside the 20-yard line, while kicking field goals 12-17-L54 (70.6) and kickoffs 37-63.8-20. Punted 41-44.0-L65 (19) in '13 with 56-64.1-38 on kickoffs. Went 0-5 on FG attempts, including two blocked. Capped his career with 65-43.8-L70-21 on punts, 71-63.4-46 on kickoffs and 11-15-L49 (73.3) on field goals. Made 108-of-110 career extra points. Invited to the Combine.

Future: Well-built, strong-legged punter who launches punts with NFL-caliber hang time. Also posted a 66-percent touchback rate his final two seasons.

Draft projection: Priority free agent.

PK JOSH LAMBO, #49 (Sr-3)

TEXAS A&M   ▶ GRADE: 5.00

Ht: 6-0 ¼ | Wt: 216 | 40: 5.05e | Arm: 29 ½ | Hand: 9

History: Married. Graduated high school in 2 ½ years before pursuing a professional soccer career — was selected in the first round of the 2008 MLS draft and spent time on the national under-20 team. After the '11 soccer season, sought out former Wisconsin kicker Taylor Mehlhaff to learn how to kick a football. Walked onto the A&M football team in '12, booking two successful extra points. Established himself in '13 when he made 8-of-10 field goal attempts (80.0 percent) with a long of 45 yards. Kicked 13-15-L50 (86.7) in '14. Missed just one extra point in 111 career attempts. Nominee for the Senior CLASS Award, the Wuerffel

Trophy, and the Burlsworth Trophy. Graduated in December with a degree in agricultural leadership and renewable natural resources. Will turn 25 during his rookie season.

Future: Powerful, right-footed kicker with terrific leg strength and deep range well beyond 50 yards. The ball jumps off his foot with rise and height. Could have some upside, as he's been remarkably accurate for a player with just two years of kicking under his belt. Mature, hardworking and cool under pressure.

Draft projection: Late draftable pick.

P KYLE LOOMIS, #29 (Sr-MILITARY)

PORTLAND STATE   ▶ GRADE: 5.10

Ht: 6-1 ⅝ | Wt: 221 | 40: 4.95e | Arm: 32 ¼ | Hand: 9 ⅞

History: Oregon native. Began his college career at Oregon State in 2006 when he punted 62 times for a 41.3-yard average with a long of 62 and 14 inside the 20-yard line. Also tossed a 27-yard completion. Left school before the '07 season and enlisted in the Army — served three years and eight months in the 2-325 Airborne Infantry Regiment - 82nd Airborne Division in Fort Bragg, N.C. Underwent two surgeries on his right ankle during his time in the military. Was medically discharged in February '12 and spent six months working for the Oregon Department of Transportation. Joined PSU in '13 thanks to his relationship with an assistant coach who was with him at OSU. On the season, punted 56-46.5-L67-18 while kicking off 37 times for an average of 57.8 yards with nine touchbacks. Led the nation in net punting average (41.7 yards). In '14, booted 75-46.0-L65-32. Led the nation in punting for the second straight season while setting a school record for career average (46.2). Will turn 28 during his rookie season.

Future: Highly productive, right-footed punter who drives the ball with distance and hang time at his best, but will have to prove he can do so consistently to hold down a job in the pros.

Draft projection: Late draftable pick.

PK JUSTIN MANTON, #17 (Sr-4)

LOUISIANA-MONROE   ▶ GRADE: 5.11

Ht: 6-2 ¾ | Wt: 196 | 40: 5.00e | Arm: 32 ½ | Hand: 8 ¾

History: Louisiana native also played basketball and baseball (left-handed) as a high schooler. As a true freshman in 2011, went 6-of-14 (42.9 percent) on field goal attempts (two blocked) and kicked off 53 times for a 54.8-yard average and zero touchbacks. In '12, made 5-9-L47 (55.6) despite three blocked, and booted kickoffs 71-60.0-22. Also punted 48 times for an average of 39.8 yards with a long of 66 and 19 dropped inside the 20-yard line. Handled all three duties the next two seasons — kicked FGs 5-9-L38 (55.6), kickoffs 53-61.4-30 and punts 80-45.8-L77-24 with four blocked (two FGs, two punts) in '13; and 20-24-L51 (83.3), 54-59.9-29 and 76-42.4-L67-20 with three blocked (two punts, one FG) in '14. Made 148-of-152 career extra points. Scheduled to graduate in May with a kinesiology degree.

Future: Long-levered, smoother-than-powerful, right-footed kicker who punches the ball with accuracy. Is dedicated to his craft and athletic for the position.

Draft projection: Late draftable pick.

P TREVOR PARDULA, #16 (Sr-4)

KANSAS   ▶ GRADE: 4.80

Ht: 6-4 ⅜ | Wt: 227 | 40: 4.95e | Arm: 32 ⅝ | Hand: 9 ½

History: Also played soccer as a California prep. Played on a 1-9 team and did not have recruiting visibility. Spent two years at De Anza College (Calif.), where he punted 48 times for a 39.8-yard average with a long of 66 and 11 dropped inside the 20-yard line in 2011. In '12, punted 47-40.9-L55 (13), while connecting on 13-of-22 field goal attempts (59.1 percent) with a long of 42 yards. Punted and kicked off for the Jayhawks — booted 84-43.7-L78-25 and 42-60.2-21 in '13; and 83-44.3-L72-24 and 41-56.7-13 in '14. Also made four tackles and forced a fumble as a senior.

Future: Tall, three-step, lefty punter whose loose, strong leg enabled the Jayhawks to finish second in the nation with a 44.0-yard net punting average. Shows ability to drop balls inside the 20-yard line, though he will have to hasten his steps in order to avoid double-thuds in the pros.

Draft projection: Priority free agent.

P BRADLEY PINION, #92 (Jr-3)

CLEMSON   ▶ GRADE: 5.20

Ht: 6-5 | Wt: 229 | 40: 4.95e | Arm: 32 ¼ | Hand: 10 ⅛

History: USA Today All-American also played baseball and soccer (goalkeeper) as a North Carolina prep. Drew national attention after he drilled a 100-yard kickoff at a high school kicking showcase. Was not the primary punter or kickoff man as a true freshman in 2012, but had nine punts averaging 39.4 yards with three dropped inside the 20-yard line and had 26 kickoffs averaging 63.7 yards with 18 touchbacks. Took over in '13 when he punted 56-39.4-L56-24 and kicked off 79-60.7-38. In '14, paced Atlantic Coast Conference punters in punts inside the 20, breaking his own school record — booted 75-42.6-L60-28 (just two touchbacks) while notching 74-62.0-36 on

kickoffs.

Future: Tall, long-levered, strong-legged, right-footed punter who looks and plays the part. Capable of booming punts that bring rain and pin opponents deep in their own territory. Could challenge for a job as a rookie.

Draft projection: Late draftable pick.

PK JARED ROBERTS, #47 (Sr-5)

COLORADO STATE   ▶ GRADE: 4.95

Ht: 5-11 ¾ | Wt: 210 | 40: 5.10e | Arm: 30 ⅛ | Hand: 9

History: Colorado native prepped at Mullen High, where he was a soccer player before joining the football team and winning two state championships. Did not make the Rams' roster until 2012 when he made 9-of-10 field goal attempts (90.0 percent) with a long of 49 yards and kicked off 52 times for a 61.2-yard average with 20 touchbacks. Set a CSU single-season scoring record in '13 when he racked up 121 points — drilled 21-24-L54 (87.5) with 94-60.4-31 on kickoffs. In '14, kicked field goals 12-20-L53 (60.0) and kickoffs 81-63.3-38. Capped his career with a game-winning 46-yard field-goal over Utah State. Converted 144-of-147 career extra points, including a Mountain West-record 111 straight. Graduated in May with a business degree and is working on a master's degree.

Future: Right-footed kicker with a strong, quick leg. Drilled 5-of-6 attempts beyond 50 yards the last two seasons, and isn't afraid to make a clutch kick. Hard working, competitive prospect who blends well in the locker room.

Draft projection: Priority free agent.

P SPENCER ROTH, #36 (Sr-4)

BAYLOR   ▶ GRADE: 4.85

Ht: 6-4 ¼ | Wt: 227 | 40: 5.00e | Arm: 32 ¼ | Hand: 9 ½

History: Prepped at Knoxville (Tenn.) Catholic. Handled the Bears' punting duties all four years in Waco. Had 29 punts for a 40.5-yard average with a long of 64 and six dropped inside the 20-yard line in 20, as the Bears punted fewer times than any team in college football. Totaled 36-43.8-L65-13 in '12; 52-45.8-L72-17 (one blocked) in '13; and 47-43.4-L69-19 in '14. His 43.7-yard career average ranks second in school history.

Future: Big, experienced punter who wasn't called upon often in college, but is adept at pinning returners near the boundary. Shows some polish, including low-effort mechanics as well as the ability to alter his drop for "coffin-corner" kicks or hasten his steps in the face of the rush.

Draft projection: Priority free agent.

SPECIALISTS

DRAFT NEEDS

AFC NORTH

BALTIMORE RAVENS	RK		CINCINNATI BENGALS	RK
OC - Marc Trestman (1)	8/13		OC - Hue Jackson (2)	6/21
DC - Dean Pees (4)	4/23		DC - Paul Guenther (2)	20/20
ST - Jerry Rosburg (8)	5		ST - Darrin Simmons (13)	6
CLEVELAND BROWNS	RK		PITTSBURGH STEELERS	RK
OC - Joe Defilippo (1)	17/20		OC - Todd Haley (4)	16/2
DC - Jim O'Neil (2)	32/8		DC - Keith Butler (1)	6/27
ST - Chris Tabor (5)	17T		ST - Danny Smith (3)	21

AFC EAST

BUFFALO BILLS	RK		MIAMI DOLPHINS	RK
OC - Greg Roman (1)	25/18		OC - Bill Lazor (2)	12/17
DC - Dennis Thurman (1)	11/3		DC - Kevin Coyle (4)	24/6
ST - Danny Crossman (3)	2		ST - Darren Rizzi (6)	12
NEW ENGLAND PATRIOTS	RK		NEW YORK JETS	RK
OC - Josh McDaniels (4)	18/9		OC - Chan Gailey (1)	3/32
DC - Matt Patricia (4)	9/17		DC - Kacy Rodgers (1)	5/14
ST - Joe Judge (1)	3		ST - Bobby April (1)	20

AFC WEST

DENVER BRONCOS	RK		KANSAS CITY CHIEFS	RK
OC - Rick Dennison (1)	15/4		OC - Doug Pederson (3)	10/29
DC - Wade Phillips (1)	2/9		DC - Bob Sutton (3)	28/2
ST - Joe DeCamillis (1)	19		ST - Dave Toub (3)	8
OAKLAND RAIDERS	RK		SAN DIEGO CHARGERS	RK
OC - Bill Musgrave (1)	32/26		OC - Frank Reich (2)	30/10
DC - Ken Norton Jr. (1)	22/16		DC - John Pagano (4)	26/4
ST - Brad Seely (1)	22		ST - Kevin Spencer (3)	29

AFC SOUTH

HOUSTON TEXANS	RK		INDIANAPOLIS COLTS	RK
OC - Bill O'Brien (2)	5/24		OC - Pep Hamilton (3)	22/1
DC - Romeo Crennel (2)	10/21		DC - Greg Manusky (4)	18/12
ST - Bob Ligashesky (3)	15T		ST - Tom McMahon (3)	7
JACKSONVILLE JAGUARS	RK		TENNESSEE TITANS	RK
OC - Greg Olson (1)	21/31		OC - Jason Michael (2)	26/22
DC - Bob Babich (3)	27/22		DC - Ray Horton (2)	31/15
ST - Mike Mallory (3)	27		ST - Steve Hoffman (3)	28

Following is a breakdown of the coordinators for each team with the number of years they have served in the position in parentheses. Where they finished ranked in the league on offense, defense and special teams is also included, with yards per game used as the benchmark for offense and defense.

The first number represents where the offensive unit finished ranked in rushing yards per game and the second in passing yards per game. For example, the Ravens finished ranked 8th in run offense and 13th in pass offense. Defensively, rush yardage allowed and passing yardage allowed are the fields displayed. For example, the Ravens finished 3th in run defense and 23rd in passing defense. Sportsday's rankings based on a calculation of 22 special teams categories was used as the benchmark for special teams rankings. Free agency will continue to shape needs prior to the draft, but the following chart should provide an idea of where teams have the most room to improve.

NFC NORTH

CHICAGO BEARS	RK	DETROIT LIONS	RK
OC - Adam Gase (1)	27/15	OC - Joe Lombardi (2)	28/12
DC - Vic Fangio (1)	17/30	DC - Teryl Austin (2)	1/13
ST - Jeff Rodgers (1)	26/30	ST - Joe Marciano (2)	15T

GREEN BAY PACKERS	RK	MINNESOTA VIKINGS	RK
OC -Tom Clements (4)	11/8	OC - Norv Turner (2)	14/28
DC - Dom Capers (7)	23/10	DC - George Edwards (2)	25/7
ST - Ron Zook (1)	32	ST - Mike Priefer (6)	10

NFC EAST

DALLAS COWBOYS	RK	NEW YORK GIANTS	RK
OC - Scott Linehan (2)	2/16	OC - Ben McAdoo (2)	23/7
DC - Rod Marinelli (2)	8/26	DC - Steve Spagnuolo (1)	30/18
ST - Rich Bisaccia (3)	13	ST - Tom Quinn (9)	25

PHILADELPHIA EAGLES	RK	WASHINGTON REDSKINS	RK
OC - Pat Shurmur (3)	9/6	OC - Sean McVay (2)	19/11
DC - Billy Davis (3)	15/31	DC - Joe Barry (1)	12/24
ST - Dave Fipp (3)	1	ST - Ben Kotwica (2)	30

NFC WEST

ARIZONA CARDINALS	RK	ST. LOUIS RAMS	RK
OC - Harold Goodwin (3)	31/14	OC - Frank Cignetti Jr. (1)	20/23
DC - James Bettcher (1)	13/29	DC - Gregg Williams (2)	14/19
ST - Amos Jones (3)	11	ST - John Fassel (4)	9

SAN FRANCISCO 49ERS	RK	SEATTLE SEAHAWKS	RK
OC - Geep Chryst (1)	4/30	OC - Darrell Bevell (5)	1/27
DC - Eric Mangini (1)	7/5	DC - Kris Richard (1)	3/1
ST - Thomas McGaughey (1)	23	ST - Brian Schneider (6)	17T

NFC SOUTH

ATLANTA FALCONS	RK	CAROLINA PANTHERS	RK
OC - Kyle Shanahan (1)	24/5	OC - Mike Shula (3)	7/19
DC - Richard Smith (4)	21/32	DC - Sean McDermott (5)	16/11
ST - Keith Armstrong (8)	4	ST - Bruce DeHaven (3)	31

NEW ORLEANS SAINTS	RK	TAMPA BAY BUCCANEERS	RK
OC - Pete Carmichael, Jr. (7)	13/3	OC - Dirk Koetter (1)	29/25
DC - Rob Ryan (3)	29/25	DC - Leslie Frazier (2)	19/28
ST - Greg McMahon (10)	14	ST - Kevin O'Dea (2)	24

PLAYER RANKINGS

GRADE SCALE

9.0 — A once-in-a-generation player (e.g. Bo Jackson, Deion Sanders).

8.00-8.99 — Perennial All-Pro (e.g. Anthony Munoz).

7.00-7.99 — Eventual All-Pro.

6.50-6.99 — Sure-fire first-rounder should make immediate impact.

6.00-6.49 — Likely first-rounder capable of starting readily.

5.60-5.99 — Likely second-rounder with immediate starter potential.

5.40-5.59 — Likely third-rounder minimally with sub-starter potential.

5.21-5.39 — Should make a roster and contribute on special teams

5.11-5.20 — Potential late-rounder with fair chance to earn a roster spot.

4.75-5.10 — Late draftable or priority free agent capable of battling for a roster spot.

4.00-4.75 — Solid free agent capable of being invited to an NFL training camp.

ALERT SYMBOLS

Jr. — Player is a junior.

Soph-3 — Player is a third-year sophomore.

QB — Can also play quarterback or the position that is listed, such as RS for return specialist.

Ch. — Character (i.e. history of arrests, team suspensions or off-field problems) can affect draft status.

X — Has a current injury situation that could affect camp status.

XX — Past or present durability concerns could affect draft status.

XXX — Serious injury concern.

About the player printout: Players are ranked according to their grades, not necessarily in the order they will be drafted. Factors such as a drafting team's needs and the abundance or scarcity of available talent at a given position can cause a player to be drafted higher or lower than his grade would indicate. All grades take into account workouts up to and including the Indianapolis Scouting Combine. Post-Combine workouts were not factored.

QUARTERBACKS

RK. NAME	SCHOOL	GRADE	NOTES
1. Jameis Winston	Florida State	6.80	Soph-3, Ch.
2. Marcus Mariota	Oregon	6.70	Jr.
3. Bryce Petty	Baylor	5.52	
4. Brett Hundley	UCLA	5.42	Jr.
5. Sean Mannion	Oregon State	5.32	
6. Garrett Grayson	Colorado State	5.36	
7. Bryan Bennett	Southeastern Louisiana	5.22	
8. Jerry Lovelocke	Prairie View A&M	5.20	
9. Shane Carden	East Carolina	5.18	
10. Cody Fajardo	Nevada	5.12	
11. Brandon Bridge	South Alabama	5.10	
12. Terrance Broadway	Louisiana-Monroe	5.04	
13. Taylor Heinecke	Old Dominion	5.02	
14. Blake Sims	Alabama	4.90	RB
15. Anthony Boone	Duke	4.80	
16. Tyler Murphy	Boston College	4.80	
17. Chris Bonner	Colorado State-Pueblo	4.80	
18. Justin Worley	Tennesseee	4.75	
19. Connor Halliday	Washington State	4.75	
20. Gary Nova	Rutgers	4.75	
21. Brandon Doughty	Western Kentucky	4.75	
22. Devin Gardner	Michigan	4.75	WR
23. Ryan Williams	Miami (Fla.)	4.50	
24. Jake Waters	Kansas State	4.50	
25. Kevin Rodgers	Henderson State	4.50	
26. Rakeem Cato	Marshall	4.50	
27. Andrew Hendrix	Miami (Fla.)	4.50	
28. Cole Stoudt	Clemson	4.50	
29. Bo Wallace	Mississippi	4.75	
30. Hutson Mason	Georgia	4.50	
31. Taylor Kelly	Arizona State	4.75	
32. Dylan Thompson	South Carolina	4.50	
33. Trevor Siemian	Northwestern	4.50	
34. Mark Myers	John Carroll	4.50	
35. Matt Joeckel	TCU	4.50	
36. Austin Sumner	South Dakota State	4.50	
37. Grant Hedrick	Boise State	4.50	
38. Garrett Safron	Sacramento State	4.50	

FULLBACKS

RK. NAME	SCHOOL	GRADE	NOTES
1. Jalston Fowler	Alabama	5.24	
2. Mike Burton	Rutgers	5.09	

3. Connor Neighbors	LSU	5.09	
4. Joey Iosefa	Hawaii	4.97	RB
5. Aaron Ripkowski	Oklahoma	4.75	
6. Mark Weisman	Iowa	4.50	
7. Jimmay Mundine	Kansas	4.50	
8. Larry Dixon	Army	4.50	
9. Channing Fugate	Eastern Kentucky	4.50	
10. Mike Marrow	Georgetown (Ky.)	4.50	
11. Paul Lasike	Brigham Young	4.50	
12. Hunter Joyer	Florida	4.50	
13. Zack Zwinak	Penn State	4.50	
14. Malcolm Johnson	Mississippi State	4.50	

RUNNING BACKS

RK. NAME	SCHOOL	GRADE	NOTES
1. Todd Gurley	Georgia	6.60	Jr., X, KR
2. Melvin Gordon	Wisconsin	6.27	Jr.
3. Tevin Coleman	Indiana	5.89	Jr., KR
4. Jay Ajayi	Boise State	5.81	Jr.
5. Duke Johnson	Miami-Fla.	5.57	
6. Ameer Abdullah	Nebraska	5.52	RS
7. T.J. Yeldon	Alabama	5.52	Jr.
8. Buck Allen	USC	5.48	Jr.
9. Jeremy Langford	Michigan State	5.42	
10. David Cobb	Minnesota	5.39	
11. David Johnson	Northern Iowa	5.39	KR
12. Mike Davis	South Carolina	5.37	Jr.
13. Josh Robinson	Mississippi State	5.28	Jr.
14. Cameron Artis-Payne	Auburn	5.24	
15. Malcolm Brown	Texas	5.24	
16. Karlos Williams	Florida State	5.23	KR
17. Matt Jones	Florida	5.22	Jr.
18. John Varga	Yale	5.22	FB
19. Trey Williams	Texas A&M	5.20	Jr., KR
20. Marcus Murphy	Missouri	5.20	RS
21. Terrence Magee	LSU	5.17	
22. Thomas Rawls	Central Michigan	5.17	
23. Zach Zenner	South Dakota State	5.16	FB
24. Dominique Brown	Louisville	5.12	
25. John Scheuerman	Lafayette	5.10	WR, KR
26. Gus Johnson	Stephen F. Austin	5.09	
27. Jahwan Edwards	Ball State	5.07	
28. Dee Hart	Colorado State	5.03	
29. B.J. Catalon	TCU	5.00	Jr., X, KR
30. Braylon Heard	Kentucky	4.95	Jr.
31. Michael Dyer	Louisville	4.92	
32. John Crockett	North Dakota State	4.85	
33. Kenny Hilliard	LSU	4.82	FB
34. Synjym Days	Georgia Tech	4.75	
35. Akeem Hunt	Purdue	4.75	
36. Kevin Parks	Virginia	4.75	
37. Tony Creecy	North Carolina State	4.75	
38. Jake Stetson	The Citadel	4.50	
39. Brandon Wegher	Morningside	4.50	
40. Prince-Tyson Gulley	Syracuse	4.50	
41. Malcolm Agnew	Southern Illinosi	4.50	
42. Ricky Seale	Stanford	4.50	
43. Terrell Watson	Azusa Pacific	4.50	
44. Joe Bergeron	Texas A&M-Commerce	4.50	

45. Marlin Lane	Tennessee	4.50	
46. Kenny Williams	Texas A&M	4.50	
47. Dreamius Smith	West Virginia	4.50	
48. Malcolm Agnew	Southern Illinois	4.50	
49. Abou Toure	Tennessee-Martin	4.50	
50. Joe Hill	Utah State	4.50	
51. Jordon James	UCLA	4.50	
52. Venric Mark	West Texas A&M	4.50	
53. Nick Hill	Michigan State	4.50	
54. Bill Belton	Penn State	4.50	
55. Travon Van	Montana	4.50	

WIDE RECEIVERS

RK. NAME	SCHOOL	GRADE	NOTES
1. Kevin White	West Virginia	6.75	
2. Amari Cooper	Alabama	6.65	Jr.
3. Devante Parker	Louisville	6.27	
4. Jaelen Strong	Arizona State	5.97	Jr.
5. Nelson Agholor	USC	5.92	Jr., RS
6. Dorial Green-Beckham	Oklahoma	5.85	Jr., Ch.
7. Devin Funchess	Michigan	5.67	Jr., TE
8. Devin Smith	Ohio State	5.64	RS
9. Breshad Perriman	Central Florida	5.57	Jr.
10. Sammie Coates	Auburn	5.56	
11. Tyler Lockett	Kansas State	5.52	RS
12. Phillip Dorsett	Miami-Fla.	5.47	RS
13. Tre McBride	William & Mary	5.47	RS
14. Rashad Greene	Florida State	5.46	PR
15. Mario Alford	West Virginia	5.42	KR
16. DeAndre Smelter	Georgia Tech	5.39	X
17. Jamison Crowder	Duke	5.38	PR
18. Ty Montgomery	Stanford	5.38	RB, RS
19. Stefon Diggs	Maryland	5.37	Jr., X
20. Justin Hardy	East Carolina	5.36	
21. Dres Anderson	Utah	5.35	X, KR
22. Tony Lippett	Michigan State	5.34	CB
23. Chris Conley	Georgia	5.33	
24. Antwan Goodley	Baylor	5.31	
25. Vince Mayle	Washington State	5.29	
26. Kenny Bell	Nebraska	5.27	
27. Josh Harper	Fresno State	5.27	
28. Darren Waller	Georgia Tech	5.26	TE
29. Titus Davis	Central Michigan	5.25	
30. Evan Spencer	Ohio State	5.24	
31. Dez Lewis	Central Arkansas	5.23	
32. Deandrew White	Alabama	5.19	
33. Rannell Hall	Central Florida	5.12	KR
34. Kaelin Clay	Utah	5.10	RS
35. Davaris Daniels	ex-Notre Dame	5.10	Jr.
36. J.J. Nelson	UAB	5.10	RS
37. Da'Ron Brown	Northern Illinois	5.09	
38. Devante Davis	UNLV	5.09	
39. Deon Long	Maryland	5.09	
40. Cam Worthy	East Carolina	5.09	
41. Tello Luckett	Harding	5.07	RB, KR
42. Chris Jones	Alabama	5.05	RS
43. Geremy Davis	Connecticut	5.01	

44. Keith Mumphery	Michigan State	4.88	
45. Ezell Ruffin	San Diego State	4.82	
46. Nigel King	Kansas	4.75	
47. Austin Hill	Arizona State	4.75	
48. Deontay Greenberry	Houston	4.75	Jr.
49. Andrew Turzilli	Rutgers	4.75	
50. Jake Kumerow	Wisconsin-Whitewater	4.75	
51. Zach D'Orazio	Akron	4.75	
52. Kasen Williams	Washington	4.75	
53. Jordan Taylor	Rice	4.75	
54. Matt Miller	Boise State	4.75	
55. George Farmer	USC	4.75	Jr.
56. Andre Davis	South Florida	4.75	
57. DeAndre Carter	Sacramento State	4.75	
58. Jordan Leslie	Brigham Young	4.50	
59. Levi Norwood	Baylor	4.50	
60. Nick Harwell	Kansas	4.50	
61. Jaxon Shipley	Texas	4.50	
62. Tacoi Sumler	Appalachian State	4.50	Jr.
63. Addison Richards	Regina (Can.)	4.50	
64. Andre Debose	Florida	4.50	
65. Rodney White	Florida Atlantic	4.50	
66. Andrew Opoku	Delaware	4.50	
67. Bud Sasser	Missouri	4.50	
68. Neal Sterling	Monmouth (NJ)	4.50	
69. Chris Harper	California	4.50	
70. Alex Wheat	Coastal Carolina	4.50	
71. Shak Phillips	Boston College	4.50	
72. David Frazier	Miami (Ohio)	4.50	
73. R.J. Harris	New Hampshire	4.50	
74. Glenn Coleman	Florida International	4.50	
75. Kyle Prater	Northwestern	4.50	
76. Damiere Byrd	South Carolina	4.50	
77. Issac Blakeney	Duke	4.50	
78. Daniel Rodriguez	Clemson	4.50	
79. Malcome Kennedy	Texas A&M	4.50	
80. Demetrius Wilson	Arkansas	4.50	
81. Christian Green	Florida State	4.50	
82. Kenny Cook	Gardner-Webb	4.50	
83. Michael Bennett	Georgia	4.50	
84. Justin McCray	Kansas	4.50	
85. Kevonte Martin-Manley	Iowa	4.50	
86. Keyarris Garrett	Tulsa	4.50	
87. Jarrod West	Syracuse	4.50	
88. Quinton Dunbar	Florida	4.50	
89. Tyrell Williams	Western Oregon	4.50	
90. Keanon Lowe	Oregon	4.50	
91. North Carolina State	North Carolina State	4.50	
92. Keiwone Malone	Memphis	4.50	
93. Michael Johnson	Delaware	4.50	
94. Shane Wynn	Indiana	4.50	
95. Jalen Fitzpatrick	Temple	4.50	
96. Jonathan Rumph	Georgia	4.50	
97. Drew Carswell	Indiana (Pa.)	4.50	
98. Ian Hamilton	UTEP	4.50	
99. Javess Blue	Kentucky	4.50	

100. Dallas Burroughs	Boise State	4.50	
101. Chase Cochran	Ohio State	4.50	
102. Jaquel Pitts	Trinity International	4.50	Jr.
103. Eli Rogers	Louisville	4.50	
104. Bradley Marquez	Texas Tech	4.50	

TIGHT ENDS

RK. NAME	SCHOOL	GRADE	NOTES
1. Maxx Williams	Minnesota	5.72	Jr.
2. Tyler Kroft	Rutgers	5.62	Jr.
3. Clive Walford	Miami-Fla.	5.40	
4. Busta Anderson	South Carolina	5.32	
5. Jeff Heuerman	Ohio State	5.31	
6. Nick Boyle	Delaware	5.26	
7. AJ Derby	Arkansas	5.24	
8. Blake Bell	Oklahoma	5.22	QB
9. Jesse James	Penn State	5.22	Jr.
10. Nick O'Leary	Florida State	5.22	FB
11. Gerald Christian	Louisville	5.21	
12. E.J. Bibbs	Iowa State	5.18	
13. Wes Saxton	South Alabama	5.18	
14. Mycole Pruitt	Southern Illinois	5.14	
15. Jean Sifrin	Massachusetts	5.10	Jr.
16. Eric Tomlinson	UTEP	5.10	
17. Ben Koyack	Notre Dame	4.97	
18. Cameron Clear	Texas A&M	4.93	
19. Randall Telfer	USC	4.92	
20. C.J. Uzomah	Auburn	4.75	
21. Casey Pierce	Kent State	4.75	
22. Khari Lee	Bowie State	4.50	
23. Tonga Westlee	Utah	4.50	
24. Devin Mahina	BYU	4.50	
25. Matt Lengel	Eastern Kentucky	4.50	
26. Brian Vogler	Alabama	4.50	
27. Khari Lee	Boise State	4.50	
28. Tyreese Russell	Eastern Michigan	4.50	
29. Steve Borden	Kentucky	4.50	
30. Jack Tabb	North Carolina	4.50	
31. Ray Hamilton	Iowa	4.50	
32. Gabe Holmes	Purdue	4.50	
33. James O'Shaughnessy	Illinois State	4.50	
34. Travis Dickson	LSU	4.50	
35. Jeff LePak	Eastern Illinois	4.50	
36. Will Tye	Stony Brook	4.50	
37. Shane Young	Sam Houston State	4.50	
38. Jon Davis	Illinois	4.50	
39. Andrew Gleichert	Michigan State	4.50	
40. Mitchell Henry	Western Kentucky	4.50	
41. Brian Parker	Albany	4.50	
42. Kevin Haplea	Florida State	4.50	
43. Kennard Backman	UAB	4.50	
44. Connor Hamlett	Oregon State	4.50	
45. Sam Arneson	Wisconsin	4.50	

CENTERS

RK. NAME	SCHOOL	GRADE	NOTES
1. Cameron Erving	Florida State	6.12	OT
2. Hroniss Grasu	Oregon	5.58	
3. Ali Marpet	Hobart	5.49	OG

RK. NAME	SCHOOL	GRADE	NOTES
4. Reese Dismukes	Auburn	5.26	
5. Andy Gallik	Boston College	5.23	
6. Max Garcia	Florida	5.20	OG, OT
7. B.J. Finney	Kansas State	5.19	
8. Greg Mancz	Toledo	5.13	OG
9. Cornelius Edison	Portland State	5.10	OG
10. Chad Hamilton	Coastal Carolina	5.09	OT
11. Shaq Mason	Georgia Tech	4.75	
12. Dillon Day	Mississippi State	4.50	
13. Jake Smith	Louisville	4.75	
14. Chris Jasperse	Marshall	4.75	
15. Shane McDermott	Miami (Fla.)	4.50	
16. Brandon Vitabile	Northwestern	4.50	
17. David Andrews	Georgia	4.50	
18. Nick Easton	Harvard	4.50	
19. Austin Barron	Florida State	4.50	
20. Steve Gurrola	Arizona	4.50	
21. Joe Townsend	Vanderbilt	4.50	
22. Robert Waterman	UNLV	4.50	
23. Elliott Porter	LSU	4.50	
24. Betim Bujari	Rutgers	4.50	
25. Mike Criste	Washington	4.50	

OFFENSIVE GUARDS

RK. NAME	SCHOOL	GRADE	NOTES
1. La'el Collins	LSU	5.95	OT
2. Donovan Smith	Penn State	5.77	Jr., OT
3. A.J. Cann	South Carolina	5.75	
4. Laken Tomlinson	Duke	5.68	
5. Tre' Jackson	Florida State	5.66	
6. Josue Matias	Florida State	5.38	OT
7. John Miller	Louisville	5.38	
8. Jarvis Harrison	Texas A&M	5.28	OT
9. Arie Kouandjio	Alabama	5.28	
10. Jamil Douglas	Arizona State	5.27	OT
11. Mark Glowinski	West Virginia	5.26	C
12. Robert Myers	Tennessee State	5.16	
13. Jon Feliciano	Miami (Fla.)	5.12	
14. Takoby Cofield	Duke	5.12	OT
15. Bobby Hart	Florida State	5.10	OT
16. Edison Cornelius	Portland State	5.10	
17. Adam Shead	Oklahoma	5.07	
18. Al Bond	Memphis	5.01	OT
19. Quinton Spain	West Virginia	4.75	
20. Miles Dieffenbach	Penn State	4.75	
21. Matt Rotherman	Pittsburgh	4.75	
22. Antoine Everett	McNeese State	4.50	
23. David Wang	Virginia Tech	4.50	
24. Ben Beckwith	Mississippi State	4.50	
25. David Beasley	Clemson	4.50	
26. Ian Silberman	Boston College	4.50	
27. Terrence Jones	Troy	4.50	
28. Quinterrius Eatmon	South Florida	4.50	
29. Terrence Jones	Troy	4.50	
30. Caleb Farris	Virginia Tech	4.50	
31. Torrian Wilson	Central Florida	4.50	
32. Junior Salt	Utah	4.50	
33. Cody Wichmann	Fresno State	4.50	

RK. NAME	SCHOOL	GRADE	NOTES
34. Hamani Stevens	Oregon	4.50	
35. Andy Phillips	Central Michigan	4.50	
36. Dallas Lewallen	Wisconsin	4.50	
37. Chris Grisbhy	Oklahoma	4.50	
38. Christian Lombard	Notre Dame	4.50	
39. Chris Slade	Auburn	4.50	
40. Bill Vavau	Utah State	4.50	
41. Jake Cotton	Nebraska	4.50	
42. Rowdy Harper	Houston	4.50	
43. Solomone Kafu	Brigham Young	4.50	
44. Mitchell Bell	Louisiana Tech	4.50	
45. Leon Brown	Alabama	4.50	
46. Tyler Moore	Florida	4.50	
47. Daniel Quave	Louisiana Lafayette	4.50	
48. Collin Seibert	Eastern Illinois	4.50	
49. Scott Inskeep	Texas-San Antonio	4.50	
50. Cole Manhart	Nebraska-Kearney	4.50	
51. Cameron Jefferson	Arkansas	4.50	
52. Garrett Gramling	Texas A&M	4.50	

OFFENSIVE TACKLES

RK. NAME	SCHOOL	GRADE	NOTES
1. Brandon Scherff	Iowa	6.52	OG
2. Andrus Peat	Stanford	6.45	Jr.
3. Ereck Flowers	Miami (Fla.)	6.32	Jr.
4. D.J. Humphries	Florida	6.08	Jr.
5. Jeremiah Poutasi	Utah	5.62	Jr.
6. T.J. Clemmings	Pittsburgh	5.56	
7. Jake Fisher	Oregon	5.54	
8. Cedric Ogbuehi	Texas A&M	5.42	X
9. Tyrus Thompson	Oklahoma	5.42	
10. Mitch Morse	Missouri	5.32	C
11. Ty Sambrailo	Colorado State	5.32	OG
12. Corey Robinson	South Carolina	5.31	
13. Daryl Williams	Oklahoma	5.27	OG
14. Jamon Brown	Louisville	5.26	
15. Laurence Gibson	Virginia Tech	5.26	
16. Rob Havenstein	Wisconsin	5.26	
17. Andrew Donnal	Iowa	5.25	
18. Trent Brown	Florida	5.22	OG
19. Rob Crisp	North Carolina State	5.21	
20. Chaz Green	Florida	5.14	
21. Austin Shepherd	Alabama	5.12	
22. Sean Hickey	Syracuse	5.11	
23. Terry Poole	San Diego State	5.05	
24. Tayo Fabuluje	TCU	5.02	
25. Brett Boyko	UNLV	4.95	
26. Darryl Baldwin	Ohio State	4.92	
27. Darrian Miller	Kentucky	4.78	C
28. Sean Donnelly	Tulane	4.75	
29. Pat Lewandowski	Kansas	4.75	
30. Antonio Johnson	North Texas	4.75	
31. Jake Rodgers	Eastern Washington	4.75	
32. Brey Cook	North Carolina State	4.50	
33. Garrett Frye	Georgia Southern	4.50	
34. Cameron Jefferson	Arkansas	4.50	
35. Eric Lefeld	Cincinnati	4.50	
36. Mickey Baucus	Arizona	4.50	

37. Mitch Hatchie	Washington	4.50
38. Jermaine Barton	Illinois State	4.50
39. Ian Silberman	Boston College	4.50
40. Quinterrius Eatmon	South Florida	4.50
41. Tyler Loos	Northern Illinois	4.50
42. Jack Rummells	Northern Iowa	4.50
43. Blaine Clausell	Mississippi State	4.50
44. Clarence Clemmons	Western Kentucky	4.50
45. Jacob Gannon	Iowa State	4.50
46. Desmond Harrison	Texas	4.50
47. Tyson Chandler	North Carolina State	4.50
48. Sean Donnelly	Tulane	4.50
49. Paul Jorgensen	Northwestern	4.50
50. Jermaine Barton	Illinois State	4.50
51. Cory Keebler	Cincinnati	4.50
52. Ben Riva	Washington	4.50
53. Tyler Loos	Northern Illinois	4.50
54. Kyle Roberts	Nevada	4.50
55. Patrick Miller	Auburn	4.50
56. Trevor Greger	South Dakota State	4.50

DEFENSIVE ENDS

RK. NAME	SCHOOL	GRADE	NOTES
1. Randy Gregory	Nebraska	6.60	Jr., Ch.
2. Vic Beasley	Clemson	6.34	OLB
3. Arik Armstead	Oregon	6.04	Jr.
4. Mario Edwards	Florida State	5.87	Jr.
5. Markus Golden	Missouri	5.53	OLB
6. Preston Smith	Mississippi State	5.52	DT
7. Za'Darius Smith	Kentucky	5.42	
8. Marcus Hardison	Arizona State	5.38	DT
9. Danielle Hunter	LSU	5.36	Jr., OLB
10. Ryan Russell	Purdue	5.32	QUOTE
11. Trey Flowers	Arkansas	5.26	
12. Anthony Chickillo	Miami-Fla.	5.26	
13. Zack Wagenmann	Montana	5.22	
14. Ryan Delaire	Towson	5.18	
15. B.J. Dubose	Louisville	5.18	
16. Corey Crawford	Clemson	5.17	
17. Henry Anderson	Stanford	5.17	
18. Tyeler Davison	Fresno State	5.17	
19. Cedric Reed	Texas	5.14	
20. Obum Gwacham	Oregon State	5.10	
21. Frank Clark	ex-Michigan	5.05	Ch.
22. Tavaris Barnes	Clemson	5.02	
23. Martin Ifedi	Memphis	4.92	
24. Lynden Trail	Norfolk State	4.85	TE
25. Deion Barnes	Penn State	4.85	Jr., OLB
26. Ray Drew	Georgia	4.75	
27. Shaq Riddick	West Virginia	4.75	OLB
28. Brock Hekking	Nevada	4.75	
29. Andrew Hutson	Washington	4.75	
30. Cory Morrissey	Iowa State	4.50	
31. Jordan Allen	Arizona	4.50	
32. Sonny Puletasi	Wyoming	4.50	
33. Brian Mihalik	Boston College	4.50	
34. Steve Miller	Ohio State	4.50	

35. Beau Martin	Boise State	4.50
36. Ryan Mueller	Kansas State	4.50
37. Konrad Zagzebski	Wisconsin	4.50
38. Zach Patt	Rice	4.50
39. Deiontrez Mount	Louisville	4.50
40. Beau Yapp	Hawaii	4.50
41. Jordan Allen	Arizona	4.50
42. Carlos Thompson	Mississippi	4.50
43. Trevor Harris	Houston	4.50
44. Sage Harold	James Madison	4.50
45. Nordly Capi	Akron	4.50
46. Rashod Flavors	Oklahoma	4.50
47. Angelo Pruitt	Connecticut	4.50
48. Sam Wren	Oklahoma State	4.50
49. Mike Hardy	Iowa	4.50
50. Will Schwarz	Saginaw Valley	4.50
51. Jordan Williams	Tennessee	4.50
52. Kendall Montgomery	Bowling Green	4.50
53. Anthony Bass	Tennessee State	4.50
54. Jordan Dewalt-Ondijo	Duke	4.50
55. Art Norman	North Carolina State	4.50
56. Andre Monroe	Maryland	4.50
57. Kazeem Olaniyan	Penn State	4.50
58. Christian Ringo	Louisiana-Lafayette	4.50
59. Justin Delaine	West Alabama	4.50
60. Darius Kilgo	Maryland	4.50
61. Markus Pierce-Brewster	West Texas A&M	4.50

DEFENSIVE TACKLES

RK. NAME	SCHOOL	GRADE	NOTES
1. Leonard Williams	USC	7.20	Jr., DE
2. Malcom Brown	Texas	6.22	Jr., DE
3. Eddie Goldman	Florida State	6.20	Jr., NT
4. Jordan Phillips	Oklahoma	5.84	Jr., NT
5. Danny Shelton	Washington	5.72	NT
6. Carl Davis	Iowa	5.72	DE
7. Mike Bennett	Ohio State	5.54	
8. Darius Philon	Arkansas	5.37	Jr.
9. Xavier Cooper	Washington	5.34	Jr.
10. Christian Covington	Rice	5.34	Jr.
11. Grady Jarrett	Clemson	5.28	NT
12. Deon Simon	Northwestern State	5.27	NT
13. Derrick Lott	Tennessee-Chattanooga	5.26	
14. L.T. Walton	Central Michigan	5.20	
15. Rakeem Nunez-Roches	Southern Mississippi	5.19	Jr.
16. Leon Orr	ex-Florida	5.18	OT
17. David Parry	Stanford	5.18	NT
18. Joey Mbu	Houston	5.14	NT
19. Angelo Blackson	Auburn	5.12	
20. J.T. Surratt	South Carolina	5.12	
21. Bobby Richardson	Indiana	5.10	
22. Gabe Wright	Auburn	5.09	DE
23. Louis Trinca-Pasat	Iowa	5.06	
24. Ellis McCarthy	UCLA	4.97	Jr., OG
25. James Rouse	Marshall	4.90	X
26. Chrishon Rose	East Carolina	4.85	
27. Toby Johnson	Georgia	4.85	

RK. NAME	SCHOOL	GRADE	NOTES
28. Darius Cummings	Florida	4.75	Jr.
29. Ashaad Mabry	Texas-San Antonio	4.75	
30. Deshawn Williams	Clemson	4.75	
31. Isiah Dunning	Grand Valley State	4.75	
32. Desmond Hollin	Florida State	4.75	
33. Brandon Ivory	Alabama	4.50	
34. Xavier Williams	Northern Iowa	4.50	
35. Olsen Pierre	Miami (Fla.)	4.50	
36. Kristjan Sokoli	Buffalo	4.50	
37. Quayshawne Buckley	Idaho	4.50	
38. Thomas Teal	North Carolina State	4.50	
39. Justin Hamilton	Louisiana Lafayette	4.50	
40. Daryl Ward	Western Ontario (Can.)	4.50	
41. Kalafitoni Pole	Washington State	4.50	
42. Trey Williams	East Carolina	4.50	
43. Antwan Crutcher	Ohio	4.50	
44. Ekino Watson	South Florida	4.50	
45. Bud Delva	Oregon State	4.50	
46. Cameron Botticelli	Minnesota	4.50	
47. Keon Stowers	Kansas	4.50	
48. Charles Tuaau	Texas A&M Commerce	4.50	
49. Chuka Ndulue	Oklahoma	4.50	
50. Josh Watson	Clemson	4.50	
51. David Irving	Iowa State	4.50	
52. Marquel Combs	SE Louisiana	4.50	
53. Patrick Mertens	Wyoming	4.50	
54. Mike Thornton	Georgia	4.50	
55. Chucky Hunter	TCU	4.50	
56. James Castleman	Oklahoma State	4.50	

INSIDE LIENBACKERS

RK. NAME	SCHOOL	GRADE	NOTES
1. Eric Kendricks	UCLA	5.86	
2. Benardrick McKinney	Mississippi State	5.74	Jr.
0. Otephone Anthony	Clemson	6.62	
4. P.J. Dawson	TCU	5.46	
5. Denzel Perryman	Miami-Fla.	5.46	
6. Ramik Wilson	Georgia	5.36	
7. Jordan Hicks	Texas	5.32	
8. H.P. Pullard	USC	5.23	
9. Bryce Hager	Baylor	5.22	
10. Mike Hull	Penn State	5.22	
11. Taiwan Jones	Michigan State	5.19	
12. Amarlo Herrera	Georgia	5.14	
13. Trey DePriest	Alabama	5.10	
14. A.J. Johnson	Tennessee	5.09	Ch.
15. Damien Wilson	Minnesota	5.09	
16. Ben Heeney	Kansas	5.05	
17. Zach Vigil	Utah State	5.05	X
18. Aaron Davis	Colorado State	4.75	
19. Curtis Grant	Ohio State	4.75	
20. Jeff Luc	Cincinnati	4.75	FB
21. Quayshawn Nealy	Georgia Tech	4.50	
22. Deterrian Shackleford	Mississippi	4.50	OLB
23. John Timu	Washington	4.50	
24. A.J. Tarpley	Stanford	4.50	
25. Kaleb Eulls	Mississippi State	4.50	
26. Terrance Plummer	UCF	4.50	
27. Jabral Johnson	Oregon State	4.50	
28. John Timu	Washington	4.50	
29. Lamar Dawson	USC	4.50	
30. David Mayo	Texas State	4.50	

OUTSIDE LINEBACKERS

RK. NAME	SCHOOL	GRADE	NOTES
1. Dante Fowler	Florida	7.15	Jr., DE
2. Eli Harold	Virginia	6.32	Jr., DE
3. Shane Ray	Missouri	6.32	Jr., DE
4. Bud Dupree	Kentucky	6.12	DE
5. Shaq Thompson	Washington	5.78	Jr., RB
6. Hau'Oli Kikaha	Washington	5.74	DE
7. Owa Odighizuwa	UCLA	5.64	DE
8. Nate Orchard	Utah	5.57	DE
9. Jake Ryan	Michigan	5.52	ILB
10. Lorenzo Mauldin	Louisville	5.44	DE
11. Max Valles	Virginia	5.34	Jr.
12. Geneo Grissom	Oklahoma	5.33	DE
13. Kwon Alexander	LSU	5.28	Jr.
14. Kyle Emanuel	North Dakota State	5.22	DE
15. Martrell Spaight	Arkansas	5.22	
16. Davis Tull	Tennessee-Chattanooga	5.20	DE
17. Mark Nzeocha	Wyoming	5.19	
18. Zack Hodges	Harvard	5.17	DE
19. J.T. Tavai	USC	5.14	
20. Alani Fua	BYU	5.09	
21. Xzavier Dickson	Alabama	5.07	
22. Tony Washington	Oregon	5.03	
23. Edmond Robinson	Newberry	5.00	
24. Neiron Ball	Florida	4.95	
25. Yannik Cudjoe-Virgil	Maryland	4.87	
26. Derrick Malone	Oregon	4.75	
27. Jermauria Rasco	LSU	4.75	
28. James Vaughters	Stanford	4.75	
29. Mount Deiontrez	Louisville	4.75	
30. Cole Farrand	Maryland	4.75	
31. Houston Bates	Louisiana Tech	4.50	
32. Darien Rankin	North Carolina	4.50	Jr.
33. Chi Chi Ariguzo	Northwestern	4.50	
34. Marcus Mallet	TCU	4.50	
35. Derrick Mathews	Houston	4.50	
36. Chase Williams	Virginia Tech	4.50	
37. Henry Coley	Virginia	4.50	
38. D.J. Lynch	Bowling Green	4.50	

CORNERBACKS

RK. NAME	SCHOOL	GRADE	NOTES
1. Trae Waynes	Michigan State	6.37	Jr.
2. Marcus Peters	ex-Washington	6.23	Jr., Ch.
3. Kevin Johnson	Wake Forest	6.12	
4. Jalen Collins	LSU	5.97	Jr., X
5. Senquez Golson	Mississippi	5.83	
6. Doran Grant	Ohio State	5.82	
7. Byron Jones	Connecticut	5.76	FS
8. Ronald Darby	Florida State	5.74	Jr.
9. Charles Gaines	Louisville	5.72	Jr., KR

10. P.J. Williams	Florida State	5.69	Jr.
11. Quinten Rollins	Miami-Ohio	5.58	FS
12. Jacorey Shepherd	Kansas	5.44	
13. Alex Carter	Stanford	5.38	Jr.
14. Ifo Ekpre-Olomu	Oregon	5.37	X
15. Bobby McCain	Memphis	5.36	KR
16. Josh Shaw	USC	5.36	
17. Lorenzo Doss	Tulane	5.34	Jr.
18. Eric Rowe	Utah	5.34	
19. Craig Mager	Texas State	5.33	
20. Steven Nelson	Oregon State	5.32	
21. D'Joun Smith	Florida Atlantic	5.31	
22. Jacoby Glenn	Central Florida	5.28	Jr.
23. Nick Marshall	Auburn	5.26	QB
24. Imoan Claiborne	Northwestern State	5.24	FS
25. Quandre Diggs	Texas	5.23	PR
26. Ladarius Gunter	Miami-Fla.	5.23	
27. Garry Peters	Clemson	5.19	
28. Julian Wilson	Oklahoma	5.12	FS
29. Justin Coleman	Tennessee	5.11	
30. D.C. Celiscar	Western Michigan	5.10	
31. Troy Hill	Oregon	5.10	Ch.
32. Kevin White	TCU	5.09	
33. Damian Swann	Georgia	5.08	
34. A.J. Jefferson	UCLA	5.03	
35. Tye Smith	Towson	5.00	
36. Bryce Callahan	Rice	4.85	
37. Cody Riggs	Notre Dame	4.75	
38. Cariel Brooks	Adams State	4.75	
39. Greg Henderson	Colorado	4.75	
40. Dexter McDonald	Kansas	4.75	
41. Blake Bernard	Colorado State	4.75	
42. Curtis Riley	Fresno State	4.75	
43. Cam Thomas	Western Kentucky	4.50	
44. Everett Deshazor	Texas A&M	4.50	
45. Bernard Blake	Colorado State	4.50	
46. Jonathon Mincy	Auburn	4.50	
47. SaQwan Edwards	New Mexico	4.50	
48. Jeremiah Johnson	Maryland	4.50	
49. Le'Vander Liggins	Louisiana Tech	4.50	
50. Chris Dunkley	South Florida	4.50	
51. Blair Burns	Wyoming	4.50	
52. Nick Waisome	Florida State	4.50	
53. Terell Floyd	Louisville	4.50	
54. Travis Bell	West Virginia	4.50	
55. Eric Patterson	Ball State	4.50	
56. Jimmy Jean	UAB	4.50	
57. J.J. Whittaker	San Diego State	4.50	
58. Ronnie Vinson	Tennessee State	4.50	
59. Manuel Asprilla	Boston College	4.50	
60. Nate Willis	Kentucky	4.50	
61. Keion Payne	Troy	4.50	

STRONG SAFETIES

RK. NAME	SCHOOL	GRADE	NOTES
1. Landon Collins	Alabama	6.23	Jr.
2. James Sample	Louisville	5.44	Jr.

3. Clayton Geathers	Central Florida	5.31	
4. Ibraheim Campbell	Northwestern	5.29	
5. Kyshoen Jarrett	Virginia Tech	5.29	
6. Cody Prewitt	Mississippi	5.25	
7. Jordan Richards	Stanford	5.25	
8. Adrian Amos	Penn State	5.20	
9. Tevin McDonald	Eastern Washington	5.02	
10. Roland Martin	LSU	4.75	
11. Erick Dargan	Oregon	4.75	
12. Damian Parms	Florida Atlantic	4.50	
13. Fritz Etienne	Memphis	4.50	
14. Sam Carter	TCU	4.50	
15. Corey Cooper	Nebraska	4.50	
16. John Lowdermilk	Iowa	4.50	

FREE SAFETIES

RK. NAME	SCHOOL	GRADE	NOTES
1. Damarious Randall	Arizona State	5.64	CB
2. Jaquiski Tartt	Samford	5.64	
3. Anthony Harris	Virginia	5.42	
4. Gerod Holliman	Louisville	5.40	Jr.
5. Derron Smith	Fresno State	5.39	
6. Kurtis Drummond	Michigan State	5.24	
7. Justin Cox	Mississippi State	5.20	Jr., Ch.
8. Detrick Bonner	Virginia Tech	5.09	
9. Durell Eskridge	Syracuse	5.09	Jr., X
10. Chris Hackett	TCU	5.07	Jr.
11. Dean Marlowe	James Madison	5.06	
12. Jermaine Whitehead	Auburn	5.04	
13. Parrish Gaines	Navy	4.85	
14. Cedric Thompson	Minnesota	4.75	

PLACEKICKERS

RK. NAME	SCHOOL	GRADE	NOTES
1. Justin Manton	Louisiana-Monroe	5.11	
2. Josh Lambo	Texas A&M	5.00	
3. Kyle Brindza	Notre Dame	4.95	
4. Jared Roberts	Colorado State	4.95	
5. Sam Ficken	Penn State	4.85	
6. Tom Obasrski	Concordia	4.85	

PUNTERS

RK. NAME	SCHOOL	GRADE	NOTES
1. Bradley Pinion	Clemson	5.20	Jr.
2. Kyle Loomis	Portland State	5.10	
3. Kyle Christy	Florida	5.00	
4. Will Johnson	Texas State	5.00	
5. Will Baumann	North Carolina State	4.90	
6. Spencer Roth	Baylor	4.85	
7. Keith Kostol	Oregon State	4.85	
8. Trevor Pardula	Kansas	4.80	
9. Mike Sadler	Michigan State	4.80	

LONG SNAPPERS

RK. NAME	SCHOOL	GRADE	NOTES
1. Joe Cardona	Navy	4.85	
2. Easton Wahlstrom	Arizona State	4.75	
3. Andrew East	Vanderbilt	4.50	

BEST PLAYER AVAILABLE BY GRADE

RK. POS, NAME, SCHOOL	GRADE	NOTES
1. DT Leonard Williams, USC	7.20	Jr., DE
2. OLB Dante Fowler, Florida	7.15	Jr., DE
3. QB Jameis Winston, Florida State	6.80	Soph-3, Ch.
4. WR Kevin White, West Virginia	6.75	
5. QB Marcus Mariota, Oregon	6.70	Jr.
6. WR Amari Cooper, Alabama	6.65	Jr.
7. RB Todd Gurley, Georgia	6.60	Jr., X, KR
8. DE Randy Gregory, Nebraska	6.60	Jr., Ch.
9. OT Brandon Scherff, Iowa	6.52	OG
10. OT Andrus Peat, Stanford	6.45	Jr.
11. CB Trae Waynes, Michigan State	6.37	Jr.
12. DE Vic Beasley, Clemson	6.34	OLB
13. OT Ereck Flowers, Miami (Fla.)	6.32	Jr.
14. OLB, Eli Harold, Virginia	6.32	Jr., DE
15. OLB Shane Ray, Missouri	6.32	Jr., DE
16. RB Melvin Gordon, Wisconsin	6.27	Jr.
17. WR Devante Parker, Louisville	6.27	
18. CB Marcus Peters, ex-Washington	6.23	Jr., Ch.
19. FS Landon Collins, Alabama	6.23	Jr.
20. DT Malcom Brown, Texas	6.22	Jr.
21. DT Eddie Goldman, Florida State	6.20	Jr., NT
22. OC Cameron Erving, Florida State	6.12	OT
23. OLB Bud Dupree, Kentucky	6.12	DE
24. CB Kevin Johnson, Wake Forest	6.12	
25. OT D.J. Humphries, Florida	6.08	Jr.
26. DE Arik Armstead, Oregon	6.04	Jr.
27. CB Jalen Collins, LSU	5.97	Jr., X
28. WR Jaelen Strong, Arizona State	5.97	Jr.
29. OG La'el Collins, LSU	5.95	OT
30. WR Nelson Agholor, USC	5.92	Jr., RS
31. RB Tevin Coleman, Indiana	5.89	Jr., KR
32. DE Mario Edwards, Florida State	5.87	Jr.
33. ILB Eric Kendricks, UCLA	5.86	
34. WR Dorial Green-Beckham, Oklahoma	5.85	Jr., Ch.
35. DT Jordan Phillips, Oklahoma	5.84	Jr., NT
36. CB Senquez Golson, Mississippi	5.83	
37. CB Doran Grant, Ohio State	5.82	
38. RB Jay Ajayi, Boise State	5.81	Jr.
39. OLB Shaq Thompson, Washington	5.78	Jr., RB
40. OG Donovan Smith, Penn State	5.77	Jr., OT
41. CB Byron Jones, Connecticut	5.76	FS
42. OG A.J. Cann, South Carolina	5.75	
43. ILB Benardrick McKinney, Mississippi State	5.74	Jr.
44. OLB Hau'Oli Kikaha, Washington	5.74	DE
45. CB Ronald Darby, Florida State	5.74	Jr.
46. DT Danny Shelton, Washington	5.72	NT
47. TE Maxx Williams, Minnesota	5.72	Jr.
48. CB Charles Gaines, Louisville	5.72	Jr., KR
49. DT Carl Davis, Iowa	5.72	DE
50. CB P.J. Williams, Florida State	5.69	Jr.
51. OG Laken Tomlinson, Duke	5.68	
52. WR Devin Funchess, Michigan	5.67	Jr., TE
53. OG Tre Jackson, Florida State	5.66	
54. WR Devin Smith, Ohio State	5.64	RS
55. FS Damarious Randall, Arizona State	5.64	CB
56. OLB Owa Odighizuwa, UCLA	5.64	DE
57. FS Jaquiski Tartt, Samford	5.64	
58. TE Tyler Kroft, Rutgers	5.62	Jr.
59. OT Jeremiah Poutasi, Utah	5.62	Jr.
60. ILB Stephone Anthony, Clemson	5.62	
61. OC Hroniss Grasu, Oregon	5.58	
62. CB Quinten Rollins, Miami-Ohio	5.58	FS
63. RB Duke Johnson, Miami-Fla.	5.57	
64. WR Breshad Perriman, Central Florida	5.57	Jr.
65. OLB Nate Orchard, Utah	5.57	DE
66. OT T.J. Clemmings, Pittsburgh	5.56	
67. WR Sammie Coates, Auburn	5.56	
68. OT Jake Fisher, Oregon	5.54	
69. DT Mike Bennett, Ohio State	5.54	
70. DE Markus Golden, Missouri	5.53	OLB
71. QB Bryce Petty, Baylor	5.52	
72. RB Ameer Abdullah, Nebraska	5.52	RS
73. WR Tyler Lockett, Kansas State	5.52	RS
74. RB T.J. Yeldon, Alabama	5.52	Jr.
75. DE Preston Smith, Mississippi State	5.52	DT
76. OLB Jake Ryan, Michigan	5.52	ILB
77. OC Ali Marpet, Hobart	5.49	OG
78. RB Buck Allen, USC	5.48	Jr.
79. WR Phillip Dorsett, Miami-Fla.	5.47	RS
80. WR Tre McBride, William & Mary	5.47	RS
81. ILB P.J. Dawson, TCU	5.46	
82. WR Rashad Greene, Florida State	5.46	PR
83. ILB Denzel Perryman, Miami-Fla.	5.46	
84. OLB Lorenzo Mauldin, Louisville	5.44	DE
85. CB Jacorey Shepherd, Kansas	5.44	
86. SS James Sample, Louisville	5.44	Jr.
87. QB Brett Hundley, UCLA	5.42	Jr.
88. OT Cedric Ogbuehi, Texas A&M	5.42	X
89. RB Jeremy Langford, Michigan State	5.42	
90. WR Mario Alford, West Virginia	5.42	KR
91. OT Tyrus Thompson, Oklahoma	5.42	
92. DE Za'Darius Smith, Kentucky	5.42	
93. FS Anthony Harris, Virginia	5.42	
94. TE Clive Walford, Miami-Fla.	5.40	
95. FS Gerod Holliman, Louisville	5.40	Jr.
96. RB David Cobb, Minnesota	5.39	
97. WR Deandre Smelter, Georgia Tech	5.39	X
98. RB David Johnson, Northern Iowa	5.39	KR
99. FS Derron Smith, Fresno State	5.39	
100. WR Jamison Crowder, Duke	5.38	PR
101. OG Josue Matias, Florida State	5.38	OT
102. WR Ty Montgomery, Stanford	5.38	RB, RS
103. OG John Miller, Louisville	5.38	
104. DE Marcus Hardison, Arizona State	5.38	DT
105. CB Alex Carter, Stanford	5.38	Jr.
106. RB Mike Davis, South Carolina	5.37	Jr.
107. WR Stefon Diggs, Maryland	5.37	Jr., X
108. DT Darius Philon, Arkansas	5.37	Jr.
109. CB Ifo Ekpre-Olomu, Oregon	5.37	X
110. QB Garrett Grayson, Colorado State	5.36	
111. WR Justin Hardy, East Carolina	5.36	
112. DE Danielle Hunter, LSU	5.36	Jr., OLB
113. CB Bobby McCain, Memphis	5.36	KR
114. ILB Ramik Wilson, Georgia	5.36	
115. CB Josh Shaw, USC	5.36	
116. WR Dres Anderson, Utah	5.35	X, KR
117. CB Lorenzo Doss, Tulane	5.34	Jr.
118. WR Tony Lippett, Michigan State	5.34	CB
119. DT Xavier Cooper, Washington	5.34	Jr.
120. OLB Max Valloo, Virginia	5.34	Jr.
121. DT Christian Covington, Rice	5.34	Jr.
122. CB Eric Rowe, Utah	5.34	
123. WR Chris Conley, Georgia	5.33	
124. OLB Geneo Grissom, Oklahoma	5.33	DE
125. CB Craig Mager, Texas State	5.33	
126. QB Sean Mannion, Oregon State	5.32	
127. TE Busta Anderson, South Carolina	5.32	
128. OT Ty Sambrailo, Colorado State	5.32	OG
129. DE Ryan Russell, Purdue	5.32	QUOTE
130. OT Mitch Morse, Missouri	5.32	C
131. ILB Jordan Hicks, Texas	5.32	
132. CB Steven Nelson, Oregon State	5.32	
133. WR Antwan Goodley, Baylor	5.31	
134. TE Jeff Heuerman, Ohio State	5.31	
135. OT Corey Robinson, South Carolina	5.31	
136. SS Clayton Geathers, Central Florida	5.31	
137. CB D'Joun Smith, Florida Atlantic	5.31	
138. SS Ibraheim Campbell, Northwestern	5.29	
139. WR Vince Mayle, Washington State	5.29	
140. SS Kyshoen Jarrett, Virginia Tech	5.29	
141. RB Josh Robinson, Mississippi State	5.28	Jr.
142. OG Jarvis Harrison, Texas A&M	5.28	OT
143. OG Arie Kouandjio, Alabama	5.28	
144. DT Grady Jarrett, Clemson	5.28	
145. OLB Kwon Alexander, LSU	5.28	Jr.
146. CB Jacoby Glenn, Central Florida	5.28	Jr.
147. WR Kenny Bell, Nebraska	5.27	
148. OG Jamil Douglas, Arizona State	5.27	OT
149. WR Josh Harper, Fresno State	5.27	
150. OT Daryl Williams, Oklahoma	5.27	OG

PLAYER INDEX